BEYOND THE INNER AND THE OUTER

SYNTHESE LIBRARY

STUDIES IN EPISTEMOLOGY,

LOGIC, METHODOLOGY, AND PHILOSOPHY OF SCIENCE

Managing Editor:

JAAKKO HINTIKKA, *Boston University*

Editors:

DONALD DAVIDSON, *University of California, Berkeley*
GABRIËL NUCHELMANS, *University of Leyden*
WESLEY C. SALMON, *University of Pittsburgh*

VOLUME 214

MICHEL TER HARK

BEYOND THE INNER
AND THE OUTER

Wittgenstein's Philosophy of Psychology

KLUWER ACADEMIC PUBLISHERS

DORDRECHT / BOSTON / LONDON

Library of Congress Cataloging in Publication Data

Hark, Michel Ter, 1953-
    Beyond the inner and the outer : Wittgenstein's philosophy of
psychology / Michel Ter Hark.
        p.   cm. -- (Synthese library ; v. 214)
    Includes bibliographical references and index.
    ISBN 0-7923-0850-6 (alk. paper)
    1. Psychology--Philosophy. 2. Wittgenstein, Ludwig, 1889-1951.
3. Psycholinguistics--Philosophy.   I. Title. II. Series.
BF38.H37   1990
128'.092--dc20   90-39743

ISBN 0-7923-0850-6

Published by Kluwer Academic Publishers,
P.O. Box 17, 3300 AA Dordrecht, The Netherlands.

Kluwer Academic Publishers incorporates
the publishing programmes of
D. Reidel, Martinus Nijhoff, Dr W. Junk and MTP Press.

Sold and distributed in the U.S.A. and Canada
by Kluwer Academic Publishers,
101 Philip Drive, Norwell, MA 02061, U.S.A.

In all other countries, sold and distributed
by Kluwer Academic Publishers Group,
P.O. Box 322, 3300 AH Dordrecht, The Netherlands.

Translation from the Dutch language by Anthony P. Runia.
This translation has been made possible by a grant from
the Netherlands Organization for Scientific Research (N.W.O)

Printed on acid-free paper

In memory of my brother Niels (1952-1987)
For Anne

CONTENTS

PREFACE

Wittgenstein's aphoristic style holds great charm, but also a great danger: the reader is apt to glean too much from a single fragment and too little from the fragments as a whole. In my first confrontations with the *Philosophical Investigations* I was such a reader, and so, it turned out, were most of the writers on Wittgenstein's later philosophy. Wittgenstein's remarkable ability to bring together many facets of his thought in one fragment is fully exploited in the critical literature; but hardly any attention is paid to the connection with other fragments, let alone to the many hitherto unpublished manuscripts of which the *Philosophical Investigations* is the final product. The result of this fragmentary and ahistorical approach to Wittgenstein's later work is a host of contradictory interpretations. What Wittgenstein really wanted to say remains insufficiently clear. Opinions are also strongly divided about the value of his work. Some authors have been encouraged by his aphorisms and rhetorical questions to dismiss the whole Cartesian tradition or to halt new movements in linguistics or psychology; others, exasperated, reject his philosophy as anti-scientific conceptual conservatism.

After consulting unpublished notebooks and manuscripts which Wittgenstein wrote between 1929 and 1951, I became a very different reader. Wittgenstein turned out to be a kind of Leonardo da Vinci, who pursued a form from which every sign of chiselling, every attempt at improvement, had been effaced. As a result, the reader of the *Philosophical Investigations* only sees Wittgenstein's solutions, but not the problems with which he wrestled, only the apt formulation, but not the formulation capable of improvement. We are fortunate that Wittgenstein, unlike Leonardo da Vinci, did not destroy his sketches, so that the reader can often follow the development and argumentative context of his thought step by step in the notebooks and manuscripts. My assumption is that the published work can only be understood properly if one has entered into this historical and argumentative context. That is not to detract from the number of excellent studies of Wittgenstein's published work; I am merely saying that even in those cases the reader lacks sufficient exegetical evidence to decide adequately on the correctness of an interpretation.

The main objective of this book is to understand Wittgenstein's ideas about the nature of psychological concepts in the historical context of his published and above all unpublished writings between 1929 and 1951. I am concerned with reconstructing, not evaluating, his work. And although I shall regularly refer to the critical literature on Wittgenstein, the debate with other interpreters is secondary. I have learned a great deal from studies by Stanley Cavell, Gordon Baker & Peter Hacker, and Merrill & Jaakko Hintikka, but they do not pay specific attention to Wittgenstein's philosophy of psychology or extensively consult unpublished material. Another distinctive feature of this book is that it closely examines the relation between the Gestalt psychology of Wolfgang Köhler and the philosophical psychology of William James on the one hand and Wittgenstein's philosophy of psychology on the other. Contrary to common practice, I will not dwell on Wittgenstein's relation to authors whom he did not read (seriously), like Descartes, Locke, or Hume, but will rather look at authors with whom he actually enters into a debate: Köhler and James.

The exegetical restriction to Wittgenstein's own work and that of some of his contemporaries does not mean that this book is merely of historical interest. Virtually all the themes which it addresses are relevant to current developments in philosophy, linguistics, and (cognitive) psychology. Some of the topics that come under review are: the importance of language for the nature of psychological phenomena, the relation between rationality and a way of life, the tension between self-knowledge and public standards for that knowledge, the relation between certainty and uncertainty about knowledge of other minds, and the many misleading tendencies in introspective, behaviouristic, and Gestalt-psychological explanations of psychological phenomena, such as perception, emotion, and willing. In the last chapter I will explicitly illustrate the relevance of Wittgenstein's philosophy of psychology to current positions in cognitive psychology and artificial intelligence.

Given the pronounced holistic character of Wittgenstein's philosophy, no study of his foundations of psychology can afford to ignore his philosophy of language and action. After a chapter explaining various aspects of Wittgenstein's Nachlass and particularly the genesis of *Philosophical Investigations*, § 243-421, the next two chapters deal with the embedment of the meaning of concepts in language-games and forms of life and with rule-guided behaviour and the primacy of actions. Chapters 4 and 5 explore the basis of Wittgenstein's philosophy of psychology; the first discusses the status of psychological concepts in the first person, the second the use of those concepts in the third person. Both chapters present a large amount of unpublished material that sheds light on the relation between the first and the third person, the private language argument, the question of whether Wittgenstein is a behaviourist, and the nature of 'Menschenkenntnis'. Chapters 6 and 7 focus on Wittgenstein's analysis of individual psychological concepts, an area that has been sorely neglected in the critical literature. Important sources here are the *Remarks on the Philosophy of Psychology* I and II and the *Last Writings*, published in 1980 and 1982 respectively, as well as unpublished material.

Use of the Nachlass necessitates frequent citation. I have therefore kept quotations from published work to a minimum, often paraphrasing rather than quoting the original. The material from the Nachlass has been translated from the German by Anthony Runia and myself. The original German versions have been added in an appendix and, in contrast to the English translations, include alternative formulations (marked between double slashes). In all other respects the English translations are identical with the original German versions. Words underlined by Wittgenstein in his manuscripts or notebooks have been italicized. Squiggly lines in quotations correspond to squiggly lines under a word in the manuscript, which Wittgenstein used to indicate uncertainty about a formulation. Words in brackets are also bracketed in the manuscripts. I have mentioned deletions only where they seemed important in the context. The interpunction in the translations has been adapted to English usage as far as possible; in German it has been kept intact as far as possible.

This book is a revision of my thesis, which I started to write in 1984 and finished at the University of Amsterdam in 1988. Chapter 1 is new, chapters 2 and 4 have been largely rewritten. My access to Wittgenstein's Nachlass was greatly facilitated by the library of the Faculty of Philosophy of the Free University in Amsterdam, where a microfilm of the Cornell University version of the Nachlass is kept. I thank the librarian for kindly allowing me to consult this valuable possession. I also thank the copyright owners of Wittgenstein's Nachlass, Professor G.E.M. Anscombe, the late Professor Rush Rhees, and Professor G.H. von Wright, for graciously permitting me to quote from unpublished and post-humously published work by Wittgenstein.

I am deeply indebted to Professor O.D. Duintjer for his detailed and often spiritual criticism of the entire manuscript. Grateful acknowledgement is also due to the late Professor H.G. Hubbeling, Professor T. de Boer, and Professor R. Bartsch for their comments on my work. Dr D.H.K. Pätzhold deserves many thanks for his correction of the German quotations from the manuscript. I am obliged to Anthony Runia for the measure in which he was able to retain the style of the original Dutch in his fine translation. I wish again to express my gratitude to Henriëtte van Aalst for accurately typing out the original manuscript. Professor T.A.F. Kuipers and Professor B. McGuinness were kind enough to recommend the manuscript to the publisher.

Karen was able to support and stimulate me while carrying on her own demanding work, but I am even more grateful to her for the birth of our daughter during the birth of this book.

CHAPTER 1

ON THE ORIGIN OF THE *PHILOSOPHICAL INVESTIGATIONS*

In one of his meditations on psychoanalysis Wittgenstein asks why Freud's significance as a psychologist is so closely bound up with his style. Far from showing a failure to appreciate the content of Freud's work, the question rather reflects an appreciation of the importance of style, or form, for content. For what the psychologist says or writes must be recognized and acknowledged by the reader or the patient as being characteristic of his behaviour; the analysis will only be successful if the patient can identify with the mirror that is being held up to him. Obviously, this recognition by the patient depends on the way in which the therapist formulates, the extent to which he is able to express the content of his thoughts aptly.

The apt word is also Wittgenstein's word. His remark about the importance of Freud's style is therefore partly autobiographical. One of the most critical and difficult tasks which Wittgenstein sets himself is to express errors of thought so characteristically that the reader will recognize and acknowledge them immediately. Indeed, it is the reader rather than the writer who determines the correctness of the philosophical formulation. That is why so many passages in the *Philosophical Investigations* are assigned to an imaginary discussion partner. The book is a dialogue in every sense of the word.

But are there readers who can really identify with the mirror that is being held up to them? The many divergent interpretations of the *Philosophical Investigations* would seem to deny this. The problem may lie in the myopia of readers, but also in Wittgenstein's inability to get the mirror image across. Wittgenstein's many comments on his own style show him to be more than sceptical of his success in formulating errors of thought aptly. Often he also apologizes for his style. Thus while deliberately seeming to choose a non-linear and aphoristic style, he seems at the same time to regret this choice, as if he would have preferred to write a 'good book', a book in a more conventional and discursive style. But it is doubtful whether Wittgenstein could have written differently from the way he actually did – which is not to say that he did not want to write the way he actually did. In any case the many unpublished manuscripts in his Nachlass have a style which differs little from the form in which the *Investigations* are cast. That can also be inferred from the many versions of the famous preface to the *Investigations*. The earliest versions, written when the book itself was far from finished, utter the same 'complaints' as the definitive version. Thus in one of the very first drafts in 1936 he wrote:

> This book represents my views on the philosophy as I developed it in the last eight years. I have done it as well as I could; but still in many respects it turns out unsatisfactory. Striking conciseness is lacking, the style is laborious. What should have been drawn in one line, I had to do in ten lines, hence unclearly. (MS 152, p. 13)

And on 15 September 1937:

> When I think for myself without wanting to write a book, I run roundabout the theme; this is the only natural way of thinking for me. Being forced to think in a straight line is a torture for me. Should I henceforth attempt it at all??
> I *waste* unspeakable effort in putting into order thoughts which may be absolutely worthless. (MS 118, 15-9-1937)

It is therefore an illusion to think that the many unpublished works from the Nachlass present a completely different Wittgenstein. Yet a study of the entire Nachlass is indispensable for a proper understanding of the *Philosophical Investigations* and later work.[1] The Nachlass shows us Wittgenstein in action. We see how certain passages evolve in an entirely different context

---

[1] All references to the Nachlass are to the Cornell University Library microfilm version of Wittgenstein's papers (made in 1967). I refer to the place of specific passages in a manuscript or typescript either by following Wittgenstein's pagination or by supplying my own where Wittgenstein has none. In one or two cases only a date is referred to. For the designation of the manuscripts and typescripts themselves I have made grateful use of the system of reference devised and published by von Wright in his 'The Wittgenstein Papers' (1982), which originally appeared in the *Philosophical Review* 78, 1969.

from the context in which they were published. And as Wittgenstein himself teaches us, a changing context can reveal new aspects of something, a picture, a word, or an aphorism. Sometimes extremely condensed aphorisms turn out to have a fairly discursive past. And almost all fragments in the *Investigations* are compilations of parts of different manuscripts from different periods. It is precisely the compilation and selection of fragments which cost Wittgenstein a great deal of time and work and which continued to dissatisfy him.[2] It pays therefore to examine the sources in order to get a clearer picture of the history and selection of the *Investigations*.

In this chapter I want to throw more light on the Nachlass itself and particularly on the history of that part of the *Investigations* which is regarded by many as the *pièce de résistance* of Wittgenstein's philosophy of mind, sections 243-421. This digression on the Nachlass takes its cue from the pioneering work of von Wright in his articles 'The Wittgenstein Papers' and 'The Origin and Composition of the *Philosophical Investigations*'.[3] Both articles are so authoritative that they have been accepted as a correct account of the genesis of the *Investigations* by almost everyone who has written about Wittgenstein, including those who have written about his Nachlass, such as G.P. Baker and P.M.S. Hacker.[4] We are, in short, dealing with a standard view of the genesis of the *Investigations*. However, study of the Nachlass shows that on many counts this standard view is not only incomplete and in need of supplementation but also wrong and in need of correction. Since the standard view also contains many correct elements, the task I have set myself in the following is to

---

[2] Thus he writes in 1937: 'I do not feel quite at ease in compiling my remarks' (MS 118, p. 84). And there are more comments to this effect.

[3] Like 'The Wittgenstein Papers', this indispensable article is included in von Wright (1982, pp. 111-137).

[4] See Baker & Hacker (1980, p. 7, note 1) and Baker & Hacker (1985, pp. 3-4). Hilmy (1987, pp. 25-40) also breaks with the standard view, but his book confines itself to the genesis of the language-game philosophy and focuses almost exclusively on the so-called 'Big Typescript' (TS 213). My concern is above all with Wittgenstein's philosophy of mind and I shall consult quite different manuscripts from Hilmy or Baker & Hacker.

offer a serious improvement rather than a refutation.[5] First I look at the history of the *Investigations* as a whole and then at *Philosophical Investigations*, § 243-421.

The standard view of the genesis of the *Investigations* broadly reads as follows. The work is historically divisible into four parts: § 1-188, § 189-421, § 422-693, and part 2. Returning to Cambridge in 1929 after an absence of almost ten years, Wittgenstein does not immediately start working on § 1-188. He first goes through a number of stages before embarking on his second major work. Between 1929 and 1933-1936 he passes through an 'intermediate phase', of which the beginning is marked by the *Philosophical Remarks* and the end by *The Blue and Brown Books*. The first work follows on from the *Tractatus* and Wittgenstein's contacts with the Vienna Circle. In *The Blue and Brown Books*, on the other hand, the transition is made to the philosophy of the *Investigations*; a transition also announced by the *Philosophical Grammar*, compiled by R. Rhees from material dating back to 1932 and 1933. In August 1936 Wittgenstein works on a German revision of *The Brown Books* and calls it *Philosophische Untersuchungen, Versuch einer Umarbeitung*. He is not satisfied with it, leaves it unfinished, but starts in Norway in December 1936 on what is now *Philosophical Investigations*, § 1-188, also called the *Proto-Investigations*. The original manuscript (MS 142) has been lost, but there exists a typescript version from 1937 (TS 220), which was made in Norway as well. Between September and November 1937 Wittgenstein writes a sequel to TS 220, TS 221, which he initially presents in combination with TS 220. Later he removes TS 221 from the 'definitive' version of the *Investigations*; it will be posthumously published as part of the *Remarks on the Philosophy of Mathematics*. In the autumn of 1938 Wittgenstein negotiates with the Cambridge University Press for publication of the *Proto-Investigations*, including the part on mathematics (TS 221). He abandons the project at the last minute, presumably because he saw problems in the integration of the part on mathematics (TS 221) and the part on language and meaning (TS 220 and so PI, § 1-188). According to von Wright, his attention is subsequently

---

[5] Von Wright himself indicates that his historical outline is incomplete on certain points (von Wright, p. 112).

engaged by philosophy of mathematics to the extent that he writes about nothing else until 1944. After TS 220 and the combination of TS 220 and 221 intended for the Cambridge University Press, the third sequel to the *Proto-Investigations* is written in the second half of 1944. This 'Intermediate Version' is the present text of *Philosophical Investigations*, § 189-421. The definitive version of part 1 of the *Investigations* is completed in 1945, when Wittgenstein adds the present sections 422-693 of the *Investigations* to the *Proto-Investigations* and the 'Intermediate Version', sections which he selects from manuscripts going back to 1930. Part 2 of the *Investigations* is then composed between 1946-1949 from material written in that period.

At the risk of overstatement I propose to call this view of the genesis of the *Philosophical Investigations* the 'brainwave theory'. The gist of the theory is that the main parts of the *Investigations* are the fruit of a short period of brilliant insights. Von Wright suggests that both § 1-188 and § 189-421 were written in a very short period and that they mark a break with what went before rather than being continuous with it.[6] To the extent that the 'brainwave theory' emphasizes the sudden and brilliant insight, it thus neglects the possible historical continuity. I do not wish to deny that Wittgenstein's work is sometimes the result of sudden insights and least of all that these insights bear the stamp of genius; I claim only that these brilliant insights also have a context, a history, and that von Wright presents a distorted picture of Wittgenstein's method by confining the genesis of the *Investigations* to circumscribed, short periods.

Thus the genesis of the *Proto-Investigations* (PI, § 1-188) is said by von Wright to be the outcome 'of two relatively short periods of concentrated writing – one in November-December 1936 and

---

[6] Von Wright might counter that he has limited himself to the most recent sources of the *Philosophical Investigations*, as he also says on page 131. Notwithstanding this restriction it is clear enough that von Wright regards recent sources as more or less primary and original sources. Thus he writes about the composition of TS 228: 'Then follow some 130 remarks from MS 129 (and one from MS 124), that is, from the period 1944-45' (p. 128). Nor does he suggest anywhere else that MS 129 has a history, something he does claim for TS 228 (see further pp. 8 ff. of this chapter).

another in September-November 1937, both periods in Norway'
(von Wright, p. 118). And von Wright remarks of the 'Intermediate Version' (PI, § 189-421):

> ... it seems safe to say that only a very minor part of the *Investigations* stems
> from the years 1937-43 inclusive. During those seven years Wittgenstein's
> main concern was with the philosophy of mathematics. In 1937-38 he wrote
> what was originally the second half of the early version of the *Investigations*
> printed as Part I of the *Remarks on the Foundations of Mathematics*... In the
> beginning of 1944 Wittgenstein was still writing about the philosophy of
> mathematics – but then he shifted to work on the philosophy of psychology,
> which was to become a source for a new version of the *Investigations*. (von
> Wright, p. 125)

In other words, the 'nucleus' of the *Investigations* was written in
little more than a year's time.

Von Wright's history of the *Philosophical Investigations* is
almost exclusively based on typescripts or fair-copy manuscripts,
that is, writings which are *already* a compilation of material written earlier. To trace these earlier sources is a painstaking labour,
not only because there are so many of them, but also because
Wittgenstein's handwriting here is often difficult to decipher and
the text contains many deletions and alternative formulations.
Nevertheless research into these most original sources has an
important bearing on the history and interpretation of the *Investigations*. As far as the genesis is concerned, these earliest sources
often present a *different scenario* from the most recent sources
cited by von Wright. I will briefly illustrate this with regard to the
Investigations, § 1-188, since the groundwork here has already
been laid by S. Hilmy;[7] I will deal at greater length with virgin
territory: the earliest sources of *Philosophical Investigations*, §
189-421.

Wittgenstein in fact compiled the *Proto-Investigations* (PI, § 1-
188) in 1937, but it is wrong to conclude that he largely based this
work on a manuscript (MS 142) from November and December
1936; a manuscript which for that matter no longer exists and has
never been seen by von Wright.[8] A substantial and crucial part of
§ 1-188 was written much earlier than 1936, either in its present

---

[7] See Hilmy 1987 (pp. 25-39).
[8] Von Wright says this himself (1982, p. 117).

published form or in some kind of draft thereof. Thus Hilmy[9] has shown that nearly all Wittgenstein's own comments on his later approach to philosophy and his philosophical method (PI, § 87-133) assumed their final form in TS 213, the 'Big Typescript' from 1932-1933, which is in turn a compilation of manuscripts going back to 1930. Rhush Rhees's widely accepted view that Wittgenstein's later method only developed between 1933-1936 is therefore untenable.[10] The same applies to the established idea that the notion of language-games was not introduced until the *Blue Books*. Backer & Hacker, for instance, claim that in the period preceding the *Blue Books* Wittgenstein used a so-called 'calculus model' of meaning which has much more in common with the formal calculus of the *Tractatus* than the later language-game philosophy.[11] Indeed, the rejection of this 'calculus model' is supposed to be Wittgenstein's main motive for introducing the language-game philosophy around 1933-1934. But Hilmy has convincingly shown that the shift from 'calculus model' to 'language-game model' was no more than *terminological* and that the term 'language-game' already occurs before 1930, just as the term 'calculus' is used long after 1933 to indicate what is meant by language-games.[12]

There are more facts supporting the view that the genesis of § 1-188 goes back much farther than 1936 or even 1933. In TS 213 Wittgenstein already dispenses with the traditional notion (also common to the *Tractatus*) that the definition of a concept requires the specification of necessary and sufficient conditions for its application. According to this notion, a statement like 'The ground was completely covered with plants' can only be understood if an

---

[9] See Hilmy (1987, pp. 34-35). Most of the remarks about philosophy in TS 213 go back to still earlier manuscripts.

[10] In the preface to the *Blue and Brown Books* Rhees says of the period 1933-1936; 'Philosophy was a method of investigation, for Wittgenstein, but his conception of the method was changing' (p. viii).

[11] See Baker & Hacker (1980, pp. 47-53) and also Bogen (1972, pp. 180 ff.).

[12] See Hilmy (1987, pp. 98-107). For an early (1931-1932) but characteristic use of 'language-game', see also the quotation from MS 113, p. 104 on page 12 of this chapter.

exact definition of 'plant' has been given (cf. PI, § 70). But, writes
Wittgenstein:

> ... the blurred boundaries belong to my concept of the plant, as it is now, i.e. as
> I use this word now and it characterizes this concept that I say for instance: I
> have not determined in advance whether I should call this thing a plant or
> not. (TS 213, p. 251)

This important characteristic of language-games, the indeterminacy of the boundaries of language-games, is discussed by Wittgenstein notably in *Philosophical Investigations*, § 75-87, and most
of these fragments come from TS 213, pp. 248-263.[13] And not only
this major characteristic of language-games was conceived before
1933-1936, but also the first version of what is often called
Wittgenstein's 'definition' of meaning; his statement '... the
meaning of a word is its use in the language' (PI, § 43) is already
written in 1931: 'To understand the meaning of a word means to
know, understand, its use' (MS 153a, p. 117). I could cite more
facts proving that *Philosophical Investigations*, § 1-188 already
takes shape in 1930 instead of between 1933 and 1936, but I want to
leave it at this and expand on the genesis of the 'Intermediate
Version' of the *Investigations*.

In von Wright's account the 'Intermediate Version' of the
Investigations (§ 189-421) was composed in two stages. In the
second half of August 1944 Wittgenstein starts work on a long
manuscript (MS 129) and in January 1945 he completes a typescript
version (TS 241) of it. Together with TS 220 and some remarks
from TS 221, TS 241 forms the 'Intermediate Version' of the
Investigations. Next, Wittgenstein draws up a compendium of
remarks from manuscripts some of which go back to the thirties.
This typescript is called *Bemerkungen* (TS 228) and comprises 698
remarks. About 400 remarks from TS 228 are included in the final
typescript of part 1 of the *Investigations*. A number of these are
incorporated in the 'Intermediate Version',[14] but most are added

---

[13] But in this 'chapter' of TS 213 there are also a large number of passages about
the indeterminacy of rules which have not been incorporated in the
Philosophical Investigations.

[14] Von Wright does not particularize, but the remarks concerned mainly go into
the present paragraphs 398-411, which generally have MS 120 as their earliest
source (see chapter 4, § 2 (a)). Other examples of fragments from TS 228 which

to the end of it (i.e. PI, § 422-693). With about 400 remarks TS 228 makes the largest contribution to the *Investigations*. However, 231 of the total of 698 remarks in TS 228 derive from MS 116 and about 130 from MS 129, some of which are left out of the *Investigations*. Of the manuscripts, therefore, MS 116 and MS 129 are the largest contributors to the *Investigations*: the first provides 155 remarks, the second 204. MS 129 gives most of its remarks to § 189-421;[15] the remarks of MS 116 are more evenly distributed over the entire first part of the *Investigations*. MS 129 is evidently crucial for the history of *Philosophical Investigations*, § 243-421.

Von Wright seems to suggest that MS 129 only contains original fragments, for he says nothing about the possible history of this manuscript in a fair copy. On one occasion, however, he alludes to such a history. Asking when pp. 136-264 of MS 116 were written, he observes that this part of MS 116 is a revision of MS 120, a manuscript from 1937-1938, and goes on: 'I should hazard a conjecture that it was actually written late in that period, i.e. 1938-1944 perhaps as late as as 1944. There is internal evidence – closeness of the thoughts to those in MS 129 written in the autumn of 1944 – to support this conjecture' (von Wright, p. 125). But apart from this rather vague conjecture, nothing is intimated about a specific history of MS 129 and so about a large part of *Philosophical Investigations*, § 243-421. Everything seems to indicate that the history of this part simply and largely coincides with MS 129, for in the period prior to the manuscript, 1937-1944, Wittgenstein is said by von Wright to be almost exclusively concerned with philosophy of mathematics.

But study of *manuscripts* and *notebooks* instead of fair copies and typescripts shows that, contrary to von Wright's claim, a

---

have filtered into the 'Intermediate Version' are the present paragraphs 297 and 308. Most remarks in TS 228 deriving from MS 129 and MS 116 have earlier sources themselves. The history of two random examples is: *Philosophical Investigations*, § 297 (MS 120, p. 47; MS 116, p. 207; TS 228, p. 41), *Philosophical Investigations*, § 405 (MS 120, pp. 158 and 203; MS 116, pp. 157-158; TS 228, p. 34).

[15] Mainly between pages 1 and 92 in MS 129 one finds most of the final sources for *Philosophical Investigations*, § 243-421. The manuscript is important because of the different way in which this part of the *Investigations* is composed. But it has little relevance to the history of fragments, since most of them have already been cast in their final form.

major part of Wittgenstein's philosophy of mind *did* evolve between 1937 and 1944, and at the beginning of that period rather than the end. Two manuscripts in particular supply many *first* sources of § 243-421: MS 119 (24-9-1937/19-11-1937) and MS 120 (19-11-1937/26-4-1938). Of the latter manuscript von Wright states merely that MS 116, pp. 136-264 are a revision of it.[16] That tallies as far as MS 116 is concerned, but is seriously inadequate to MS 120, since the latter contains many passages that have been left out of MS 116 but included in *Philosophical Investigations*, § 243-421, for instance the fragments that belong to the most widely discussed of Wittgenstein's philosophy of mind: § 244, 246, 248, and 265. And MS 119 also contains the first versions of the equally important paragraphs 258 and 270. If we are to believe the critical literature on the 'private language argument', these paragraphs form the lynchpin of Wittgenstein's revolutionary contribution to the philosophy of mind. Thus the 'nucleus' of Wittgenstein's philosophy of mind was not written in the second half of 1944, as von Wright would have it appear, but already at the end of 1937 and beginning of 1938.

And there is more to be mined from MS 119 and MS 120. MS 119 contains the first sources of a number of paragraphs in the so-called part about rules (PI, § 189-242).[17] What we find between

---

[16] The first part of MS 116 (pp. 1-136) is a revision of TS 213. See Hilmy (1987, pp. 25-33) for a difference of opinion with von Wright about the period in which this part of MS 116 was written and, indirectly, about the importance of TS 213 for the genesis of the *Investigations*. MS 116 (pp. 136-264) mainly supplies material to *Philosophical Investigations*, § 664-693. Many of these fragments in turn go back to MS 120 (pp. 187 ff.).

[17] The correspondences between sources in MS 119 and paragraphs in *Philosophical Investigations* is:

Philosophical Investigations	MS 119 (pages)
191	35
192	36
193	28-31
194	36-40
195	41-42
196	42-43
197	44-46
215	46-47
216	47-49

pages 99 and 148 is even more interesting. For fifty pages Wittgenstein writes in a surprisingly discursive style about the logical relations between the concepts 'doubt' and 'certainty', between 'certainty' and 'action', about 'certainty' and the 'beginning of language-games', and about all this in relation to the concept 'form of life'. Although some of these remarks were published isolated from the rest of the manuscript,[18] it would be unwise to disregard the importance of this part of MS 119 for the genesis of the *Investigations*... and of *On Certainty*. For Wittgenstein arrives at his fundamental insights into the relations between 'doubt', 'certainty', and 'action' as early as 1937 in MS 119, and not as late as 1949-1951 in *On Certainty*. Moreover, these pages in MS 119 make it clear that there is an intrinsic connection between Wittgenstein's logical or grammatical description of language-games and forms of life and his analysis of epistemic concepts like 'doubt' and 'certainty', so that the basis for the traditional, purely epistemological interpretation of *On Certainty* is cut away (see chapter 3, § 2). From page 170 through to the end (page 295) this manuscript is devoted to the question of 'private language' and the status of first person statements. And although the number of protoversions of fragments from the *Investigations* is comparatively small, there are many *other* fragments about the *same* themes, so that we can safely say that a very important and large part of § 189-421 already crystallizes in 1937 in MS 119.

The same can be said about MS 120, though the number of protoversions and final versions from the *Investigations* is considerably greater here. We can take for instance § 398-411, a part that receives less attention in the debate over the 'private language argument' than parts which precede it in the published text. But the manuscript sources prove that § 398-411 originate *earlier* than all other paragraphs addressing the 'private language argument' and that it forms a substantial part of that argument, namely the part criticizing the fallacious idea that the term 'I' refers to a metaphysical person or owner. Manuscript sources also show that the genesis of § 398-411 goes back even further than 1938 (MS 120); early in 1932 (MS 113, pp. 245-251) Wittgenstein already warns

---

[18] Under the title 'Ursache und Wirkung: Intuitives Erfassen' in *Philosophia* vol. 6, 1976, pp. 391-408.

against the application of concepts derived from the physical space to the 'visual space', a comparison of which he says in *Philosophical Investigations*, § 398: 'The "visual room" is the one that has no owner. I can as little own it as I can walk about it, or look at it, or point to it.' In MS 113 he writes:

> When we speak of the visual space we are readily seduced by the picture as if it were a kind of peep-show that everyone carries with him. That is, we then use the word 'space' analogously to the case in which we call a room a space. (p. 248)

> My visual field does not display any incompleteness that could lead me to turn around and look what lies behind me. In the visual space there is no 'behind me'... (p. 249)

Wittgenstein continues this discussion[19] in 1932-1934 in MS 156b[20] and subsequently formulates the final version of § 398-411 in 1938 in MS 120.

The history of § 398-411 already showed how little Wittgenstein can be said to work according to the 'brainwave' method, but the history of what is perhaps the most celebrated paragraph of the *Investigations*, § 244, offers the best proof of this. This single fragment gradually evolves in the period 1932-1944. The first proto-version reads as follows:

> The transition from the toothache to the statement 'I am in pain' is simply quite different from the transition from the noise to the statement 'someone is in this room'. That means the transitions belong to quite different language-games. (MS 113, p. 104)

Besides proving that Wittgenstein already uses the term 'language-game' seriously before 1933-1936, this fragment from 1931-1932 also shows him anticipating the later idea in § 244 that 'words are connected with the primitive, the natural, expressions of the sensation and used in their place'. We might add that Wittgenstein wrote this passage in MS 113 as a critique of his earlier view that first person statements are based on an immediate

---

[19] Wittgenstein closely gears this discussion to the 'No ownership' theory (see Strawson 1959, pp. 95-99) which he already describes in *Philosophical Remarks*, § 57 ff. Paragraph 398 is the extremely complex result of this equally complex discussion.

[20] This manuscript is discussed at length in chapter 4, § 2 (a).

acquaintance with subjective experience.[21]   Paragraph 244 takes firmer shape in MS 120:

> I have not learnt the words 'I have' so that it was said to me for instance: observe who is in pain and if it is you, point to yourself etc. But these words of mine are the direct translation of an uttered complaint. (MS 120, p. 33)

One notebook from the same period (1938)[22] is in fact wholly devoted to the exact formulation of the logical character of expressions. The conclusion of § 244, 'So your are saying that the word "pain" really means crying? – On the contrary: the verbal expression of pain replaces crying and does not describe it', is finally reached in a way that might have given less cause for behaviouristic interpretations than the published fragment:

> 'So you are saying that the word "pain" originally means the crying of pain?' – On the contrary. It replaces crying, but does not say that someone cries. The words 'I am in pain' become a part of the pain-behaviour; and hence do not say that someone behaves thus.   And like this all the linguistic expressions of sensations are connected with the primitive expressions of sensations. (MS 124, pp. 223-224)

I confine myself to these few examples since later chapters in this book quote extensively from MS 113, MS 156, MS 158, MS 119, and MS 120 and make it even plainer how and how far the genesis of § 243-421 goes back to 1937 and even farther. Later chapters will also show that the strict division which von Wright seems to make between Wittgenstein's work in philosophy of mathematics and philosophy of psychology is not entirely correct. In MS 120, for instance, we find large-scale application of insights from philosophy of mathematics to philosophy of psychology (see chapter 7, § 4). Moreover, in manuscripts from the second half of 1938 and later Wittgenstein writes about philosophy of psychology as well as about philosophy of mathematics. Examples are MS 121 (26-4-1938/9-1-1939), where Wittgenstein devotes a good many pages to his idea in the *Investigations*, § 303 that a sensation 'is not a *something*, but not a *nothing* either!', and to a lesser extent MS 123

---

[21] For a verificationistic and also behaviouristic interpretation of Wittgenstein's philosophy of mind between 1929 and 1931, see my article 'The Development of Wittgenstein's Views about Other Minds' (forthcoming) *Synthese*.

[22] This notebook contains 94 pages and is written in English from page 70 onwards.

from 1941.[23] So we have enough material to prove that between 1937 and 1944 Wittgenstein works continuously on first and final versions of § 243-421, besides his work on philosophy of mathematics.

I have drawn up a table in order to give a more complete and accurate idea of the *first* manuscript sources of a large part of § 243-421 (see table 1.2). But first I want to comment on von Wright's table of *latest* manuscript sources of part 1 of the *Investigations* (see table 1.1).[24]

This table invites the following comments. As von Wright notes in his own commentary, only the latest sources are accounted for in the table and it is a task for future research to track down the earliest sources. Thus the table does not indicate when and where fragments from the *Investigations* were originally written nor where the first protoversions of these fragments can be found. One of the problems is that the table itself – and the same is usually true of von Wright's article 'The Wittgenstein Papers' – fails to make it clear which manuscripts have contributed to which parts or paragraphs of the *Investigations*. By way of clarification I will therefore briefly sketch the contents of some manuscripts that contribute largely to the *Investigations*. My main reason for doing so is to show that von Wright's historical analysis of § 243-421 in fact stops with manuscripts from 1944-1945.

MS 114, MS 115 (1), and MS 116 (1) are all revisions of TS 213 from 1932-1933. This so-called 'Big Typescript' contains only one section that is related to material from § 243-421, but only one fragment from this section has found its way to the *Investigations*, which allows us to conclude that MS 114, MS 115 (1) and (2), and MS 116 (1) do *not* contribute to § 243-421.[25] An exception has to

---

[23] In this manuscript (between 16-5-1941 and 6-6-1941) Wittgenstein criticizes for the first time his own and Carnap's logical behaviouristic construction of third person statements about other minds. See also my article 'The Development of Wittgenstein's Views about Other Minds' (forthcoming) *Synthese.*

[24] See von Wright (1982, p. 130).

[25] But *Philosophical Investigations*, § 257 and 353-356 do derive from MS 115 (see table 1.2). The section from TS 213 is called 'Schmerz haben' and is part of the chapter 'Idealismus, etc.'. This chapter contains 19 fragments from *Philosophical Remarks*, chapter 6.

Table 1.1 Latest manuscript sources of remarks in the *Philosophical Investigations*

MS	Year of Writing	Number of selected Bemerkungen (or parts of them)	Randbemerkungen (or parts of them)
108	1930	2	
109	1930-1931	1	
110	1931	8	
112	1931	5	
153a	1931	1	
114	1933-34	38	4
115 (1)	1933-34	79	2
110	1933-34	1	
116 (1)	1934? (1937?)	47	5
115 (2)	1936	26	
152	1936	34	
157a	1937	11	
157b	1937	13	
117	1937	14	
119	1937	10	
121	1937-38	1	
162b	1939-40	4	
163	1941	3	
116 (2)	1938-44	46	
116 (3)	1944?	28	1
124	1944	16	
127	1944	1	
128	1944	3	
180a	circa 1945	1	
129	1944-45	201	3
130	1945?	15	
116 (4)	1945	29	
Total		637	16

be made for MS 115, which does contribute solidly to the paragraphs on the concept of willing (PI, § 611-632) in the form of
seven all but definitive fragments.[26] MS 152 has a more provisional status than most other manuscripts from the table. It mostly contains sources for § 1-189, such as the discussion centring
around the concept of reading (PI, § 156-178). And one also finds
here the earliest of many versions of the preface to the *Investigations*.

The fact that MS 119 has been included in the table, after what I
said about this manuscript before, might suggest that it forms an
early contribution to § 243-421. But this is not so. I have already
identified nine passages out of ten as sources for § 191-216, a
section dealing with the concept 'rule'.[27] The next big contribution comes from MS 116 (2). This manuscript does in fact
supply material to § 243-241, but we already noted that it is a
revision of a manuscript from 1938, MS 120, whereas MS 116 (2)
should be assigned to 1944, according to von Wright. It is
therefore a very late contribution to § 243-421. MS 116 (3) and MS
128, both from 1944, are important sources for *Philosophical
Investigations*, § 633-647 (see chapter 7, § 5). Neither manuscript
can be dated with precision, according to von Wright; he conjec-
tures that both were written in 1944. In any case MS 128 con-
tributes *more* to § 633-647 than the three fragments mentioned by
von Wright; nine fragments from MS 128 are more or less final

---

[26] The correspondences are:

Philosophical Investigations	MS 115	MS 157a
611	104 + 107	25
612	104	
613	105 + 111	43-44
617	103	
618	106	22
620	107	
621	108	37

[27] See note 17.

sources of § 633-647.[28] MS 116(4) contains sources for a wide variety of fragments in the *Investigations*. One finds here for instance the paragraph on the concept of imagination (PI, § 370), but also the paragraph on the genesis of the problem of dualism and behaviourism (PI, § 308). The last major contribution occurs in MS 129 from 1944. This manuscript contains very many sources for § 243-421, but as I noted above, it is a fair copy based on *earlier* manuscripts. The conclusion is that von Wright's table, however valuable it may be, does not in fact trace the earliest sources of the *Philosophical Investigations* in general and § 243-421 in particular. The sources of § 243-421 are confined to fair copies from 1944 (MS 116(2) and MS 129). The sources cited by von Wright dating from before 1944 have little or no relevance to § 243-421, so that one is apt to conclude that the genesis of this important part of the *Investigations*, in contrast to other parts, goes back no farther than 1944. Table 1.2 shows that the ancestry of § 243-421 is much longer and that it is divided between various manuscripts.

This table calls for some comments too. In the first place it is incomplete; for a number of fragments I have been unable to trace any sources. Possibly I have overlooked them, but it may also be that there are no manuscript sources. Secondly, I have designated MS 129 as a source when I have been unable to find an earlier source. Conversely, I have *not* designated MS 129 as a source when I have been able to find an earlier source. Thirdly, it may be that there are earlier sources of fragments which I have over-

---

[28] The correspondences are:

Philosophical Investigations	MS 128
633	34
634	35
638	2
639	7
640	8
642	9
644	11
645	14
646	26

looked, or which no longer exist – since a number of manuscripts in the Nachlass are missing. Fourthly, it should be realized that this table indicates the earliest sources, so that the sources are mostly not identical with their final version in the *Philosophical Investigations*. Sometimes a source contains only part of a fragment from the *Investigations*, sometimes the whole fragment but with a number of changes. But in each case there is a clear family resemblance between the source and the paragraph in the *Investigations*. For an illustration of this I refer to the quotation of sources of § 244 on pages 12-13 . The quotation from MS 113 is perhaps the most extreme example of a source in the table which only slightly resembles a published fragment. The two other examples are representative of the degree of resemblance between sources mentioned in the table and fragments in the *Investigations*. Finally, I wish to point out that a number of manuscripts in this table are not mentioned at all in von Wright's table. These are: TS 213, MS 158, MS 120, MS 165. But my table too omits a number of manuscripts which contain important material for a proper understanding of § 243-421, such as MS 113, MS 156a and b, and MS 123. And if some manuscripts scarcely figure in the table, such as MS 121 and MS 158, this does not mean that they supply only a small amount of relevant material.

Finally, a few remarks about the genesis of part 2 of the *Investigations*. Von Wright's account here seems to me quite accurate, and so with the publication of *Zettel*, the *Remarks on the Philosophy of Psychology*, and the *Last Writings* we now have almost the full history of part 2 of the *Investigations*. But two criticisms are warranted. In the first place it is not true that the *entire* second part evolves in 1945-1946.[29] Thus Wittgenstein's analysis of the concept 'seeing as' occurs much earlier, for instance in MS 123 from 1941 (see chapter 6, § 3 and 4). In the second place von Wright underestimates the importance of MS 169 for part 2 of the *Investigations* when he writes: 'There are also some remarks selected from the pocket notebook MS 169' (von Wright, p. 134). This manuscript opens with a number of paragraphs that have been almost entirely incorporated in part 2: *Philosophical Investi-*

[29] Von Wright suggests this (1982, pp. 115 and 134).

gations II viii, ix, x, and a number of remarks about 'seeing as' in xi. Moreover, one finds in this manuscript protoversions and alternative versions of fragments about 'pretending', 'mathematical certainty', and 'knowledge of other people's feelings' (PI II xi, pp. 222-229) (see chapter 5, § 2 and 4).

Table 1.2 Correspondences between *Philosophical Investigations*, § 243-421 and early manuscripts

Philosophical Investigations	Original Source	Page/date
243	MS 124 (1944)	213, 221-223
244	MS 110 (1931)	105
	MS 120 (1937-38)	35
	MS 180a (1944)	21-22
	MS 124 (1944)	222
245	MS 124 (1944)	270
246	TS 213 (1932-33)	209
	MS 120 (1937-38)	35, 157
	MS 180a (1944)	224-225
248	MS 120 (1937-38)	225
	MS 116 (1937-44)	179
249	MS 120 (1937-38)	185
	MS 121 (1938)	29
250	MS 124 (1944)	269
253	TS 213 (1932-33)	510
254	MS 129 (1944)	41
255	MS 163 (1941)	6-9-1941
256	MS 124 (1944)	226
257	TS 213 (1932-33)	207
	MS 115 (1933-36)	91
258	MS 119 (1937)	241-246, 255, 258-259
	MS 124 (1944)	226-227
259	MS 163 (1941)	6-9-1941
260	MS 124 (1944)	227
261	MS 121 (1938)	8-9

Philosophical Investigations	Original Source	Page/date
	MS 124 (1944)	227-228
263	MS 119 (1937)	138-139
264	MS 119 (1937)	183
265	MS 120 (1937-38)	135
267	MS 120 (1937-38)	137
268	MS 119 (1937)	199
	MS 120 (1937-38)	138
269	MS 119 (1937)	252-253
270	MS 119 (1937)	207-211, 235
	MS 165 (1941-44)	160-162
	MS 124 (1944)	282-283
271	MS 120 (1937-38)	109
	MS 124 (1944)	271
272	MS 165 (1941-44)	179-180
	MS 124 (1944)	291
273	MS 165 (1941-44)	178-179
	MS 124 (1944)	291
274	MS 165 (1941-44)	180-181
	MS 124 (1944)	291-292
275	MS 165 (1941-44)	181-182
	MS 124 (1944)	292
276	MS 163 (1941)	6-9-1941
277	MS 120 (1937-38)	3-4
	MS 165 (1941-44)	183-184
278	MS 163 (1941)	6-9-1941
280	MS 129 (1944)	23
281	MS 165 (1941-44)	201
	MS 124 (1944)	238
282	MS 110 (1931)	58
	MS 165 (1941-44)	188-189
	MS 124 (1944)	239
283	MS 120 (1937-38)	97
	MS 157a (1934-37)	14-15
	MS 124 (1944)	240
284	MS 165 (1941-44)	56
	MS 124 (1944)	242-243

Philosophical Investigations	Original Source	Page/date
285	MS 124 (1944)	244
286	MS 179 (1944)	64
287	MS 165 (1941-44)	188
288	MS 119 (1937)	279
	MS 165 (1941-44)	160
	MS 124 (1944)	245
289	MS 121 (1938)	14-15, 33
	MS 124 (1944)	272
290	MS 119 (1937)	222-223, 264-265, 279
	MS 158 (1938)	7
	MS 120 (1937-38)	119
	MS 124 (1944)	286
291	MS 163 (1941)	6-9-1941
293	MS 124 (1944)	256-257
294	MS 120 (1937-38)	51
	MS 116 (1937-44)	209
295	MS 124 (1944)	258-259
296	MS 121 (1938)	9
	MS 124 (1944)	259
297	MS 120 (1937-38)	47
	MS 116 (1937-44)	207
298	MS 124 (1944)	260
300	MS 119 (1937)	255
	MS 162b (1939-40)	62-63
301	MS 162b (1939-40)	68
302	MS 120 (1937-38)	21-22
	MS 129 (1944)	18
303	MS 129 (1944)	62-63
304	MS 121 (1938)	14, 40
	MS 165 (1941-44)	163-164
305	MS 120 (1937-38)	244
306	MS 120 (1937-38)	123
307	MS 120 (1937-38)	125
	MS 121 (1938)	21
	MS 161 (1939)	79

Philosophical Investigations	Original Source	Page/date
310	MS 165 (1941-44)	171-172
	MS 124 (1944)	288
311	MS 165 (1941-44)	173-174
	MS 124 (1944)	288-289
312	MS 165 (1941-44)	175-176
	MS 124 (1944)	289-290
313	MS 165 (1941-44)	178
	MS 124 (1944)	290
314	MS 124 (1944)	271
315	MS 165 (1941-44)	162
	MS 124 (1944)	286
317	MS 117 (1937-38)	134
318	MS 164 (1941-44)	157-158
	MS 124 (1944)	215
319	MS 124 (1944)	218
320	MS 180a (1944)	17
323	MS 124 (1944)	216-217
324	MS 153a (1931)	152
	MS 180a (1944)	19
	MS 124 (1944)	220
325	MS 153a (1931)	152
	MS 113 (1931-32)	105
	MS 115 (1933-36)	101
326	MS 112 (1931)	221
327	MS 165 (1941-44)	206
328	MS 165 (1941-44)	207-208
329	TS 213 (1932-33)	223
336	TS 213 (1932-33)	224
	MS 117 (1937-38)	135
337	MS 164 (1941-44)	162-163
339	MS 110 (1931)	2-4
	MS 117 (1937-38)	127-128, 133
	MS 165 (1941-44)	3-4
340	MS 165 (1941-44)	20
342	MS 165 (1941-44)	195-196
343	MS 120 (1937-38)	206

Philosophical Investigations	Original Source	Page/date
344	MS 165 (1941-44)	192-193
345	MS 165 (1941-44)	197-198
346	MS 165 (1941-44)	209-211
347	MS 165 (1941-44)	194
348	MS 165 (1941-44)	198-199
350	MS 119 (1937)	226-227
	MS 116 (1937-44)	141-142
351	MS 116 (1937-44)	142-143
353	MS 115 (1933-36)	71-72
354	MS 115 (1933-36)	74
355	MS 115 (1933-36)	74
356	MS 115 (1933-36)	74
357	MS 165 (1941-44)	200-201
359	MS 110 (1931)	35-36
360	MS 110 (1931)	58
361	MS 165 (1941-44)	204-205
362	MS 129 (1944)	11
363	MS 124 (1944)	262-263
366	MS 124 (1944)	250
367	MS 116 (1937-44)	207
368	MS 162b (1939-40)	90-91
372	TS 213 (1932-33)	255
374	MS 120 (1937-38)	120-121
376	MS 120 (1937-38)	118-119
377	MS 165 (1941-44)	183-184
380	MS 180a (1944)	64
381	MS 180a (1944)	66
384	MS 124 (1944)	284
385	MS 124 (1944)	252
386	MS 124 (1944)	272
387	MS 124 (1944)	273
388	MS 165 (1941-44)	190-191
391	MS 129 (1944)	13
392	MS 129 (1944)	14
393	MS 129 (1944)	14-15
398	MS 113 (1931-32)	245-251

Philosophical Investigations	Original Source	Page/date
	MS 120 (1937-38)	55-57
399	MS 120 (1937-38)	79
400	MS 120 (1937-38)	87
401	MS 120 (1937-38)	84
402	MS 120 (1937-38)	71
403	MS 116 (1937-44)	154-155
404	MS 120 (1937-38)	31-37
405	MS 120 (1937-38)	158, 203
406	MS 116 (1937-44)	158
407	MS 120 (1937-38)	154
409	MS 120 (1937-38)	149, 152
410	MS 120 (1937-38)	147
411	MS 120 (1937-38)	158-160
412	MS 124 (1944)	264-265
413	MS 124 (1944)	266
414	MS 120 (1937-38)	79
415	TS 213 (1932-33)	408
416	MS 124 (1944)	275
417	MS 124 (1944)	275-276
418	MS 124 (1944)	227
419	MS 124 (1944)	238
420	MS 124 (1944)	277-278
421	MS 124 (1944)	285

CHAPTER 2

LANGUAGE-GAMES AS CONTEXT OF MEANING

When Wittgenstein returns to Cambridge in 1929, there are many intersecting paths in his thought, and we would do him wrong by following just one path and seeing in this path the only true starting-point of his later philosophy of psychology. In the preface to the *Philosophical Investigations* he remarks that he is obliged to move criss-cross in all directions through a vast area of thought, and we should take this remark seriously. In this chapter, therefore, I shall follow a path without cutting off all kinds of other paths and intersections; many of these other paths, however, will be traced more extensively in the following chapters. In this chapter I start by focusing on Wittgenstein's reaction to the psychological or causal theory of meaning developed by Russell and Odgen & Richards, since this reaction illustrates a number of ramifications occurring in Wittgenstein's thought in 1929 and the first years after. At the same time Wittgenstein's reaction to the psychological or causal theory of meaning provides a convenient link to his emphasis on language-games as the reference point for his logical or grammatical inquiry into the meaning of concepts. Section 1 deals with the psychological theory of meaning, section 2 with language-games.

1. The psychological theory of meaning

Comparing the first work which Wittgenstein published after his return to Cambridge, the *Philosophical Remarks* (PR), with the manuscripts on which it is originally based,[1] one is not surprised that Wittgenstein's familiarity with the psychological theory of

---

[1] The manuscripts are: MS 105, MS 106, MS 107, and the first half of MS 108.

meaning of Russell and Odgen & Richards and his rejection of it have received so little attention in the critical literature.[2] The authors in question are mentioned only once in the *Philosophical Remarks* (§ 21), whereas they are cited more frequently in the Nachlass. Moreover, Wittgenstein enlarges there on the general characteristics of the theory argued by Russell and Odgen & Richards and in this criticism one sees the germination of an important facet of his philosophy of language-games.

In MS 107 the following fragment precedes what is now published as *Philosophical Remarks*, § 16:

> There is a kind of philosophy – one might call it psychologistic philosophy, but I have not yet found a good name for it – which always speaks of associations and the simultaneous or vaguely simultaneous occurrence of events A, B and C; of similar constituents of two events having the consequence that the whole crosses one's mind when a part comes before our eyes. A typical philosophical dead-end. The combination of attempted exactness and actual irrelevance. (MS 107, p. 235)

This is directly followed by Wittgenstein's first critical discussion of Russell's causal explanation of the meaning of 'expecting', i.e. *Philosophical Remarks*, § 16. That by the 'mixture of attempted exactness and actual irrelevance' Wittgenstein is thinking of the approach of Russell and Odgen & Richards appears explicitly from a fragment occurring among a number of drafts for the preface to the *Philosophical Remarks*,[3] the preface in which Wittgenstein claims that his thought goes against the current of the times: 'The thought is completely described by its expression. A description which lies outside of the expression of the thought does not concern us, for it belongs to psychology or physiology' (MS 109, p. 210).

He goes on to remark about the effect of sentences, i.e. their causal relations: ' ... these interest the psychologist, not us. To that extent Odgen & Richards are right with their causal view, except that they don't see the other aspect'. (MS 109, p. 210). Since it is now clear that Wittgenstein dissociates himself – to put it mildly – from the psychological theory of meaning of Russell and Odgen

---

[2] An exception must made for S. Hilmy (1987), to whom this section owes much.

[3] Hilmy (1987, p. 301, quote 429) argues convincingly that the several drafts for a foreword in MS 109 were intended as a foreword to TS 213 and not to what is published as *Philosophical Remarks*.

& Richards, we have to know what this theory says. In general, according to these authors, the meaning of a word is its psychological effect on the mind. By way of association a word evokes certain impressions and images. One has used a word in its correct sense and communication has succeeded if the sign evokes those associations of impressions and images in the listener which the speaker in fact wished to convey. In Russell's *The Analysis of Mind* from 1923 these ideas can be found quite specifically. He defines the meaning of words in terms of associations of 'images and sensations'. 'Image associations' are called 'mnemic phenomena', that is, 'responses of an organism which, so far as hitherto observed facts are concerned, can only be brought under causal laws by including past occurrences in the history of the organism as part of the causes of the present response' (Russell, p. 78). According to Russell, the causal nature of meaning can be summed up in the general law of 'mnemic causation' to which Wittgenstein alludes in the quotation at the beginning of this section: 'If a complex stimulus has caused a complex reaction B in an organism, the occurrence of a part of A on a future occasion tends to cause the whole reaction B' (Russell, p. 86).

The further details of Russell's theory are unimportant here, as are the refinements added to it by Odgen & Richards in their book *The Meaning of Meaning*.[4] The fact is that Wittgenstein was familiar with both works soon after they were published, as Hilmy has shown.[5] It is also clear that Wittgenstein wishes to mark off the causal theory of meaning from his own grammatical inquiry into meaning. But this demarcation will turn into rejection once the causal theory of meaning claims an ability to explain all aspects of meaning. Sometimes Wittgenstein seems also to suggest that the causal theory of meaning says nothing at all about meaning, only something about side effects. Before showing how far the philosophy of language-games was a reaction to the psychological theory of meaning, I want to examine various offshoots of this theory which in Wittgenstein's view are equally products

---

[4] Odgen & Richards put less emphasis on 'images' and their terminology can more readily be interpreted in a behaviouristic fashion. See Hilmy (1987, pp. 118-119).

[5] See Hilmy (1987, pp. 110-112).

of conceptual confusion and which are all accorded a prominent position in the *Philosophical Investigations* and other works.[6]

I just mentioned Wittgenstein's logical analysis of 'expecting' and 'intending' as alternative to and correction of the psychological explanation of their meanings by Russell. Wittgenstein's lifelong preoccupation with the correct analysis of these concepts has been pointed out before by critics, but the origin of this preoccupation is rarely talked about. As indicated by the above-cited fragment that precedes *Philosophical Remarks*, § 16 in MS 107 – Wittgenstein's first debate with Russell's explanation of 'expecting' and 'intending' – the issue at stake in Wittgenstein's analysis of these concepts is the 'psychologistic' philosophy of Russell and Odgen & Richards. Russell's explanation of 'expecting' and 'intending' exemplifies for Wittgenstein a mixture of attempted exactness and actual irrelevance. Later he will attack the application of the causal theory of meaning to other psychological concepts and will take the work of William James in particular (see chapter 7) as a source of conceptual confusions. One can therefore conclude that the causal theory of meaning forms a crossroads in Wittgenstein's analysis of individual psychological concepts. This crossroads is further complicated by the fact that Wittgenstein's lifelong fascination with colour concepts is also aroused by the causal theory of meaning. The causal theory of meaning explains the meaning of colour concepts in terms of introspective recognition of colour experiences and this idea is of course rejected by Wittgenstein (cf. PR, § 16), just as he rejects the explanation of the meaning of 'pain' in terms of introspective recognition.

A third path crossed by the causal theory of meaning, in Wittgenstein's view, has to do with the nature of rule-guided behaviour. In a discussion about obeying rules (carrying out orders) he writes:

---

[6] I am not saying that the attack on the psychological meaning-theory and its various offshoots were Wittgenstein's sole point of departure. On the contrary, it is one of many. Other points of departure are two topics that were discussed by the Vienna Circle in the 1920's, the relation of physical space to visual space and the problem of solipsism and other minds (see further chapter 4, §1a). Still another point of departure has of course to do with the philosophy of mathematics, which is not our topic here, however.

> Don't we have here the essence of the motive in contrast to the cause. Clearly
> yes. The order, when I obey it, becomes the motive of my way of acting.
> And the motive is not hypothetical. I cannot be mistaken in the motive, it is
> contained in my action but not so its cause.
> (Odgen & Richards's and Russell's theory of meaning is thus based on a
> confusion, or equation, of motive and cause.). (MS 110, p. 94)

An explanation of rule-guided behaviour in terms of causes goes
beyond the practice of rule-guided behaviour and is thus irrelevant to the obeying of rules. Confusion is created by reducing
rule-guided behaviour to the causal level and adducing causes
where reasons should be given. In particular the normative aspect of rule-governed behaviour is shut out in this way (see § 2
and chapter 3). Finally, there is a fourth path. But this path is less
specifically linked to the causal theory of meaning than the other
three; in chapter 4 and 5 we shall see that the idea in question also
arises in the context of self-knowledge and knowledge of other
minds. After observing in MS 107 that we are dealing with a
'psychologistic' philosophy, Wittgenstein writes between what is
now published as *Philosophical Remarks*, § 17-18:

> As long as one conceives of the soul as a *thing*, a *body* that is in our head, this
> hypothesis is *not* dangerous. The danger does not lie in the incompleteness and
> roughness of our model, but in its non-transparancy (unclarity).
> The danger starts when we realize that the old model does not suffice, but do
> not change it, but as it were sublimate it. As long as I say the thought is in my
> head, everything is all right, but it would be dangerous if we say: the thought
> is not in my head but in my mind. (MS 107, pp. 238-39; PR, § 229)

In relation to the psychological theory of meaning, the sublimation of the concept 'Seele' entails the following. The meaning of
words first of all becomes a philosophical problem because it is
realized that the linguistic signs themselves, the scratchings on
paper, the sounds, have no meaning. The psychological theory of
meaning believes that the problem can be solved by looking for
something *behind* the signs, a 'Geist', and by seeing the signs
themselves, therefore, as a façade behind which all kinds of
psychic processes take place:

> If one says, the thought is a psychic activity, or an activity of the mind, one
> thinks of the mind as a cloudy, gaseous being, in which much can happen, that
> cannot happen outside of this sphere. And from which one <u>can</u> expect much,
> that is not possible otherwise...

> The thought, as it were, is the organic part of the symbol, the sign the inorganic. And that organic part can achieve things that the inorganic couldn't. (TS 213, p. 286)

The suggestion is that in postulating a hidden mind-mechanism one has been misled by the analogy with bodily processes which are caused by all sorts of internal organic mechanisms. Psychic processes occurring in the magic medium of the mind have to breathe life into 'dead' signs, according to the psychological theory of meaning. It is this sublimation of the concept of the mind as a magic and omnipotent medium of thoughts, images, and internal representations which Wittgenstein reduces to its proper proportions. As was said before, this sublimation of the concept of the mind is not confined to the psychological theory of meaning, but also determines how the relation between body and mind is conceived (cf. LW, § 979).

Wittgenstein's rejection of the psychological theory of meaning provided one of the main impulses for his philosophy of language-games. In the *Philosophical Remarks* but more extensively in TS 213 one sees Wittgenstein presenting his logical approach to the problem of meaning as an *alternative* to the psychological explanations prevalent in the thirties. A fragment that represents this development in some detail is the following:

> The meaning is a definition, not experience. And therefore not causality. What the sign suggests one finds through experience. It is experience that teaches us which signs are least misunderstood. The sign, insofar as it influences the mind by suggestion, interests us only as a move in a game: term in a system that is autonomous.
> It would be characteristic for a specific erroneous view if a philosopher believed a sentence would have to be printed in a red colour, since only in this way would it completely express what the author wants to say. (Here we would have the magical view of signs instead of the logical one.)[7]
> The investigation of whether the meaning of a sign is its effect is a grammatical investigation.
> I believe that to the causal theory of meaning one can simply answer that if someone received a push and fell, we don't call the fall the meaning of the push...

---

[7] After this the following has been deleted: (The magical sign would work like a drug and the causal theory would be correct for it.)

The sense of language is not determined by its effect. Or what one calls the sense, the meaning in language is not its effect. (TS 213, pp. 40-41)

That Wittgenstein is opposing the causal theory of meaning in this fragment requires no further comment, but something more can be said about the way in which he does this. At the beginning of this chapter we saw that Wittgenstein found a 'mixture of attempted exactness and actual irrelevance' in the causal theory of meaning. In particular the meaning of 'exactness' is not unambiguous. A clue is offered by the manuscript version of the first part of this fragment. After the statement 'The meaning is a definition', Wittgenstein writes: 'What is exact is the internal relation.' (MS 153a, p. 136). From this we can infer that the psychological theory of meaning, in which meaning is explained via external relations, is not exact. The following fragment justifies this conclusion: 'Frege about psychological logic. All his remarks are about the inexactness of psychological considerations in contrast with logic' (MS 153a, p. 228). In the following chapter it will be argued that Wittgenstein's grammatical description of internal relations is a description of criteria for the application of concepts. Criteria are contrasted by him with symptoms. Consequently, the causal explanation of the meaning of concepts via external relations can be called an investigation of symptoms. Within the causal inquiry we can then talk about 'attempted exactness' in the following way. In the investigation of, for instance, thought processes, certain phenomena are discovered in psychology – and certainly the psychology of Watson, Russell, and James – that can be measured, such as chronometry of the understanding of individual letters. A method is now thought to have been found which enables us to measure 'thinking' and 'understanding'. According to Wittgenstein, however, what is really problematical about thinking remains unsolved here: not the phenomenon itself has been investigated but a side effect; a measurable symptom and not a criterion; something which is externally related to the phenomenon and not internally.

The following needs to be said about this distinction between criteria and symptoms. In the first place it does not serve to drive a permanent wedge between the logical and the empirical, since by Wittgenstein's own account (BLB, p. 25) the borderline between criteria and symptoms is indefinite. Thus it is a standard scientific procedure to call phenomena which can be accurately measured criteria. 'Rain', for instance, is defined in terms of points on the barometer, and if the barometer were also to function in everyday life as a standard by which the meaning of 'rain' is explained, instead of the customary standard, a feeling of wetness, the reading of a barometer would be a criterion and not a mere symptom. Secondly, this division between criteria and symptoms by no means serves to reject causal explanations in psychology in favour of conceptual analyses[8] and so promote a conceptual conservatism. What Wittgenstein warns against is merely a *confusion* of criteria and symptoms. This confusion occurs for instance in psychology when on the one hand 'thinking' is used in the normal sense of the word and on the other hand is regarded as measurable in terms of (physiological) reactions. Wittgenstein does not say that this kind of measurement is impossible, but only that it involves an *entirely different* phenomenon from what 'thinking' is normally understood to mean. As he puts it: 'There are gradations of expecting, but it is nonsense to speak of a measurement of hoping, if one allows the word "hope" its use' (MS 115, p. 73). So while Wittgenstein does not presume to deprive psychologists of their causal method, he does want to demarcate his philosophical work from scientific work. Philosophy is (among other things) the description of criteria. Criteria are not objects of knowledge but a standard of knowledge.[9] Thus criteria are learned in an entirely different way from symptoms. One learns that something is a symptom for something else by being given (specific) information (indications on the barometer in the case of rain). By contrast, one cannot learn a criterion as an object of knowledge, since any information that is supplied – wet trousers, raindrops on the window, etc. – presupposes familiarity

---

[8] See especially Fodor (1975, pp. 2-9) for this misleading interpretation of Wittgenstein and also Ryle.

[9] In saying that criteria are not an object of knowledge in the sense that the description of criteria does not inform us about something we did not know previously, I dissociate myself from the standard epistemological view of criteria, initiated by Albritton (1957). The best criticism of this tradition is found in Cavell (1979).

with the criterion, i.e. the criterion that the meaning of 'rain' depends on what rain looks like, what it feels like: 'Whether a phenomenon is a symptom of the rain, experience teaches; what counts as a criterion of the rain is a matter of agreement, of our determination. (Definition)' (MS 115, p. 72).

2. Horizontal and vertical language-games

The rejection of a psychologistic explanation of meaning leads Wittgenstein to undertake a logical description of the context of meaning. In this investigation he proceeds like the Adolf Loos of philosophy. Just as the Viennese architect wanted to exclude all decorations and frills as pointless details from truly functional design, so Wittgenstein excludes all empirical elements as super-fluous decoration from his logic of meaning: 'What is un-necessary in logic, is no use either. What is unnecessary, is super-fluous' (TS 213, p. 90). It is unnecessary and therefore superfluous to appeal to psychic processes in order to explain a meaning; it is enough to shift one's view to the context of meaning. In this section I limit myself to a more or less structural description of language-games and forms of life as context of meaning. I do this mainly in order to give a more specific character to the concept of language-game, which is often characterized in a merely sche-matic and global fashion in the critical literature.

Our starting-point is the following fragment:

> 'Because of the fact that I *mean* the sentence, it gets life'. But I have to give it a quite *definite* life, not just life. *This* meaning, not another. If I mean it, I must mean it *thus*. The words have to glance at their meanings. – But the lively glance of the word at its meaning is based on the steady movements in the field of application. (MS 129, p. 94)

'Field of applications' is a more prosaic term for language-game and form of life. The simplest – and most current – interpretation of language-game is that it is a primary linguistic context of agreements from which words and verbal utterances derive their meaning.[10] But the logic of language-games is much more

---

[10] Hintikka (1986, pp. 217 ff.) also opposes this linguistic interpretation, but he

complex. We can mention, among others, the following two considerations. One: Not all language-games function on the same logical level. The failure to distinguish these differences in level I call the 'ground-floor fallacy'. Two: Language-games do not just consist of actual verbal moves: the potentiality, the technique or skill of the game is much more important. The corresponding fallacy I call the 'actuality fallacy'. Both fallacies have led to sophistic interpretations, such as behaviourism and introspective psychology or philosophy and scepticism.

In order to help chart the structure of language games I split up the general relationship of concepts to language-games into *horizontal* and *vertical* relations.[11] A horizontal relation expresses a relation of a concept *within* language-games, a vertical relation expresses a relation *between* language-games. The first relation applies to all concepts, the second to some concepts. Some concepts, therefore, are not only horizontally embedded in a language-game, but are also embedded in a vertical relation to other language-games. To put it more simply: all concepts are horizontally embedded in language games, but not on the same level. For instance, the expression 'to feel pain' is horizontally embedded in the language-game of sensations (which in this case is essentially an expressive language-game), and the expression 'to pretend to feel pain' is horizontally embedded in the language-game of pretending, but the latter game itself presupposes in a vertical sense the language-game 'feeling pain'.

With these vertical relations I want to emphasize two points: not all language-games function on the same logical level, but there is instead a hierarchy of logically more and less fundamental language-games; within fundamental language-games the linguis-

---

forgets to involve the meaning of 'forms of life' in the discussion. See for 'forms of life' chapter 3, § 2 and 3.

[11] The same sort of distinction is made by Hintikka (1986, chapter 11). His terminology ('primary versus secondary language-games') is misleading, however, for it is in these terms that Wittgenstein describes one specific example of vertical relations between language-games, i.e. the language-games of primary word-meanings and secondary word-meanings. These language-games have rather idiosyncratic features that cannot be predicated of all language-games vertically related to other language-games. See chapter 6, § 5 for the logic of secondary word-meanings.

tic element is less prominent than in less fundamental language-games. I first discuss the horizontal relations of language-games.

In the first place the horizontal relations of language-games include more than just actual verbal moves. Via a horizontal relation a concept is not embedded in a language-game as a link in a syntactic and semantic chain. In a language-game it constantly moves in a field of 'Anwendungen'. The meaning of 'Anwendung', even more than 'Gebrauch', is to employ, use, or apply something for a certain purpose; in any case it is a way of doing something, of acting, and not just a way of talking. In the second place – and this is the crucial point – the actual speaking and acting presuppose familiarity with a rule-guided praxis. Taking the (non-) verbal part to be the whole of language-games has led to the actuality fallacy. Wittgenstein was already wary of this: 'One sees the terminology, but fails to see the technique of applying it' (RPP I, § 911). 'Technique' is a term derived from Spengler for the rule-governed praxis which forms the real structure of horizontal relations.[12] This structure of rules constitutes the meaning of concepts in the language-game:

> The concept of pain is simply embedded in our life in a certain way. It is characterized by very definite connexions.
> Just as in chess a move with the king only takes place within a certain context, and it cannot be removed from this context. – To the concept there corresponds a technique. (The eye smiles only within a face.) (RPP II, § 150)

> And put more generally: 'To understand a sentence means to understand a language. To understand a language means to be master of a technique' (PI, § 199).

Mastery of a technique is a designation for the whole body of rules which gives the horizontal relations of language-games

---

12 Not only his *Der Untergang des Abendlandes* (1923) but also his far less well-known *Der Mensch und der Technik* (1931) contain passages that probably influenced Wittgenstein's use of 'technique'. Spengler defines 'technique' as the 'Anwendung', the practical handling of things (p. 8). The products of technique are not the result of abstract reasoning but of a practice. Just as a way of acting underlies thinking, so speaking underlies grammar. The opposite relations are considered by Spengler to be typical of rationalistic philosophy, a philosophy based on the prejudice 'that the sentence expresses a judgement or thought' (p. 41). For a striking resemblance with this quote, see *Philosophical Investigations*, § 317.

their normative character. In the course of this study the horizontal relations of specific concepts will be dealt with extensively; here I confine myself to general characteristics of rules. The following five characteristics are attributed by Wittgenstein, if not very systematically, to technique (and so to rules).
(a) Rule-guided behaviour is not the same as merely regular behaviour. (b) Rule-guided behaviour is learned. (c) Rules enable people to give reasons and justifications for behaviour. (d) Rule-guided behaviour implies criteria for the correctness of behaviour. (e) Rule-guided behaviour is recognizable behaviour for others. Characteristic (a) clarifies what rule-guided behaviour is *not*: merely regular behaviour. Language-games constitute the meaning of concepts then and only then when rules are actually obeyed. Failure to recognize this distinction soon leads to the actuality fallacy: rule-governed behaviour is identified with actual behaviour, which can always be described in the form of generalizations. What is typically human about rule-guided behaviour is lost as well, since the behaviour of animals and even the way that computers and brains function can be described via generalizations too. Wittgenstein guards against this inflation of the rule in two ways: behaviour that is guided by rules is not necessarily capable of description in a blueprint of rules and behaviour that can be thus described is not necessarily rule-guided.

With regard to the first point: many authors have represented Wittgenstein as wanting to subject the use of words to a strict diet of rules or criteria, ultimately trimming language down to something abstract. But in fact one finds in Wittgenstein the view that language is, rather, like something vegetable or animal, naturally grown rather than abstract. And to expect logic (in the sense of strict rules) from this kind of naturally selected idiom is to expect people to be able to find their way around town via an exact geographical map in their minds. Wittgenstein, by contrast, points out that if we were to make such a map, assuming that we could, our undisturbed traffic from home to work and vice versa would be disrupted at once (RPP I, § 556). He also points out that there are situations where even in retrospect actions cannot be meaningfully described in terms of strict rules. In *Philosophical*

Investigations, § 83 he pictures a group of people who seem to be playing different kinds of ball games at the same time and are also chasing each other with the ball and demonstrating other forms of 'pointless' behaviour. This 'undisciplined' playing he recognizes in language too, as appears from the earlier version of this fragment in TS 213, p. 254. He says there about the statement 'N has died':

> Of course, the sentence is taken away from somewhere, and if you like, he is also playing now a game with very primitive rules; for it remains true after all that I got an answer to the question 'who is N', or a series of answers that were not completely erratic. – We can say: Let's investigate the rules of the language. If it has no rules there and there, then that is the upshot of our investigation. (TS 213, p. 254)

As for the second point: not all behaviour that actually conforms to rules is rule-governed. Otherwise actions would no longer be distinct from conditioned responses or reflexes. Once-only, compulsive, gratuitous, or stereotype reactions would have to be called rule-guided too. Wittgenstein takes a very different view. In *Philosophical Investigations*, § 199 he emphasizes that one person cannot make a statement or give an order only once in his life. Rule-guided behaviour is not random, spontaneous behaviour or behaviour which shows no hesitation whatsoever. He is very clear about this in MS 165. Rule-guided behaviour presupposes the mastery of a certain skill. These skills manifest themselves in actual behaviour, but are not identical with it: they make the behaviour possible and comprehensible for others: 'Is it correct to say: Someone follows a rule only when he can *do* certain things. (And this stipulation of course refers to a length of time)' (MS 165, pp. 68-69). To master a skill implies normally that actions are learned, repeated, corrected, and reattempted. This applies to all activities extending in time. That a rule-guided praxis is a skill and no actuality also appears from the fact that it is learned (b). Wittgenstein, as he himself says (RPP II, § 337), connects the meaning of concepts with learning. And elsewhere: 'As children we acquire concepts and what one can do with them simultaneously' (MS 169, p. 71). As children we acquire the rules for the meaning of concepts through our upbringing and education. A variation of *Philosophical Investigations*, § 199 is also

illustrative here. Obeying a rule, he says in § 199, is a 'Gepflogenheit' and between parentheses he adds, a custom, an institution.
In MS 180a 'Gepflogenheit' is followed only by 'Übungen', that is,
by practical exercises. Characteristic (b) already suggests that playing a language-game according to rules is a normative activity;
characteristic (c) leaves no doubt whatsoever on this point. Only
where a rule-guided praxis is in force is it possible to determine
whether something is justified or founded. 'For to justify, establish, or criticize something means to measure something by a
certain standard, and then to examine whether or not it agrees
with this standard, whether or not it is legitimate' (Duintjer, 1977,
p. 76). To adduce a reason for something means that this reason
meets a certain standard determining what a right reason is.
Rule-guided practices, language-games, or forms of life are such
normative standards on the basis of which we can distinguish
between founded and unfounded. The practice or standard itself
is neither founded nor unfounded (cf. PI, § 482). The essential
idea that 'the standard has no grounds' (PI, § 482) is formulated by
Wittgenstein as early as 1932 in MS 113. Straight after the first
draft of § 482 Wittgenstein formulates his idea even more
explicitly:

> 'Why do you assume that he will be in a better mood because I tell you that he
> has eaten? is that a good ground?' – That is a good ground, for experience
> teaches me that eating has an influence on his mood. And that one could also
> say like this: 'Eating makes it really more probable that he will be in a good
> mood'.
> However, if one should like to ask: 'And is all that you adduce from the
> previous experience a good ground to assume that it will also be like that this
> time'.
> I cannot say now: yes, for that makes the occurrence of the supposition
> probable. Above I have justified my ground with the help of the standard of
> good grounds; now however I cannot justify the standard. (MS 113, p. 113)

In other words: at a certain point justification is no longer possible
(PI, § 217). However, the import of this crucial idea is for later (see
chapter 3, § 2).

The technique of language-games implies that there are criteria
which determine what a correct or incorrect execution or continuation of a rule is (e). Wittgenstein supplies too many examples of
such criteria to enumerate – they will be amply dealt with in the

course of this study. His central idea in any case is that in the absence of criteria there are no correct or incorrect results and that the technique in question cannot be learned and mastered either. To learn a technique implies correction and criticism and there-fore a standard (criterion) to which one appeals.

If a technique manifests itself in actions, verbal and non-verbal, and if one can appeal to criteria determining whether someone applies a rule correctly, then this also implies the possibility of public judgement (e). As Wittgenstein says, to believe that one is obeying a rule is not the same as obeying a rule (PI § 202). The latter is a practice, the former a pseudo-practice. This is a rather problem-ridden point, however, which I shall discuss in chapter 3, § 1. For the present it is enough to say that such public standards do not necessarily presuppose a social community. Robinson Crusoe can also appeal to them. (see chapter 4, § 1)

The meaning of concepts can only be described within this kind of rule-guided system of horizontal relations; outside of it nothing can be described. This boundary of inside and outside implies a form of relativity (which is not the same as relativism) that will be discussed in chapter 3, § 3. But I take it that Wittgenstein also uses the term relativity in a vertical sense, to refer to a logical relation between certain language-games. In *Remarks on the Philosophy of Psychology* II, § 313 he writes: 'For I describe the language-game "Bring something red" to someone who can him-self already play it. Others I might at most *teach it*. (Relativity.)'. The context shows that Wittgenstein is thinking of a relation in which one kind of language-game logically presupposes the other. In this case the language-game in which colour impressions are described and that in which things are described according to their colour, more generally the language-games of imagining and perceiving. The latter forms a logical condition for the former – later we shall see in what way. In the language-game of imagina-tion the expression 'it looks red to me' may occur, but in the language-game of perceiving 'a person does not occur as per-ceiving subject' (RPP II, § 317). The language-game of perceiving is unable to accommodate introspective accounts on a horizontal level; it can accommodate them on a vertical level, but has then become an entirely *different* language-game. The widely held notion that Wittgenstein denies the possibility of introspective language-games is therefore an instance of the ground-floor fallacy (see chapter 4, § 3). We can take another example. In MS 169, p. 54 Wittgenstein writes: 'A problem of relativity'. The immediate context is a discussion about pretending to feel pain. The logic of this kind of language-game, according to Wittgenstein, is based on the language-game of the spontaneous expression of pain or that of the meaning of pain. Without these language-games as logical conditions, pretending to have pain would not even exist as a language-game. So here too we have a vertical relation between language-games.

A general characteristic of language-games vertically related to other language-games is that in a horizontal context they are almost entirely linguistic. They are linguistic not accidentally but necessarily: language is *constitutive* for the (psychological) phenomena in question: 'Someone who has a soul has to be capable of pain, joy, sadness, etc. And if furthermore he also has to be able to remember, to make decisions, to make up his mind, he needs the linguistic expression' (MS 173, pp. 41-42). To the latter list Wittgenstein might have added 'to expect', 'to hope', 'to believe', 'to think', and 'to intend', but not 'fear' or 'anger'. The reason for this is made clear by comparing 'hope' and 'anger'. It is easy to recall the angry face of somebody one knows and to imitate his expression. But what about somebody who hopes something? That is more difficult. Hope has no natural expression or typical gestures. 'How does hoping that someone will return express itself?' (LW, § 357). The answer is: in the verbal expression 'I hope he will return'. The horizontal relations by which 'hoping' is embedded in language-games are primarily linguistic relations, and not physiognomical ones. However, the linguistic relations do presuppose, in a vertical sense, the physiognomical relations. Wittgenstein indicates this in the first fragment of *Philosophical Investigations* II when he says that the phenomena of hope are 'modes of this complicated form of life'. 'Modes' because 'hoping' remains embedded in a way of life and is not suddenly *sui generis* in being a primarily linguistic phenomenon; 'complicated' because it has a number of vertical relations with other language-games. The following fragment plainly attests to this complexity:

> Someone says: 'Man hopes.' How should this phenomenon of natural history be described? – One might observe a child and wait until one day he manifests hope; and then one could say 'Today he hoped for the first time'. But surely that sounds queer! Although it would be quite natural to say 'Today he said "I hope" for the first time'. And why queer? One does not say that a suckling hopes that ..., but one does say it of a grown-up. – Well, bit by bit daily life becomes such that there is a place for hope in it. (RPP II, § 15)

For babies this 'hope' of vertical relations is not a vain hope, but it is for animals: 'The crocodile doesn't hope, man does' (RPP II, § 16). One can imagine a crocodile being angry, happy, afraid, or sad (crocodile tears!), but not hopeful. His life is not complicated enough, that is to say, a crocodile lacks the medium of language in which the very essence of 'hoping' lies.

Wittgenstein does not say that animals do not speak because they are intellectually inferior. This may be well the case, but precisely for that reason it is a hypothesis, and Wittgenstein has nothing to say about hypotheses. Not so Otto Weininger, another animal lover. According to Weininger, a dog can recognize his master after many years, but he cannot hope for his return or think about him in his memory. He does not have the mental capacity for this. The same dog occurs in the *Philosophical Investigations*, but there he cannot hope (PI II i, p. 174), feel remorse (RPP II, § 308), simulate (PI, § 541-542), or talk to himself (PI, § 357), because he has no language, quite apart from the (empirical) fact why it is that he has no language. More is required for this kind of phenomena than the concrete here and now of physiognomical expressions prevailing in the animal kingdom. Human beings are capable (logically, that is) of this 'more' thanks to vertical relations between language-games.

With this constitutive role of language we also have a division between more and less fundamental language-games. By this Wittgenstein does not mean that the more linguistic phenomena are less fundamental in the sense that we can easily imagine living without them. On the contrary, commanding, asking, recounting, chatting are as much a part of our natural history as walking, eating, drinking, and playing (PI, § 25). They have become a kind of second nature. But this does not alter the fact that certain concepts are more closely bound up with a way of life than others. Not surprisingly, Wittgenstein mentions the example of 'pain'. Is it possible to imagine that a legislator would abolish the notion of pain? The answer is: 'Certain concepts are so closely interwoven with the most fundamental ones in our way of life, that for that reason they are inviolable' (MS 169, p. 71). These inviolable concepts are embedded in our form of life via the highly specific horizontal relations of facial expressions and natural reactions. Purely linguistic language-games are based on physiognomy and in this logical respect they are less fundamental.

Two other types of language-games need to be mentioned. They are also vertically related to others, but if possible in an even more complicated way than in the examples given: the language-games of seeing-as and secondary meanings. These language-games are dealt with in chapter 6, so I can confine myself here to the following note. In *Philosophical Investigations*, § 43 Wittgenstein introduces a restriction in his definition of meaning as use: the definition applies to a large class of cases, but not to all. We are not told which words are excluded. In chapter 6, § I shall show that Wittgenstein may have been thinking of seeing-as and secondary meanings. In fact, these more aesthetic facets of the concept of meaning seem at first sight to resist incorporation in a field of applications. But the same chapter will show that late in his career Wittgenstein was able to bring them into line with his definition of meaning as use via a system of extremely complicated vertical relations.

CHAPTER 3

AGREEMENT IN FORMS OF LIFE

Movements in a language-game, actions, verbal utterances are guided by horizontal and often also vertical relations of rules. On the basis of these rules or rule-guided and normative practices it is logical to distinguish between a correct and incorrect or between a founded or unfounded statement; the regulative practice functions as normative standard for all kinds of justifications and criticisms. As a standard or norm the practice itself is neither founded nor unfounded: at a certain point justification and substantiation are no longer possible. Wittgenstein refers to this end point of justification inherent in every practice by the expression 'agreement in forms of life'. The present chapter deals with this 'agreement in forms of life' and its relation to the context of the foundational argument. Wittgenstein introduces 'agreement in forms of life' at the end of a long discussion on the obeying of a rule (PI, § 143-242). An example of the obeying of a rule which specially interests Wittgenstein is the continuation of an arithmetic series and in particular the question of how a general arithmetic formula can determine the way in which somebody must continue an arithmetic series at a certain point:

> When I now build up an extension, what does it mean that I build it up *according* to that general expression?
> That is like asking: how does one obey an – or this – order? How is what I do connected with these words? (But I do not mean causally connected.) Well, of course only through a general practice. (MS 165, p. 79)

This problem was long overshadowed by the so-called private language argument, but particularly since Kripke's essay 'Wittgenstein on rules and private language' the tables have been turned.[1]

---

1 I will be referring to Kripke's article in Block (1981).

Kripke's essay has rightly been criticized by Baker and Hacker;[2] other authors accept his views unthinkingly.[3] Since Kripke's approach is symptomatic of a long – mainly sceptical – epistemological tradition, I shall only discuss his position so far as it illustrates this tradition. In § 1 I show that it is wrong to attribute a sceptical starting-point to Wittgenstein and that, on the contrary, Wittgenstein sees sceptical problems as being based on a misconception of rule-governed behaviour. Section 2 discusses at greater length the pointlessness of sceptical approaches, with reference to unpublished manuscripts and *On Certainty* (OC). In § 3, finally, I reject biologistic and sociologistic interpretations of Wittgenstein's discussion of rules and agreement and instead argue an 'internalistic' interpretation.

1. Internal relations

The problem brought up by Wittgenstein occurs under many forms in his work. In its most abstract form it concerns the internal relation between language and reality, between sign and meaning – Wittgenstein talks about the 'harmony of language or thought and reality' (cf. PI, § 429; PG, § 113). In slightly less abstract terms it deals with the internal relation between a mathematical rule and its applications, and more and more concretely it deals with the internal relation between a desire and its fulfilment (PG, § 86 ff.), between an expectation and its fulfilment (PI, § 444-445), between an order and its execution (PI, § 431 ff.), or between pain and its expression.

According to a number of authors, all these formulations have a sceptical intention. Kripke, for instance, claims that they express an epistemological scepticism about the meaning of words and the possibility of language in general. He bases this claim on *Philosophical Investigations*, § 201, where Wittgenstein formulates the paradox that no action can be constituted by a rule, because every action can be carried out in accordance with the rule. And if that

---

[2] See Baker and Hacker (1984) and for a more elaborate account Baker and Hacker (1985). This section owes much to the last work in particular.

[3] See for example Strawson (1983, p. 77) and Malcolm (1986, pp. 157-169).

is true, then every action can also conflict with the rule and there would be neither agreement nor disagreement here. In Kripke's opinion, this fragment and others raise the question of how I can know whether my present use of a word, for example 'plus', is coherent with what I used to mean by it, assuming that my present use is a new application. Nothing in the instructions which I received or gave myself forces me to continue the series 2, 4, 6, 8 ... in this way, starting from 1000: 1002, 1004, 1006, 1008 ..., or in this way: 1004, 1008, 1012, 1016 ... Both continuations can always be squared with the instructions. Nor can my memory help me determine whether I am still using the first meaning of 'plus', or any other word, as I used it before. To use a word in accordance with a rule is therefore impossible. The dramatic conclusion is that nobody can ever consistently mean anything by a word and that meaningful language is an illusion (Kripke, 1981, pp. 267-268). Kripke believes that this sceptical paradox is only equalled, in terms of its profundity and disastrous consequences, by Hume's scepticism about induction. Wittgenstein's solution is Humean as well (Kripke, 1981, pp. 268-269). Just as Hume bridges the gap between experience from the past and statements about the future by an appeal to habit-formation – and so concedes to scepticism that the problem is rationally insoluble – so Wittgenstein bridges the gap between rule and actions by appealing to the voice of the community: since the community has decided and insists that these actions conform to these rules, the logical gap is doubt-proof. In this view, therefore, Wittgenstein accepts the premises of the sceptical argument, but not the conclusion.

There will be more to say about this sceptical solution presently. Is it true that Wittgenstein sees the sceptical paradox as a paradox? No. In his view, the paradox is based on a misunderstanding (cf. PI, § 201). The paradox that every action can be interpreted as according with a rule is based on a misunderstanding about rule-guided behaviour. The alternative version of *Philosophical Investigations*, § 201 in MS 180a is instructive here. Unlike the text in *Philosophical Investigations*, this fragment is preceded by a lengthy discussion about how I know that this is red. A psychologistic interpretation of this knowledge is rejected by Wittgenstein, i.e. the idea that the colour is first recognized introspectively

as red and that this recognition subsequently mediates between
the perception and the verbal statement:

> I realize it is *thus*. And now I have to make a transition to words, or actions.
> (Before) my problem was that no course of action could be determined by a rule,
> because every course of action can be made out to accord with the rule. The
> answer was: if everything can be made out to accord with the rule, then it can
> also be made out to conflict with it. And so 'conflict' and 'accord' would lose
> their meaning completely here. (MS 180a, pp. 72-73)

'Agreement' and 'contradiction' lose their meaning here; the paradox is not real but apparent and is based on a misunderstanding.

Generally speaking, I think, the misunderstanding is based on a
failure to recognize the internal relation between rule and action,
between order and execution, or between pain and its expression.
In the *Philosophical Investigations* Wittgenstein contests more
and less explicitly the following external explanations of the relation between, among other things, rule and action. (1) The relation between rule and action is explained via a third, psychological kind of step: a mental image, an interpretation, a conditioning;
I call this the psychologism fallacy. (2) The relation can be
explained via the third step of human biological nature; I call this
the biologism fallacy. (3) The relation can be explained via the
third step of social pressure; I call this the sociologism fallacy.

While the critics have generally agreed that Wittgenstein
opposes (1), they have sought his means of doing so either in
biological or in sociological circumstances. Fallacies (2) and (3)
have therefore been produced by the critics and not by Wittgenstein. And although Wittgenstein does not discuss fallacies (2)
and (3) explicitly as he does (1), one can show that he sufficiently
guarded himself against them. In this section I shall confine
myself to (1), dealing with (2) and (3) in section 3.

The question of how we know whether a certain action accords
with a certain rule derives its relevance mainly from the fact that
many rules are 'only' learned through examples. Mathematical
rules, like the order 'add 2' (cf. PI, § 185), are typically taught to
children via examples, even if there are general formulations for
them. There are also rules, like the continuation of a geometrical
pattern (cf. PI, § 208), which cannot be summed up in a general
formula at all and can only be expressed via a series of examples.

From a strictly logical point of view, such illustrative formulations of rules do not tell us which continuations accord or conflict with the rule. The gap between the limited number of examples and the often unlimited extension of the rule can only be bridged, it seems, by an interpretation of the rule. How otherwise can a child that has only learned the example 2, 4, 6, 8 ... know that it must continue at 1000 with 1002, 1004 ... and not with 1004, 1008 ...?

This problem, which sceptics blow up to the mysterious proportions of a paradox, is the result of a misunderstanding about the nature of the relation between rule and action. This relation is internal and the psychologism fallacy describes it as external. 'Internal relation' is a term which occurs only once in the *Philosophical Investigations* – and not in an explanatory or defining sense (cf. PI II xi, p. 212). From this fragment and also from others[4] we can infer that Wittgenstein assigns the following three characteristics to internal relations. (i) It is impossible that both *relata* do not have this relation to each other. (ii) The relation is not mediated by a third term. (iii) The internal relation exists in a practice, in language. Wittgenstein was already convinced of (i) in the *Tractatus*, but of (ii) and (iii) only in his later work.

The terms of an internal relation cannot but have this relation to one another (i). In other words, the identification of A is *eo ipso* the identification of B. Or in more Wittgensteinian fashion: the criterion for the identity of an action is the criterion for the identity of a rule. What the psychologism fallacy amounts to is that it presents the comprehension of a rule as being independent of its application:

> It seems so clear here: it is one thing 'to *understand* a word' and another 'to *apply* it'. And that is why we are accustomed to accept the ostensive explanation as an adequate answer to the question 'Do you understand the word...?' For it seems as if we could give ourselves an ostensive explanation of the question 'Do you understand what "memory image" means', by conjuring up (such) an image before one's mind. (MS 116, pp. 144-145)

Comprehension is not one thing and application another. A rule is only understood if it is correctly applied. To understand a rule

---

[4] See *Philosophical Remarks*, III, § 21.

is *eo ipso* to know what accords and what conflicts with the rule. The psychologism fallacy makes the mistake of thinking that a rule can be explained by an interpretation or mental image of the rule. In actual fact this is merely the substitution of one formulation of the rule for another. This kind of substitution is only an explanation if the translation of the first formulation can itself be applied. Nothing has been explained if the application of the translation is as unclear as the application of what has been translated. And a mental image, like a material image, can always be applied in different ways. Comprehension of a rule is a skill, a practice. The practice is the criterion for mastery of the skill and so for comprehension of the rule. The rule 'add 2' would not be the rule it is if continuation of the series 2, 4, 6, 8 ... with 10, 12, 14, 16 ... were not in accordance with it. To write down a different continuation is to disobey the rule 'add 2'. For another person this is a sign that the pupil does not understand the rule.

The fact that a certain action must go with a certain rule does not mean that there are no actual situations in which the rule does not lead to the action. Rules admit of exceptions, exceptions are possible, but rules cannot be exceptions. However, rules are not so restrictive that every move in the language-game is predetermined. For instance, a constitutive rule of the language-game of imagination is that fantasy is represented. This does not rule out the possibility of borderline cases, such as 'I can imagine it in every detail, but can't possibly put it into words'. 'A game allows for borderline cases – a rule for exceptions. But the exception and the rule could not change place without destroying the game' (RPP II, § 145).

A rule admits of exceptions, but that does not mean that the rule can be an exception. One cannot determine *a priori* when and where the rule and the exception change roles, but there is a point at which our attitude will abruptly change to 'That is no longer a ...'. It is a logical property of rules to allow room for exceptions and deviations. It is certainly not true that by admitting exceptions Wittgenstein indicates a breach in logic, so that the distinction between logical and empirical capsizes. On the contrary, the logic of rules is such that exceptions are allowed for.

This hospitality does not turn a rule into an empirical regularity (see further § 3).

Wittgenstein gives more of these exceptions: 'It is compatible with the concept of order that orders are not followed, but not that an order would never be followed' (MS 165, p. 81). Meaning in the language-game of orders presupposes the mastery of a skill, that is to say, the playing of the game. Sure enough, games can be invented without ever being played, but it is inconceivable that games would never be played but only invented (cf. PI, § 204). Nothing is solved by the assumption that understanding a rule is a separate process leading to an interpretation which can then tell us whether an action accords with the rule (ii). No interpretation – and no intermediary – can bridge the gap because it in turn creates a gap between itself and the action: the action does not now have to be harmonized with the rule but with an interpretation of the rule. The same problem now returns: how do I know that my action accords with the interpretation? The transition from rule to action remains unexplained. The problem has merely been shifted to an area where it manifests itself even more mysteriously: the mind. The obeying of rules has not yet been adequately described; it only seems to have been explained (cf. PI, § 202).

It is interesting that the 'paradox' about rules (PI, § 201) and the 'solution' of this 'paradox' (PI, § 202) is historically preceded by a different discussion from the discussion about (mathematical) rules in the *Philosophical Investigations*. Versions of *Philosophical Investigations*, § 201-202 occur in MS 180a in a discussion of the perception of colours and the verbal communication of these perceptions (what is now PI, § 377-381).[5] The suggestion which Wittgenstein wants to do away with is that an introspective act of recognition mediates between seeing a colour and saying that it is red, just as he rejects the idea that an interpretation mediates between a (mathematical) rule and a continuation of that rule. The following account of the discussion in MS 180a shows

---

[5] The link between the problem of colour perception and the problem of rules is explicitly commented upon by Wittgenstein in MS 118: 'How do I know that in continuing the series +2 I will have to write 200004, 200006 and not 200004, 200008?'

The question is akin to: 'how do I know that this colour is red?' (MS 118, p. 1).

Wittgenstein rejecting a phenomenal language on the basis of a conceptual analysis of 'rule' and 'practice'. The idea which Wittgenstein is out to reject in this manuscript is that we first identify a colour introspectively and then say what colour it is on the basis of this identification. The appeal to this kind of mediating introspective recognition is compared by Wittgenstein to the situation in which you have lost your way and somebody shows you the way like this: the road on which he is leading you '... suddenly comes to an end. And now my friend says: "All you have to do now is to find the way home from here"' (MS 180a, p. 70). The appeal to introspective recognition is pointless because the transition to words still has to take place, just as the lost person still has to find his way home. After a draft of *Philosophical Investigations*, § 201 Wittgenstein writes that none of the rules we appeal to for this transition will help us: 'The rules leave us in the lurch, because there is no transition from seeing that it is *thus* to seeing that it is *red*' (MS 180a, p. 74). The 'rules' are left hanging in midair, since there is no technique and no practice for their application. And there is no practice, since the 'transition' takes place in the private domain of the inner. In other words: 'The transition from what is seen to words is *private*. That is why the rules are a castle in the air. If the transition from looking to the word 'red' cannot be made all at once, then it cannot be made via rules either' (MS 180a, p. 75). This is followed by a version of PI, § 202, i.e. the idea that a rule cannot be obeyed privately, but only if there is a practice. The possibility of a phenomenal language (in this case for colours) has therefore been rejected on the basis of a conceptual analysis of 'rule' and 'practice'.

An internal relation exists in a practice (iii), not in the hidden medium of the mind or in a theory. Only within a practice, within a way of life, can one say that this rule means this, that this action obeys this command. Tertiary terms, far from unambiguously establishing the meaning of rules, lead to an infinite regression of interpretations and so create an unbridgeable gap. The rules are left hanging in midair because there is no technique, no practice which establishes their meaning unambiguously: 'Hence the words "obeying a rule" refer to a practice that cannot be replaced by the semblance of a practice' (MS 180a, p. 76; cf. PI, § 202).

Unlike its counterpart in the *Philosophical Investigations*, this fragment is directly followed by part of PI, § 242: 'This seems to abolish logic, but does not do so'. The possible problem detected by Wittgenstein here is described as follows in MS 165: 'Should I say now that the meaning of the word "red" is based on the agreement of people? That namely the practice is based on the agreement?' (MS 165, p. 82). Wittgenstein is here anticipating what I have called the sociologism fallacy. Talking about 'beruht' suggests that a practice is justified by prior agreement. But Wittgenstein's view will be that a practice is not justified by anything, since a practice is a standard of justification. 'Agreement' is rather introduced by him to make this nature of a practice explicit, i.e. the fact that it is neither founded nor unfounded. In this way, as we shall see, Wittgenstein dissociates himself from a sceptical solution to the relation between the foundational argument and agreement. We already saw that he also dissociates himself from a sceptical formulation of the problem: the sceptical formulation which Kripke attributes to Wittgenstein is due to a misunderstanding about the nature of the relation between, generally, sign and meaning; this relation is not external but internal.

Before going into this incorrect sceptical 'solution' of the relation between practice and agreement – and the biologism fallacy – I first want to pay more attention to Wittgenstein's notion that a pseudo-practice leads to an infinite regression of interpretations and that there is a point at which justification is no longer possible. Only then does it become clear that by 'agreement in forms of life' Wittgenstein wants to stress the meaninglessness rather than the meaningfulness of sceptical positions. I shall call his approach non-epistemological in the sense that Wittgenstein does not want to prove the incorrectness of scepticism, since such a proof presupposes the meaningfulness of scepticism.

2. Justifications without end, end without justification

A number of passages in the *Philosophical Investigations* seem to have an existential resonance, namely those in which Wittgenstein posits a practice as the final limit for interpretations and

justifications. He says that the justifications which one can supply
for the continuation of rules soon give out and that one then acts
without a basis (PI, § 211). After justifications have been ex-
hausted, the spade is turned by the bedrock of action (PI, § 217),
and in the end rules are not obeyed deliberately, but blindly (PI, §
219). We have already seen one reason for this primacy of the
practice: an interpretation of a rule is no more than an alternative
formulation of this rule and as such does not constitute rule-
guided behaviour, because an interpretation has to be used itself
first. With a little imagination, moreover, every action can be
interpreted in accordance with a rule. Another reason is never
mentioned in this connection. I am referring to Wittgenstein's
remarks about certainty. The critical literature has only discussed
this subject in an isolated context, i.e. Wittgenstein's criticism of
Moore's refutation of scepticism.[6] The isolated edition of *On Certainty* has doubtless led to this restricted focus. In their preface the
editors would have it that Wittgenstein worked on this book
exclusively in the period 1949-51 and that it was an entirely new
theme for him.[7] But this is simply not true: Wittgenstein was
writing extensively about certainty as early as 1937.[8] In MS 119 he
devotes more than 50 pages to the subject. It is remarkable that

---

[6] Norman Malcolm and in his footsteps Anthony Kenny have encouraged an
epistemological reading of *On Certainty*. Kenny, for instance, writes: 'Wittgenstein being preoccupied with the theory of meaning was comparatively unin-
terested in epistemology for much of his life ... Toward the end of his life while
staying with Norman Malcolm in Ithaca in 1949 he was stimulated by the study
of Moore's articles to begin to write on epistemology' (Kenny, 1973, p. 204).
Malcolm persists in the epistemological reading of *On Certainty*, as isolated
from the main themes of *Philosophical Investigations*, in his latest book on
Wittgenstein (Malcolm, 1986, pp. 201 ff.).

[7] For the same point of view, see von Wright (1982, p. 59).

[8] In fact, Wittgenstein writes much earlier on certainty and doubt, although not
as systematically and elaborately as in MS 119. For example, at 3-2-1931 he says
in the context of a discussion on solipsism: 'The words "being certain that" can
only be used in connection with a hypothesis. It is pointless to say "I am certain
that I have a toothache" except in a sense in which it is possible to doubt that I
have a toothache ... What does it mean, being certain that one will have a
toothache. (If one *cannot* be certain, one is not allowed by the grammar to use this
word in this connection.)' (MS 110, pp. 31-32). There will be some terminological
changes later: instead of 'I am certain', Wittgenstein will say 'I know'.

the fragments, while largely following the argumentation in *On Certainty*, are discussed here in the context of agreement in forms of life. As such they advance a supplementary rather than completely new reason for the primacy of the practice. I first look at MS 119 and then at *On Certainty*.

Wittgenstein opens his discussion of certainty on p. 101 by asking whether a language-game can start with doubt. After dismissing this proposal – we shall presently see why – he diagnoses this typically philosophical idea as follows:

> The game does not begin with doubt whether someone has a toothache, for that would not correspond – as it were – to the biological function of the game in our life. Its elementary form is a reaction to the complaints and gestures of the other, a reaction of pity or the like. We console, want to help. One can think: it is the most important thing to start at once with doubt, because doubt is a refinement, in a certain sense, an improvement of the game. (Similarly one thinks that because it is often good that a judgement is founded, the chain of reasons would have to go on *ad infinitum* in order to reach complete justification.) (MS 119, pp. 111-112)[9]

From a philosophical point of view, scepticism seems to offer the deepest insight. This kind of doubt does not stop at a certain point, just as providing a basis for judgements has to go on and on. Not to doubt, therefore, would not be the obeying of a rule, but a way of burying one's head in the sand. Not to doubt is to overlook the possibility that something may be very different from what it seems. Only an intellectualistic and sceptical attitude can prevent blindness.

---

[9] The last phrase in this quotation about the 'chain of reasons' occurs in a different form in *Philosophical Investigations*, § 211 and 326, where Wittgenstein famously says 'But the chain of reasons has an end'. The genesis of this insight goes back even further than 1937. In 1931 he says 'I could also ask it like this: Why do you long for explanations? When they will have been given, you will after all again stand before an end (vor einem Ende stehen). They cannot bring you further than where you are now' (MS 110, p. 96). And toward the end of 1931, in the context of a discussion of the philosophy of mathematics, he composes the first draft of *Philosophical Investigations*, § 326: 'The chain of reasons comes to an end and that in this game (namely at the end of the game) (namely at the limit of the game)' (MS 112, p. 221).

Wittgenstein sets a limit to this 'intellectualism'. That is to say, his emphasis on practice is an emphasis on the fact that this intellectualism is embedded – without lapsing into irrationalism.

> Reason – I might say acts for us as the graduator *par excellence* according to which everything we make and all the language-games are measured and judged. We can say: we are so preoccupied with the contemplation of a standard, that we are incapable of letting our views *rest* at certain (appearances or) pictures. We are, as it were, accustomed to dispose of this by saying that they are unreasonable, correspond to a lower level of the intellect, etc. Our view is held captive by the standard and is again and again withdrawn from these appearances. (MS 119, pp. 127-128)

Intellectualism refuses to submit to a practice, afraid as it is of surrendering to irrationalism. From Wittgenstein's point of view, however, the discrepancy between rational and irrational is not applicable at the level of the practice in question here:

> One would like to give grounds and grounds and grounds! Having the feeling that where there is a ground, everything is all right. If there is no ground present, the subject is irrational, and therefore not interesting to us. ('Irrational' is used similarly to the word 'falling' in the sentence: 'If the earth were not held fast somewhere, it would have to fall'.) We would not simply like to describe what happens, but we would always like (just) to explain. (MS 116, p. 128)

In my opinion, Wittgenstein does not give up an argument *ad infinitum* out of despair or resignation because the goal can never be achieved. There is no goal outside the language-game, and so it is meaningless to say that this goal cannot be achieved. Just as 'standing firm' and 'falling' do not apply to the earth but do apply to houses and apples, so the concepts of 'verification', 'falsification', 'justification', 'knowing', and 'doubt' do not apply to language-games. They are concepts which belong to a higher order: they belong in language-games which typically have a vertical relation with more fundamental language-games. Or to put it more precisely with regard to 'knowing' and 'doubt': doubt can only be a vertical or secondary move in a game that is played with certainty.

The intellectualistic prejudice that scepticism cannot be taken too far is itself taken to absurd lengths by Wittgenstein. For the sake of argument he assumes that an action starts with doubt. He goes on to infer that this kind of 'doubt' can no longer be regarded as doubt and concludes that language-games cannot start with doubt; they presuppose certainty.

Wittgenstein chooses an example involving non-verbal 'doubt', a mother's response to a crying child. Normally, says Wittgenstein, this kind of comforting and caring response expresses the very opposite of doubt, but let us assume that the mother is 'sceptical':

> Now let us imagine the mother that is sceptical from the very first: When the child cries, she shrugs her shoulders and shakes her head; possibly she takes a scrutinizing look, examining it; in exceptional cases she makes a vague attempt to comfort or tend. Were we to see such a conduct, we would not call it in the least sceptical, it would strike us (only) as curious and crazy. 'The game cannot start with doubt' means: we would not call it 'doubt' if the game were to start with it. (MS 119, pp. 114-115)

Doubt is possible only when included in a second order language-game. The point of the example is that doubt is essentially an exception to the rule. The mother's behaviour is conceivable and can be described in detail, but it is impossible for us to give it the predicate 'sceptical': the way we apply the predicate is excluded here. The mother uses it in a context where scepticism is a rule and certainty an exception, whereas language-games have a context of certainty and regularity in which scepticism is exceptional. A practice which as such admits of no possibility of error or doubt is a condition or precondition of the possibility of doubt. For to play a game requires mastery of a technique as a *conditio sine qua non*. And this skill is only acquired by acting regularly, not just once, in accordance with certain words.

An especially relevant example in the discussion on the limit of justifications is the language-game of cause and effect. Wittgenstein devotes a great deal of space to this topic.[10] Suppose one notices a flex moving in one's room. One explores and finds somebody who has tugged at the flex. Now how does one know for certain that this is the cause: is it not safer and wiser to discover by experiment whether there is another explanation? And if so, is it not always better to start with such experiments and to adopt a sceptical attitude from the outset, since one never knows what causes anything? Wittgenstein's answer is that this

---

[10] See MS 119, pp. 124-129.

kind of intellectualistic point of view makes it impossible even to talk about a beginning of a language-game:

> But then we do not need to speak of the *beginning* of the game, but we can say: the game 'searching for the cause' *consists* especially and mainly in the fact that we practise. There appears also something that we can call doubt and uncertainty, but this is a feature of a second order. Just as it is characteristic for the functioning of the sewing-machine that its parts wear out and bend, and that the spindles can shudder in their bearings, but it is a feature of a second order compared with the normal movement of the machine. (MS 119, p. 145)

Both Wittgenstein and intellectualistic epistemology see scepticism as a refinement. They differ in where they locate this refinement: intellectualistic epistemologies locate it at the beginning of all thought, Wittgenstein in secondary moves within language-games which presuppose certainty and agreement. Within primary moves of language-games there is no possibility of doubt or error; if there is, it is within a different, more complicated – and therefore more refined – level of the language-game.

At the end of this discussion Wittgenstein draws a logical conclusion, which has been wrenched from this context, however, and planted in the miscellaneous *Culture and Value* (CV). It concerns his statement that the origin of a language-game is a reaction – the reaction of the mother, the reaction to a cause – and that complicated language-games can only develop on this foundation. Language is a refinement: 'In the beginning was the deed' (CV, p. 31; MS 119, pp. 146-147). The primitive form – the archetype – of the cause-and-effect language-game is determination of the cause, not doubt, just as the primitive attitude of the mother is that of sympathy and not of objection. In the later terminology of *On Certainty*: 'The primitive form of the language-game is certainty, not uncertainty. For uncertainty could never lead to action' (MS 119, pp. 147-148). The summarizing fragment which follows again shows clearly that the discussion about certainty is directly connected with that about agreement in forms of life; for we can regard it as a protoversion of *Philosophical Investigations*, § 241, where Wittgenstein states that agreement in forms of life is a condition for an agreement in opinions:

> I want to say: it is characteristic of our language that it grows on the basis of stable forms of life, regular ways of acting. Its function is *above all* determined by the action, of which it is the companion. We have a notion which forms of life are primitive and which forms have only originated from those. We believe that the most elementary plough was there before the complicated. (MS 119, pp. 148-149)

The import is clear: the primacy of the forms of life is the primacy of practice. Language-games, in the sense of rule-governed frameworks for more and less intellectual skills, can only develop if this practice is presupposed. If it is not, as in intellectualistic epistemologies, the game can never start, owing to an infinite regression of interpretations and justifications of rules or to an endless proliferation of doubt. In this way Wittgenstein does not put a contrived and irrational check on intellectualistic epistemologies. On the contrary, he makes them run until they cannot but hold back: their quest for a purely sceptical beginning, if carried through consistently, is a beginning without end and as such removes every basis for a meaningful application of the notions of 'game', 'doubt', or 'justification'. Their application is meaningful only as exception to the regularity of a practice.

This reconstruction of fragments from MS 119 makes it clear that as early as 1937 Wittgenstein expressly links his key notion of 'agreement in forms of life' to the conceptual nature of and relation between 'doubt' and 'certainty'; a theme which will absorb his attention entirely around the year 1950. 'Agreement in forms of life' is as much the basis of every practice as certainty is the basis of every specific language-game. As the basis or 'foundation' of every practice, 'agreement in forms of life' is the condition for the possibility of justification and criticism, but cannot itself be justified or criticized (see also § 3). Just as a form of life is neither founded nor unfounded, so it cannot be adequately characterized in terms of epistemological concepts either. For, as Wittgenstein himself says, we are not dealing with an agreement in opinions but in forms of life. We have to see that where there is agreement in opinions there may also be differences in opinions; and where there may be differences in opinion, grounds and reasons can be brought forward. But no grounds can be produced for a form of life itself, and so there is neither agreement nor difference in opinion at this level: there is no place for opinions at all here because there is no place for justification, criticism, in short: knowledge.

In *On Certainty* Wittgenstein indicates more systematically how traditional epistemological concepts like 'truth', 'knowing', 'proving' are embedded in a way of life. Or more precisely: how these concepts are accommodated in language-games which vertically presuppose more fundamental games. For this purpose he introduces a number of concepts which form limits for epistemological concepts, in this order: 'Geistesstörung' and 'Irrtum', 'glauben' and 'wissen', 'abrichten' and 'erklären', 'Einstellung' and 'Meinung'. The first concept in each of these pairs is constitutive for the second, and is therefore a condition for the possibility of the second, but cannot itself be justified. I take them to be limitative concepts which merely mark the point at which a language-game or practice is itself no longer justified. These concepts are in fact empty of content. At any rate Wittgenstein never gives them a specific content, and certainly not a psychological one. I shall now discuss them in the above order.

The way in which Wittgenstein introduces 'objective certainty' is important for the first distinction: 'If everything speaks *for* a hypothesis and nothing against it, is it objectively *certain*? One can call it that' (OC, § 203). 'Objective certainty' applies to assertions which can be supported by reasons within a certain practice, for instance the verification of a scientific hypothesis. Objective certainty is a (very certain) degree of knowledge, but no matter how objectively certain one is of something, one may still err. Objective certainty and the possibility of error itself are based on agreement: 'For man to err, he must already judge in conformance with mankind' (OC, § 156). On the basis of this agreement certain errors are inconceivable (logically impossible). What would we think of somebody who seriously claims that he cannot remember whether he has always had two hands? We no longer call this an error, but a (perhaps temporary) mental derangement ('Geistesstörung'). The difference between the two is that an error has a ground as well as a cause. That is to say: an error can still be classified in the knowledge of the person who errs (cf. OC, § 74).

An error is still part of a language-game, that is why it can be explained. The foundation of the language-game is agreement in forms of life. This agreement cannot be explained, let alone the behaviour of somebody who does not share this agreement and is apparently playing a different game. Somebody who sees an exception where we see a rule is 'mad'.

Agreement in forms of life is also constitutive for 'knowing'. Wittgenstein appears to have been inspired here by Otto Weininger, who said that 'alles Wissen auf dem Glauben beruht'.[11] Wittgenstein does not take 'believing' here in the sense of 'supposing'; the sense in which he does take it is made clear by his analysis of 'knowing'. Wittgenstein accepts a number of classical conditions for 'knowing'. A first and necessary but not sufficient condition is that one knows something if one also believes it. 'What I know, I believe' (OC, § 177). 'I know' is typically used in a situation in which something is subjectively held to be true. A second condition is that what one knows must also be true; this need not be the case with something one supposes. In turn this requires as a third condition that one can prove one's claim by producing grounds for it: 'Whether I know something depends on whether the evidence bears me out or contradicts me' (OC, § 504). According to Wittgenstein, Moore was wrong in concluding that an expression of positive certainty (first condition) entails the truth of the proposition (second condition): 'I know = I am certain that it is thus and it is' (MS 171, p. 9). But the truth of the proposition depends on whether one is able to produce reasons for it according to public criteria. If one professes to know something, there should always be the possibility of demonstration. However, if somebody's belief is such that the reasons he can produce for it are no more certain than his assertion, then he cannot maintain that he knows what he believes (cf. OC, § 243). An example of such a pointless attempt is a philosopher (Moore, for instance) who stamps on the ground with his feet to prove that the earth exists. A reason, if it is to be a reason, must be more fundamental than what it supports. In this example the reason which one can produce is no more fundamental than the

---

[11] See Weininger (1904, pp. 142-182). Weininger's thesis is that just as ethics presupposes a willing subject, logic is in need of a believing subject.

proposition to be proved: one stays on the same ground level. At this level one can no longer justify and so one can no longer speak of knowing. As Wittgenstein puts it: believing supported by reasons (i.e. supposing) is based on believing not supported (which is not the same as unsupported) by reasons (OC, § 378). Knowledge is ultimately based on acknowledgement ('Anerkennung') (OC, § 378), on something one relies on (OG, § 509). To put it somewhat differently, belief is a form of disbelief: disbelief in the opposite of what is believed. And this disbelief characteristic of our 'most fundamental' language-games pre-eminently shows itself in (or is identical to) the way we happen to act. The exact status of this kind of 'foundation' will be discussed in § 3.

Concepts somewhat akin to 'knowing' are constituted in the same way. 'Doubting', for instance. In *Philosophical Investigations* II, p. 221 Wittgenstein writes that 'I know' may mean 'I do not doubt ...' but not that 'I doubt ...' is meaningless and therefore logically excluded. For doubt one can produce certain grounds and grounds can only be produced in a language-game. Doubt cannot occur outside that language-game, so that doubt too presupposes agreement: 'The game of doubting itself presupposes certainty' (OC, § 115).

If one can only talk about 'doubt' and 'knowing' where there are grounds or reasons, then one cannot talk about 'knowing' or 'doubt' where grounds are absent. Or about 'true' or 'untrue'. Wittgenstein departs here from the tradition: philosophers have always used 'I know ...' to introduce statements for which they can no longer produce grounds, e.g. I know that I have consciousness, I doubt whether other people have consciousness. The consequences of Wittgenstein's revolutionary approach to these two statements (and others) will be dealt with in chapters 4 and 5 respectively.

In pedagogy one also finds the level at which reasons can no longer be adduced: 'Any explanation has its foundation in training. (Educators ought to remember this.)' (RPP II, § 327). 'Abrichtung' too is introduced as a limitative concept, marking the end of explanations: ultimately one can explain a rule in arithmetic only by teaching a child actually to apply the rule. A child that asks whether the teacher has made an error in saying that 12 x 12 = 144 and whether he can produce a rule that excludes this kind of error, forgets that it is the practice of saying one's tables, not a rule, which teaches us this (OC, § 44). And the teacher who is asked by a clever pupil à la Berkeley whether a chair is still a chair if he turns around and no longer sees it, will not only lose his patience but also observe that the pupil has not yet learnt how to ask questions (cf. OC, § 315). One can only look for something if it is somewhere; just so one can only ask questions which admit of answers. Asking for the justification of a language-game does not lead to an answer, but at the most to a demonstration of the game.

I can be brief about the last contrast, that between 'Einstellung' (attitude) and 'Meinung' (opinion); it will be extensively applied in chapter 5. In *Philosophical Investigations*, § 241 Wittgenstein said that the agreement in forms of life is not an agreement in 'Meinungen'. In *Philosophical Investigations* II, p. 178 he writes: 'My attitude towards him is an attitude towards a soul. I am not of the *opinion* that he has a soul.' The two terms are contrasted here. 'Einstellung' too does not point to a justification, but to a condition for justification. Once again it is a limitative concept which, especially in the problem of 'other minds', marks the point at which no (analogical) arguments can be given for the existence of other 'minds'. Such arguments themselves ultimately turn out to be based on the presupposition that other people have minds. The following fragments from MS 169, p. 61 show that this last contrast is also significant in the discussion about constitutive rules. 'But what is the difference between an attitude and an opinion?

I would like to say: the attitude comes *before* the opinion. In an opinion one can err. But what would an error look like here?' (MS 169, pp. 60-61). [12]

---

[12] The same thought also occurs in the Remarks on Frazer's Golden Bough: 'A religious symbol does not rest on any opinion. And error belongs with opinion' (p.3).

3. Forms of life and constitutive rules

The conclusion of § 1 was that rule-guided behaviour presupposes a practice. For if there is no practice of action according to rules, both the expressions 'in accordance with the rule' and 'in conflict with the rule' are deprived of all sense. A conclusion of § 2 was that a practice is ultimately an agreement in forms of life and that this agreement cannot be described via epistemological concepts such as 'knowing', 'doubt', 'opinion', or 'justification'. The relation between the foundational argument and agreement in forms of life makes for a certain instability in the 'foundations' of Wittgenstein's philosophy, though more in the countless interpretations of these 'foundations'. Most authors have sought these 'foundations' in Wittgenstein's use of the terms 'form of life' and 'agreement' and have given an interpretation of these terms which amounts to either the sociologism fallacy or the biologism fallacy. The disastrous effect of both paralogies is that the internal relation between rule and action, sign and meaning, or pain and expression falls apart into an empirical, causal, external relation: according to the sociologism fallacy this relation should (moreover) be explained via a third term, social convention; according to the biologism fallacy it should (moreover) be explained via the third term of human nature, in which we are all alike. In this section I raise the following three questions: in what respect can agreement in forms of life be called a 'foundation' for the foundational argument (A) and how does Wittgenstein avoid the biologism fallacy (B) and the sociologism fallacy (C)? The answer to (A) brings us back to the *Philosophical Grammar* and the corresponding manuscript TS 213, where Wittgenstein discusses at length what he calls 'the autonomy of constitutive rules'. In *Philosophical Grammar*, § 133 he writes: 'Grammar is not accountable to any reality. It is grammatical rules that determine meaning (constitute it) and so they themselves are not answerable to any meaning and to that extent are arbitrary' (PG, § 133). In this extremely condensed fragment the following crucial links are made: between the 'autonomy' of grammatical rules and their constitutive function, and between this function and the arbitrary (conventional) character of those rules. An explication of the constitutive nature of rules also entails therefore a clarification of their autonomous and conventional nature. These characterizations cannot be strictly distinguished, however. The autonomy of rules is a recurrent theme throughout Wittgenstein's oeuvre. As early as the *Notebooks* he wrote, 'Logic must take care of itself' (p. 1), in *Philosophical Grammar*, § 2, 'Language must speak for itself', and in *On Certainty*, § 139 he still writes, 'the practice must speak for itself'. Why do logic, practice, and language have to speak for themselves and why is there nothing else that can speak for them? The answer is: 'The limit of language is shown by the impossibility of describing the fact which corresponds to a sentence (is the translation of it), without simply repeating the sentence. (This has to do with the Kantian solution of the problem of philosophy.)' (CV, p. 10).

I call the fundamental position which Wittgenstein adopts here 'internalism'. It is a confirmation of the following two theses. (a) The meaning of words and signs is not given independently of constitutive rules, language-games, forms of life, but is internal to them. (b) The description of these rules, language-games, forms of life is not itself an empirical statement.

The import of (a) is broader than the earlier argument that the relation between a rule and an action is internal. The broader philosophical implication is that there is no point at all in talking about 'objects', 'states of affairs', or even 'impressions' as a sphere unaffected by our rules, language-games, and forms of life. Even the criterion for the identity of pain, no matter how biological pain may be, turns out to be non-independent of such rules (see chapter 4). Objectivity is always a human cross-section of reality.

The consequence of (a) is that one cannot say anything about the correspondence between language and reality, at least not without repeating oneself. In any case the correspondence cannot be pointed out from a metaphysical vantage-point, a vantage-point outside language-games. As Wittgenstein puts it on various occasions: the harmony between thinking/language and reality is to be found in the grammar of language. In other words, one cannot place a statement next to reality, step back, and say, pointing to both: 'that corresponds to that'.

When one asks someone 'how do you know that the description renders what
you see' he could answer for instance 'I *mean* that by these words'. But what is
this 'that', if it is not itself again articulated, that is, language. Consequently, 'I *mean* that' is no answer at all. The answer is an explanation of the
meaning of the word. (TS 213, p. 190)

The meaning of words cannot be defined ostensively, either publicly or privately; such definitions in turn presuppose language-
games. The problem of how language can refer to reality can only
be approached within the limits of language. A metaphysical
explanation of this relationship via entities 'outside' language-
games is circular: these entities in turn need to be thought or
talked about and this is only possible through a medium,
language. But the problem in fact was how language can refer to
something 'outside' of itself. Within the limits of language-games
one should not expect too much of a 'solution' either. For, asking
about the correspondence between language and reality, one's
answer is again a linguistic formulation, so that in a certain sense
one repeats oneself. That is the gist of *Culture and Value*, p. 10.

This constantly presupposed role of language-games and constitutive rules is discussed explicitly by Wittgenstein in § 1 of the
Philosophical Grammar and more extensively in the typoscript
version of these fragments. 'Can one *understand* something else
as a sentence? Or: Is it not only a sentence when one understands
it? Thus: Can one understand something else as a sentence?' (TS
213, p. 2). Can 'something non-linguistic' be understood as
language? No: 'What is spoken can only be explained in language
and so (in this sense) language cannot be explained' (TS 213, p. 2).
One can interpret and translate language, but this still presupposes
language: 'I want to say: one cannot interpret the whole language.
An interpretation is only one as opposed to another. It attaches
itself to the sign and incorporates it into a broader system' (TS 213,
p. 2). Not only is language as a whole incapable of being interpreted into something non-linguistic, language is not interpreted
in this way at all. If, for instance, one asks somebody, 'What do
you mean', one gets the answer, 'I mean that you should come
along', or something to that effect. In any case one does not say –
as a continual interpretation of language would imply – 'I mean
what I mean by "coming along"'. Or in Wittgenstein's example: if

you ask somebody something, you are satisfied with an answer and you will not complain that this answer is merely a linguistic sign, since its true meaning is supposedly hidden behind this sign and still needs to be interpreted. You expect nothing but an answer: 'It is clear that nothing else could be expected and that the answer presupposes the use of language. Like everything that can be said' (TS 213, p. 3).

This presupposing role of rules and language-games entails that they cannot be justified or explained via empirical statements. Constitutive rules cannot be founded on a simple method of empirical verification: such methods themselves presuppose constitutive rules. In other words: grammatical rules cannot be justified by a reference to or description of reality, since 'reference to', 'description of', and *a fortiori* 'justification' are themselves certain forms of language which also presuppose agreement in forms of life. Only where certain constitutive concepts and standards are actually being employed can these 'references' and 'descriptions' get off the ground. But this means that the grammatical rules themselves determine what counts as a description of or reference to reality. That is why it is meaningless to talk about founding such rules via extra-linguistic facts. Grammatical rules and language-games cannot be empirically justified and are in this sense conventional, autonomous, and arbitrary. For a better understanding of these logical features, Wittgenstein compares them with other kinds of rules.

Wittgenstein compares grammatical rules with culinary rules. The rules for cooking are not autonomous, not arbitrary, and so not constitutive. Why not? 'Because I think of the concept "cooking" as defined by the aim of cooking, and I don't think of the concept "language" as defined by the aim of language' (PG, § 133). The similarity between both kinds of rules is of course that they establish a certain normativity and regularity for typical ways of speaking and acting. The crucial difference seems to be that the justification present in both types as such also applies to the culinary rules themselves, but not to the grammatical rule itself. For besides the regularity which culinary rules establish in the kitchen, they themselves are also justified by something in the stomach: appetite, i.e. the goal. Cooking is not essentially an activity conforming to culinary rules, but above all an activity with a certain result. This result is more or less independent of the culinary rules themselves. If a chef breaks with the rules of traditional recipes, culinary critics will still judge it to be culinary art, as long as the desired result (eatable to very eatable food) is achieved. Wittgenstein, not surprisingly a lover of plain cooking, gives us this recipe: 'It is for instance a rule that eggs are boiled for three minutes in order to get soft boiled eggs; if owing to some or other circumstance the same result is achieved after five minutes cooking, one does not say "that is not what is called 'boiling soft eggs'".' (TS 213, p. 236). As long as the culinary rules produce the desired result, they are justified, that is, in an empirical-causal sense. Justification here is always a certain effect, for instance a dish which makes one's mouth water.

Culinary rules are what Duintjer has called modifying rules: they modify behaviour that exists independently and is independently identifiable (cf. Duintjer, 1977, pp. 45-52). This means that they are constituted by something external to them, a cause, a result, and this result is causally dependent on the activity of cooking and on the natural fact that eggs are sooner cooked than potatoes. In this respect culinary rules are not autonomous. Grammatical rules themselves are not justified by something external to them. They are autonomous and an example of constitutive rules: rules that define a practice and do not admit of alternatives, since these involve a departure from the practice. Grammatical rules cannot occasion a discussion as to whether they give a correct rule for a certain word. For without these rules the word has no meaning. These rules are constitutive, arbitrary, or autonomous in the sense they give words their meaning in the first place. Modifying or technical rules like culinary rules are different: here one can obey other rules or flout existing ones and yet it is still possible to indicate a goal, even if it can now no longer be achieved, for example eatable food. With grammatical rules this is impossible: the goal of grammatical rules is conceptually dependent on the rules themselves: 'The aim of grammar is just the aim of language' (TS 213, p. 194). Mistakes made by not obeying grammatical rules are excluded. Without grammatical rules there is no language at all, not just wrong or

careless language. According to Wittgenstein, constitutive rules
can be meaningfully compared with methodological rules, for
instance rules for determining units of measure (cf. PG, § 133).[13]
The sense in which a unit of measure is arbitrary is *not* that in any
given case one can choose the unit one prefers. Arbitrary, conventional, means that the act of indicating a unit of measure is
not itself an empirical measurement of, for instance, length. It is
constitutive for a measurement of length and in this sense
practical or unpractical, useful or useless, but not true or untrue.
True or untrue applies to the measurement of length, given the
constitutive rules for the measurement of length. This constitutive rule should not and cannot therefore be confused with
an empirical measurement of length. The same goes for grammatical rules.

> One can call the rules of grammar 'arbitrary' if by that it is meant that the
> *aim* of grammar is just the aim of language. And it is nonsense to say: language
> must contain substantives, property-words, verbs and numerals, because there
> are things, properties, activities and numbers and the like. As if the case
> were comparable with: Astronomy has to speak of four Jupiter moons because
> there are four Jupiter moons. (MS 116, pp. 134-135)

A constitutive rule for the use of a word is not the same as an
empirical statement in which the word is used. The first statement is logical, the second empirical; the logical statement is constitutive for the empirical one.

What conclusions can now be drawn from this first aspect of
Wittgenstein's internalism with regard to the kind of 'foundation'
which a practice or form of life is? We have already seen that a
form of life cannot itself be called founded or unfounded since a
form of life is a condition for distinguishing between founded and
unfounded. Wittgenstein's internalism and the resulting autonomy of grammatical or constitutive rules have made it clear that
forms of life are not founded by something external to them-

---

[13] The comparison between grammatical rules and methodological rules is
possibly inspired by Einstein. Wittgenstein mentions Einstein a few times; for
instance, in a discussion about criteria for inner experiences he responds to an
adversary as follows: 'You forget what Einstein, as I surmise, has taught the
world: that the method of time measurement belongs to the grammar of time
sentences' (MS 119, pp. 226-227).

selves. Forms of life and grammatical rules are not foundations
in the sense that they supposedly correspond to the 'objective
facts' or the 'essence of nature'. For the grammatical rules
themselves determine what is to be regarded as 'objective fact' and
as 'the essence of nature'. (This is not to say that Wittgenstein
does not recognize physical or physiological facts which are not
part of a rule-guided practice. On the contrary, the grammatical
rules *are* 'accountable to reality' in the sense that, if reality were
quite different in certain respects, our rules and language-games
would lose their value and meaning.) Forms of life and
grammatical rules are 'foundations' in the sense that they
constitute the meaning of our concepts in the first place and that if
we were to change the rules, the concepts would have an entirely
different meaning or no meaning at all. A further characterization of 'foundation' in this sense will be given when we
discuss the second aspect of Wittgenstein's internalism.

But first we have to reject two interpretations of 'agreement in
forms of life': the biologism fallacy (B) and the sociologism fallacy
(C). The biologism fallacy is the idea that forms of life and so also
rule-guided behaviour have their basis in human biology. A first
objection to this idea will by now be clear: a form of life is not
founded by any goal or fact outside itself, including biological facts.
This does not mean that biological causes play no role in the
genesis of rule-governed behaviour and the meaning of words.
But on principle Wittgenstein does not concern himself with this
kind of genesis. His inquiry into the validity of rules is conducted
within language-games and not on the hypothetical plane of
external (biological) causes. A second objection to (B) is that what
Wittgenstein calls our form of life is not exclusively biological, but
rather cultural, social, and anthropological. That much is already
shown by a fragment (RPP I, § 630) which I quoted in the previous
chapter. This fragment instances the following 'Tatsachen des
Lebens' of which forms of life consist: punishing certain actions,
giving orders, reporting something, describing colours, and being
interested in another person's emotions. In short, facts which can
be called social and cultural, but not biological. When Wittgenstein does draw a comparison between man and animal, as in *On
Certainty*, § 359, where he calls the agreement in forms of life

something 'Animalisches', he does so by way of analogy: an analogy for the fact that forms of life cannot be called founded or unfounded.

Wittgenstein steers clear of the sociologism fallacy (C) too. A practice is not 'based' on prior agreement, but shows agreement. Kripke, in particular, presents agreement as a kind of contract and form of decision-making. But Wittgenstein writes: '"Contrat Sociale". In this case *no* treaty has actually been made; but the situation is more or less akin to, analogous to, the one we were in when ... And it is of great value to view it from the perspective of such a treaty' (TS 213, p. 196). In the first place there is no contract because Wittgenstein thinks it possible that Robinson Crusoe is capable of playing language-games (cf. chapter 4, § 1). In the second place agreement between people is not agreement in opinions but in language-games and forms of life (cf. PI, § 241). As we saw in § 2, consultation, deliberation, decision-making, etc. are appropriate at the level of opinions, but not at the level of 'Einstellung', attitude. There considerations are no longer reconsidered, but make place for action. Agreement therefore does not mean decision-making, as in Kripke: as if individuals get together and then reach a consensus democratically. Decision-making itself already presupposes agreement in forms of life (cf. Z, § 429-431).

The second characteristic (b) of Wittgenstein's internalism was that descriptions of forms of life are not empirical statements. The description of a form of life is a clarification of a practice which we already 'know'. The 'knowledge' this produces is not comparable with the information given by empirical statements, but is 'knowledge' in the sense of recollection or explication. This characteristic can shed further light on the kind of 'foundation' that forms of life are and the kind they are not in the following way. Certainly at an elementary level (for instance in physiognomical language-games), the rules forming the 'foundation' of our justifications and criticism are so interwoven with a way of life that we do not learn them specifically and can only state them retrospectively, e.g. as philosophers: 'I do not explicitly learn the propositions that stand fast for me. I can *discover* them subsequently like the axis around which a body rotates. This axis is not fixed in the sense that anything holds it fast, but the movement around it determines its immobility' (OC, § 152). The form of life is not 'held fast' by anything and we do not have the form of life as something which we ourselves 'hold fast': 'What stands fast does so, not because it is intrinsically obvious or convincing ...' (OC, § 144). The 'foundation' which the form of life is is something which we ourselves are, our way of life, not something we have and on which we can base ourselves as an independent foundation. This characteristic too is liable to be misunderstood. Above all it seems open to the charge of conservatism: apparently we are so settled in our forms of life that we will not tolerate alternative ones. It might even be said that we cannot imagine alternative forms of life because we are so immured in our own.

The impossibility of alternatives is in fact implied in the nature of constitutive rules. This is fairly innocuous in the case of chess, cards, or football. If one plays chess according to other rules than the existing rules, or if one plays patience with two people, one is not so much playing incorrectly as playing a completely different game. On the other hand, if one cooks according to other rules than the standard rules, one either cooks badly or one cooks in a very special way, but in any case one cooks. In view of this rule-independent goal of cooking (the desired result), culinary rules are not arbitrary and therefore not constitutive either.

The impossibility of alternatives is much more dramatic when we look at the constitutive rules that Wittgenstein is concerned with. Although he often compares his themes with the game of chess, language-games are much more serious. Constitutive rules for language-games are not conventions in the conventional sense of the word: arrangements which one can change according to convenience. If we were to change constitutive rules for 'pain', 'colours', 'meaning', 'emotions', etc., we would not escape as lightly. These concepts are so fundamentally embedded in our way of life that other rules would imply a radically different mode of existence.

It is in this light that we should consider Wittgenstein's frequent allusions to imaginary tribes and his description of hypothetical language-games. The method of hypothetical language-

games, particularly of those involving an imaginary anthro-
pology, serve a dual purpose: to show via 'abnormal' language-
games what the normal circumstances, the constitutive rules, are
that provide our language-games with their logic; and to show via
'abnormal' language-games the limits of our normality. This
seems to me the important moral and cultural implication of
Wittgenstein's philosophy. At the end of the *Philosophical Investigations* Wittgenstein writes that he is interested in the correspondence between concepts and very general facts of nature, but
that he next imagines these facts to be different from what they
are, so that other concepts and relations between concepts become
more 'intelligible'. And in *Remarks on the Philosophy of
Psychology* I, § 48 he writes 'natural' instead of 'intelligible'.
Concepts different from our own are first of all difficult to
imagine because we are hardly conscious of those very general
facts. But once we imagine those facts to be different, other
concepts no longer seem unnatural and the imperialism of our
conceptual system is broken down. Wittgenstein gives many
examples of such alternative societies. I quote just one:

> If people really could, as I assumed, see the working of the nervous system of
> another person and adjusted their behaviour toward the other, they simply
> would not, I believe, have our concept of pain (e.g.), though perhaps a related
> concept. Their life *would look quite different* from ours (MS 169, p. 65)

> That is: I consider this language-game as autonomous. I only want to describe
> it, not justify it. (MS 169, p. 65)

The charge of conservatism sometimes levelled at Wittgenstein is
unwarranted.[14] Wittgenstein would be guilty of conservatism if
he were in fact to undertake a justification, if he were to describe
our concepts as the only right and possible concepts, so that people
who do not share our concepts apparently fail to see something
we do see. However, Wittgenstein does not opt for a prompt and
facile relativism either. He does not hold that we can put
ourselves in the position of everybody and everything by simply
drawing up an inventory of alternative language-games. On the

---

[14] This charge is brought by Marcuse (1964, pp. 173 ff.). A more recent version is
given by Nyiri (1982). For a convincing criticism of Nyiri, see Janik (1985, pp.
116-136).

contrary, that still often leaves us without an exact idea of these alternatives, let alone that we could live them. A world in which people can see and also respond to each other's physiology seems inconceivable to us because we have no concepts (we only have 'pain') to express their lack of concepts (they have no 'pain' but only 'stimulation of C fibres'). The example of colours make this even clearer than pain. Imagine a world in which the colour red-green occurs; Wittgenstein posits this on several occasions. Even if we imagine this world, still we often have no idea of what we have achieved by doing so, since this colour cannot be what we call red-green, but it cannot be what they call red-green either. For this final step is only possible if we have a concept for a thing of which we have no conception ('green-red'). If we lack this concept, it seems inevitable that we describe their colour precisely in terms of those concepts ('red', 'green') which only we in turn have, but not they.

In the end, therefore, we have to be satisfied with the vague but rigorous observation that their life is completely different. A real relativist does not leave it at that. He says more about it than he can. He often thinks that he can indicate precisely how a different way of life, a different upbringing, different interests and worries lead to a way of thinking that functions in the same way as ours. For him it *is* possible to imagine a different way of thinking.

CHAPTER 4

MY MIND: FIRST PERSON STATEMENTS

It would be misleading to call this chapter 'The private language argument'. The term derives from the critical literature on Wittgenstein and usually refers to what is regarded as his main contribution to the philosophy of mind. But the unanimity of the critics does not go beyond this appreciation of the argument's importance and opinions differ widely on the content and even the location of the argument in the *Philosophical Investigations*. The earliest tradition, headed by Kenny, has the argument begin at § 243 and end at § 257 ... or at § 265, or 270, or 293, or 315! In the latest tradition, led by Kripke, the argument starts much earlier, at § 143, and ends much earlier too, at § 243, where it begins according to the old school.

Stanley Cavell has been one of the few to express doubts about the point of localizing the argument: 'I find little said [i.e. in § 243-315] especially about privacy and language, that is not said, generally more clearly, elsewhere in the *Investigations*, so that the very fame of this argument suggests to me that it has been miscast' (Cavell, p. 343). In fact, problems connected with psychological statements in the first and third person are not discussed exclusively or even exemplarily by Wittgenstein in *Philosophical Investigations*, § 243-315. It is not even true that this part of the *Philosophical Investigations* was conceived earlier than later sections dealing with the first and third person. The first attack on private languages, as I shall argue in this chapter, occurs in *Philosophical Investigations*, § 398-411. The many manuscripts in the Nachlass devoted to the problem of the first person show that § 398-411 of the *Philosophical Investigations* were conceived between 1929 and 1937 and that many fragments between § 243 and 315 took shape later.

In this chapter I shall draw more extensively on the Nachlass than I have done so far, in order to map the genesis of Wittgenstein's analysis of first person statements as fully as possible. The reconstruction of his analysis of the third person follows in chapter 5.

1. Robinson Crusoe and private language

The gist of Wittgenstein's discussion on rule-guided behaviour was that the relation between a rule and an action which accords with it is internal. Attempts to support or explain this relation via a third term were called fallacies: the psychologism, biologism, and sociologism fallacies. Although it is generally agreed that Wittgenstein opposes the psychologism fallacy, many still believe he adheres to a form of biologism or sociologism. In chapter 3, § 1 I have shown that Wittgenstein, far from adopting these positions, in fact opposes them as fallacies. But the sociologism fallacy is persistent and particularly affects the private language argument. It is widely thought that, since a private language lacks every kind of social dimension, Wittgenstein's emphasis on the practice of rule-guided behaviour spells death to such a language. For, in this line of thought, 'practice' is synonymous with 'social use'. So that the problem of defining whether an action is or is not in accordance with a rule can only be solved in terms of what a social community regards as a standard practice.

I have already shown that this appeal to a social community is a fallacy. An explanation of the relation between rule and action via the pressure of social circumstances involves a third term and so fails to do justice to the internal nature of the relation: the relation is made external. In this section I moreover want to show that a rule-guided Robinson Crusoe existence is by no means a conceptual absurdity for Wittgenstein and that 'private' should not be taken in the sense of the doings of a physically isolated individual. In fact, authors[1] guilty of the sociologism

---

[1] See Strawson (1954, p. 85), Ayer (1963, p. 4), Fodor (1975, p. 71), and Malcolm (1986, pp. 157 and 171). Authors who also criticize the sociologism fallacy and hence the purported impossibility of Robinson Crusoe speaking a rule-guided

fallacy tend to produce Robinson Crusoe as the prototype of some-body who speaks or, rather, thinks he speaks a private language. Of course the choice of this unsocial prototype is natural if such heavy emphasis is put on the social community as the guarantor of consistent rule-governed behaviour. The idea is that Crusoe, acting in isolation, cannot distinguish between actions which merely seem to him to be in conformance with a rule and those that really are. He can only make this distinction by comparing his actions with those of others and by learning from the feedback which only others can provide. His social isolation precludes this, so that all his actions can be interpreted as according with a rule. And this means that there is no agreement or conflict. The basis for that distinction lies in the social community and the control it imposes on individuals.

Robinson Crusoe and similar solitary individuals are also pro-duced by Wittgenstein in various manuscripts: MS 116, p. 117, MS 124, p. 221, MS 165, pp. 74, 116, 117, and MS 180a, p. 59. In all these passages Crusoe serves to illustrate, not an 'impossible private language', but a *possible* one – even if this sometimes proves most difficult. Although Robinson Crusoe is not actually men-tioned in the *Philosophical Investigations*, the first part of § 243 is a compilation of fragments from manuscripts in which his name does occur. This is most clearly the case in MS 124. In a proto-version of the first part of § 243 Wittgenstein writes:

> There are cases in which we say that someone admonishes himself; orders, obeys, punishes, reprimands, questions and answers himself. This means that human beings can exist who only know the language-games which everybody plays with himself. Indeed, it could be imagined that these humans possessed a rich vocabulary. We can imagine that an explorer came to their country and watched how everyone of them accompanied his activities with articulated sounds, but without turning to others. Somehow or other it occurs to the explorer that these people hold conversations with themselves, he listens to them during their activities and he succeeds in giving a probable translation of their speech into our language. By learning this language he is also able to predict actions that are performed subsequently by these people, for much of what they say is the expression of resolutions and decisions. (How these people could have been able to learn their language is indifferent here). (MS 124, pp. 213-214)

---

language are McGinn (1984, pp. 78-79) and Baker & Hacker (1985, pp. 169-179).

A few pages down Wittgenstein refers to this language as follows:

> The private language that I described above is such that for instance Robinson
> could have spoken it to himself on his island. If someone had listened to him
> and watched him, he could have learned this language of Robinson's. For the
> meanings of the words showed themselves in Robinson's way of acting. (MS
> 124, p. 222)

This is followed by versions of the second part of § 243 and § 244.
It is striking that activities with a clearly private nature are called
language-games in these fragments. Apparently the dividing line
between what Wittgenstein still calls language-games and what he
calls 'private language' does not coincide with the boundary
between a community and an individual that lives outside of it or
between a community and a number of eccentrics. Robinson's
private codes and language can be called language-games if his
solitary actions are not random but correspond to a regular pattern
of actions. In other words, a study of his actions must show that
he knows a skill. For only if he knows a skill, a technique, however idiosyncratically, will his actions show a certain regularity
which can then be used by another person as a basis for predictions. Robinson's solitary actions can therefore be considered
rule-guided if in principle they are comprehensible for others.
That is to say, *for* others, not through others. Rules are not
corrective measures and rule-guided behaviour is not behaviour
allowed by virtue of communal sanctions.[2] Rule-governed behaviour does presuppose mastery of a technique, a complex of
skills that primarily manifests itself in different, often very intri-
cate 'patterns of life'. In Robinson's private and solitary pattern of
life these skills are no doubt hard to distinguish, but the problem
is not a fundamental one.

His private mode of life does not in fact coincide with that of
the speaker introduced in the second part of *Philosophical Investigations*, § 243. Wittgenstein suggests there a language of which
the words refer to immediate private sensations known only to
the speaker; others cannot understand his language. In the light
of the above, this incomprehension would imply that no mastery

---

[2] Kripke interprets rules as such corrective measures when he says: 'When the
community denies of someone that he is following certain rules, it excludes him
from various transactions...' (1981, p. 287).

of a technique is manifested in the language concerned; for a language can only be comprehensible for another person, he can only recognize a pattern in it, if it is the manifestation of a technique. The paradigm of this kind of language, which does not presuppose any knowledge of a technique, is of course phenomenal 'language', the 'language' of consciousness, of sense data, etc. In the previous chapter we already saw Wittgenstein drawing a clear parallel between his rejection of a phenomenal language for the meaning of colour concepts and his rejection of psychological interpretations of rule-governed behaviour (see chapter 3, pp. 49 ff.). However, the application of phenomenal languages is perhaps most persistent in the case of first and third person statements about my mind and other minds and Wittgenstein's analysis here is profound and complex. But although this case is more complex and according to Wittgenstein more difficult than those of colour concepts and rule-governed behaviour, yet it seems pointless, given the way these three cases are interrelated, to call one of them the focal point or essence of the *Philosophical Investigations*. Nevertheless one still finds critics doing just this, even if the 'focal point' has been shifted from *Philosophical Investigations*, § 243 ff. to § 189 through 242. Kripke goes so far as to claim that the heart of the *Investigations* is § 202 and that § 243 ff. deal with the 'problem of sensations'.[3] But this is too narrow. Sections 243 and further sweep a much broader field and the sensation of 'pain' is mainly used by Wittgenstein as a striking example of the many intersecting problems here. This more illustrative role of the pain concept is reconfirmed by various manuscript versions of § 243 ff. Directly after the above-cited first version of § 243 in MS 124 Wittgenstein discusses psychological concepts which tend to be included in private languages, and his examples are not 'pain' but 'thinking', 'sudden insight',[4] 'finding

---

[3] According to Kripke, the private language argument is the application of general conclusions about language reached in § 138-242 to the 'problem of sensations' (1981, pp. 239-240).

[4] He writes for instance: 'Mozart writes in a famous letter that he could see a complete musical work in a flash in his mind. How is that possible, did he hear it played in his mind at breakneck speed; or thus that all the tones resounded simultaneously? And what justified him to say that he perceived a piece of

the right word' (MS 124, pp. 215-221). And he rescues these concepts from the nebula of private languages in a way that is analogous to how he will describe 'pain' in horizontal relations of language-games: via internal relations with their more or less natural expressions. 'Do not conceive of thinking as the words that accompany the melody of a song, but rather as the "expression" with which the song is sung' (MS 124, p. 215).

Yet Wittgenstein chooses 'pain'. Why? The answer has two parts. First of all, 'pain', in contrast to 'thinking', 'hoping', and 'meaning', has a natural expression: a face contorted by pain, a cry for help, etc. He could not have found a more striking example of his idea that the meaning of psychological concepts is internally related to (natural) expressions. In the second place he chooses pain, and not anger or joy, which also have a specific physiognomy, because the sensation of pain is more direct, more temporary, more physical than the experience of emotions. More than emotions, pain is usually an acute state of consciousness. Wittgenstein links the following strategy to this: if it is possible in the case of pain, where the inner sensation is so emphatic that introspective naming of it seems completely straightforward, to demonstrate the necessity of a public language-game as unit of meaning – the language-game of expression – then this necessity applies *a fortiori* to phenomena where either inner sensations are not as immediate but more gradual – joy, grief, etc. – or characteristic inner sensations seem absent rather than present – expecting, wishing, meaning, etc. In this respect 'pain' plays a strategic as well as an illustrative role.

If there is a 'problem of sensations', it is not in § 243 ff., but in *Philosophical Investigations* II viii,[5] where Wittgenstein discusses the problem of kinaesthetic sensations (see chapter 7, § 1). The main issue in § 243 is what Wittgenstein in the *Blue Books* calls 'personal experience' (pp. 44-45) – this notion is not the central problem of *Philosophical Investigations* II, as Hallett wrongly assumes.[6] By this term Wittgenstein refers to the well-known

---

music in his mind? How did he know that a piece of music corresponded to what he perceived? (MS 124, pp. 216-217).

[5] See also RPP I, § 382-408 and 765-786 (see chapter 7, § 1).

[6] Hallett (1977, pp. 53-54).

distinction between propositions describing material reality and propositions describing our personal experiences, e.g. visual experiences. Wishing now to concentrate on the analysis of the language for personal experiences, Wittgenstein assumes that the impossibility of a phenomenal language in general has been demonstrated – including such a language as a basis for propositions describing material reality. What remains is the rejection of the many proposals to explain the concepts of personal experiences in phenomenal terms and the attribution of these concepts to specific language-games[7] as their units of meaning. And perhaps this is Wittgenstein's most daunting problem, as he says at the beginning of a long discussion on private languages and personal experiences:

> The area in which we find ourselves here rightly counts as one of the most difficult ones in philosophy; namely because the surface grammar is extraordinarily misleading here and the ground is churned up by the countless, criss-cross wheel tracks of philosophizing people, so that it is almost impossible to know the *way* here.
> If one wished to speak of a personal experience in the sense that its grammar would be independent of the expression of the experience, then it would be quite indifferent *which sort* of experience we postulated behind the expression and indifferent whether we assume that I recognize it correctly or incorrectly. In *this* sense I may err again and again in saying that I have a toothache, because each time I have a fundamentally different experience; but it is all the same. – But what sort of meaning of the word personal experience is it that functions *thus*. Where do we take it from; how does it arise? (MS 119, pp. 226-227)

In this fragment, which forms the beginning of a long series of protoversions of § 243 through 293, Wittgenstein clearly shows how the general explanation of public language by a private, phenomenal language affects the specific case of psychological concepts in the first person. The other side of the coin, statements about personal experiences in the third person, is shown in e.g. *Philosophical Investigations*, § 246: 'In what sense are my

---

[7] Wittgenstein is not out to eliminate subjective experiences from language-games. On the contrary, he wants to emphasize that language-games of subjective experiences are *different* from language-games of objective experiences. For his and Köhler's use of 'subjective experience' versus 'objective experience', see chapter 7, note 18.

sensations *private*? – Well, only I can know whether I am really in pain; another person can only surmise it.' The problem brought up by Wittgenstein in § 243 is not the problem of sensations, not the problem of a phenomenal language in general; I see the problem as turning on the application of phenomenal language to the meaning of psychological concepts in the first and third person. The idea of a phenomenal language was that the meaning of linguistic signs is to be explained by an underlying domain of inner experiences. This domain is supposedly the cause to which every facet of meaning can be reduced; the signs themselves are no more than a concomitant effect. The *application* of a phenomenal language to *first* and *third* person statements can then be reconstructed as follows.

A. The meaning of the non-verbal and verbal expression of pain must be causally explained by the present sensation of pain.

B. As a concomitant effect the expression is externally related to the crucial inner sensation.

C. In the first person the expression is based on direct acquaintance with the sensation; sensation and expression can be perceived side by side and can be connected with one another.

D. In the third person only the concomitant effect, the expression, is perceived.

E. Knowledge in the third person is therefore based on indirect, external grounds; the inner sensation can only be hypothetically deduced from the effect.

Propositions (D) and (E) are dealt with in the following chapter, (A), (B), and (C) in the present one, if not systematically. (A) through (E) I call the *symmetrical view* of first and third person statements. Both perspectives are constructed according to the same symmetrical scheme: in the first person there is knowledge and observation based on direct, inner evidence, in the third it is based on indirect, outer evidence. The distinction between direct and indirect does not disturb the symmetry but on the contrary preserves it: I know that I am in pain and the other can only suppose so, I suppose that the other is in pain, he knows that he is in pain.

To annul this symmetrical image is the main destructive purpose of § 243 ff., while rehabilitation of an *asymmetrical* logic is
the main constructive objective. Roughly speaking – a specific
interpretation will follow presently – this asymmetry means that
the first person, unlike the third person, involves neither observation nor a claim to knowledge. As a result, Wittgenstein will
dispense with the phrase 'direct, inner evidence' in his analysis of
the first person and with 'indirect, outer evidence' in his analysis
of the third person. In the final section of this chapter I shall talk
about the relation between Wittgenstein's analysis of the mainly
expressive use of the first person and its descriptive use.

2. Four misleading analogies

The problem and the solution are not as simple as the above
would seem to suggest. The symmetrical view cannot be cut
down to a single characteristic, and the asymmetrical logic cannot
be set out recipe-wise. Moreover, the virtuosity of Wittgenstein's
method here often seems hard to follow. Nevertheless I shall not
start by introducing terms – privacy in the sense of 'incommuni-
cability' and in the sense of 'inalienability'[8] – which are not used
by Wittgenstein himself and which give the problems an inappro-
priate epistemological flavour. The Nachlass clearly shows that
Wittgenstein is fighting a whole series of misleading analogies:

> Or really, a hundred misleading comparisons seem to meet each other here:
> Something is conceived to be an ostensive definition which is none; something
> a description which is none; something a proper name which is none; some-
> thing knowledge which is not knowledge. ('inner and outer') (MS 120, p. 67)

The philosophical theory opposed here by Wittgenstein is based
on everyday experience. Because of the familiarity of this experience, the theory is much less alert to prejudices and metaphors
than a philosophical theory about some or other abstract subject.
One is much more liable to speak in terms of metaphysical
images, such as 'I can only feel my pain' or 'It is impossible for me

---

[8] These terms were introduced by Kenny (1975, pp. 185 ff.). For my criticism of
Kenny, see note 16.

to know what he is feeling'. Wittgenstein was well aware of this and in the manuscripts dealing with the first person he warns against the intrusion of metaphysical tendencies in our thinking: 'Oh, how difficult it is to pass from metaphysics to grammar here' (MS 120, pp. 122-123). 'Philosophy works against the myth-forming tendencies in our mind' (MS 158, p. 49).

Although no single analogy is to the fore of Wittgenstein's mind, the conceptual confusion underlying some analogies is analysed more fully than others. For this reason I shall begin my reconstruction by looking at the way Wittgenstein unravels the knots in the conception of the ego (seeing a proper name where there is none).

a. I and my sense data

In discussions of the private language argument a series of frag-ments is mostly and in any case largely left unconsidered, namely *Philosophical Investigations*, § 398-411. I shall try to show in this section that this part of the *Philosophical Investigations* can right-ly be called Wittgenstein's first argument against the privacy of immediate experiences. The facts of the Nachlass show that the definitive version of § 398-411 was completed prior to the defini-tive version of most of the fragments in § 243-315, where most authors situate Wittgenstein's private language argument. The essence of my interpretation of § 398-411 and especially the history of this part of the Nachlass will be that Wittgenstein refutes solipsism and phenomenalism here. More specifically, he simul-taneously exposes the grammatical confusion underlying the theory of the solipsistic or metaphysical ego and that underlying the theory of sense data.

As early as the *Tractatus* Wittgenstein felt challenged by the theory of solipsism. In T, 5.62 he says enigmatically that what the solipsist means is correct but that it cannot be said. The subject, as Wittgenstein states in T, 5.632, is not part of the world but forms its limit. To clarify this point he gives the following analogy. The relation between the metaphysical subject and the world is like the relation between the eye and the field of vision (cf. T, 5.633-5.6331). The existence of the field of vision demonstrates the existence of the eye. But the eye itself is not seen in the field of vision; it is its source. The same applies to the ego. The ego is the source of consciousness and as such is no object of consciousness. Nor can it be localized in experience, just as the eye cannot be localized in the field of vision. Since it bounds the world, nothing can be said about it: it merely shows itself. The correct meaning behind solipsism is that I hold a perspective on the world which is limitless, just as the field of vision is limitless (T, 6.4311). But this truth behind solipsism cannot be said and solipsism is the confused result of the attempt to say this truth nevertheless. As soon as the solipsist tries to formulate an intention which is correct in itself, he arrives at the absurd position that only I exist and only I have experience of anything.

Wittgenstein's first explicit rejection of phenomenalism dates from the end of 1931 and beginning of 1932. He probably rejects phenomenalism as early as 1929, but the facts are ambiguous and I do not wish to discuss the matter here.[9] Nor will I discuss the extremely complicated question whether and how far Wittgenstein occupies a phenomenalist point of view in the *Tractatus*. What we do know is that members of the Vienna Circle and also Russell are phenomenalists and that Wittgenstein opposes their views.

As was said before, Wittgenstein's rejection of phenomenalism before 1931 is not entirely unambiguous and the debate over the following fragment is proof of this: 'I do not now have phenomenological language, or "primary language" as I used to call it, in mind as my goal. I no longer hold it to be necessary' (PR, § 1). In the Nachlass the term 'phenomenological language' is more frequent and from the context it clearly refers to a language which is the most direct description of the immediate experience. 'Phenomenological language: The description of immediate sense experiences, without a hypothetical addition' (MS 113, p. 246). The continuation of this fragment shows that Wittgenstein is not only

---

[9] There are passages in MS 105 and MS 107 where Wittgenstein countenances a phenomenalistic description of the visual space, for instance MS 105, pp. 49-51: 'Now it is a proposition to say: Red is here. 'Here' is here a designation of a place in the visual field and this designation also indicates the form of the red spot, for the form stems from the position of the red spot. But how is this position really to be described?'

thinking of the sense data theory. After attempting to describe the immediate experience in ordinary everyday language, he concludes that any attempt at an even more direct description can no longer be called a description, and as an example he mentions Driesch's statement: '"Ich habe, um mein Wissen wissend, bewusst etwas"' (MS 113, p. 247).[10] But the main examples of a phenomenological language are certain descriptions of the visual space ('Gesichtsraum') as opposed to physical space and memory time ('Gedächtniszeit') as opposed to physical time. As the following fragment shows, Wittgenstein is not out to declare that descriptions of the visual space or memory time are impossible; in the first place he wants to diagnose the appeal of this kind of phenomenological language and subsequently provide a less esoteric and magic description of the immediate experience:

> (How important then is the description of the present experience that can become for us an *idée fixe*. That we suffer from it that the description cannot describe what takes place while we read the description. It seems as if the preoccupation with this question is almost foolish and we find ourselves in a dead-end. And yet it is a significant dead-end, for all of us are lured into it, as if the final solution of the philosophical problems were to be looked for there – It is as if with this picture of the present phenomenon one gets into a enchanted swamp, where everything tangible dissappears.)
> On the other hand we do need a way of expressing the phenomena of the visual space in isolation from experiences of a different kind. (MS 113, pp. 247-248)

Phenomenological language is an *idée fixe* for many philosophers because they think they can solve philosophical problems with it. And above all two problems: the problem of the relation between immediate experiences and physical reality and the problem of the ego. Wittgenstein discusses these two problems side by side in the following fragment:

> When we speak of the visual space we are readily seduced by the picture as if it were a sort of peep-show that everyone carries with him. That is, we then use the word 'space' similarly to when we call a room a space. In reality, however, the word 'visual space' relates to a geometry, I mean, to a part of the grammar of our language. In this sense there are no 'visual spaces', each of

---

10 Because of its idiosyncrasy I have not translated this remark. To my knowledge Wittgenstein mentions Driesch only once.

them with its owner. (And for instance also such erratic ones that belong to no one.) (MS 113, p. 248)

This fragment is preliminary to the extremely complicated text in *Philosophical Investigations*, § 398. The analogy of the peep-show will disappear, but not that of the room; in § 398 Wittgenstein talks about a 'visuelle Zimmer' to denote the phenomenal 'space' of sense data and the like. The 'possessor' of this 'space', the solipsistic ego, als recurs in § 398. But a term which no longer occurs is 'geometry'. Nevertheless it is precisely this less metaphorical terminology that Wittgenstein uses between 1931 and 1938 in his attempts to provide a more adequate description of the ego and the field of vision. 'Geometry' is moreover the term which supplies a direct link between the rejection of solipsism in the *Tractatus* and the later work. I will now first reconstruct his later criticism of the solipsistic ego.

Characteristic of this later criticism is its emphasis on the grammatical analysis of conceptual confusions. In the *Tractatus* Wittgenstein says the following about his approach:

> 'There is nothing in the visual field to show etc.' (L. Ph. Abh.). This means so to speak: You will look in vain for *the one who sees* in the visual space. He is nowhere to be found in the visual space. But the truth is: You only *act as if* you are looking for something. (MS 120, pp. 113-114)

Wittgenstein is suggesting that, while the search for an 'I' still seemed meaningful in the *Tractatus*, he now believes that 'searching' is used here wrongly or misleadingly. The following fragment shows the same emphasis on the misleading use of words: 'Solipsism could be refuted by the fact that the word "I" has no central position, but is a word like any other word' (TS 213, p. 508). But a striking point of agreement with the *Tractatus* is that Wittgenstein retains and expands the analogy of the eye and the visual space: 'There is no metaphysical subject in language, just as there is none in the visual space' (TS 213, p. 508).

To clarify the notion that there is no metaphysical subject in the visual space, Wittgenstein distinguishes between two ways in which our perception converges in one point: in a physical eye and a geometrical eye.[11] The physical eye is the point where the

---

11 See *Blue Books*, p. 64. The same distinction is made in MS 156b.

rays of light converge, the geometrical eye is the focus behind the
field of vision. It is the geometrical point that lies at the beginning of the field of vision's axis. The point of the comparison is
that, just as the geometrical eye cannot be equated with the physical eye, so the metaphysical ego cannot be equated with the ego in
the sense of a person. The criteria for the identity of the ego are
completely different in kind from those for the identity of a
person, just as the criteria for the identity of the geometrical eye
are completely different in kind from those for the identity of the
physical eye.

In the following fragment Wittgenstein describes the temp-
tation to rank the geometrical eye in the same category as the
physical eye: 'I wish to say: "Behind what is called the description
of my experience stands something that has no neighbour, that is
unique, with which I compare the description"' (MS 156b, p. 114).
'Geometrical eye' does not in fact mean the same as 'physical eye';
to this extent the solipsist is right. But on the basis of this difference he is inclined to make 'geometrical eye' and 'physical eye'
refer to different *things*, and this is wrong. By making 'geometrical eye' refer to anything at all, he puts it in the same category of
the demonstrable as 'physical eye'. It is this inclination which
leads to the absurdity of solipsism: 'The tendency is to say "only
what *I* see is really seen". I look at my surroundings and say "*that*
is seen". If someone else says that he sees such and such, I say
"only that is *seen*". What is seen has no *neighbour*' (MS 156b, p.
88). Wittgenstein does not deny that the field of vision has no
neighbour, but he does oppose the solipsistic conclusion which is
drawn from this, namely that I (the geometrical eye) am the
unique and sole centre of perception, that I am the only one who
sees. The 'discovery'[12] of this focus behind the field of vision
makes it seem as if I can point to something which I cannot point
out to another person. And again Wittgenstein does not deny
that there is something which one cannot make known to

---

[12] In *Philosophical Investigations*, § 400 Wittgenstein says that the 'visual
room' seems like a discovery, but is in fact only a new way of speaking. In MS 120
he indicates *why* it seems like a discovery: 'For it is precisely because of the fact
that we are not always conscious of it that we think we *discovered* it' (MS 120, p.
87).

another person by pointing to it; what he denies is that one can point it out to *oneself*: 'Can I point out to another what I see? Not in the sense in which only I can see it. But can I point it out to *myself*, if to no one else ("That is here")' (MS 156b, p. 104). According to Wittgenstein, only a grammatical inquiry into the different uses of 'geometrical eye' and 'physical eye' can make it clear that the two do not belong to the same category of demonstrable objects:

> We combat the conception that my visual field is close to me. That is, we want to use 'visual field' in a sense in which it is not a part of the physical space. We must ask ourselves again: how do we use the word 'visual field'? (MS 156b, p. 111)

What confuses us, according to Wittgenstein, is that first we take the ego as a place (the physical eye) in Euclidean space and then as a place (the geometrical eye) in the field of vision. The transfer of predicates applicable to Euclidean space to the field of vision is illegitimate. 'Here' is not the name of a place, says Wittgenstein in *Philosophical Investigations*, § 410. In other words, there is no 'here' in the field of vision, so that one cannot say 'It looks like this from here'. The solipsist thus finds himself in a situation where what he wishes to say makes no distinction. For if he says 'only what I see is real' and in doing so refers to his geometrical eye, he points to objects in Euclidean space. But that is not actually his intention, for what he wishes to say is not intended for physical space but for the field of vision. In the field of vision, on the other hand, it is meaningless to talk about 'here' or 'I'. In the field of vision there is no 'behind me' or 'in front of me'. Nor is the field of vision incomplete in the sense that one would like to turn around to get a more complete picture.[13] The field of vision is limitless, one cannot move in it. One cannot point to anything in the sense that one cannot distinguish between a part in the foreground and a part in the background. This contrast cannot be made since the field of vision has no neighbour and so there is not a relative but an absolute position. And since a meaningful use of 'here' or 'I' is conditional on the possibility of

---

[13] See the quotation from MS 113, p. 249 in chapter 1, p. 14.

making a contrast, these terms cannot be applied to the field of vision.

If the terms 'I' and 'here' are not applicable to the visual space, the visual space cannot be considered linked with an 'I', a 'here', a 'possessor':

> But to what extent is the visual space only connected particularly with *you*? For of which 'I', in which sense of your person do you speak here? Of your picture in the visual space? No. Of the body L.W.? (MS 156b, pp. 94-95)

And a few pages back:

> What justifies me in saying 'Only I see...' Who is I? But I could say that W sees and mean that his body is now visible around the geometrical eye. 'I see' does not mean anything at all to me, as long as I do not know who I am. (MS 156b, p. 89)

The analogy of the 'geometrical eye' served to point up the solipsistic inclination to postulate a metaphysical subject as a point of reference independent of the environment and the body. For an experience like pain the solipsist demands a possessor, an 'I', besides a place in the body. In connection with this solipsistic tendency Wittgenstein asks: 'I have here pain (in my tooth). That I have it in my body belongs to experience. But also that *I* have it?' (MS 156b, p. 76). 'The person appears as the object of experience, but also seems to appear differently: essentially as subject, not as object' (MS 156b, p. 73). In *The Blue and Brown Books*,[14] dictated in the same period that MS 156 was written, Wittgenstein distinguishes between 'I-as-subject' and 'I-as-object'. I-as-object is the person as object of experience. I-as-subject is what is essentially subject, but now no longer in a metaphysical or solipsistic sense: what is meant by the solipsistic subject is now brought down to its true everyday proportions, i.e. to the use of 'I' in the language-game of expression. In *The Blue and Brown Books* and manuscripts from the same period Wittgenstein has not yet explicitly formulated the use of I-as-subject in terms of the language-game of expression; this only happens around 1937. The use of I-as-object, writes Wittgenstein in *The Blue and Brown Books*, implies the recognition of a certain person and it is possible to err here. Examples of this use are: 'My arm is broken'

---

14 See *Blue Books*, pp. 61 ff.

and 'I have grown 6 centimeters'. The use of I-as-subject does not imply the recognition of a certain person and errors are ruled out here. Examples of this use: 'I see so-and-so' and 'I feel pain'.

As the examples make clear, statements in which I-as-subject occurs are about immediate experience. Immediate experience is in fact expressly mentioned in a text from 1932 which can be seen as moving towards the distinction between I-as-subject and I-as-object.

> What should it mean: he is in this pain? except, he is in such pain: that is, pain of such a degree, kind, etc. But only in this sense can also I be in this pain. That means that the subject-object form is not applicable here. The subject-object form is related to the body and the things around it that act on it.
> In the non-hypothetical description of what is seen, heard – these words mean here grammatical forms – the I does not appear, there is no question here of subject and object. (TS 213, p.508)

Before looking at why there can be no talk of an object here, we need to find out in what way there can be no talk of a subject, an ego. In *Philosophical Remarks*, § 57 Wittgenstein suggests that it is instructive to eliminate the word 'I' from statements about immediate experience; so instead of saying 'I feel pain' we should say 'pain' or 'there is pain'. His idea is that the use of 'I' in these statements is superfluous, since they express no relation of something to the body. They say nothing about one's own body; no person is made the object of experience.[15] In 1937 Wittgenstein will put it like this: 'I feel pain' is analogous to a complaint and a complaint says nothing about the body. In 1933, not having fully developed the logic of expressions, he describes the peculiar character of 'I feel pain' somewhat more primitively by saying that the subject need not say that *he* feels pain, that he need not use the personal pronoun, since he has no choice in the matter and it goes without saying that he feels pain. 'The man who cries out with pain, or says that he has pain, *doesn't choose the mouth which says it*' (BLBK, p. 60), is his answer.

In a manuscript where Wittgenstein arrives at the final version of *Philosophical Investigations*, § 398-411 the expression 'I-as

---

[15] This view of Wittgenstein has been called by Strawson the 'No-ownership-theory' (1959, pp. 95-99).

subject' no longer occurs and is replaced by the analogy between 'I feel pain' and a cry:

> Does not everything amount to this, that the words 'I am...' correspond to a moaning or cry? That when I groan out of pity, it cannot be inferred from this who the sufferer is, but that for that a sign is necessary, whereas the cry of the one who suffers leads (us) to him. (MS 120, p. 30).

> One can even say: I can say that I am in pain without knowing who is in pain. (MS 120, p. 31)

'I have' (or 'I feel') is not used in these fragments as a statement about my body. Therefore the subject-object relation is not applicable and so there is no question of an 'I' or an owner who possesses something. In the following long passage, which explains much of *Philosophical Investigations*, § 411, Wittgenstein introduces a contrast between the reflexive and possessive use of 'mine' and it is clear that the former refers to I-as-subject and the latter to I-as-object:

> I might define with an ostensive gesture: '"my" nose is *this* nose.' Might I now also similarly explain: '"my" pain is *this* pain?' I might (surely at least) explain: '"My complaint" is the one that is uttered by *this* mouth.' It would be the essence of this explanation that the pointing-gesture is *reflexive*.
> It is different when I say: 'I call *these* books "my books".' 'I call *these* books "my books" because *I* always use them.'
> 'Mine' *reflexive* or *possessive*.
> 'Mine' is what I *have*; and *that* (with a reflexive gesture) is I. So if you want to know whether something is mine, check who the owner is; *if I have it*, it is *mine*. This explanation could (for instance) be applied to these books: If you discover that *I* read them, then you know that they belong to me. But can one apply this explanation to 'my face'? And to 'my pain'? (MS 120, pp. 159-161)

The possessive meaning of 'I' and 'mine' belongs only to I-as-object and not to I-as-subject.[16] The use of these words is possessive if they express a relation to my body. In that case 'mine' means what I possess. It is an assertion, since somebody who wants to know whether it is mine can put this to the

---

[16] Kenny's use of 'inalienability' (see p. 81 and quotation 8) does not sufficiently distinguish between 'I-as-subject' and 'I-as-object', for he treats the sentences 'Only I can have my pain' and 'Only I can have my bank account' in the same way, whereas Wittgenstein would precisely emphasize that these two examples cannot be compared, since in the latter case the use of 'my' is possessive but in the former merely reflexive. See Kenny, 1975, p. 188.

question. He can find out who the owner is, just as a contract of sale shows that this is my house. The possessive use is not applicable to I-as-subject. There is no meaningful way of carrying out the order 'Check whether this is my face or my pain'. There can be no doubt that I feel pain; doubt is logically excluded here.

The use of I-as-subject has to be distinguished from third person statements as well, such as 'he feels pain'. But if Wittgenstein has just said that 'I' can be eliminated from statements about immediate experience, then there now seems no way of distinguishing between 'I' and 'you' and 'he'. Wittgenstein anticipates this objection: 'But surely you use "I" in contrast to "he". So you do (thereby) differentiate, after all, between persons' (MS 158, p. 158).

His answer is that 'I' and 'he' do not function on the same level. The relation between the first and the third person is *asymmetrical*. The use of 'he' in 'he feels pain' is only meaningful if there are criteria for the identity of a person (cf. PI, § 404), if 'he' is used together with a description, a name, or a demonstrative gesture. We are taught the meaning of 'he' by the action of pointing to people. We can do something similar in relation to ourselves. If somebody asks 'Who is MtH?', I can raise my finger and say 'That's me'. The following question seems but is not identical: 'Who's me?'. In any case we are not taught an answer to this question in the same way we are taught an answer to the question 'Who's he?'. There the answer refers to a person. But what we are taught in the case of the first question, if anything, is to make a reflexive gesture; we are taught to bend our arm. We are not taught the use of I-as-subject (the expressive use) by means of criteria for the identity of a person (cf. PI, § 404): '"Have I then asserted that I have something"? I have only complained and I have been taught the complaint "I am in pain"' (MS 120, p. 203). 'But surely you do not leave open whether you or someone else is in pain?' I leave everything open, I merely *complain*' (MS 120, p. 204). Our view of the logic of expressions is obscured by metaphorical language: 'The complaint "I am in pain" is about me and about the fact that I have something in a *metaphorical sense*. But it is not used as a statement about me, i.e. my body' (MS 116, p. 175). The use of 'have' and 'I' (in the German) is metaphorical in the sense that if somebody expresses his pain he is not trying to say that he *has* something, that something has a special episte-mological relation to his body. As an expression of pain, 'I feel pain' tells us no more *who* is feeling pain than the more primitive 'Ouch!': 'How is it: do I tell somebody who is com-plaining by saying: "I am complaining"? Do I tell somebody who is saying the word "yes" by saying "yes"?' (MS 120, p. 217).

Earlier on in this section (see pp. 84 ff.) we saw that Wittgen-stein's criticism of solipsism is connected with his criticism of phenomenalism, i.e. he criticizes both the notion of a unique subject and a unique object of experience. There is reason to look more closely at his criticism of sense data theories, particularly in view of the widespread complaint that he fails to take an explicit stand on the matter. This is a fair complaint insofar as Wittgen-stein mainly talks in metaphorical terms about phenomenalism and sense data in *Philosophical Investigations*, § 398-411. But the genesis of these fragments reveals a remarkably unambiguous point of view.

In the quotation from MS 113 Wittgenstein observed that the term 'visual space' is often misleadingly compared to a kind of peep-show that everyone carries around with them. 'That is, we then use the word "space" similarly to when we call a room a space' (p. 248). The confusion is that the field of vision is first regarded as *analogous* to physical space and then, differently, as something that is inalienably mine, which physical space ob-viously is not. In *Philosophical Investigations*, § 398 Wittgenstein describes this confusion in terms of 'visuellen Zimmer' and 'materielle Zimmer'. Somebody is sitting in his (material) room but then goes on to talk about his 'visual room', that is to say, he thinks he can look into his field of vision and perceive objects there like a 'visual room'. According to Wittgenstein, the ex-pression 'looking into one's field of vision' is nonsense.

Significantly, Wittgenstein does not deny that it makes sense to talk about visual experiences. His point is a purely grammatical one: visual experiences cannot be conceived of as quasi-physical appearances, as sense data each of which has its own possessor (cf. PI, § 401). This is made clearer by a very discursive fragment, which in MS 120 comes after *Philosophical Investigations*, § 399.

Wittgenstein states there that the 'possessor' of the visual room is essentially identical with it.

> 'The visual room has no owner' means so much as: it has no neighbour.
>
> But how is the expression 'the visual room' *used*? How, when you say to someone: 'I have *this* image...' and now describe an image while you immerse yourself in it – so you have this image – but the image is not an object of a subject. One can also say: The body before your eyes is object and your sense subject. But in contrast to that the image is not object: one cannot say of that: it is *seen*, nor does it stand *before* a subject, for it is *bounded by nothing*, is not part of a space. I stand before this stove but not before the image of this stove.
>
> My visual body stands before the visual stove – but my visual body cannot see. Therefore we might indeed say: there is no subject here – and consequently no object either. (MS 120, pp. 79-81)

If visual experiences are thought of as sense data, they are conceived of as a (private) part of physical space, as things which can therefore be seen in the same way that things in physical space can be seen. If Wittgenstein attacks this misrepresentation, it is not to eliminate visual experiences, but to eliminate a *physicalistic way* of thinking about visual experiences. To put in a somewhat un-Wittgensteinian manner: visual experiences are not representations of physical things, representations which can in turn be seen themselves. Visual experiences do not represent reality but present it:

> I see something before me; that is surely *seen*; but is it not just *there*, is it actually *seen*? Does one see that it is seen? 'Seeing' is connected with a picture of the effect of an object on the subject. I say 'I see this curtain'; but should I also say 'I see a vision'?
>
> I wish to say: in the visual space nothing is seen, there are no rays of light that go from an object to the one who sees.
>
> What then do I normally have before me: the visual space or the physical space? No, it is not like that. The visual room is not as it were a different peep-show from the physical one. When I say: 'no rays of light are going through the visual space', that means only that I say only of a <u>visual phenomenon</u> that it is in the visual space.
>
> And as only that which is seen is an object in the visual space, one cannot say that something is *seen* in the visual space. (MS 120, pp. 114-115)

With this quotation we leave Wittgenstein's criticism of the theory of sense data, phenomenalism, criticism which is already formulated in 1932.

b. Introspective recognition

In the Augustinian idea of language (see PI, § 1-27), defining by ostension is an important way of giving words meaning. Wittgenstein's objection is that ostensive ceremonies can only be meaningfully conducted within horizontal relations of language-games. An ostensive definition of 'ball' is only meaningful if it is already clear what can and cannot be done with a ball. The possibility of ostensive definitions is conditional on the use of the concept within a language-game. So the meaning of a concept is not its reference but its use. The identification of meaning and reference is an example of what I have called the actuality fallacy (see chapter 2, § 2). A somewhat dramatic manifestation of this fallacy occurs in the case of someone who has died: the reference of the name, the bearer, is no more, and yet the name keeps its meaning. In my view the actuality fallacy also underlies the (ostensive) definition of first person statements. In 'I feel pain' 'pain' has to have an actual experience as its bearer. Otherwise, according to the argument, the phrase is meaningless and an inanity. But here too it is forgotten that pain can be talked about without anybody *actually* being in pain, and this already suggests that the meaning of a concept is not its reference and that private ostensive definitions are impossible.

Wittgenstein 'uses' the private ostensive definition mainly in *Philosophical Investigations*, § 258, 268, 277, and 293. In the final fragment he calls this mode of definition the 'object and designation' model and his positive conclusion is: 'if we construe the grammar of the expression of sensation on the model of "object and designation" the object drops out of consideration as irrelevant'. Wittgenstein is saying here that the application of the ostensive definition to the expression of pain makes the relation between expression and sensation fall apart into a causal, external relation. Although the private ostensive definition was introduced by psychologists and philosophers in order to save sensations, the 'existence' of sensations is in fact *threatened* by it. That is the moral of § 293. A concern to save the inner sensation has indeed privileged the introspective method of the private ostensive definition, as we can hear in this cry of despair which

Wittgenstein puts in the mouth of the introspective philosopher: '"Yes, but there is *something* there all the same accompanying my cry of pain. And it is on account of that that I utter it. And this something is what is important – and frightful"' (PI, § 296). Proposition (A) of the symmetrical representation can now be split up into two:

(i) there must be something – some or other sensation – for otherwise my cry has no reference, and so no meaning, and is merely hollow-sounding;

(ii) that something must be present *now*, at the moment in which we cry out (cf. PI, § 277).

(i) and (ii) together offer the best proof of the actuality fallacy. 'Pain' has to refer to something, just as a proper name has to have an actual bearer. Moreover, unlike proper names and names for physical objects, 'pain' has to refer to a present sensation. Since one only knows one's own pain – according to the symmetrical theory – one can only explain what pain is to somebody else by hitting him and saying: 'What you are now feeling is what I mean by pain'. This reference to a 'now' seems the only way of preventing sensations from vanishing in the mist of consciousness. Wittgenstein explicitly refers to (ii) in MS 179, pp. 42-43:

> I want to appeal to the momentary experience, but this again appears elusive, something that cannot be fixed, cannot function as a piece in a game.
> Or again: it is the result of a false interpretation of language. One wishes to say namely: there is something that is only the present and not the past (nor the future).

Now a typical introspective, ostensive ceremony proceeds as follows. Feeling something, one cries out. Because the cry is accompanied by a feeling, it can be named: an expression of pain. This definition proceeds broadly along the same lines as the ostensive definition of proper names and names for physical objects. The difference, of course, is that the definition is private: the naming does not consist of externally observable circumstances, but of inner ones. Mental 'pictures' in one's 'mind's eye' seem now (from an introspective point of view) the most natural bearers of vocabulary for sensations. Inner concentration and minute attention can therefore attach names for sensations to their bearers.

This connection is the starting-point for Wittgenstein's criticism: 'How do words *refer* to sensations?' (PI, § 244). The point of this question tends to be misunderstood. The question is not epistemological – how can we recognize and then name our sensations?[17] – but logical: how can we *apply* names for sensations? On the whole critics have acknowledged that Wittgenstein rejects the epistemology of introspective recognition, but have interpreted his own position as an alternative epistemology – usually behaviouristic or criterionistic. Wittgenstein does not ask the question of how we can recognize our sensations introspectively and then name them, because this question already suggests an external, psychological relation. But his diagnosis of this question is meant to draw our attention to the internal relation between the application of names and the technique of the language-game of expression. Recognition of the entirely non-problematic nature of this relation is impeded, according to Wittgenstein, by a preconception about the way language functions: the meaning of words is thought to be their reference. In the case of psychological concepts this preconception is supported by many characteristics of their surface grammar. Thus first person statements ('I feel pain') in fact take the form of descriptions and an introspective and ostensive explanation seems self-evident. Another preconception is that mental images and flashes of memory are 'pictures' in one's mind's eye. The grammar for 'image' seems to be that of 'picture', albeit in the variant sense of a private picture seen only by the person who imagines or remembers something (see chapter 7, § 3). Such preconceptions have helped to generate the psychologistic question of how I can name my sensations:

> How does one name an image? For instance like this: One has it right now, concentrates one's attention on it and speaks the words: 'that should be called "Z"'. Is it now named? And what is the use of this magical process? We forget completely the aim of what we call the naming of an object. It is as if

---

17 The contrast between an epistemological and a logical phrasing of the question is suggested in this fragment: 'Do not ask: "how can I name my sensation?" so much as: "how can one apply the names of the sensations?"' (MS 179, p. 25).

we appointed dolls or also other objects lieutenants, captains and generals by pinning onto them the badges of these ranks. (MS 119, pp. 257-258)

Clearly, only in a rule-guided game, whether this is Stratego or the army, are pieces or people entitled to the rank of general or lieutenant. The same applies to sensations. Only *within* the language-game of expressions is a word related to a sensation; outside of the language-game it is no more than a decoration on a jacket which nobody ever wears.

The famous diary passages are concerned with this naming of sensations *outside* of their language-games. Prior to the first passage (PI, § 256) Wittgenstein asks *per impossibile* how sensations can be linked to names if not via natural and verbal expressions (PI, § 256). Keeping a diary provides a solution. If there were no natural expression of pain, one could try to register the sensation of pain by making a certain sign in a diary. Every time one feels the pain, one enters the sign in the diary on the day in question. The moral of these passages is that it is pointless to link names to sensations via this kind of procedure. And if this is pointless, the hypothesis that sensations are *not* related to natural expressions is *pointless* too. The negation of this negation provides conclusive evidence for Wittgenstein's thesis that sensations are internally related to natural and verbal expressions. The diary passages thus have the structure of a *reductio ad absurdum*. The diary language-game is fictitious and merely has heuristic value for Wittgenstein: by describing it rather extensively we come to the conclusion that our concept of pain does not work in the same way at all. In this way the fictitious introspective language-game sheds light on our actual language-game of natural and verbal expressions, of which Wittgenstein says at the outset (cf. § 244) that it is non-problematic. But before it can be judged non-problematic, it has to be formulated in terms of a problem.

In the absence of natural and verbal expressions the diarist cannot resort to words or gestures for his 'definition' of feelings. His only refuge, it seems, is an introspective recognition of the feeling, a recognition which he gives the minimal name 'E'. Wittgenstein's objection is that this private ostensive definition cannot establish the meaning of 'E'. The only thing the definition achieves is that in the future the writer will remember the relation between 'E' and the sensation. But in this situation he has no criterion for the correctness of his memory: 'whatever is going to seem right to me is right. And that only means that here we can't talk about "right"' (PI, § 258). The writer's appeal to his memory is compared by Wittgenstein to someone who wants to be sure about the departure of his train and therefore checks his memory by means of the imaginary page of the time-table in his memory. This second memory is of no help, 'for this process has got to produce a memory which is actually *correct*. If the mental image of the time-table could not itself be *tested* for correctness, how could it confirm the correctness of the first memory?' (PI, § 265).

Critics[18] often see an epistemological thrust behind these comparisons: as if Wittgenstein wanted to show that a private ostensive definition of sensations is unfeasible because the memory is always capable of cheating. To support this interpretation a fragment in *Philosophical Investigations* II xi, p. 207 is usually cited, where Wittgenstein proposes to eliminate the private object by supposing that it continually changes without our being aware of it, because we are cheated by our memories. But the value of this suggestion is no more than heuristic: Wittgenstein wants to distract attention from the inner and clear the way for a logical description of language-games, just as he wants to distract attention from physiological explanations by supposing that human beings have no central nervous system.[19] The point of these comparisons has nothing to do with a good or bad memory. On the contrary, the passages do not deal with the memory at all, or at least not with the language-game of remembering. In subsection (c) it will become clear that remembering can only be spoken of in very special language-games and certainly not in the so-called language-game of the diarist. To explain these passages as if they are concerned with the inherent inadequacy of the memory implies that in any case they can be said to deal with remembering. Wittgenstein's point is entirely logical: the appeal

---

[18] See for instance Ayer (1985, p. 98).

[19] In chapter 7, § 1 I will refer to this strategy as Wittgenstein's physiological agnosticism; see p. 3 and note 4.

to recognition leads to a *regressus ad infinitum* analogous to the explanation of rules by interpretations of those rules (see chapter 3, § 2). In a fragment that anticipates the diary passages, Wittgenstein formulates this regression rather explicitly:

> But do we not judge that something is the same inner experience simply by memory? Memory is to be sure a further inner experience – And what does it mean to *'judge'* by memory? If judging is again an inner experience, I do not know how I finally can get to the use of *words*. If to judge already means: to *say* something, then I do not know what it should mean to be *guided* by the inner experience, if the *rule* by which I am guided is lacking; the rule that should then assign - by a table *for instance* – the inner experience to the word. (MS 119, pp. 209-210)

The diarist, if we apply this to him, wants to name a certain feeling and tries to establish this relation via introspective recognition. The problem is that the recognition of the sensation is a sensation itself too, so that one has to ask how the diarist recognizes the latter sensation, and so on *ad infinitum*. This infinite regression prevents the diarist from ever achieving a rule-governed procedure of naming, a real practice. Since he can only appeal to a recognition of a sensation which is in turn a sensation, this recognition cannot be called an adequate judgement of the first sensation; as a sensation the recognition needs to be judged in turn. This endless series of judgements of judgements prevents the diarist from ever achieving a meaningful use of words and concepts. He is continually faced by a new sensation, namely the sensation of recognizing another sensation. And so private ostensive definitions float in the air like the interpretations of rules. The private ostensive definition is a pseudopractice, not a real practice. All the words which one would use within this pseudo-practice, such as 'identical sensation', 'recognizing', 'remembering', etc., are inapplicable. Even the word 'diary' has no place here:

> Imagine again a diary and the entry of private feelings. The recognition does not show him that this is the same feeling that he had, but it is now merely a new inner experience. But for that we must not use the word 'recognition', for this was reserved for a certain public use. Thus we have to give it a new name, which is useless however. He can write a sign in his diary and observe it again and again, and that is all we can say about what takes place. But is that a diary? (MS 119, pp. 237-238)

The diarist lacks not so much a good memory, therefore, as a technique for explaining the meaning of 'E'. Although he substitutes sensation (2) for sensation (1), these substitutions only result in an explanation of meaning if the application of (2) is understood. If the application of (2) remains as obscure as that of (1), there is no definition. The diarist's error is to suppose that language has two functions, a public and a private (cf. PI, § 277), and that the private justifies the public. 'Pain', it is thought, refers to the really important inner sensations which are hidden from others as well as to openly observable actions. Wittgenstein's point is that no language-game can be played with this kind of private language. The public language-game, the specific body of rule-guided horizontal relations, is constitutive for the meaning of pain, not the private language.

The question is: why then postulate such an incomprehensible private language, if what it should explain is so obvious? Wittgenstein's diagnosis here is identical to his explanation of the need for interpretations of rules (see chapter 3, § 2). He explained this need from strong *intellectualistic* preoccupations, as if only an interminable series of explanations can really guard us against all kinds of misconceptions and errors. Again he uses the 'falling earth' here as an image for the unquenchable intellectualistic thirst for justification:

> 'He has the same sensation as I do' – Criteria of identity. But what is the criterion of identity when I say: 'I now feel the same pain as before?' Should I say: 'I recognize immediately that it is the same?' Thus I *recognize immediately* that the word 'same' fits it? Or that the picture ++ fits it? And *how* does it fit it? – But do you want to say that I merely *say* the word 'same' without it being justified one way or another? The word 'merely' is erroneously applied here. The word that the expression 'same' is not justified here gives you the same uneasiness as many people feel when hearing the expression that the earth floats freely in space without being supported (and that is not ridiculous). (MS 121, pp. 42-43)

The typical intellectualistic tendency is to suppose that the statement 'I feel pain' should be justified by an inner sensation, making it more than a hollow phrase. Wittgenstein's rejoinder is to point out that this hypothesis does not take us far enough, or rather takes us too far, since it leads to an infinite regression: the sensations which one postulates constantly imply other sensations, just as a foundation of the earth implies another foundation, etc. The philosophy of language-games and forms of life is an antidote to such dizzying intellectualistic falls. The earth is not supported by anything. 'Supporting' and 'falling' do not apply to our planet. This safeguards the existence of trees, houses, and human beings: their foundation is the earth and the earth itself needs no foundation, being its own 'foundation'. The same is true of 'pain'. 'I feel pain' is supported by the relevant language-game. And this language-game starts rather than ends with the expression of pain (cf. PI, § 290). Ending with it, the language-game would itself be supported by something, an introspective and ostensive definition of a pain. By analogy with the logic of rules, Wittgenstein concludes that 'pain' cannot be provided with an inner foundation, since this foundation is a bottomless pit. 'I feel pain' has meaning only if there is already a practice. This practice is the language-game of expression (of pain). That language-game is the foundation for the use of 'I feel pain', but is neither founded nor unfounded itself: it is its *own* foundation. It is asymmetrically related to language-games in the third person: expressions of pain in the first person present tense are not based on (introspective) observation and definition, but in the third person ('he feels pain') they are identified via observation.

This asymmetry of the first and third person possibly savours of behaviourism. Wittgenstein wonders whether he is a behaviourist in disguise (PI, § 307), someone who in the final analysis calls everything a fiction except human behaviour. His reply is that, when he talks about fictions, he means grammatical fictions. The meaning of this has never been satisfactorily construed, not even by those who do not accuse Wittgenstein of behaviourism.[20] The meaning of a statement related to it has also been subject to merely rough and speculative 'explanations', as Stroud (1983, p. 340) has rightly remarked. In *Philosophical Investigations*, § 304 Wittgenstein's opponent asks whether there is no distinction between pain behaviour with and without pain. Wittgenstein starts by saying that no difference can be greater. His opponent counters that Wittgenstein is nevertheless increasingly inclined to

---

[20] See for instance Vesey (1974, p. 152).

say that the sensation itself is nothing. 'Not at all. It is not a *something*, but not a *nothing* either!' In what way do these words deny both a behaviouristic rejection of inner sensations and an introspective acceptance of them?

The suspicion of behaviourism is aroused because Wittgenstein says that there is nothing 'behind' the expression of pain. However: 'The sentence: "Behind the expression of the sensation stands nothing" is a *grammatical* one – hence it does not say that we feel nothing' (MS 124, p. 6). I take the fiction to be grammatical in the sense that psychologistic theories assume that words can only have meaning if they refer to 'something'. In relation to 'I feel pain' this means that, although the reference of the statement is invisible for others, I myself must be able to indicate it if I am to say anything meaningful. The object of this, shall we say, dualistic grammar is of course the incongruence of 'feeling pain' and 'behaving in such-and-such a way'. But in actual fact statements about the inner and the outer are made *congruent* by this dualistic grammar: in both cases they are construed as observations, namely observations of the inner and observations of the outer. In this way the grammar of such statements is pinned to a symmetrical scheme. Wittgenstein's asymmetrical logic therefore brings out the diversity of 'feeling pain' and 'behaving in such-and-such a way' even more sharply than the philosophy which sets itself against behaviourism: 'Indeed, their use is more *different* than is represented by the philosophers who speak against behaviourism' (MS 124, p. 20).

His criticism is not aimed at inner sensations but at an excessively narrow explanation of the language for these sensations. He does not claim that we feel nothing when we feel pain and merely make a grimace, but that the meaning of the (verbal or non-verbal) expression of pain is not based on introspective observation.

The feeling of pain is neither 'something' nor 'nothing', or put somewhat differently: 'It is as if there were something elusive here – One asks: "Is here something, or nothing?" and neither fits. The word "pain" designates neither a thing nor a void' (MS 121, p. 41). Wittgenstein's point is that the dualistic tendency to talk about 'something' is elicited by the behaviouristic tendency to talk about 'nothing' and vice versa. The dualistic tendency is caused by a 'horror vacui': if nothing 'accompanies' the expression of pain, if there is nothing 'behind' it, there is no justification for it; it is 'merely' an empty cry, comparable with the empty space through which the earth wanders if it is not supported by anything. But the postulation of a 'something' leads to 'nothing'. The commmon error is to assume that a private ostensive definition can establish whether the expression of pain is accompanied by a feeling and so is justified, as opposed to a simulated expression. As we already saw, nothing can be justified via a private ostensive definition; such 'inner justifications' merely lead to an infinite regression and the very emptiness one feared is created by such 'stop-gap explanations'. But if an 'inner justification' is no justification and if it cannot tell me or the other person (since I cannot show him anything) whether I am talking about the 'same' sensation, then we have to conclude that a 'nothing' serves the same purpose as a 'something' which cannot be talked about (PI, § 304). Wittgenstein's diagnosis of 'inner justifications' is essentially this: 'behind' the expression one can just as easily imagine something that is always the same as something that is different each time. It makes no odds. But if it makes no odds whether it is something or nothing, there is no point in describing sensations in terms of this contrast. In this grammatical sense they are neither something nor nothing. Once again, elimination of such grammatical fictions does not mean that Wittgenstein opts for a behaviouristic position. He does not claim that we express ourselves without feeling anything, but that we express ourselves without observing 'anything' and so justifying the expression:

> If one said only 'I am in pain' and *were not* in pain, pain would be nothing frightful. – Naturally, if one is not in pain, there is nothing frightful about it. 'If one only had the pain behaviour and nothing else, then there would be nothing disagreeable about it.' – Naturally: holding your hands to your cheeks is not disagreeable – the toothache is what is disagreeable. (MS 121, pp. 7-8)

c. Memory

The memory has to do the trick for James and his followers. The 'private object' which confronts them is near at hand but also elusive, like a dream which leaves a frame but no photo after waking. A good memory, and also keeping a diary, might help frame the photo. Hence Wittgenstein's interest in this genre. Another misleading use of terms is to talk about 'description' here. It is misleading in two ways: (1) descriptions in the first person present tense are neither descriptions of the inner (2) nor descriptions of the outer. I first discuss (1).

In (b) we already discussed a first objection to (1). If, for the reasons mentioned there, first person statements are not observations of my mind, then there can be no descriptions on the basis of these observations either. Descriptive interpretations of the first person fail to do justice to the asymmetrical logic of expressions. At this point I want to look at a second objection which Wittgenstein is less explicit about: descriptive interpretations of the first person also fail to do justice to what we call descriptions. And since these introspective 'descriptions' typically take the form of 'memories', they fail to do justice to the language-game of remembering as well. People have been misled here by the syntactic surface structure of memory statements like: 'All at once I vividly recalled him'. This statement seems a 'description' of an inner picture. Philosophers have gone on to model all kinds of psychological statements on this type of 'description', thus not only overlooking the asymmetrical logic of expressions (of pain), but also the logic of the kind of description that is constitutive for memories. To reduce such descriptions to 'descriptions' and memories to 'memories' is a ground-floor fallacy: all psychological concepts are reduced to the same introspective type.

In MS 119 and MS 120 one finds many variations of the diary passages and the use of the concepts of description and memory. If the *Philosophical Investigations* are already quite clear about it, these manuscripts show unambiguously that Wittgenstein does not base his argument against private language on the fallibility of the memory. Indeed, the diarist has a particularly good memory: a memory that like a seismograph registers the slightest change in his inventory as an earthquake. Wittgenstein's idea, however, is that the introspective 'description' of 'inner objects' offers an incorrect account of both the logic of (non-)verbal expressions and the language-game of remembering (cf. PI, § 305). He does not deny inner sensations, for that would be to deny that anybody ever remembers anything (PI, § 306).

A fragment occurring in MS 116 has an ending similar to *Philosophical Investigations*, § 293. According to Wittgenstein, it is possible for somebody to say: 'yesterday I saw this as green, now I see it as red'. If this phenomenon can be explained physiologically, the statement may make sense. But if somebody says this kind of thing the whole time, without any reason, others will no longer be inclined to say that he is remembering something, only that he claims to be remembering something. And what that means nobody knows:

> If someone now replied: 'Well, he has precisely the experiences that we call "memory experiences"' – we would suddenly be inclined here to brush it aside as an irrelevant remark; we would not know what to do with the idea of the inner experience, and are inclined to abandon it. Suddenly it becomes unnecessary to speak of 'a certain inner experience' (James's quotation from Ballard). (MS 116, p. 203)

Neither here nor in *Philosophical Investigations*, § 293 is Wittgenstein belittling the importance of inner sensations when somebody remembers something. Nor is his suspicion aroused by the subjective and personal nature of such sensations. For as the diary passages show, even if 'memory images' are translated into a medium accessible to others, e.g. letters or drawings, the problems for the meaning of concepts do not disappear. Even if somebody makes accurate drawings of the memories he sees in his mind, still his intentions are basically unintelligible to others. Granted that the diarist wishes to record the meaning of concepts on the basis of an acquaintance with his sensations, he may still do this in a way that offers no information to others. Each day he may give the same sensation a different name or, conversely, he may make the same drawing although it fails to agree with the original situation. In short, the result of all his efforts is no more than an external relation between sign and sensation. The associations which he creates between sounds or signs and whatever facts thus have an *ad hoc* character. This *ad hoc* character can never guarantee the identity and meaning of concepts. Comprehending signs or intending something by them is only possible if the signs *already* function in a certain language-game and not if they are invented on the spot, *ad hoc*.

The following variation of the diary passages shows that Wittgenstein's approach is logical and not epistemological, aimed at the conceptual absurdity of *ad hoc* explanations of meaning and not at the (un)reliability of memory:

> Let us imagine a diary that is kept by means of a number of independent signs. Every page has a date and is, like a timetable, divided into 24 parts; and now 'A' is called in our language: I go to sleep, 'B': I get up, 'C': I eat; etc. How does he know that what he notes down by 'A' is always the same? He refers to his memory. But that does not get us any further. The expression of the memory then in fact goes together with the sign (Imagine that instead of the memory he used a dice, and (now) he throws the dice to decide what he has to write). (MS 116, p. 135)

Wittgenstein is as little interested in the (un)reliability of the memory as in, for instance, the (un)reliability of the senses. He is solely interested in the question of how we understand the language of the senses or the language of memories. The procedure followed in the diary is an *ad hoc* procedure which is incomprehensible both to others and to the diarist. 'Memory pictures' tell him nothing, not even if he manages to achieve a perfect synchrony between sign and sensation via compulsive diary notes: the relation remains an external one (the memory merely 'gesellt sich', links itself, to the sign). The same 'memory pictures' may present themselves at the sight of quite different objects, people, and situations. The diarist may undergo the same sensation while looking at cars from a window or reaching for his wallet, just as Proust summoned up entire episodes from his childhood by dipping a 'petite madeleine' in his tea, but also by inhaling the smell of the carpet on the stairs. Although such sensations are characteristic of memory, they are not referred to simply by describing them introspectively and linking them to signs. The relation between sign and sensation is no less *ad hoc*, the sensation no less isolated, than somebody who is travelling alone, but who is constantly in my thoughts.[21]

---

[21] '(As a man can travel alone, and yet be accompanied by my good wishes; or as a room may be empty, and yet full of light.)' (PI, § 673).

In the diary nothing is described, nothing is communicated, nothing is remembered. For in the diary it makes no difference whether I have correctly recognized the sensation or not (PI, § 270). But the language-game of remembering is essentially the language-game of remembering *correctly*. And that means that there are criteria, in the strict sense of tests, for the truth or falsity of memories. But we have to watch our step now. This kind of criteria has commonly[22] been applied to all psychological concepts, and in particular to 'pain'. But this generalization is based on the ground-floor fallacy. All psychological concepts are thus again reduced to one and the same type, whereas Wittgenstein's concern is precisely to show that remembering is a much more complicated concept than pain. For remembering we need criteria of truth and falsity, which we do not need for pain, or at any rate for pain in the language-game of sincere expression. The natural expression of pain is no criterion of pain, but is a *part* of pain (see further under (d)). Remembering has no 'Naturlaut' as pain has. The place of this concept in forms of life is more complicated: the language-game of remembering is vertically related to more fundamental language-games and language is constitutive for this language-game:

> (Naturally) one thinks of 'memory experience' first and foremost as something like – memory-image. Of course there are memory-images, – I can readily call some to mind. But how do I call it to mind, in which surrounding of thoughts? And if I look at it, fix it separately, is *it* itself the memory? I say for instance: 'I see myself walking there and there with a friend.' But – how do I know that it is *me* and my friend? Are the portraits such a good likeness? Of course not. But I *say* that it is me with my friend, I make this transition from the picture (from the image) to words or from this picture to certain other pictures, etc. (MS 116, p. 137)

The words with which I express my memory are my memory reaction, writes Wittgenstein (PI, § 343). A protoversion of *Philosophical Investigations*, § 305, 306 makes it plain what Wittgenstein means by 'Ausdruck' or 'Reaktion' in relation to memories:

> 'Memory is surely an inner process' is a grammatical remark; it really says that the language-game starts with the *expression* of memory.

---

[22] An exception has to be made for Hintikka (1986, pp. 284-286). See also subsection (d).

> The sentence, however, seems to justify our making some or other assumption about the inner processes of a person. – But one can say: *Because* memory is an inner process, an assumption about memory-processes is senseless if it is not an assumption about the expression of these processes. (MS 120, p. 121)

The implication of 'reaction' is not that remembering is a conditioned response, but that saying the *words* 'I see my self walking there with my friend' itself constitutes the phenomenon of remembering. To call these words a reaction means that saying them creates the relation between sensation and memory: saying them is not a claim on introspective grounds that this relation exists. They are a reaction insofar as they are not an introspective description. Wittgenstein brings out this non-introspective quality by calling a first person statement in the present tense an 'Ausdruck', 'Äusserung', or 'Reaktion' (cf. RPP, II 63). This is made clear by the way in which he introduces this terminology for the first time:

> One could call this kind of statement 'utterance', 'utterance of pain', 'utterance of memory', etc. (MS 120, pp. 206-207)

> But how is it with: 'I *was* in pain'. This is surely no complaint. In general it will be a memory-statement. But one who says: 'I remember...' expresses a memory and does not say that he remembers... (MS 120, p. 206)

Although Wittgenstein often uses these terms interchangeably, it is useful to distinguish between them. I reserve 'expression' ('Ausdruck') for the language-games of pain and emotions, language-games constituted by natural physiognomical expressions. I reserve 'utterance' ('Äusserung') for those language-games which are not constituted by natural expressions but by linguistic formulations, e.g. that of remembering (see further chapter 7). This terminological distinction between 'Ausdruck' and 'Äusserung' also does more justice to the different roles played by expressions of pain and 'utterances' of memories in their language-games. The utterance of a memory is typically used as a statement, in contrast to an expression of pain. And the criteria applying to the language-game of statements are different from those for the language-game of pain expressions: 'You did not learn the use of the *expression* by being shown a phenomenon that is described by these words' (MS 120, p. 227).

The expression of pain, non-verbal and verbal, is not a description of behaviour either (2). This is indicated as follows in *Philosophical Investigations*, § 244: '"So you are saying that the word 'pain' really means crying?" – On the contrary: the verbal expression of pain replaces crying and does not describe it.' Yet many anti-behaviouristic authors have taken exception to this statement.[23] But they have simply been misled by a syntactic construction: 'it' does not refer back to 'pain' but to 'crying'. In itself this misreading is no disaster, for if 'it' were to refer to 'pain' then the sentence says that the verbal expression does not describe pain and this is correct to the extent that the logic of expressions is non-introspective. It is wrong to infer from this that pain can never be described; Wittgenstein also recognizes a retrospective use of the pain concept (see § 3). But in the second instance this syntactic error is disastrous: 'I feel pain' is taken to describe the crying. And in that case Wittgenstein is a logical behaviourist à la Carnap:[24] someone who claims that the meaning of psychological concepts can be exhaustively described in terms of behaviour. To achieve this Carnap and also Ryle opt for a third person perspective. In the third person, statements about others are typically based on observations of behaviour. The same is true for the first person, although this does not seem so: 'I am excited', to use Carnap's example, is shown by a logical analysis to mean no more than 'I see that my hands are shaking'. That is to say, the 'content' of 'I am excited' is the same as the content of 'I see that my hands are shaking'. With regard to the traditional first person perspective, Carnap's comparison with the third person seems revolutionary. But Wittgenstein's approach makes it painfully clear how conservative Carnap's revolution is: the shift from the first to the third person is completely insignificant as long as the symmetry remains intact. And the symmetry remains intact since both cases involve observation and description. The different examples chosen by Carnap and Wittgenstein are telling in this connection. 'I feel pain' is a statement whose 'content of experience' is much harder to omit or equate with a physicalistic statement than

---

[23] See for instance Gustafson (1979, pp. 149-166).
[24] See Carnap (1928) and especially Carnap (1932-1933).

Carnap's example 'I am excited'. Since the relevance of the 'content of experience' to the pain concept seems beyond dispute, a theory like Carnap's, which cannot do justice to the 'content of experience', is inadequate. Wittgenstein felt challenged to do justice to the 'content of experience' without lapsing into the customary introspectionistic alternative. His ingenious approach is to do justice to this content without proceeding from the contrast between inner and outer. In the case of 'pain' the 'content of experience' can be adequately described by charting the *role* which the pain concept plays in the language-game where it belongs. And that role is expressive.

Expressions have two important roles. In the first place an expression is not a description. This emerges from *Philosophical Investigations*, § 244, but is shown even more clearly in the following protoversions.

> I did not learn the words 'I am' by being told: observe who is in pain and if you are the one, point to yourself, etc. But these words of mine are the direct translation of an uttered complaint. (MS 120, p. 33)

> 'So are you saying that the word "pain" originally means the cry of pain?' – On the contrary, it replaces crying, but does not say that someone cries. The words 'I am in pain' become a part of pain-behaviour; and hence they do not say that someone behaves thus. And in this way all the linguistic expressions of sensations have become connected with the primitive expressions of sensation. (MS 124, pp. 223-224)

In the second place an expression is to be described as the beginning of a certain kind of interaction or communication. The very role of pain expressions in our form of life goes to illustrate this. An example – again perhaps chosen by Wittgenstein to demonstrate the inhuman character of a behaviouristic approach – is the relationship between doctor and patient. If a doctor asks the nurse whether the patient is in pain, she answers 'Yes, he is groaning', but the patient himself does not say 'I am groaning': he groans! (cf. PI II v, p. 179). The intention of this kind of expression is that somebody comes to the patient, or in any case does not leave him. The result of the expression must be that attention is turned to the patient, that he is helped and comforted. The patient's complaint is therefore no statement in the sense that it is not told for the mere sake of giving information: 'What I say to him is not the point; but what he does with that' (MS 158, p. 15).

Without making an epistemological appeal to the contrast between an inner and an outer, Wittgenstein's description of the logic of expressions does more justice to the content of our direct experiences than Carnap's streamlined symmetrical construction of the first and third person.

d. Self-knowledge

The last misleading analogy is that one is inclined to say 'I know I feel pain' although the use of 'knowing' here makes no sense. The reason for this will by now be clear. If first and third person statements are symmetrically construed, as logical behaviourists and mentalists do, one can talk about 'knowing' in the first person as well as the third person. But the implication of the three previous comparisons is that 'knowing' is applicable to observations of other people's behaviour, but not to the first person: nothing is observed here (see (b)); that 'knowing' is applicable to descriptions of other people's behaviour, but not to the first person: nothing is described here (see (c)); and that 'knowing' is applicable when assertions are made about other people's behaviour or about one's own body, but not when a cry is uttered: an expression is not an assertion (see (a)). The logic of knowing is exclusive to second order language-games, where something is asserted and where assertions can be motivated, tested, verified, and falsified on the basis of criteria. And these are language-games in which errors are possible as well (see chapter 3, § 2). The result of this approach, as I see it, is that there is no place in the language-game of expression for criteria in the strict sense of grounds for the truth or falsity of utterances. Although Wittgenstein does state this in *Philosophical Investigations*, § 290, there is a tradition[25] which persists in failing to appreciate the difference

---

[25] The tradition headed by Kenny (1973, p. 258) and Pitcher (1972, p. 137). More specifically, this tradition qualifies the application of all the concepts in terms of one general criteriological relation. Hence it has often ignored the very typical 'criteriologcial relation' between expressions and their 'content', which is incorrigible. That is, in this kind of language-game criteria for truth and falsity of statements are not used. For the same point of view, see Hintikka

in kinds of criteria for expressive and descriptive language-games. According to this tradition, Wittgenstein rejects the idea that first person expressions of pain are based on inner criteria, but not that in those language-games outer criteria are used – and in fact Wittgenstein fails to make this distinction explicit in *Philosophical Investigations*, § 290. The interpretation outlined here goes far enough to show that the use of criteria, in the sense of adduction of evidence, does not function on the level of expressive language-games, but on a second order level. Nevertheless there is also material which clearly demonstrates that Wittgenstein denies an appeal to both inner and outer criteria in expressive language-games. In a discussion about keeping a diary Wittgenstein first notes that no private ostensive definition can be given of a memory experience. If somebody claims to remember something, we normally have outer criteria for this. The objection that such an appeal to outer criteria is unnecessary, since we do not use it in our own case, is countered by Wittgenstein as follows:

> ... I do not need an outer, but neither an inner criterion. If I 'express' such an 'inner experience', then it is precisely this expression that functions in the game and I have to assume that the other also uses an expression that is called the expression of the memory-experience. (MS 119, p. 223)

This interpretation is also confirmed at the end of *Philosophical Investigations*, § 288, where Wittgenstein points out that if one assumes the abrogation of the normal language-game with the expression of pain, one needs a criterion for the identity of the pain; in that case there is also the possibility of error. The conclusion seems to be that criteria (of a certain kind) are unnecessary in the normal language-game. But by abolishing the normal language-game, it might still be objected, Wittgenstein is thinking of a situation which precedes the normal language-game, a kind of natural state without language-games. In fact, however, Wittgenstein is thinking of a situation that *follows* rather than precedes the normal language-game, i.e. a language-game that is vertically related to the physiognomical language-game, as appears from his remark that in the non-normal situation there is the possibility of error. For in a situation without language-games

---

(1986, pp. 284-286).

there is no possibility of error at all, as the following reconstruction of a number of fragments shows. A situation which comes fairly close to a situation without language-games is described by Wittgenstein in *Remarks on the Philosophy of Psychology* I, § 309. Suppose someone knows that a child who possesses no expression at all feels pain and he wants to teach the child to express this sensation.   How should he link an action to a sensation so that one is the expression of the other? Can he for instance teach the child 'Look, this is how you express something: this is the expression of that. And now you are expressing pain!' (cf. RPP I, § 310)? This kind of teaching implies that the child can first give a private ostensive definition of the sensation and can then link the expression to it.   But the separation which this brings about between pain and expression is absurd: the relation between the two is internal, so that the identity of one is inextricably joined to that of the other.   In my view the use of criteria for the truth or falsity of statements plays no role in expressive language-games in the sense that there are no criteria for the identity of pain *independent* of physiognomical expression.   There can only be criteria in expressive language-games in the sense that one repeats or demonstrates the expression of pain. Wittgenstein tries to bring out the difference in the following way:

> Is the cry true or false? What if I said it is real or not real?

> Not, of course, as if the word 'real' would be more correct than 'true'! It reminds us only of a grammatical distinction that is ignored or misunderstood. (MS 124, p. 280)

But this involves criteria which are completely different from grounds for the truth or falsity of statements. But does it still make sense to talk about 'error' in a situation preceding the normal language-game? Wittgenstein would deny this. In that kind of abnormal situation one would never be able to recover the reason for the error; the 'inner' error can never show itself. But a groundless error is no longer an error (see chapter 3, § 2). So if an error *is* possible, there must be outer criteria for it; the error must show itself in some actual application.   The situation in *Philosophical Investigations*, § 288, where the possibility of errors is said to be meaningful, must in fact refer to a language-game which comes after or is vertically related to the physiognomical language-game. In the language-game of expression there is after all no place for criteria of truthfulness or untruthfulness, and so there is no place for errors either: 'To be sure, one cannot be deceived about one's immediate experience: but not because it is so certain. The language-game allows for senseless utterances – even though not for "false" ones' (LW, § 187). One cannot be wrong about direct experience inasmuch as the language-game starts precisely with an expression, with spontaneous behaviour, and for this no justification can be offered. To assume an 'inner' error here is pointless, since no public reasons can ever be put forward for such an 'error'. But errors are possible and so criteria of truth and falsity are necessary in language-games of the second order, such as the language-game of 'pretending' (see chapter 5) or that of remembering. Reasons (criteria) can be produced both for correct and for incorrect memories (errors).

3. Description of one's inner

Expressions are not descriptions which refer boomerang-like to the inner; rather they form the beginning of a game. Because of Wittgenstein's strong emphasis on expressions, however, his discussion of descriptive first person statements has been neglected. What is more, critics have unanimously assumed that he rejects this use of the first person and have taken him to task accordingly.[26] But Wittgenstein does recognize the descriptive use; he merely denies that it is the most current form of the first person (cf. RPP I, § 693). Not only is it a language-game that is played less frequently than the expressive language-game, it moreover requires more skill. It requires observant, thoughtful, and retrospective behaviour, an attempt at precision, an ability to correct oneself, to compare (cf. LW, § 51). In everyday life these descriptions of the inner do not occur all that often and their

---

[26] After writing this chapter I saw that Hacker (1987) in his revision of Hacker (1975) corrects his 'avowal' interpretation by also attributing to Wittgenstein a descriptive use of first person utterances.

context is fairly specialized: the psychological laboratory, Freud's sofa, Proust's bed.

Wittgenstein gives examples of the descriptive use in *Philosophical Investigations* II ix. One finds earlier versions of a number of these fragments in MS 120. Before turning to these examples, let us look at the beginning of this section:

> 'Observing' does not produce what is observed. (That is a conceptual statement.)
>
> Again: I do not 'observe' what only comes into being through observation. The object of observation is something *else*. (p. 187)

Since the reader, having reached this section, is by now used to the conceptual nature of the *Philosophical Investigations*, one wonders why Wittgenstein confirms it in so many words here. The reason for this is that the idea concerned can and has been taken in an empirical sense. Philosophers like Comte, Mill, Brentano, and James[27] – the first three are discussed in James's work – have all pointed out that the phenomenon to be observed during introspection, for instance grief, suffers from this attention. The grief does not stay the same, but tends to disappear when the person is forced to observe his grief coolly and with detachment. In this way the state which one wished to observe is changed and thus produced.

Put like this, the objection to introspection seems negotiable and more a sign of the empirical difficulties inhering in this method. The conceptual point of Wittgenstein's comment is that, given the logic of the concept of observation, it makes no sense to talk about observation here. A characteristic of this logic is that the result of observation can also be used in those cases where *no* observation takes place (cf. RPP I, § 690). This characterization aligns Wittgenstein to Köhler rather than James, Mill, or Comte. Köhler stated that the result of introspection has to be constantly recreated by an act of introspection.[28] The flaw here becomes

---

[27] See James (1890, I, pp. 185-187). Köhler (1929, pp. 7-8) has the same objection as James.

[28] Köhler (1929, pp. 8-9) remarks about the introspective definition of 'direct experience': 'You cannot, as the physicists seem to do, make your two statements about one and the same event... You have two events in two experiences. What is your evidence for assuming that under the same conditions the ultimate data of

evident when one wants to tell others about one's inner discoveries: one constantly has to state the conditions under which the experience in question will occur. There is no question here of an observation or definition as in physics, where it is enough to give an exact definition, so that everybody can understand what is meant. According to Köhler, the object of introspective attention needs to be recreated each time anew if everybody is to grasp its meaning.

Instead of 'introspection' Wittgenstein prefers to speak of 'receptive attitude' ('rezeptive Einstellung') (cf. PI, § 672). What misleads us when we speak of introspection or a receptive attitude, according to him, is the analogy between pointing and introspectively directing one's attention. Just as we sometimes talk about things or people by pointing to them, so it is thought that we can talk about sensations and impressions by 'pointing', i.e. introspectively directing one's attention to them (cf. PI, § 672). But, says Wittgenstein, if one wishes to call 'directing one's attention to impressions or sensations' a kind of 'pointing' to something, 'then that something is not the sensation we get by means of it' (PI, § 672). The analogy with public pointing is misleading in the sense that one conceives of introspection as a kind of 'inner pointing' to an 'inner object'. The question which of course arises then, according to Wittgenstein, is how we could have learned to detect this kind of 'inner object' via this kind of 'inner pointing'. His intention is not at all to *deny* that we do sometimes have a receptive attitude to our impressions; but in that case the attitude has to be *part* of a language-game, that is, it has to have a *function* in the language-game. This can be be seen in the following draft of *Philosophical Investigations*, § 671 and 672:

> *How* can the inner gesture belong to the sentence? to the language-game? It 'accompanies it' not in the sense in which a gesture accompanies it; it is simply no gesture. A receptive attitude (listening e.g.) to be sure can be a gesture and function as a pointing, but the sensory impression (hearing e.g.) that we get by means of it does not correspond to the object which was pointed to. By the gesture of listening I do not point to what one calls 'my auditory impression'. (MS 120, pp. 188-189)

---

experience are the same for both of you?' For Köhler's positive account of 'direct experience', see chapter 7, note 18.

In the language-game, directing one's attention to an impression is not an 'inner pointing' to an 'inner object' but a kind of observation, that is, an activity that we have learned to perform publicly in relation to an object that can be described publicly. We have learned to observe our subjective experiences and to describe them in such a way that the observation can be said to be correct or incorrect[29] – which cannot at all be said of an 'inner pointing or observing'. As Wittgenstein puts it:

> Indeed, an 'inner pointing' takes place, or often takes place, (and) this characterizes the situation in which these words are pronounced. But if I proceed with 'I meant my pain', then I do not do so on the basis of an observation of an inner phenomenon of meaning. Rather I substitute afterwards the word pain for the word 'it'. I proceed in the calculation and the way I proceed in the calculus, that is the meaning. (MS 120, pp. 176-177)

The language-game in which introspection corresponds to an observation which can be corrected is of course a second order language-game. It is the language-game in which something is described, for instance: a touch which was still painful yesterday is no longer so today, or today I only feel the pain when I think about it (PI II ix, p. 187). These statements describe something and do not merely point to something. The statement 'I hoped all day...' describes a 'genuine duration' of experiences (RPP II, § 722); 'I have long been wanting...' or 'I keep on hoping' describes a certain development (RPP II, § 726); and 'I was less afraid of him now than I used to be' moreover describes a comparison (ibid.). First person statements are therefore quite capable of being descriptive in those cases where the duration, the development, the intensity, etc. of experiences is described. To speak of introspection or observation is misleading, since Wittgenstein rejects these conceptions as they are traditionally understood. He therefore suggests a terminology also chosen by Brentano[30] after his criticism of introspection: 'The word "observe" is badly applied here. I try to remember this and that' (RPP I, § 467).

---

29 For instance, we can indicate the *place* where we feel pain or hear the noise (cf. PI, § 671).
30 See Brentano (1924, pp. 49-50).

CHAPTER 5

OTHER MINDS: THIRD PERSON STATEMENTS

Doubts about the inner disposition of other people are seen in everyday life as a sign of arrogance or unremitting paranoia rather than as a serious attitude. Scepticism here seems academic, a pose and not a position. But recognition of the difference between a pose and a position still leaves a philosophical – and so theoretical – problem: what is our knowledge of other minds based on and in what way does it differ from knowledge of one's own mind and physical reality? There is no reason to assume that this philosophical inquiry will help to ease contacts between men and women, therapists and clients, and people in general. Not that it will make contacts more difficult, although some people, after reading sceptical literature, may be more pessimistic about their ability to judge human character. Scepticism about our knowledge of other minds can take various forms: how can I know what you think or see, how can I know that you see what I see, or, worse, how can I know that you think at all, that you are a human being and not an automaton? In all these cases the sceptic is not so much concerned to show that our insight into human nature is false as to show that it is inadequate. Inadequate, that is, compared with our knowledge of mathematics or the location of cities. Predictions of human behaviour are more like weather forecasts than mathematical deductions. If we regard that kind of deduction as the paradigm of certain knowledge, then our knowledge of other human beings seems shrouded in obscurity; accounting for actions is much more hazardous than calculating square numbers.

Two more specific sceptical theses are relevant to Wittgenstein's analysis of third person statements. One relates to the difference in method between knowledge of other minds and knowledge of one's own mind, the other to the inferior quality of the former kind of knowledge compared with the latter. They can broadly be formulated as follows: (A) we cannot know other minds in the same way that we know our own mind; (B) knowledge of our own mind is certain and direct, knowledge of other minds is uncertain and indirect.[1] Although Wittgenstein does not systematically distinguish between the two theses, it makes sense to deal with them separately. In the first section I shall deal with Wittgenstein's criticism of (A), in sections 2 and 3 with his criticism of (B). In both cases I shall emphasize in what way his criticism is logical and not so much directed at the correctness or incorrectness of scepticism as at its *meaningfulness*. Section 4 looks at Wittgenstein's highly original, constructive description of the concept of 'Menschenkenntnis', which for want of a better translation will be rendered as 'knowledge of human nature'.

A few remarks on the primary literature. Wittgenstein writes about the problem of other minds mainly in the last fragments of *Philosophical Investigations* II. These are highly compressed, moreover, so that it is no surprise to find that few critics have given attention to them.[2] More fragments dealing with the subject are collected in later publications of work from the period 1945-1949.[3] But most of this material has not (yet) been published. The manuscripts concerned are 169 (1949), 171 (1949 or 1950), 173 and 174 (1950), and 176 (1950).[4] The last three manuscripts also collect remarks about certainty and colours. Besides these two themes, therefore, Wittgenstein's last period systematically addresses a third theme, that of our knowledge of other minds. There are at least two reasons for involving this unpublished

---

[1] James (1890, I, p. 197) appeals to this distinction when he warns against the 'psychologistic fallacy', i.e. the assumption that an external observer has a grasp of a subject's experiences that is superior to the subject's own 'direct acquaintance' with that experience: 'The mental state is aware of itself only from within; it grasps what we call its own content and nothing more. The psychologist, on the contrary, is aware of it from without...' But Russell too appeals to the distinction between 'introspection by acquaintance' and 'knowledge by description'. See Russell (1910-1911).

[2] If any attention has been paid to this theme at all, it has mainly been on the basis of isolated aphorisms. See for instance Cavell (1979, pp. 431 ff.).

[3] See RPP I, § 137-149; RPP II, § 586-737; LW, § 181-206, 224-271, 859-979.

[4] Another manuscript from an earlier period which treats of the same problems is MS 123 (1940-1941).

material in our interpretation.   In the first place we can
supplement the summary selection of material in *Philosophical
Investigations* II xi and so throw more light on the purport and
structure of Wittgenstein's argumentation.   But does the content
of this material justify an exegesis?   The second reason answers
this question: the content of the unpublished material is important because Wittgenstein's analysis of the first person is incomplete.   As he himself says: 'One has to consider the concepts "being
in pain" and "acting as if in pain" in the *third and first* person.
Again: the infinitive precedes all persons and tenses.   Only the
whole is the instrument of the concepts' (MS 169, p. 59).   To complete chapter 4 on the first person we therefore need this chapter
on the third person.   An additional reason is the high quality of
the material.   That will have to be borne out by this chapter too.

1. The asymmetry of observation and expression

Problems (A) and (B) are closely interwoven.   The statement (A)
that the method of knowing other minds differs from the method
of knowing my mind readily leads to the evaluative distinction
(B) that in the first case there cannot be the same claim to knowledge as in the second.   The connection between the two is not so
surprising, given the common genesis of both problems.   In a
Wittgensteinian diagnosis the principles of the philosophical
problem of other minds are as follows.
(a) The meaning of psychological concepts is their reference.
(b) Their reference lies in the realm of consciousness, the concepts
are names for various kinds of immediate experiences.
(c) In the first person these sensations can be observed introspectively.
(d) In the third person introspection is out of the question; only
outer behaviour can be observed.
(a) and (b) are the well-known premises of the causal, psychologistic theory of meaning criticized by Wittgenstein; (c) is a major
source for the philosophical problem of self-knowledge and (d) for
that of other minds.   Now the methodical aspect means that we
can never know another person's mind in the way that he or she

knows it or in the way that we are familiar with our own mind: via introspection (c). The mind is only visible to one person: its owner. The evaluative aspect follows directly from this methodical deadlock. For the implication of (c) is that (i) knowledge in the first person is based on direct, inner facts and of (d) that (ii) knowledge in the third person is based on indirect, outer facts. The result of (i) is certain knowledge, the result of (ii) is uncertain knowledge. Knowledge of other minds is thus inferior to knowledge of one's own mind. The following fragment shows that Wittgenstein in fact attributes a similar line of reasoning to his opponents:

> The main difficulty arises because one conceives of the experience (pain for instance) as a thing for which we naturally have a name, which makes the concept easily comprehensible. Thus we always want to say: What 'pain' means we know (namely *this*) and thus the problem is only that one cannot determine this with certainty in the case of another person. (MS 169, pp. 69-70)

I confine myself to the methodical aspect in this section.

It can be seen that the relation between (c) and (d) is a symmetrical one: both involve observation, if introspective observation in the case of the first person; both, too, involve a claim to knowledge. In view of this symmetrical construction Wittgenstein may be expected to pursue the following strategy: in order to demonstrate the asymmetry of (c) and (d) he will argue that (e) the difference in status between the first and the third person is only significant *if* knowledge is also claimed for the first person and that (f) since there is no such claim for the first person, only the third person can be said to involve observation. I will analyse his strategy in this order.

As we saw in chapter 4, the language of the inner is above all metaphorical. 'I feel pain' turned out to be a metaphor, at any rate philosophically speaking. In the hands of philosophers 'I feel' or 'I have' reflects the cupidity of a grasping ego. Logical analysis showed that the meaning of words like 'to feel', 'I', or 'mine' is not possessive (see § 2, (a)). 'I feel pain' is as far from referring to an owner as 'Ouch!'; from a logical point of view it is expressive, like a cry. This analogy does not mean that the language of subjective experiences lacks eloquence, only that this language cannot claim an owner or a possession or a unique epistemological relation between the two. An expression of pain is not a description of pain, but is itself part of the pain. And if it is no description there is no reason for verification, falsification, or any kind of justification. Psychological concepts in the first person present tense – with the exception of the descriptive use – are not claims to knowledge.

This makes the difference in status between the first and third person negligible. Indeed, one can no longer really talk about a difference, according to Wittgenstein: only in the third person is there a claim to knowledge. And in fact it is a similarity rather than a difference which has troubled the philosophers. The reason for their increasing problems with the difference in observation is that they have interpreted first person statements as observation statements, just like third person statements. Now that this similarity has been proved invalid by the logical analysis of a certain type of first person statements, there is also less call to be perturbed. The difference that remains has no bearing on the dispute. For the fact that I lay claim to knowledge in the third person, but not usually in the first, is a conceptual truth. The relation between the first and third person is therefore not symmetrical but asymmetrical: in the third person statements are identified via observation (f), but not in the first; in the third person something is communicated, but not in the first (Z, § 472; RPP II, § 63).

It is this asymmetry of expression and observation that Wittgenstein has in mind when he writes in *Philosophical Investigations* II ix, p. 189 that a cry cannot be called a description, though it can function as an object of description. What he is saying is that a cry is not a description of a psychic state, but that somebody else can infer such a state from it. Instead of dealing with a reduction[5] of the inner to an outer cry, we are rather dealing with the opposite: the 'secrets' of the inner are no longer the exclusive property of autobiographical statements, for 'even' a cry reveals something about the inner. Wittgenstein's insight is that even if I do not say so, my cry says something about my state of mind; my

---

[5] For such reductionistic interpretations, see for instance Fodor (1967) and Fodor (1975, chapter 2).

cry may not be meant as information, but it is information – for somebody, that is. Another person can *infer* from my cry that I am in pain, that I need help, that I cannot help myself, etc.

So with this asymmetrical construction of the first and third person Wittgenstein has moved away from the symmetrical construction proposed by Carnap. But has he moved away far enough not to be called a behaviourist? Yes he has, as far as his analysis of the first person is concerned, as we saw in the previous chapter. But his analysis of the third person and especially his idea that third person statements are based on observation of behaviour can be interpreted behaviouristically. At first this seems to be Wittgenstein's own view too. When at the end of 1930 he formulates his idea that first person statements about direct experience[6] are non-hypothetical, in the sense that they cannot be verified by reference to phenomenal experiences, he suggests that third person statements are hypothetical and calls this approach behaviouristic: 'If I make myself understood by him in language, then it has to be understanding in the sense of behaviourism. That he has understood me is a hypothesis, as is that I have understood him' (MS 110, p. 8). The suggestion is that behaviourism is involved in the sense that we can only communicate indirectly and hypothetically about other people's experiences; that is, we cannot communicate about such experiences at all, we can only communicate about physical stimuli and responses. In section 3 we shall see that around 1938 but especially between 1946 and 1950 Wittgenstein plays down the intellectualistic equation of third person statements and hypotheses, and takes such hypotheses to be preceded by a more primitive level of spontaneous reactions of, for instance, sympathy and antipathy. I will show there how this involves neither behaviourism nor the classical argument by analogy.

But Wittgenstein's criticism of behaviourism takes place much earlier than 1938. As early as 1932 he discusses an objection habitually urged against behaviourism by dualists or mentalists,

---

[6] Wittgenstein's first explicit rejection of an introspective interpretation of first person utterances occurs in MS 113, pp. 102-105. Reference is usually made to Moore (1954, p. 12), but Moore's notes give no datings and their content is only suggestive.

but without opting for a dualistic or mentalistic position himself. The objection is that from a behaviouristic perspective there is no way of distinguishing between a case in which somebody really feels pain and a case in which somebody merely pretends to feel pain. In the second case a behaviourist would have to draw the same conclusion as in the first, since in both cases only behaviour is observed. The behaviourist, then, cannot do justice to the fact that the behaviour in the second case means something quite different from that in the first. Wittgenstein analyses this controversy as follows:

> Behaviourism. 'It seems to me that I am sad, my head droops so.'
> Why does one not have pity when a door is unoiled and weeps in opening and closing? Do we pity the other that behaves as we do when we are in pain, – on philosophical grounds that have led to the result that he suffers as we? Physicists might just as well make us scared by assuring us that the earth is not compact after all, but consists of loose particles that wander around erratically. 'But we would not pity the other if we knew that it is just a doll, or that he merely feigns his pain?' – Naturally – but we do have quite specific criteria for something being a doll, or for someone feigning to be in pain and these criteria oppose those we call criteria for something not being a doll (but for instance a human) and for someone not feigning his pain (but really being in pain). (TS 213, p. 509)

Not until much later, in 1949-1950, does Wittgenstein discuss what the criteria are for pretending to be in pain. This is the subject of the next section.

2. The hidden inner

Although observations can tell us something about the inner man, they can only do so as long as we are not being fooled. And human behaviour is a prime instrument for doing just that. Of course, there are situations in which people are obviously fooling, but sometimes it is not at all easy to make out. Take the following comedy of errors: two people acknowledge each other in the street, but neither can remember where they have met before. A tentative conversation follows, in which both are at great pains to pretend that they know where their acquaintance was made. They scrupulously avoid any detail that might show their ignorance, hoping that a slip of the tongue will reveal the true identity of Mr or Mrs X. And it is also possible, though rare, for people to simulate to the second degree. As Wittgenstein notes, people can simulate hypocrisy (RPP I, § 137).

Such naive observations are at the basis of a highly contrived sceptical position vis-à-vis other minds. The simple fact that observation does not always supply information about some-body's inner – at least not the information one would wish to have – gives substance to the philosophical idea that another person's inner is hidden and perhaps even hidden in principle. And if that is the case, there is not just a difference in status between the first and third person, but the status of the third person is inferior to that of the first person.

This intuition can be formulated step by step:[7]
1. Knowledge of other minds is based on evidence or signs: the observations of somebody's actions.
2. This evidence is indirect and for that very reason creates uncertainty.
3. The criterion for evidence is that something is evidence if the relation between the evidence and what it is evidence of can be demonstrated.
4. The relation between outer and inner can only be demonstrated by another reference to the outer; it can therefore only be proved via a circular argument.
5. In the case of other minds this evidence is therefore spurious.
6. Knowledge of other minds is not real knowledge: solid grounds are lacking.

This argument is attributed by Wittgenstein to opponents, if not along such systematic lines. But the argument can be reconstructed from a large number of passages in his work without undue effort; in the present and following sections I shall show how. The brunt of Wittgenstein's attack is directed at (2), (3), and (4). In his attack he does not opt for the other well-known epistemological position, demonstration of the contrary of (6): the classical argument by analogy. Instead, both the sceptical argument and the argument by analogy are undermined by his logical analysis of

---

[7] For a similar argument, see Don Locke (1968, pp. 46-47).

concepts. I discuss (2) in this section and (3) and (4) in the next.
Wittgenstein only accepts premiss (1) of the sceptical argument.
In the course of this and especially the following section it will
become plain how the observation of behaviour presupposes an
internal relation between the concepts of inner and outer. That
Wittgenstein attributes (2) to his opponent appears from the
following remark, for example: '"But you can't recognize pain
with *certainty* just from externals"' (RPP II, § 657). The double
quotation marks, but also the continuation of the fragment, which
I shall cite later, indicate that this is the view of an opponent.
Wittgenstein's criticism of this view clearly emerges from another
fragment:

> The distinctive feature of the inner seems to be that it has to be guessed at
> from the outer of the other person and is *known* only from within.
> But when through accurate consideration this conception vanishes into thin
> air, the inner indeed has not become the outer, but for us there is no longer
> direct inner evidence and indirect outer evidence for the inner. (MS 173, p. 33)

I will postpone discussing the cancellation of the distinction between direct, inner signs and indirect, outer ones; first I confine
myself to a further diagnosis of (2).

In the most neutral sense of the word, 'evidence' means that
which provides us with knowledge about a certain state of affairs.
Knowledge of physical reality is often based on direct evidence: I
know that my house-keys are lying on the table because I can see
them lying there. Often this knowledge is indirect too: a great deal
of information is passed on to us second-hand, for instance
through newspapers. Nevertheless it is possible in such cases to
check the indirect evidence, to find out whether the evidence is
direct as well and whether there is in fact a correlation between
what the newspaper says and what is actually the case. Indirect
evidence for other minds, according to the sceptic, is not merely
this kind of gradual assessment: in principle the evidence can
never become direct. Evidence for the fact that somebody is sad,
resentful, or is toying with a certain idea never refers to these
feelings and ideas themselves, but to something different: to what
the other says, does not say, does and does not do.

The sceptic's next move is to point out that, given this necessarily roundabout approach to other minds, we are always in the dark about other minds. We cannot rule out the possibility that our interpretations of other minds are completely wrong and that others merely simulate. And with a great talent for over-statement – often essential to sceptical positions – the sceptic now advances the categorical claim that the inner of other people must always remain a sealed book. As a source for our knowledge of their inner the behaviour of others now immediately loses prestige: it is imperfect and leaves scope for error; uncertainty is a flaw in the outer. The outer now turns into a barricade and becomes the code rather than messenger of the other's mind – a code without a key. The sceptic's mainstay in this dramatic con-clusion is the phenomenon of 'pretending'. Yet this pheno-menon is no more than a very special case of uncertainty about other minds; people under an anaesthetic, or from a different culture, or with an introverted nature, equally make us guess at their inner. First I shall discuss the problem in general, therefore, and afterwards the more specific case of pretending.

'Hidden' is a seductive and at the same time misleading meta-phor. The meaning which this concept has assumed in philo-sophical language is typically the product of a symmetrical logic: just as I *know* what I feel, so this must be *hidden* for another (PI II ix, pp. 220-221). And just as this symmetrical logic leads in the first person to a metaphysical private property, so the meaning of 'hidden' is metaphysical too. The similarity between the two areas is in fact perfect, for here too the normal meaning of a word has been given a sublimated meaning, here too an ordinary concept, 'hidden', is described in philosophical superlatives. In *Philoso-phical Investigations* II xi, p. 223 Wittgenstein remarks that the guessing of thoughts does not make the thoughts more hidden than a hidden physical process. Material from the Nachlass makes this statement less enigmatic.

In MS 176 Wittgenstein asks:

> 'Is the impossibility of knowing what goes on in another person physical or logical. And if both – how are they connected?'
> First: you could imagine possibilities of investigating another that actually do not exist. Consequently, there is a physical impossibility.

The logical impossibility consists in the fact that exact rules for the evidence are lacking. (Hence we often express ourselves like this: 'We can always be wrong, we can never be sure, what we see can always still be pretending.' Although pretending is just one of many possible causes of a false judgement.) (MS 176, pp. 50-51)

In philosophy these two impossibilities are not kept distinct, in Wittgenstein's view. What is physiologically or psychologically impossible is held to be logically impossible. The empirical fact that people only feel pain in their own body or can keep their thoughts to themselves is interpreted logically or, rather, metaphysically: as if they are 'hiding' something from us which is unfindable to start with. Precisely these two impossibilities are confusing and the usual meaning of 'hidden' seems to have been given an unusual, metaphysical meaning. In the usual sense 'hidden' means that one cannot find something, but that it *can* be found. In the philosophical sense the term refers to something that is not just hard to find, but cannot be found at all: it is *impossible* to find. Wittgenstein says of this confusion of logical and empirical aspects: 'This would be a metaphysical hiding' (RPP II, § 586). What is impossible from a logical point of view is interpreted as if something is being metaphysically hidden. In the following fragment Wittgenstein points out that 'metaphysically hidden' is meaningless: 'One can say: "He hides his feelings". But that means that they are not *a priori* always hidden. Again: there are two conflicting statements. One is that feelings are essentially hidden; the other that someone hides his feelings from me' (MS 169, pp. 55-56).

The absurdity of this metaphysical hide-and-seek is clear, I think. For if somebody 'hides' something which can never be experienced, felt, or heard by me, then strictly speaking nothing is being hidden. Something can only be hidden if it can also be found. And only then is what is being hidden relevant: something that can never be found is irrelevant and falls outside the scope of language-games. Of course, the absurdity of this metaphysical hide-and-seek follows directly from the absurdity of the metaphysical notion of private property: since I do not 'own' anything, there is nothing I can keep 'hidden' from others either. This involves no 'loss', since I never 'owned' anything. If one wants to talk about hidden, therefore, it should be in the usual sense of something which can be found. Only then is the hidden object relevant. It is precisely the asymmetry of the first and third person which does justice to this more common meaning:

> The inner is hidden from us means it is hidden from us in the sense that it is not hidden from him. And it is not hidden from the owner in the sense that he *expresses it* and that we give credence to the expressions under certain circumstances and that no error exists there. And this asymmetry of the game is expressed by the sentence, the inner is hidden from us. (MS 169, pp. 56-57)

Although Wittgenstein is not out to reform language with his grammatical descriptions, yet it would make for clarity here to drop the term 'hidden'. He suggests that it is less misleading to say: my thoughts are not (metaphysically) hidden from another person, but are *manifest* in different ways to me and her: to me as expressions, to her as observations of those expressions. For an expression I do not appeal to facts, not even direct, inner ones; this does away with the need to talk about indirect facts in the third person: 'It is not as if I in me have direct evidence for my inner and he only indirect. But he has evidence for it, I (however) do not' (MS 173, p. 42).[8]

In other words, my uncertainty about somebody else's mind is not opposed to his certainty. A major support for the sceptic's claim has thus been cancelled, since he sees knowledge in the third person as being inferior by the superior standards of first person knowledge. But if superior is not a viable term here, then neither is inferior.

After this general diagnosis of the sceptical argument for the dubious quality of third person knowledge, it is time to look at the phenomenon which provides the sceptic, by his own account, with the main reasons for his pessimism: pretending. When people pretend, an absolute gap seems to be created between observation of behaviour and the true facts of the behaviour. And even if one prefers, like Wittgenstein, to talk simply about evidence rather than 'indirect outer evidence', there is still a problem: pretending seems to devalue, to annul, all evidence. The behaviour shown can stand for anything and also for nothing. So

---

[8] Variations of this remark can also be found in PI II xi, p. 224; PI, § 246; and LW, § 894, 963.

the uncertainty in the third person seems to involve a hidden psychic medium after all. Wittgenstein's opposition to the sceptical consequences attached to pretending can be reconstructed in three stages. (i) A hidden psychic medium is irrelevant. (ii) There is evidence for pretending. (iii) Pretending is a language-game which is vertically related to other language-games.

Of course, uncertainty tends to be thought of in terms of situations where one feels that one is being deceived or duped. In these situations somebody deliberately conceals something and disguises his behaviour in such a way as to make his inner unrecognizable (i). But Wittgenstein gives a number of instances where uncertainty is created by precisely the opposite situation: 'Consider that we not only do not understand the other when he hides his feelings, but also often not when he is not hiding them, indeed when he is doing his utmost to make himself understood' (MS 169, p. 43). Uncertainty here has nothing to do with a 'hidden' inner which lies beyond one's reach, but rather with an outer which remains closed, like a handwriting that cannot be deciphered. It is also possible to hide one's thoughts from somebody by expressing them in a language unfamiliar to him (RPP II, § 564) or by withholding one's diary (LW, § 974). These cases do not involve a 'hidden psychic medium': on the contrary, there is relevance in what is being hidden here. The irrelevance of a hidden psychic medium can also be illustrated by means of fictitious language-games. For instance, people who, because the physiognomy of their face automatically betrays their feelings and thoughts, cover their faces to prevent others from discovering the real meaning of their actions. Uncertainty in this kind of society has nothing to do with an inner that is kept hidden, but with the fact that faces cannot be read because they are covered (LW, § 226-227). In all these cases the uncertainty cannot be attributed to the fact that one only possesses indirect evidence and that what the evidence should prove remains elusive. The examples show clearly enough that it is not elusive, so that Wittgenstein remarks: 'One might even say: The uncertainty about the inner is an uncertainty about something outer' (MS 174, p. 13).

There is evidence or there are signs for pretending (ii), not accidentally but essentially. 'Above all, pretending has its characteristic outer signs. How else could one speak of pretending at all?' (MS 169, p. 68). There must be signs for pretending, since it would otherwise be impossible to expose somebody as an impostor: one can only expose somebody if one knows, no matter how, that he is wearing a mask. The conceptual link between pretending and evidence is most notably exploited in the theatre: 'But you can portray a pretender on the stage. So there is such a thing as an *appearance* of pretence...' (LW, § 863). Histrionic talent, Wittgenstein is saying, already presupposes the ability to pretend: in order to play a role one must be able to dissemble. The fact that there are professionals who play roles already shows that there is evidence for pretending: acting is the stylization of these signs. Moreover, the fact that an actor may be cast in the role of an impostor shows that there are signs from which the audience can conclude that somebody is a hypocrite and somebody else is not. So the theatre proves two things: the signs are *uncertain,* since actors play at being sad, although actually they may not be sad at all, and the signs are also quite *real* and not just counterfeit, since there are evidently typical signs of grief, deception, or suspicion, witness the roles that are so cast. But one need not go to the theatre to expose traitors. In everyday life too there are incontestable signs for contestable behaviour: 'I say "This man conceals his inner". How does one know that he conceals it? There are accordingly signs for it and also signs for the opposite' (MS 169, p. 50). Deception and hypocrisy may make it more difficult to judge the facts, but they are not substantially different from transparent behaviour: 'After all, from a person's behaviour you can draw conclusions not only about his pain but also about his pretence' (LW, § 901). Thus Wittgenstein has no reason to abandon his idea that inner processes too have meaning only within the horizontal relations of language-games and forms of life. He is explicit about this with regard to pretending: 'Also what goes on in him is a game and pretending is not *present* in him like a feeling, but like a game' (MS 169, p. 49). In other words, to ask whether somebody is posing or not is to ask about the *kind* of language-game that is being played, not about our knowledge of the relation between his behaviour and something inside him.

Pretending is a different kind of language-game from the language-game of spontaneous expression of feelings, pain, etc. (iii). I take it to be a language-game that is vertically related to (see chapter 2, § 2) and based on these spontaneous language-games: 'The expressions of my feelings can be unreal. In particular they can be feigned. That is a different language-game from the primitive language-game of genuine expressions' (MS 169, p. 63). If we connect the meaning of 'pretending' with the way in which the concept is learned, these vertical relations soon become apparent. A child has a great deal to learn before it can dissemble (LW, § 942), so that we only talk about pretending in a fairly complicated pattern of life: 'If pretending were not a complicated pattern, it would be possible for a newborn child to pretend' (MS 171, p. 1). And: 'A child has to learn all sorts of things before he can pretend' (LW, § 868). What the child has to master, in a logical-conceptual sense, are above all linguistic concepts. For instance, the statements 'I think he's in pain', 'He thinks I'm in pain, but I'm not'. This language-game is a level up from the language-game where the child is only capable of misleading others with his behaviour. Via a simple process of conditioning he has learned, for instance, that crying always leads to sympathetic responses in mothers; next he starts to cry on purpose, because of the sympathy which he can expect. Yet this is still no pretending, though it is a root (LW, § 867). One only speaks of pretending in various cases and degrees of deception, in contrast to the experience of pain.

Language proved constitutive for vertically related language-games, and pretending is no exception. For like little children animals do not have the ability to pretend: a dog does not dissemble, nor is it sincere (PI II xi, p. 229b). Normally only somebody who knows a language can be sincere; which is not to say that people necessarily express sincere gratitude or dissimulated feelings in language: adults sometimes show this kind of behaviour without speaking a single word, by a mere look or gesture. But one has to be grown-up for this subtle way of exploiting one's physiognomy. Children are not born with a cunning look. The physiognomy of pretending is complicated as well and presupposes familiarity with many concepts. Hence this conclusion:

Feigning and its opposite exist only when there is a complicated *play of expressions*. (Just as false or correct moves exist only *in a game*.) (LW, § 946)

And if the play of *expression* develops, then indeed I can say that a soul, something *inner*, is developing. But now the inner is no longer the cause of the expression. (LW, § 947)

A complicated game of (linguistic) expressions is constitutive for the ability to describe one's feelings and thoughts at will, to conceal them and keep them to oneself, to disguise them and pretend, in short, for what is called the inner.

These vertical relations have important consequences for the scope of scepticism.[9] The sceptic says that we must always be on our guard against the possibility of dissimulation, but according to Wittgenstein this possibility cannot be universally present. For pretending that one feels pain is a language-game that vertically presupposes the spontaneous expression of pain. And on this fundamental level there is no place for scepticism. Only in *special* situations is certain behaviour to be regarded as simulated.[10] The simple fact that our natural attitude to other people can be different, that somebody's complaints of pain may meet with indifference in one person and compassion in another, does not mean that deception is involved. For the language-game of pretending there is in any case a reason, a motive, and a certain suspicion on the part of the untrusting person (LW, § 912) – in detective stories this conceptual environment is often elaborated with great subtlety. The concept of pretending is involved in very special situations and events in human life; that is why not all behaviour under all circumstances can be deceptive (LW, § 253). The language-game has extremely tenuous vertical branches and so is fairly specialized. To ignore this specialism is to deprive the language-game of its vertical stays, and the result is a universal

---

[9] Austin (1964, p. 116) has a similar remark when he says: '... it does seem that philosophers, who are fond of invoking pretending, have exaggerated its scope and distorted its meaning.'

[10] The concept of lying is also embedded in a language-game that is vertically related to 'honest' language-games, as can be seen from this remark: 'To what extent can one say that the game of lying is based on the language-game without lying? Surely merely because we would not use the word lying for something that is not in a specific way an exception' (MS 121, p. 29).

crisis in the knowledge of human nature. However, from a logical point of view the uncertainty can never assume such philosophical proportions, but remains practically confined to special situations (RPP II, § 558). By this Wittgenstein is saying that the very need for feigned behaviour can only arise if I know that I am not always a mystery to others. As he puts it: 'If I can *never* know what he feels, then he cannot pretend either' (MS 169, p. 56).

Vertically related language-games are made possible by more fundamental language-games, but they function autonomously, according to Wittgenstein. The internal relations between sensation and expression in the language-game of spontaneous expression of pain remain *intact*, regardless of the possibility of pretence. Dissimulation and deception form a *different* language-game. This language-game does not disturb the original pattern, but makes the concept of pain more complex. 'Thus I wish to say that there is an original, genuine expression of pain; thus that the expression of pain is not to the same extent connected with pain and pretending' (MS 171, p. 1). In 'I feel pain', the sincere expression, the relation between expression and sensation is internal; the expression *is* the sensation and cannot be conceived of without the sensation. Otherwise the expression is embedded in the language-game of pretending to feel pain. The relation between expressions and sensations is not internal here; expression and sensation can be separated – that is indeed the main feature of the game. That the relation is not internal also appears from the fact that there is no primary and spontaneous expression in this language-game. At any rate 'I am merely pretending that I feel pain' is not regarded as an expression of pretending, in the way that 'I feel pain' is regarded as an expression of pain. The spontaneous expression of pain functions on a more fundamental level than the language-game of pretending, in the sense that the certainty in the sincere language-game is not prejudiced by the possible uncertainty in the insincere language-game. On the contrary, precisely the fact that there is room for doubt and uncertainty in the insincere language-game – and more generally in the language-game of the third person – implies that there is certainty too, witness Wittgenstein's logic of 'knowing' and 'certainty' (see chapter 3, § 2). Just as it is meaningless to talk about doubt and therefore about knowing in the language-game of the first person, so it is meaningless *not* to talk about certainty, if on a different and more fundamental level, where it is possible to talk meaningfully about doubt and knowing: the language-game of the third person. Wittgenstein seems consistently to apply this fundamental idea about 'knowing' and 'certainty' to the concepts of 'inner' and 'outer'. The conclusion is that the sceptic cannot use the intriguing phenomenon of pretending to support his claim that knowledge in the third person is inferior. There is uncertainty – just as there is certainty – but it need not be explained by a dualistic gap between evidence and what it is evidence of. Wittgenstein has shown that both signs for deception and signs for sincerity 'inside' can be recognized on the outside. So the issue is not a dualistic contrast between inner and outer. And likewise there is no need to talk about a quasi-causal relation between indirect outer evidence and a metaphysically hidden inner. The question of whether deception is involved should not be judged by an epistemological inspection of other people's inner lives, but by a description of the kind of language-game that is being played.

3. 'Einstellung zur Seele'

Premiss (3) of the sceptic's argument was that something counts as a sign only if it can be proved that it is a sign of something. Wittgenstein does not furnish such a proof, not out of despair or resignation, but on logical considerations: the language-games in which we express a sceptical view of other minds presuppose more fundamental language-games in which there is no room for proving or disproving. Wittgenstein, I think, subscribes to the following ideas about these fundamental language-games in which certainty rules: (a) signs for other minds need not be proved since they cannot be doubted either; (b) if a proof is senseless, then so is the classical answer to scepticism, the argument by analogy; (c) the expression of other minds is seen immediately. I shall discuss (a), (b), and (c) in that order.

In *Philosophical Investigations* II v, p. 179 Wittgenstein describes a dialogue between a nurse and a doctor. The doctor asks
the nurse how the patient is feeling and the nurse answers that he
is groaning: a description of his behaviour. But, continues Wittgenstein, need there be any question for them whether the
groaning is genuine? Might they not immediately conclude that
the patient needs a painkiller? And the same fragment in *Last
Writings*, § 352 adds: 'But in the context of these thoughts can't the
report about behaviour be *used as* a report about a person's mental
state?' A statement about the outer is used as a statement about
the inner. The statement is about inner and outer, 'not side-by-
side, however, but about the one *via* the other' (PI II v, p. 179).
The terms inner and outer are *internally* related here, not
externally, in juxtaposition. That the patient has an inner and
feels pain is not for instance a separate, if tacit, presupposition, for,
as Wittgenstein says, where there is a presupposition there is also
doubt (PI II v, p. 180). The suggestion here is that there is no doubt
in this case and that there is always a point at which presup-
positions come to an end. Thus, when we send someone to the
shop, we do not presuppose that he is human and that the shop is
not a fata morgana (LW, § 354). The relation between inner and
outer is not mediated here by a separate presupposition. The
point of the dialogue is rather that the immediate reaction of
nurse and doctor to the patient's behaviour shows that inner and
outer are internally related: insofar as they treat the patient as a
human being, they treat him *eo ipso* as somebody with an inner.
There is no question of a supposition that the thing lying in bed
there and groaning is a human being. On the contrary, we are
dealing with an attitude to a human being and an attitude to a
human being is at this level an attitude to an inner.

This internal relation is the point of Wittgenstein's statement:
'My attitude towards him is an attitude towards a soul. I am not
of the *opinion* that he has a soul' (PI II iv, p. 178; LW, § 324). I said
earlier on that an attitude is logically antecedent to an opinion, an
assumption, a view (see chapter 3, § 2). But if 'knowledge' of
another person's mind is an attitude towards another person –
and in this section attitude always means attitude to an inner –
then a proof is in fact pointless: a proof has point only where there

is room for doubt and error. An attitude is precisely the absence of such room. 'But what would an error look like here' (MS 169, p. 61). And a few pages earlier: 'There are surely cases in which only a madman could take the expression of pain (e.g.) to be unreal' (MS 169, p. 51). Wittgenstein's emphasis on attitude is far from having behaviouristic implications, as Kripke supposes.[11] He does not think that a belief in other minds is a sort of superstition, a gratuitous, unreasoned hypothesis and certainly not 'real' knowledge. It is not a (hypothetical) belief *at all*. Nor does an attitude of certainty here mean that one buries one's head in the sand and shuts one's eyes against doubt: 'They are shut' (PI II xi, p. 224). This is not the blindness of somebody who is asleep. On the

---

[11] See Kripke (1981, p. 303, n. 21), who says that this slogan 'sounds much too behaviouristic to me. I personally would like to think that anyone who does not think of me as conscious is wrong about the facts, not simply "unfortunate" or "evil", or even "monstrous" or "inhuman", in his "attitude" (Whatever that might mean).' Had Kripke added 'insane' to this list, he would have shown more comprehension. The difference between 'knowing' and 'certainty' has escaped him completely. With his emphasis on the 'facts', Kripke wants to indicate that his idea that he and other people have an inner is fundamental. This fundamental character is not denied by Wittgenstein, but he does deny that it can be described in terms of 'knowing', for where 'knowing' is involved, there is also the possibility of falsification. But an 'attitude toward an inner' leaves room for neither disagreement nor agreement of opinion. In effect Wittgenstein thus indicates more correctly than Kripke in what way the 'belief' in an inner is so fundamental.

The same statement has also given rise to religious interpretations. Translations – including the English ones – already take that direction by translating 'Seele' as 'soul'. The only correct translation is 'inner' or 'psyche', as appears from, among other things, the fact that Wittgenstein uses both terms interchangeably ('a soul, something *inner*, is developing' (LW, § 947)). Unbridled religious speculations are found in Dilman (1974). This article is illustrative of many others in which a deficient knowledge of Wittgenstein's work is compensated by wide reading in another field. The author starts by quoting a few passages from Wittgenstein and fills the rest with digressions on authors with whom Wittgenstein supposedly has affinities. Wittgenstein is thus put in a tradition which runs as far as 'from Plato through Kierkegaard to Simone Weil' (Dilman, p. 191). Ignorance of the Nachlass takes its toll here too, witness the final sentence of the article: 'Perhaps if he had lived longer he would have returned to them [i.e. the discussion about 'Seele']. I do not know.'(p. 192) But we do know now: Wittgenstein was still to write extensively about 'inner-outer' and not in a religious sense, although he was not opposed to it (cf. RPP I, § 586).

contrary, one is quite alert and knows exactly what to do. One does not choose, hesitate, consult; one reacts immediately. No reasons need be produced for this reaction, precisely because such reasons presuppose this kind of reaction. With this emphasis on 'attitude' Wittgenstein puts his finger on the internal relation between inner and outer: from the perspective of this fundamental language-game of attitude, 'inner' and 'outer' cannot be separated. If we do separate them, if we take somebody's moaning to be so many hollow vibrations and not an expression of pain, then we are breaking the constitutive rule for this game and playing a different game.

In an attitude there is no room for doubt and error, and there-fore no room for proving, for knowing, believing, or supposing. 'It seems to me: if one cannot really *know* whether someone is annoyed (e.g.), one cannot believe or surmise it either' (MS 174, p. 7). And elsewhere: 'Do I *believe* in a soul in someone else, when I look into his eyes with astonishment and delight?' (RPP I, § 268). The language-game in which knowing and so believing and supposing are possible is the language-game in which veri-fication or falsification are possible. That kind of language-game also requires an appeal to criteria, in the sense of strict tests (see also chapter 4, § 2 (d)): tests verifying or falsifying the hypothesis that somebody is not an automaton, but a human being. The Turing test is such a game.[12] There it does make sense for some-one to adduce criteria in support of his notion that the person on the left behind the screen is an automaton and that the figure on the right is not. We then find ourselves in a situation referred to by Wittgenstein when he remarks at the end of *Philosophical Investigations*, § 288 that if one assumes the abrogation of the normal language-game with the expression of sensations, one needs a criterion for the identity of the sensation; but in that case the possibility of error exists as well. This seems to me to refute a commonplace in interpretations of Wittgenstein:[13] Wittgenstein

---

[12] See chapter 8 for an extensive discussion of the Turing test in relation to Wittgenstein's philosophy of other minds.

[13] Hintikka (see chapter n. 22) forms an exception to this commonplace with regard to his interpretation of Wittgenstein's remarks about the first person, but he says next to nothing in this respect about the third person.

does not hold a simple view of criteria for other minds: he does not claim that in the third person one can always appeal to criteria in the strict sense of verification and falsification. On the fundamental level of attitudes such criteria for evidence of other minds have no meaning. Contrary to what one is inclined to think, this does *not* mean that one has no knowledge of other minds. One is certain of it, as one is certain that an exercise book is lying on the table, that there is a pen in one's hand, that the book will fall if one lets go of it, or that one has not miscalculated when saying that 25 x 25 = 625: 'The following, however, is true: I can't give criteria which put the presence of the sensation beyond doubt; that is to say: there are no such criteria' (RPP I, § 137). For a moment it seems as if Wittgenstein is saying that criteria in the sense of verifications and falsifications are necessary and that since they do not exist, we have no way of knowing others. But this is an optical illusion. The point is that doubt may be removed with the help of such criteria, but only where doubt exists. An attitude leaves no room for doubt; criteria are therefore unnecessary. An attitude, an immediate reaction, reflects our certainty concerning others. This certainty may be equal to the certainty in mathematics. Section 4 will show in what way both language-games are nevertheless different.

If no proof of other minds is necessary, given the fundamental status of our attitude to others, then the claims for the traditional argument by analogy[14] can be dropped as well (b). This argument says that the correlation between inner and outer can be proved on the basis of our own situation. I know that if I feel pain I am inclined to cry, so that if somebody else cries it is no more than likely that he too feels pain. Many objections can be raised to this argument, e.g. that it savours of narcissism and does not sufficiently respect the real otherness of the other person. Wittgenstein and also Köhler object that it is too artificial. Since one does not actually make the inference on the basis of one's own situation, according to Wittgenstein, the argument by analogy can

---

[14] Authors that have defended the argument by analogy are for instance Brentano (1971, I, p. 53) and Russell (1948, pp. 482-486).

be dismissed (RPP II, § 719; Z, § 537).[15] It may be instructive to look more closely at the similarity to Köhler's position.[16]

Like Wittgenstein, Köhler calls the sceptical problem of other minds a typical philosophers' problem: it is the product of an inadequate conception of 'inner' and 'outer'. The common view of these two notions is that of two heterogeneous domains divided by an unbridgeable gap. Once this view is established, there remains but one way of closing the gap: 'Nothing but an external relation seems to exist and to be possible here, between the facts of two different worlds' (Köhler, p. 184). If the relation is in fact external, it must be relatively easy to reseparate the combination of inner and outer. However, as Köhler remarks in a 'Wittgensteinian' fragment,[17] it is very difficult to disconnect the physical configuration in a friendly look from the friendliness, especially if we view the face as a whole, without analysing it into a mosaic of coloured dots (Köhler, p. 184). Against the disparateness of inner and outer in the argument by analogy, Köhler therefore posits a striking similarity. The outer, he says, is an extraordinarily adequate 'picture' of the inner. According to Köhler, the 'objective experience' of the outer contains all the material necessary for understanding another person's mind (Köhler, p. 201). The directly observable behaviour expresses similar characteristics of the inner. If, for instance, somebody is thinking angrily about a rival, he will start to walk faster, he will raise his voice. The increased tempo of the inner agitation is matched by a crescendo and accelerando in physical movement, expression, and diction. In this way the outer is often a 'direct picture' of the inner: not indirect but direct evidence.

At first sight Wittgenstein's approach seems identical to Köhler's. He rejects the argument by analogy for similar reasons:

---

[15] This is an empirical objection also urged by Köhler: '... the whole theory seems to be an arbitrary construction, since no one explicitly draws such inferences by analogy in common life, though he may "understand" his fellow men to a considerable degree' (1929, p. 182).

[16] Köhler (1929) discusses the argument by analogy in chapter 7.

[17] It might be fairer to say 'Köhlerian', for Köhler did not know Wittgenstein's work.

That statement 'I believe he feels what I feel in such circumstances' does not yet exist here: The interpretation, that is, that I see something in myself which I surmise in him.

For in reality that is a rough interpretation. In general I do not surmise fear in him – I *see* it. I do not feel that I am deducing the probable existence of something inside from something outside; rather it is as if the human face were in a way translucent and that I were seeing it not in reflected light but rather in its own. (RPP II, § 170)

And especially Wittgenstein's statement that the human body is the best picture of the human psyche (PI II iv, p. 178) seems to indicate agreement with Köhler's view that there is an almost perfect resemblance between the inner and the outer. But Wittgenstein, as we know, is strict. Although Köhler has rightly seen that the relation is more than just external, Wittgenstein criticizes him for failing to provide an accurate description of the internal relation between inner and outer. 'Can one say that there is a *similarity* between the emotion and its expression, insofar as both are excited, for example? (I think Köhler said something like that.)' (RPP II, § 334). He calls this a wrong view because Köhler takes 'excitement' to refer to something inner as well as to something outer. This again leaves room for an external relation for which there is no place in the logic of the language-game. For Köhler's view again allows us to talk about an inner feeling *per se* and to ask how one knows this feeling. Wittgenstein takes such questions to be pointless, not because he wants to eliminate 'inner agitation', but because Köhler's view presupposes a misleading view of the meaning of concepts. 'Inner agitation' is not learned as if it stands for a specific feeling and, besides that, for typical outer manifestations. The basis for the meaning of the concept is formed by the rule-governed manifestations of facial expressions, primitive reactions and actions. The inner is not presented via this basis – as if the inner is a domain behind or parallel to the outer and something which one should also be able to know in that capacity – the inner is *expressed* in it. The outer is expressive for the inner and this expressive relation is internal. The inner can be *seen* in the physiognomy of expressions. The most salient feature of Wittgenstein's emphasis on the fact that the inner can be seen in the outer is the *qualitative* nature of our act of seeing and of what is seen. In the *Investigations* he says that our attitude

towards a dead body is completely different from out attitude
towards a living body and the difference has everything to do with
the transition from quantity to quality (PI, § 284). In the next remark he reminds us of the fact that we describe facial expressions
without being able to do so on the basis of geometrical measurements (PI, § 285). That is, our description is purely qualitative. In
MS 124 he writes the following after § 285: 'One can really say: the
soulful body feels pain. And whether a body is soulful, that one
perceives through the senses' (MS 124, pp. 244-245). This
qualitative nature of soulful expressions is our next subject.

The expression of other minds is seen immediately (c). By 'seen
immediately' Wittgenstein means that an 'Einstellung' expressing
certainty is involved. Wittgenstein gives many examples of such
attitudes, but two are recurrent: (i) the attitude to facial expressions, (ii) the attitude to confessions. We see emotion, according
to Wittgenstein (RPP II, § 570).[18] What he means is that the concepts of joy, grief, boredom are not indirect descriptions of what
one sees, as if they are inferred from a geometry of features. Far
from it, the face is immediately described as sad or happy, without
one being capable of describing it with anatomical precision. For
the concept of emotion it is constitutive that it is applied in an
internal relation to facial expressions. There is a clear parallel
here with Wittgenstein's approach to aspects: aspects in this
conceptual sense, like emotions, are seen immediately (see

---

[18] Hintikka (1986, pp. 273, 277) quotes this remark too and says that Wittgenstein also acknowledges basic physiological languages, but would have 'preferred' physiognomic language-games because he was a 'closet Tolstoyan in his
philosophy of language' (p. 275). There are two objections to this: first, if Wittgenstein has been influenced here, it has not been by Tolstoy but by Köhler and
Spengler. Spengler distinguishes between 'Ausdruckssprache' and 'Mitteilungs-
sprache' (1923, pp. 693 ff.). The former is an 'active transformation' of physiognomical expression and cannot be learned, strictly speaking. However, it is the
precondition for all manner of language learning. A similar view is found in
Bühler (1934, p. 28), whom Wittgenstein knew very well (see Bartley, 1985,
p. 128). Secondly, Wittgenstein did not simply 'choose'; for if he could have
chosen otherwise, this means he would have been able to describe a form of life
which is *completely* different from ours. And that he could not do, on account of
the 'givenness' of our form of life, which is not to say that our form of life could
never change.

chapter 6). In this conceptual sense grief is 'personified in the face' (RPP II, § 570). Not only emotions have a physiognomy. Wittgenstein also talks about a shade of consciousness in the face. Consciousness is as clear in the face and behaviour of another as in oneself (RPP I, § 927, 929). And although knowledge and opinion have no facial expression, there is a tone and gesture of conviction, at least if something is said in this tone or with this gesture (RPP I, § 928). Expression is here verbal expression. With these and other examples Wittgenstein wants to show that the attitude to other minds is based on an internal relation between inner and outer and is not an interpretation or a narcissistic projection. In these external approaches he recognizes the anthropological counterpart of the causal and psychologistic theory of meaning: just as a linguistic sign in itself was considered meaningless apart from a psychical injection, so the outer is taken to be no more than a symptom of a more important inner phenomenon (LW, § 979). But the outer need not be considered a front for psychic powers. 'Psychic' easily assumes a metaphysical meaning, especially in the hands of philosophers: '"Psychic" is for me not a metaphysical but a logical epithet' (MS 173, p. 35). And from a logical perspective the relation is not external but internal: 'Inner and outer are not only connected by experience but also logically' (MS 173, p. 37). Unlike the external, empirical relation between fever and red cheeks, the relation between a sad face and a feeling is internal: the concept of grief can only be applied in the horizontal relations of, for instance, a sad face, sad gestures, or a sad voice. Sadness itself cannot be observed apart from a medium, just as fleet-footed only means something in relation to somebody, Achilles for instance.

> Now a picture is strongly suggested to us, the picture of something incorporeal which enlivens the face (like quivering air). We have to remind ourselves that a face with a soulful expression can be painted to make us believe that colours and forms by themselves can affect us this way. (LW, § 325)

Our attitude to a soulful expression is primary and attests to our certainty about other minds. Through an expression the face becomes transparent, as it were. 'If facial expressions, gestures and circumstances are univocal, the inner seems to be the outer; only when we cannot read the outer does an inner seem to be hidden behind it' (MS 173, p. 36). But deliberately concealing one's inner can also have the opposite effect: 'If I lie to him and he guesses it from my face and says it to me, – do I still have the feeling that my inner is in no way accessible to him, is hidden? Do I not rather feel that he sees completely through me' (MS 169, p. 52). In these cases the inner is not hidden, as the cause of a stomach-ache may be hidden. The concept of inner is essentially applied in the horizontal relations of the concept of outer. If the inner seems concealed, this is not because it is hidden by the outer, but because the *outer* is hidden: one does not know how to apply the concept of 'inner' within the horizontal relations of 'outer'. The inner is therefore hidden in the way that something which is fully present may be invisible. The situation is similar to the one with visual aspects (see chapter 6). So it is not the other person's body which prevents us from knowing his mind, but rather our attitude to the other. Like blindness to aspect, one might say, there is such a thing as soul-blindness.[19] The aspect of another person's mind fails to show itself to us, it is blocked by another aspect to which we do have an attitude: 'So in this sense I only see it *this* way as long as I have this *attitude* toward it? That could be said' (LW, § 667).

Certainty about other minds is also reflected in our attitude to confessions (ii). In the *Philosophical Investigations* Wittgenstein makes one remark about confessions. He writes that the criteria for a truthful confession are not the same as for the description of a past inner event. The importance of a confession is not that an inner event is reported, but resides 'in the special consequences that can be drawn from a confession whose truth is guaranteed by the special criteria of *truthfulness*' (PI II ix, p. 222). A number of authors have linked this fragment to the problem of whether expressions can have truth value.[20] But that is not the only point. The point of the fragment is the special *role* of confessions in our form of life: a confession gives certainty to our knowledge of other people's motives and actions. Confession is thus typically a concept accommodated in the language-game of the attitude to

---

[19] See Cavell (1979, p. 369) on the application of the concept of 'aspect-blindness' to the other minds problem.

[20] See Hacker (1972, chapter 9) and Malcolm (1986, pp. 139-140).

other minds. This meaning of confessions is not evident. A more obvious interpretation is that confessions are descriptions of wrong things which somebody has done in the past, things which have been kept secret. The idea here is that the later confession reveals the person's inner. Wittgenstein's objection to this is that a description does not explain the nature of inner and outer. For a confession is something exterior too and if I do not give credence to it there is no point in it (RPP II, § 703). What is central, therefore, is not an inner state, the accuracy of an introspective report, but the confession and its consequences. One of these consequences is the fact that the confession can explain something to me about your behaviour; for instance, I may have to admit to you that my suspicions were unfounded. Or I may declare my guilt in a confession and so submit to prosecution. Although there are exceptions, it is a constitutive rule that my honest confession is more reliable than the judgement of others. We can take for instance legal proceedings, which on the whole are aimed at inducing the criminal to confess. The pursuit of this strategy is solely based on the conviction that a confession generally offers the most direct insight into somebody's motives. According to Wittgenstein, this function of confessions must rest on a general fact: 'It has to be roughly the case that I can give in general a more coherent account of my actions than the other. In this account the inner plays the role of a theory or construction that completes the rest into an understandable whole' (MS 169, p. 54). His idea is that the criteria for the reliability of confessions are different from those for the accuracy of an introspective report. The reliability of confessions is comparable in this respect with the fact that I can predict the movements of my arms and legs. Here too the criteria for reliability do not reside in the degree of introspective infallibility, but in the fact that the prediction usually proves correct. If my confession were not generally more reliable than the judgement of others and if others were unable to draw those conclusions from my confession of motives which they generally draw, then the entire language-game would not be what it is; it would not exist. The greater reliability of confessions vis-à-vis judgements is constitutive for the language-game. Our attitude to confessions illustrates this too. If somebody finally confesses to

something after concealing it for a long time, we do not again call
his confession into question. We do not say that again we do not
know what is on his mind. On the contrary, his inner has become
transparent in a facial expression or in the consequences of a
confession and certainty has been reached. A proof of the correlation between outer signs and what they are signs of (the inner)
need not be given. An attitude to the inner is involved which is
more fundamental than any furnishing of proof. At this level
inner and outer are internally related. If proof is unnecessary,
therefore, we can obviously dismiss step (4) in the sceptical argument, which says that such a proof can only be circular. Steps (5)
and (6) are dealt with in the following section.

4. 'Menschenkenntnis' and indeterminacy

The pointlessness of sceptical uncertainty does not mean that
'Menschenkenntnis' is knowledge that can be formalized. To pretend we know exactly what we are talking about here is to belittle
the mystery which other people sometimes are to us. Wittgenstein certainly has no such pretensions. As an ironic example of
such a mystery he mentions British women.[21] Knowledge of
human nature cannot be formalized; yet we find here a similar
kind of certainty to that in mathematics, and also a similar kind of
uncertainty.

In the last period of his philosophical work Wittgenstein concentrated on a description of this 'Menschenkenntnis'. By this
term, as will become clear later on, Wittgenstein does not mean
the science of psychology or his own description of psychological
concepts in general; rather it denotes a skill which some people
have a more intuitive grasp of than others. His description of this
knowledge is devoid of the sceptic's pessimism that genuine
knowledge is impossible here (step 6 in the argument), but also
lacks the optimism of analogy arguments – the idea that others
are like oneself. Again the characteristic feature of Wittgenstein's
approach is that he resists such attempts at explanation and opts

---

[21] See *Culture and Value*, p. 74.

for a logical description of the concept 'knowledge of human nature'. I take the following three propositions to be the result of this description. (A) the concepts 'human being', 'soul', 'inner', 'outer' are constituted by indeterminacy. (B) Knowledge of human nature is based on 'imponderable evidence'. (C) The rules for learning knowledge of human nature cannot be exactly described. I will discuss them in that order.

At an early stage Wittgenstein had become convinced that vagueness is inherent in language-games (A).[22] But it was only later that he became aware of a similar vagueness in the concepts 'human being', etc., as this aside from 1933 shows: 'The concept of a living being has the same indefiniteness as language. (I don't entirely understand this.)' (TS 213, p. 192).[23] Not until 1949 was he able to describe this indeterminacy without making it more focused than it is. First we must indicate what indeterminacy is *not*. In the first place indeterminacy is not a causal category. Indeterminacy, the fact that we sometimes have no idea what people's motives are, do not know what to expect or do know but not why, this kind of indeterminacy is not removed by, say, a surgical inspection of the body. Such an inspection is of course possible, but the indeterminacy remains intact: the concepts are constituted in such a way that inspection is irrelevant and if inspection were relevant, the concepts would no longer be what they are.

> One could imagine that to determine whether someone is in pain a kind of clinical thermometer is used. If a human being cries or moans, they take his temperature and only if this shows such and such a sign, they start to pity the one who suffers and to treat him the way we treat the one who is 'clearly in pain'. (MS 176, p. 50)

In this kind of situation the concept of pain would be applied in causal terms. The reading of the thermometer has a similar external relation to 'pain' as red cheeks to fever or a stomach-ache to flu. To the extent that 'pain' can subsequently be measured, the concept has been made more precise and does not have the indeterminacy of our concept of pain. This example clearly shows

---

[22] On vagueness and determinacy of sense, see PI, § 75-87.
[23] This remark can also be found in MS 116, p. 133.

that indeterminacy is not a causal category for Wittgenstein. For while the concept of pain has now been determined in the sense that it has been measured, the indeterminacy in our concept of pain has not been removed. It has not been removed because the measurable manipulation of pain produces an entirely *different* concept of pain from ours. A characteristic of our concept of pain is for instance that an expression of pain is not a claim to knowledge: the statement 'I know that I feel pain' makes no sense (see chapter 4, § 2 (d)). In the case of 'thermometer pain' the introductory clause 'I know ...' does make sense, since it now also makes sense to doubt whether one feels pain: one can doubt the reading of the thermometer like any other indication of an illness or disease. Thus indeterminacy taken in a causal sense can always be made more determinate by the addition of new knowledge, so that one has more and more grounds for knowing or doubting somebody else's inner disposition. Indeterminacy in Wittgenstein's sense does not indicate a gap in our knowledge of causal connections, nor is it removed by filling such a gap. 'But with a human being, the assumption is that *it is impossible* to gain an insight into the mechanism. Thus indeterminacy is postulated' (RPP II, § 666). The case is different from that of machines. By contrast, the behaviour of a complicated clock can become more determinate for us after we have inspected the mechanism. Of course, Wittgenstein does not want to dismiss the question of whether the logic of psychological concepts is related to the *de facto* absence of certain empirical possibilities in the way we function psychically and physiologically. But to the extent that this is a causal question he cannot answer it. Such an answer would be hypothetical and so incompatible with his descriptive method. All he can do is describe how the logic of concepts is embedded in a way of life that is important to us. Nor can he say whether we would change our form of life if we had other, perhaps more practical, physical possibilities. In that case he would fail to respect the autonomy of constitutive rules (see chapter 3, § 3). He confines himself to noting the importance of our concept of pain and so he says of 'thermometer pain': 'If measuring is not important to us, we do not measure, even though we *could*' (MS 176, p. 50).

In the second place indeterminacy does not denote a deficiency in skill or knowledge for Wittgenstein. Indeterminacy in the attribution of feelings to others cannot be compared with an inadequate command of a foreign language in which one is forced to express oneself. That indeterminacy can be remedied by a crash-course in French. Nor does indeterminacy mean hesitation or uncertainty: even if one characterizes somebody as aggressive without hesitation or a moment's thought, this characterization is qualified by indeterminacy. Indeterminacy in Wittgenstein's sense follows logically from the constitution of concepts: 'One might say: In a game in which the rules are indeterminate, one *cannot* know who has won and who has lost' (MS 174, p. 9). The meaning of psychological concepts is based on a rule-guided context of more or less primitive reactions and actions. Precisely this foundation is the reason for indeterminacy in the logical sense. What is constitutive for our psychological concepts, our psychological judgements, our more or less primitive reactions, is the 'bustle' and 'hustle' of human life (RPP II, § 626). The back-drop for psychological judgements is not monochrome, but a pattern in highly complex filigree. The behaviour, expressions and actions constituting psychological concepts are blurred; as a result the concepts lack focus and have a kind of elasticity. This lack of focus should not be interpreted negatively. It does not mean an all-pervasive vagueness. On the contrary, it is quite possible to draw sharp boundaries in the investigation of concepts – and Wittgenstein himself does this too. His grammatical inquiry shows that concepts in language-games often have a hard centre. But this centre is not exhaustive. By being embedded in human life, concepts are elastic at the edges, so to speak, and pass gradually into each other. Indeterminacy should therefore be understood in the sense of a non-exhaustive or not ultimately justifiable determinacy (see also (C)).

Indeterminacy above all shows itself in two prominent aspects of human life: (i) the irregularity of the human physiognomy, (ii) the unpredictability of human behaviour. Facial expressions are an important basis for concepts of emotion in particular and for some concepts of sensation. With regard to these expressions Wittgenstein repeatedly says that variability and irregularity are an essential part of the human physiognomy (RPP II, § 615). The variability of the face is almost as important as, say, the facial features characteristic of grief or joy (RPP II, § 627). The play of the human physiognomy is a-mechanical in every way. A comparison with more primitive animals is instructive. Thus the behaviour of spiders is far from indeterminate and yet we hesitate to attribute feelings of pain to them. As Wittgenstein notes, doubt as to whether a spider feels pain is not due to the fact that we do not know what to expect (RPP II, § 669; Z, § 564). On the contrary, doubt arises because we know so well what to expect.[24] We refuse to attribute an inner life to a spider because its members and movements are too regular, but it is less strange of cranky widows to believe that their dog has a soul: a dog is more like a human being than a being that looks human but behaves mechanically (RPP II, § 623). The point of similarity between man and dog is not form, skin colour, or anatomy, it is the behaviour and the actions of a dog, what it can and cannot do: '"Only look at the face and movements of a dog and you will see that he has a soul". But what is it about the face? Is it only the similarity with the facial expression of the human face? Is it, at least partly, the lack of stiffness'? (MS 173, p. 39) And the question of how a human body would have to behave for us to be disinclined to talk about a soul, about inner and outer states, is answered as follows: 'The *only thing* I can imagine is that this human body acts automatically and not like normal human bodies' (MS 173, p. 40). The importance of irregularity and variability of expression, I take it, emerges only when the opposite situation is described via fictitious language-games, where life does assume a regular course and determinacy instead of indeterminacy rules. A clearly defined formation of concepts is much more natural in this kind of situation. Thus we can imagine people whose faces can vary between just five positions (RPP II, § 614), and not gradually, like our faces, but one position is abruptly followed by the other.

---

[24] Doubt as to whether insects can feel pain is called philosophical by Wittgenstein and he contrasts this sort of doubt with practical or instinctive doubt. The former is universal, the latter restricted to particular cases. Hence philosophical doubt as to whether humans feel pain does not exist, for the doubt is particular and therefore presupposes certainty. See RPP II, § 659, 644, 558.

These people 'laugh' in a stiff and frozen way and it is doubtful whether we are still prepared to call it laughter. In any case we will not relate to it as we do to real laughter; above all we will not laugh ourselves.

With this example Wittgenstein graphically conveys the essence of indeterminacy. For if these people could change their faces into far more than five positions (but not into as many as ours) and also less spasmodically (but not as smoothly as ours), then it would be much harder to decide whether they were capable of real laughter. Sufficient evidence passes into insufficient evidence without a borderline, says Wittgenstein (RPP II, § 614). There is an elastic margin in which the evidence for real laughter is insufficient, but not so insufficient as to be evidence for the opposite. The evidence balances gradually between sufficient and insufficient, but does not abruptly tip to either side. If, therefore, a pattern deviates from the normal pattern, our judgement is not necessarily predetermined. The indeterminacy of our lives and concepts allows this margin.

The indeterminacy of the concepts 'soul', 'inner', and 'outer' also manifests itself in the uncertainty often produced by human behaviour. In turn this uncertainty shows itself in the unpredictability of human behaviour (ii). With the concepts of uncertainty and unpredictability Wittgenstein seems to adopt a traditional epistemological position. These characteristics of behaviour had of course been observed before and had always been explained with reference to the inner: the fact that behaviour is sometimes unpredictable was put down to the causal relation between inner and outer. The mind is a gaseous reservoir of unpredictability and the physical behaviour drawn from it carries part of this unpredictability. From the third person perspective this uncertainty thus appears as a deficiency: behaviour is a front for the unpredictable tricks of an inner. The inner cannot really be recognized in the signs offered by behaviour. These are synthetic signs, an artificial substitute for the direct, inner signs of the conjuror inside.

Wittgenstein does not use the concepts of soul and inner in this sense, in order to justify and explain indeterminacy, uncertainty, and unpredictability. The *reverse* is true: the indeterminacy of

human life provides an explanation for the use of the concepts of soul and inner. The following fragment clearly bears out this reversal of the causal approach: '"But you can't recognize pain with *certainty* just from externals." – The *only* way of recognizing is by externals, and the uncertainty is constitutional. It is not a shortcoming' (RPP II, § 657).[25]
Wittgenstein's grammatical inquiry does not focus on the fact that certain signs indicate certain feelings with only a degree of probability. It is not directed at the degree of knowledge but at the *measure* for knowledge. And in the case of other minds the measure is this: that we base predictions and explanations on a highly complex pattern of actions and situations. The uncertainty which always exists here is constitutive and has nothing do with an inner that conceals itself behind an outer, but has everything to do with the connection between elastic concepts and all but unspecifiable external circumstances. Unlike the language-game with colours and other kinds of observation statements, the situation here is marked by a lack of agreement. The indeterminacy involved in determining the genuineness of feelings is reflected in the *absence* of blind agreement: 'Concepts with fixed limits would demand a uniformity of behaviour. But what happens is that where I am *certain*, someone else is uncertain. And that is a fact of nature' (RPP II, § 683; Z, § 374). The same signs may entirely convince one person and fail to convince another. Yet we do not therefore exclude one another from society as being incapable of judgement or unsound of mind. The uncertainty is constitutive for the language-game, 'is an indefiniteness in the nature of the game, in the admissible evidence' (LW, § 888).

Before I explain the meaning of 'imponderable evidence' (proposition B), something needs to be said about the term 'Menschenkenntnis'. 'Knowledge of human nature' is not scientific and quantifiable knowledge of human beings, it is not psychology. That much is already made clear by the examples that Wittgenstein discusses: how do we recognize the genuineness of an expression of feeling, on what basis do we identify an expression of feeling as simulated, is there such a thing as an

---

[25] The English translation writes 'external' here instead of 'outer'. See for a similar remark RPP II, § 657.

'expert judgement' about the genuineness of expressions and is
proof possible here, and, finally, can knowledge of human nature
be learned, e.g. by taking a course in it at school, like arithmetic?
(PI II ix, p. 227). As Wittgenstein uses the term, knowledge of
human nature is more a kind of sensitivity; a skill which some
people have a more intuitive grasp of than others, whether by
aptitude, experience, or profession – which is not to say that
knowledge of human nature can be learned by studying
psychology. Although Wittgenstein had a low opinion of
psychology, his ironic query as to whether there is a course in
'Menschenkenntnis' is not aimed at this science. On the contrary,
psychology is not concerned with knowledge of human nature,
but with knowledge, especially quantifiable knowledge, of human
beings. But Wittgenstein's analysis of 'Menschenkenntnis' does
hold interest for psychologists.[26] His description of the use of this
term in our form of life offers the psychologist a convenient way
of translating his own quantifiable results into everyday
knowledge (see also chapter 8). Wittgenstein's analysis of 'Menschenkenntnis' is not equivalent to his analysis of individual
psychological concepts either, such as 'emotion', 'willing', or 'expecting' (see chapter 7). In his analysis of these concepts Wittgenstein, as a philosopher, does draw sharp lines and boundaries. In
this way he shows that psychological concepts within language-
games have a solid centre of meaning. Although he is convinced
that these concepts too show a certain elasticity at their edges,
since they are embedded in forms of life, this does not mean that
their meaning cannot be clearly defined within certain limits.

The 'evidence' for knowledge of human nature is to an important degree 'imponderable': 'Imponderable evidence includes
subtleties of glance, of gesture, of tone' (PI II xi, p. 228). The phrase
'imponderable evidence' is very apt. I take it to mean that in
everyday life knowledge of human nature is entirely non-
problematical and *certain* (since there is 'evidence'), but that it is
also a very *different* kind of evidence from the (universally valid)
evidence on which a claim to knowledge can be based, as in

---

[26] It particularly holds interest for cognitive psychologists who favour computer
simulations of the working of our minds, since it is seriously to be doubted
whether intuitive knowledge can be simulated at all, given the lack of rules.

science or in court (since the evidence is 'imponderable', 'un-
weighable'). Three characteristics can help to clarify the peculiar
nature of this imponderable evidence. (i) It is not based on clearly
definable grounds. (ii) It is unpredictable. (iii) There is no agreement about it. Wittgenstein formulates as follows the absence of
clearly definable grounds (i) which exclude doubt, as in mathematics: 'There is uncertainty and there is certainty; but from this it
does not follow that there are certain criteria' (MS 174, p. 11). In
this language-game we can talk about certainty (and uncertainty),
but not about knowing. To be able to talk about knowing we have
to be able to justify, verify, and falsify, in short, supply criteria. In
this case it is impossible to supply definite criteria, since the
evidence is essentially indefinite. This does not mean that one
can never be sure about someone else's feelings. One can be quite
sure about one's attitude to another person, only one cannot
know why one is so sure. This absence of definite criteria is
especially evident when I want to communicate my knowledge to
others. I can point to somebody who I think is typically pretending. If somebody asks me how I know this, I can often only
suggest that he take a good look at the face of the person in
question (RPP II, § 610). And often the only 'justification' I can
produce is that I saw a certain look in his eyes and that if you had
seen the same look you would have reached the same conclusion
(LW, § 923). But even so the statement 'I know that he was happy
about it' is not a statement of knowledge. All it means is that I
react to him in this way, without being unsure. The statement is
an expression of my attitude to him and for that very reason is not
knowledge. That is why my positive conviction will not be
accepted as evidence in a court: 'If I have known the other for a
long time, the court will also let my testimony count, lend weight
to it. But my absolute certainty will not mean *knowledge* to it.
For from knowledge it would have to be able to draw quite specific
conclusions' (MS 174, p. 12). If the reason for this conclusion
turns out to be concealed in an idiosyncratic logic, if I insist that I
am able to draw very specific conclusions even if nobody else can,
then they are not conclusions. Conclusions have to be valid for

everybody.[27] The conviction expressed by my attitude can be called intuition, but not knowledge. Once again the result is not a hopeless vagueness. The fact that there is no knowledge only means that one does not know the reason for something as often as in physics or mathematics.

The indefinable subtleties of behaviour are largely unpredictable (ii). 'What we regard as expression consists in incalculability' (CV, p. 73). If one could use knowledge of anatomical proportions to calculate exactly what kind of facial expression somebody will produce and how his face will move, then it would no longer be a facial expression. In any case we would no longer know how to react. And Wittgenstein compares this situation to people who only know the music of music boxes. We will expect these people too to make gestures to which we have no response (RPP II, § 696). Facial expressions, like soulful music, cannot be recognized or described via rules. Wittgenstein is saying that it is just as impossible to describe a facial expression in spatial, passport-like terms as it is to explain a musical theme via a paradigm. Any attempt to do so or any attempt to gives rules for expressive portraiture is likely to result in grotesqueness, in a caricature. The same musical theme can be played with genuine expression in countless ways, the same mood can be expressed in the face in countless different aspects. However, the unpredictability of behaviour involves more than the unpredictability of the physiognomy of aspects. It is also, more broadly, the fact that one cannot indicate what the essentially observable consequences are of 'inner states'. What, for instance, is exactly to be expected of somebody who is glad? Certainly there are consequences, but of a diffuse kind (PI II ix, p. 228). They cannot even be formulated in a general system and cannot in any case, according to Wittgenstein, be described like the reactions which characterize the state of a machine:

> It is important e.g. that one has to 'know' a human in order to judge which meaning has to be ascribed to his expressions of feelings and that yet one cannot describe what one knows in him. It is equally important that one

---

27 In MS 174, p. 12 Wittgenstein writes: 'And one cannot retort: "I draw specific conclusions from my knowledge, even if no one else can" – for *conclusions* have to hold for everyone.'

cannot say what the esssential consequences are of an inner state. If he was really glad, for instance, what is to be expected from him and what not? There are of course such characteristic consequences, but they are not to be described as the reactions that characterize the state of a physical object. (MS 174, p. 14)

Imponderable evidence for knowledge of human nature entails, finally, that the certainty of one person need not convince another (iii). This characteristic follows naturally from the other two. For if I am unable to produce reasons for my attitude and if I am also unable to make a prediction which has value for someone else, then my attitude of certainty need not convince another person:

> This is important: I may know from certain signs and knowledge of a person that he is glad, etc. But I cannot describe my observations to a third person; if he trusts these, convince him thereby of the genuineness of that joy, etc. (MS 174, p. 10)

Another person is not convinced here in the way that he may be convinced by a *proof*. He only becomes convinced by assuming the same kind of attitude and trusting the other person on that basis. To become convinced is to follow the same constitutive rules, to play the same language-game, and to use concepts based on the same indefinite signs.

In the third place Wittgenstein subscribes to the proposition (C) that there are no fixed, exact rules for knowledge of human nature. He asks two questions in this connection: (a) can one learn this knowledge? (b) Is there such a thing as an expert judgement here? One can acquire knowledge of human nature (a), but not by studying it as if it were a science. One may become convinced by certain signs that somebody is not pretending, but for this there are only certain overall rules, whereas the most important evidence is indeterminate (PI II ix, p. 228). The fact that the main evidence is imponderable has two consequences: (i) knowledge of human nature is mainly learned through particular instances and (ii) long experience is required.

Since it is constitutive for the language-game that sufficient evidence passes gradually into insufficient evidence, knowledge of human nature cannot be learned via fixed rules (i). The method of particular instances does not indicate a lack of psychological insight, but is the consequence of the constitution of concepts. In this connection Wittgenstein points out yet another analogy between 'Menschenkenntnis' and aesthetics. Is it possible, he asks, to describe the pattern in life's carpet of sincere and insincere expressions of feeling?

> Suppose it would really involve samples on a long conveyor belt.
> The belt passes before my eyes and I say one time 'this is sample S', one time 'this is sample V'. Often I do not know for some time which it is; often I finally say 'It was neither of them'.
> How could one be taught to recognize this sample? Simple samples are shown to me, then also more complicated ones from both types. It is almost like the way I learn to distinguish the style of two composers.
> But why does one draw this boundary between these samples that is so *hard to grasp*?
> Because it is of importance in our life. (MS 169, p. 69)

The restriction to particular instances does not mean that we do not learn, but only that we learn differently here from the way we learn arithmetic. The meaning of concepts is not definite and in view of the conceptual relation between learning and meaning this indeterminacy also displays itself in how we learn here.

Knowledge of human nature is not acquired in a (crash) course, it can only be learned 'durch Erfahrung'. 'Experience' is a risky term. It might be another word for knowledge, whereas Wittgenstein is thinking of a more fundamental, logical level. 'Erfahrung' and also the term 'Verstehen' used by Wittgenstein should not be associated with the hermeneutical tradition above all initiated by Dilthey. In that tradition 'understanding' refers to the specific kind of knowledge that we have of other people and cultural expressions. But Wittgenstein's use of 'understanding' has nothing to do with an intuition of the mental state which has led somebody to a given expressive action. This not only confines the meaning of understanding and experience to propositional knowledge, but is also too mentalistic. 'Understanding' seems to have more affinity with 'knowing how' than with 'knowing that'. It is a skill and in that sense so intimately related to our body and certain activities that we can barely provide an explicit, theoretical description of it. For instance, how does one learn to recognize that a portrait is a genuine Rembrandt? 'Not in the *same* way as one learns to calculate. A great deal of *experience* was necessary.

That is, the learner probably had to look at and compare a large number of pictures by various masters again and again' (LW, § 925).

One only gets to know the work of various masters by actually comparing paintings from various periods with each other, describing the differences between them, etc. In any case one does not get to know them by a theoretical course in art history. One needs to know people for a long time too before being able to assess the authenticity of their expressions. This is 'knowing' in the sense of 'knowing how': having talked to somebody on more than one occasion, having spent some time with him, having assumed the same attitude:

> Statement: 'I know that the bottle stood there' – How do you know that?' – 'I have seen it there' – If the statement is now: 'I know that he was glad' and it is asked 'How do you know that?' – What is the answer? Not simply the description of a physical fact. Part of it is for instance that I know the person. If in the courtroom a film could be shown in which the whole scene was reproduced, his facial expressions, his gestures, his voice, that could often be quite convincing. At least if he is no actor. But it works for instance only if those who judge the scene belong to the same culture. I would not know for instance what real joy looks like with the Chinese. (MS 174, p. 14)

Wittgenstein is not saying here that Chinese gladness must remain beyond our ken. Although Wittgenstein does not commit himself on such a question, we can infer from the way he characterizes forms of life that he holds no truck with this kind of provincialism. After all, a form of life is something that needs to a very important extent to be learned, so that it is quite possible to learn a different form of life.

The question of whether there is such a thing as professional knowledge of human nature (b) must similarly be answered by a finely shaded consideration. Here too, according to Wittgenstein, some people's judgements are better than those of others (PI II ix, p. 227). These differences need not be serious, certainly if one compares the situation here with the judgements of professional weather forecasters (cf. PI II ix, p. 228; LW, § 910, 911). Predictions are extremely hazardous even in physics, which has as regular a place in everyday life as judgements about other people. The fact that some people have a better knowledge of human nature than other people does not mean that one can indicate why their judgement is better. 'I could cite several things; but they would only be bits and pieces of a description' (LW, § 919). Fixed rules or a coherent system of rules cannot be given on account of the non-exhaustive determinacy of the language-game. Again a comparison with aesthetics is instructive. There too it is often imponderable evidence which leads a connoisseur to declare that a painting is not a genuine Rembrandt, although this can also be definitely proved by documentation. The similarity with 'Menschen-kenntnis' is that if documents are lacking, the expert will judge without giving his reasons. At any rate the reasons which he supplies are not based on generally recognized principles; they are reasons for him, his judgement is an expression of his attitude: 'A *connoisseur* couldn't make himself understood to a jury, for instance. That is, they would understand his statement, but not his reasons. He can give intimations to another connoisseur, and the latter will understand them' (LW, § 927). Once again, the non-exhaustive determinacy of 'Menschenkenntnis' does not result in an all-pervasive vagueness. For on the basis of evidence one can convince somebody that his psychological judgement is mistaken and on the basis of evidence one can teach him a better judgement. The point is that the evidence is largely indefinable, i.e. there are no *generally* recognized principles on which the evidence rests. Moreover, the vertical relations between 'knowing' and 'uncertainty' entail that the doubt which sometimes occurs in language-games based on imponderable evidence presupposes certainty. This certainty ('Einstellung zur Seele') is so enmeshed in our way of life that it can no longer itself be justified. Thus the relations discussed in chapter 3 between 'agreement in forms of life', 'certainty', and the 'foundational argument' turn out to play a crucial role in Wittgenstein's logic of self-knowledge and knowledge of other minds.

CHAPTER 6

THE MEANING OF ASPECTS

According to many critics, there is not only a lack of coherence between the fragments of part II of the *Philosophical Investigations*, but also between part I and part II themselves. In the previous chapter, however, I showed that Wittgenstein's remarks on the 'hidden inner' of other people in *Philosophical Investigations* II xi are systematically connected with the problem of psychological statements in the first person which he analyses in *Philosophical Investigations* I. The fragments about the 'hidden inner' are the least-known part of section xi and the *pièce de résistance* is formed by the richly variegated logic of 'aspect' and 'seeing-as'. Hardly anybody has known how to relate this logic to *Philosophical Investigations* I. Not surprisingly, therefore, none of the well-known monographs[1] on Wittgenstein devotes a chapter to 'seeing-as'. Those who have written about 'seeing-as' have been less concerned with its place in the *Investigations* and more interested in applying Wittgenstein's insights to philosophy of science and aesthetics.[2] In brief, those who have written about Wittgenstein have said little or nothing about 'seeing-as', and those who have written about 'seeing-as' have said little or nothing about Wittgenstein. In this chapter I want to show that the logic of 'seeing-as' does not form an island in Wittgenstein's philosophy, but is systematically connected with his definition of 'meaning' as use (PI, § 43). As a result, we have to reject the

---

[1] Fogelin (1976, chapter 4) and Finch (1977, chapter 11) are exceptions.

[2] For applications of Wittgenstein's ideas about 'seeing-as' to philosophy of science, see Hanson (1965) and Lewis (1976). Authors who have concerned themselves with the place of the logic of 'seeing-as' in the *Investigations* are, among others, Mounce (1982) and Budd (1987). Scruton (1974), Wollheim (1974), and Tilghman (1984) are among those who are interested in the application of the logic of 'seeing-as' to problems in aesthetics.

interpretation favoured by philosophers of science which takes Wittgenstein's analysis of 'seeing-as' to be an isolated study about the nature of perception. Sections 1, 2, 3, and 4 deal with the interpretation of 'seeing-as', section 5 returns to the connection between 'seeing-as' and the problem of meaning. I sketch this connection in what follows.

Dissatisfaction with the psychological theory of meaning held by Russell and James led Wittgenstein to his definition of meaning as use. The meaning of concepts is not embedded in a stream of consciousness but in a practice of language-games and forms of life. But the bed of a practice might in turn be interpreted as a form of reduction, a reduction of all kinds of meaning to a strict regime of rule-governed use. This would also involve the familiar consequences of reduction: any phenomenon which resists submission to the regime must be eliminated. The restriction which Wittgenstein imposes on himself in *Philosophical Investigations*, § 43 reveals a much more liberal attitude. He admits that his definition is too broad and cannot sufficiently account for variants of 'meaning'. The following passage in 1933 indicates which variants are concerned and also shows that he is still at sea about them:

> What do we want to understand by 'meaning' of a word? A characteristic feeling that accompanies the utterance (the hearing) of the word? (The and-feeling, if-feeling. James.), or do we want to use the word 'meaning' in a completely different way, e.g. say two words have the same meaning when the same grammatical rules apply to them? We can take it the way we want, but we have to know that these are two completely different ways of using the word 'meaning'. (Perhaps one can also speak of a specific feeling the chess-player experiences while making moves with the king.) (TS 213, p. 33)

Much later, in 1941, he specifically concludes that the Jamesian variants of 'meaning' do not coincide with use. In MS 180b he mentions a number of such meanings. The words of a poet, for instance, which may cut through one like a knife. Or words which one is reluctant to speak: an adieu, a self-confession. Such words are bearers of a significant tone and charged with all kinds of emotions. Meaning here seems to be something that is experienced rather than the rule-guided use of a word in a language-game: 'And if one wants to speak of meaning here, it does not consist in the use of words.' (MS 180b, p. 6); 'The meaning of a

word, I said, is its use. But an important addition has to be made
to this' (MS 180b, p. 8). After this fragment Wittgenstein goes on
to discuss a different but related category of psychological phenomena: feelings of tendency or, more generally, the experience of
the intention of one's words. This category too does not seem to
submit to a regime of rule-governed use.[3] A feeling of tendency
occurs, for instance, when we are about to say something. Before
speaking we clearly experience an intention and this intention is,
precisely, to give our words their characteristic meaning. But an
intention as experience seems at odds with Wittgenstein's definition of meaning as use. Wittgenstein treats at length of these
germinal experiences in *Philosophical Investigations* I, § 633-663
and II ix, pp. 217, 218, and 219 (see chapter 7, § 5). I confine myself
here to the first category, the so-called 'secondary meanings'.

Wittgenstein distinguishes between the primary and secondary
meanings of words (PI II xi, p. 216). But his example is a bizarre
one. He asks whether, given the words 'fat' and 'thin', we would
be inclined to call Tuesday 'thin' and Wednesday 'fat'. He seriously calls this secondary meaning a 'meaning', yet this 'meaning'
seems to be more private, more subjective, and more an experience than the primary, rule-guided use. Many words have such
secondary meanings, and proper names are exemplary in this
respect.[4] Prosaically speaking, a proper name is a label which is
tagged onto us at birth, its meaning being a kind of gesture
towards us. But apart from identifying its bearer a name can also
be used in a different way, on account of an autonomous secret
concealed in it: the name itself seems to have absorbed the qualities of its bearer and is replete with meaning. This aspect becomes
clear by comparing for instance the statement 'Beethoven was
born in Bonn in 1770' with the cry 'Beethoven!', on recognition of
his music. In the latter case the name has become the bearer of a
significant tone, and this tone is heard in it. Not only words but
also vowels possess this kind of secret: 'For me the vowel *e* is
yellow' (PI II ix, p. 216). The example is rather like Rimbaud's

---

[3] Despite appearances to the contrary, however, rule-guided descriptions *can* be
given of 'feelings of tendency'. See chapter 7, § 5.
[4] Wittgenstein has been inspired here by Goethe's view of proper names. See
also *Remarks on the Philosophy of Psychology* I, § 326, 336, 341.

vowel symbolism: 'A noir, E blanc, I rouge, U vert, O bleu; voyelles'.[5]

In this physiognomical respect I take secondary meanings to be related to visual aspects, to the meaning of facial expressions, e.g.: 'Goethe's signature intimates something Goethian to me. To that extent it is like a face, for I might say the same of his face' (RPP I, § 336). The name is now no longer a label tagged to the bearer, but a picture of the bearer. Alternately understanding words in a primary and secondary meaning is analogous to the recognition of different visual aspects. 'A person's name is *seen* as a portrait' (LW, § 70). This analogy also exists negatively, as when people are unable to recognize aspects or certain 'faces' by their names. Wittgenstein has this analogy in mind when he talks about 'aspect-blindness': 'The importance of this concept lies in the connexion between the concepts of "seeing an aspect" and "experiencing the meaning of a word". For we want to ask "What would you be missing if you did not *experience* the meaning of a word?" (PI II xi, p. 214). Wittgenstein also speaks of 'meaning-blindness', 'sensation-blindness', and 'Gestalt-blindness'.[6] A prototypical example of aspect-blindness is somebody who is unable to hear or see something in a certain way, as opposed to somebody who has a musical ear or a painter's eye. What does somebody lose who can only use proper names as labels? And what about somebody who has no sense of how a word loses all meaning and becomes purely acoustic when he utters it a number of times in succession? At first sight this kind of person would not seem to lose a great deal. It is a plain fact that in everyday communication proper names function as labels rather than as symbolic experiences. One takes as little interest in such experiences as in other people's dreams.

---

[5] See Rimbaud (1973, pp. 78-79).
[6] Wittgenstein uses these terms indiscriminately (cf. RPP I, § 189). To my knowledge the term 'Gestalt-blind' as such does not occur in Gestalt psychology. But Köhler does talk about a form of blindness to organization: 'After what has been said about organization, we cannot be surprised to learn that serious lesions in the optical centre of the brain may produce a kind of "blindness" in persons, who at the same time are not deprived of vision. Careful examination of such a case by Gelb and Goldstein has shown that, here, the field of vision has undergone a radical change, organization having disappeared almost completely, so that the field shows a more or less chaotic character' (Köhler 1929, pp. 129-130).

At any rate they do not form the essence of communication (cf. RPP I, § 202).

But if we take a different angle from that of ordinary communication, then secondary meaning has far more than a subsidiary role. Wittgenstein already suggests this by pointing out that secondary meanings and aspects are pre-eminently exploited in an aesthetic context. In fact, in aesthetics the world seems turned upside down: there secondary meanings and aspects are of primary importance (cf. LW, § 634).

But in Wittgenstein's view aesthetics is not a separate world, entirely independent of a more pragmatic context. On the contrary, he is convinced of the kinship between aesthetic phenomena and the meaning of concepts in language-games and forms of life: 'Why should I say at all what meaning is? Why should I not say: Language, music and much that we call similar to language is meaningful? (MS 180b, p. 6). Intonation and interpunction[7] are important musical elements in language and Wittgenstein's emphasis on the expressive as opposed to the informative use of language is most certainly inspired by the analogy with music and poetry (cf. RPP I, § 888).

The consequence of this is that secondary meanings and aspects play a more important role in ordinary communication than is generally thought. The tendency to understand words in a 'soulful' sense may not be ordinary, but neither is the opposite: 'But the opposite of being full of soul is being mechanical' (RPP I, § 324). A world devoid of such physiognomical aspects looks suspiciously like a behaviouristic geometry of stimulus and response. In this kind of world proper names may just as well be replaced by numbers – as in prisons.

Against this background it is perhaps less surprising that Wittgenstein uses rather pejorative epithets to describe those who are aspect-blind. This type of person is not only called 'prosaic' but also insensitive and even mentally ill.[8] We often feel about the mentally ill that they react and speak more like automatons, says Wittgenstein. Like the meaning-blind they will be insensitive to

---

[7] The same emphasis on musical aspects of language is found in Spengler (1923, p. 694). See also chapter 5, note 18.

[8] See *Remarks on the Philosophy of Psychology* I, § 197, 198, 216, 224.

Rimbaud's vowel symbolism and will read a poem not as a poem but as a telegram. And they will only be able to use proper names when the person in question is actually standing before them. According to Wittgenstein, secondary meanings of words and aspects most certainly do derive their meaning from their connection with forms of life, even if they are not subject to a more or less strict regime of rule-guided use. Before explaining this connection more precisely (§ 5), I first take a further look at the logic of 'seeing-as'.

1. 'Meaning-theory' versus 'Gestalt-theory'

The human eye is very expressive. One can look daggers at somebody, but also look straight through him. Yet there are psychologists and philosophers who claim that we cannot 'see' a look. According to the British empiricists Locke and Berkeley, the senses are only capable of registering form and colour, the intellect being the instrument for all other visual aspects. In nineteenth century psychology this dichotomy was developed into a division between sensation and perception. The Gestalt psychologist Köhler has called this strategy the 'Meaning-theory'.[9] An assumption of this theory is that sensation reveals simple and neutral sense data. Sure enough, we do not have such virginal impressions in everyday life, but this life is buried under a layer of habits and associations. Nevertheless there is a hard core of neutral sensations, only the wheat must be separated from the chaff. And for that one must be an introspective psychologist. Köhler opposes his own 'Gestalt-theory' to this 'Meaning-theory'. In his theory a look, a penetrating glance, is 'just as' visible as form and colour.

---

[9] Köhler discusses the Meaning-theory in his chapter 'The Viewpoint of Introspection' (Köhler 1929). The following is one of many formulations of this theory: 'A decisive motive in introspectionism is the belief that true sensations are independent of subjective attitude and depend only upon local stimulation as purely local experiences' (p. 73). According to Köhler, the experience does depend on 'attitude' (pp. 140-141) and not so much on molecular physiological processes as on molar and organized wholes in the visual field.

I submit that Wittgenstein's discussions of 'seeing-as' are primarily aimed at untangling the conceptual knots in the debate between the Meaning-theory and the Gestalt-theory. Both theories are misleading in his view. Usually, however, a different twist is given to his discussion, which is interpreted as if Wittgenstein is formulating a view of perception in general. He is supposed to be showing that what we perceive depends on concepts which we have acquired with language and that visual experiences cannot be separated from conceptual knowledge. Now this interpretation is not so much incorrect as uninteresting: the general philosophical position – Wittgenstein's internalism (see chapter 3, § 3) – that concepts regulate our view of reality was adopted much earlier by Wittgenstein in his discussion of rules and the relation of rules to empirical statements. Why then should he want to devote so many fragments to this position much later? But this interpretation is also misleading. For by incorporating the account of 'seeing-as' in traditional discussions of perception, critics[10] usually rank Wittgenstein with the opponents of the Meaning-theory – the term is avoided, but not the names of philosophers like Locke, who was certainly not consulted by Wittgenstein here and whose name only increases the risk of anachronism. Thus Wittgenstein is put in with the Gestalt-theory – a name that is also avoided, which only increases the confusion. As we shall see (in § 3), Wittgenstein has serious reasons for rejecting the approach of Gestalt psychology too. He agrees with Köhler that the look in somebody's eyes can be seen, but not with his argument that the look is a visual property. An additional drawback of putting Wittgenstein in either of both camps is that the logical point of his account is undervalued. Both the Meaning-theory and the Gestalt-theory are genetic-psychological approaches aimed at explaining the nature of perception. The insight that Wittgenstein wants to reach here must be capable of being reached without an explanation. For any explanation of the phenomenon requires the same conceptual clarification as the unexplained phenomenon itself. This is clearly indicated by his criticism of the Meaning-theory, which

---

[10] Vesey (1976) and Lewis (1976) 'clarify' Wittgenstein's view by contrasting it with Locke's theory of perception.

says that the 'pure' perception must be disconnected from associations and habits: '"What I *see* can't be the expression, because the recognition of the expression depends on my knowledge, on my general acquaintance with human behaviour." But isn't this merely an historical observation?' (RPP I, § 1073). In any case it is not a conceptual observation. Köhler's theory is not conceptual either, convinced as he is that the Meaning-theory is based on a physiological prejudice and his own Gestalt-theory on a physiological judgement:

> 'When you get away from your physiological prejudices, you'll find nothing in the fact that the glance of the eye can be seen.' Certainly I too say that I see the glance that you throw someone else. And if somone wanted to correct me and say I don't really *see* it, I should hold this to be a piece of stupidity. (RPP I, § 1101)

So Wittgenstein does not give in to Köhler's view either, the view that a look in somebody's eyes is a visual property. In fact, Köhler's approach is for him an exemplary case of the problems in psychology: the experimental method and the problem fail to mesh. The Gestalt psychologist and his introspective opponent both believe that they can solve the problem of 'seeing-as' by making the concept 'seeing' more exact, i.e. more physiological. This way of refining concepts may serve purely scientific purposes, but not philosophical ones, according to Wittgenstein. And the problem of 'seeing-as' is largely philosophical, and so conceptual. Wittgenstein's philosophical inquiry draws conceptual boundaries and has nothing to do with physiological hypotheses (RPP I, § 1104). He does not explain one psychological phenomenon ('seeing') by the other ('seeing-as'), or vice versa, but by noting similarities and differences they are grouped or ordered with regard to each other and related phenomena. Only by ordering the phenomena in this kind of way, according to Wittgenstein, can the mystery of 'seeing-as' be solved.

What is mysterious about 'seeing-as'? It is that a visual experience changes although nothing changes optically. If I suddenly see my brother in my father's face, if I see the face of an acquaintance in a crowd, the object of perception seems to undergo a metamorphosis. At any rate something changes in my way of seeing things, the crowd looks different from the way it did before, now that I have noticed an acquaintance. Before describing this enigma further, we need to look at the different kinds of aspect-changes that Wittgenstein distinguishes.

One kind is optical aspects (RPP I, § 970, 1017). Purely optical aspects occur automatically and change shape rather like after-images – which does not affect Wittgenstein's internalistic view that optical aspects too are conditional on familiarity with concepts and practices. A favourite example is this figure, derived from Köhler. A change of aspect occurs if one first sees a black cross against a white background and next a white cross against a black background.

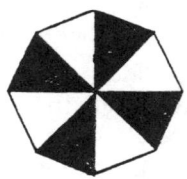

A sub-class of optical aspects is formed by organization aspects (cf. LW, § 529-530). These aspects also involve simple modifications of visual impressions, but are created by a certain arrangement of the impression. In this figure one can first see the lines closest to each other as 'belonging to each other', with three wide spaces in between, and next the lines farthest apart as 'belonging to each other', with three narrow spaces in between (LW, § 444).

No concepts other than visual ones are really necessary for the description of optical aspects and organization aspects. I may say that I see a 'white windmill' with 'four sails' in the double cross or that I see the white cross as 'four corners of a piece of paper', but people will shrug their shoulders. We are less indifferent about such descriptions when dealing with a second class distinguished by Wittgenstein, conceptual aspects (RPP II, § 509). For these aspects there is often an apt formulation. Not only that, the experience of aspect can *only* be expressed by other than visual concepts: '"See F as "

ㅓ

could not be understood before something quite different has been said. For would I understand "See this triangle as that triangle"? There must first be a conceptual connection' (RPP II, § 510). We need here, say, the indication that this F has to be seen as an F 'facing left'. Facial expressions, in my view, are more important examples of conceptual aspects. For instance, somebody's face can suddenly turn from expressionless to expressive and this change of aspect can only be described by concepts like 'gloomy', 'mean', or 'friendly'. In fact, a 'purely visual' or geometrical description is hard to imagine. As Wittgenstein aptly puts it, a painter can paint a 'staring eye' and so render staring by form and colour, yet he need not be able to describe staring geometrically (RPP I, § 1077).

Mainly on the basis of the fact that the description of conceptual aspects requires mastery of many alternative concepts (LW, § 699), Wittgenstein concludes that optical aspects are more funda-mental. A child who cannot yet talk is quite capable of indicating the aspects of the double cross simply by pointing alternately to the white and black crosses (LW, § 701). The distinction in level is emphatically a conceptual distinction in language-games. By observing that optical aspects are more fundamental than con-ceptual aspects, Wittgenstein is not for instance siding with Köhler's view that the perception of aspects and meaning is in any case determined by the purely optical principle of organization (see § 3). According to Köhler, the optical organization of wholes in the field of vision precedes the learning and attribution of meaning. Köhler accuses the associationists of paying no atten-tion to wholes and only to parts on the retina, but ultimately his own description of wholes falls into parts too: a purely visual part, in which units are formed and separated, and a meaning-part which slavishly follows the shadings of the first part and is in fact

made possible by it. For why is it, asks Köhler,[11] that of their own
accord so few people see a 4 in this figure?

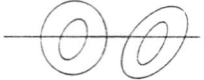

Obviously because they do not see the appropriate lines for it as
belonging together. And in general Köhler claims that we cannot
take something for something if we cannot see it as a whole. But
that would mean, according to Wittgenstein, that a child first
learns to answer the question 'How do you see that?', and only
then the question 'What is that, what does it mean?'. It would
mean that the child first has to see a chair as a visual whole in
order to recognize it ultimately as a piece of furniture: 'Do I grasp
that chair visually as a thing, and which of my reactions shews
this? Which of a man's reactions shew that he recognizes something as a thing, and which, that he *sees* something as a whole,
thingishly?' (RPP I, § 978). The point here is that the question is
senseless, since an answer leads to a position outside of language-
games, which is impossible according to Wittgenstein's internalism. Optical aspects are not fundamental because they are
supposed to be the truest copy of reality, but because less conceptual skill is required for their description. But even the
primitive reaction of a child to an optical aspect (pointing) is not
yet an expression of seeing-as (RPP I, § 1048). The pointing can
only be called an expression of seeing-as in combination with
other expressions showing a certain way of treating things, a skill.
Optical aspects cannot be described by ostensive definitions alone.

   After this inventory of aspects it is time to look at Wittgenstein's account of aspect-seeing. The following fragment provides
a fairly complete description:

> If this constellation is always and continuously a face for me, then I have not
> named an *aspect*. For *that* means that I always *encounter* it as a face, treat it
> as a face, whereas the peculiarity of the aspect is that I see something into a
> picture. So that one might say: I see something that isn't there at all, that

---

[11] See Köhler (1929, p. 155). Wittgenstein draws this figure too and mentions
Köhler. See *Remarks on the Philosophy of Psychology*, § 982, 983, 987.

does not reside in the figure, so that it may surprise me that I can see it (at least, when I reflect upon it afterwards). (RPP I, § 1028)

The phenomenon seems to be characterized by three features. (1) When an aspect is registered, the object of perception does not undergo any change in colour, form, or distance to the observer. That is why the change to two ways of seeing something is so mysterious, for how can a change of experience be accounted for if optically and geometrically speaking everything stays the same? The best way of bringing out the paradox, according to Wittgenstein, is to say that nothing, and yet everything, has changed, or that everything has stayed the same and yet everything is new (RPP II, § 474). If there is any geometrical or optical change, no matter how slight, the mystery immediately disappears, since a physical explanation can be given. (2) We only become conscious of aspects in a certain change ('Wechsel') (RPP I, § 1034). Only when foreground and background change in the double cross figure does the viewer become conscious of an aspect. Wittgenstein also describes this feature via three other conceptual characteristics. (i) An aspect does not remain fixed, but dawns (RPP I, § 1021; LW, § 518). If an aspect were to remain fixed, it would belong to the object as a physical property. But the physical shape of the object does not change, so that an aspect is not a new physical property of the object and cannot remain fixed, no matter how briefly. (ii) The expression of a perception of aspect is essentially the expression of a new perception (LW, § 518). It cannot be the expression of an earlier or older perception, as the perception of all relevant physical properties does not reveal the aspect. The perception of an aspect in this figure

is essentially unstable; a fact which is expressed by a statement such as 'it could also be a duck, it could also be a rabbit', or by an expression like 'Now it is this, now it is that'. Not that this formulation follows invariably; the point is that one does not normally say 'Now it is this' *before* a change of aspect (LW, § 521). (iii) The experience of an aspect is akin to the expression of astonishment (LW, § 565). This is not a psychological characterization either, but a logical one. An aspect does not remain fixed, but dawns. Therefore the attention needed to see a dawning aspect cannot logically speaking be static; it is dynamic (RPP II, § 512). The attention is a form of astonishment and astonishment cannot logically speaking be static either (RPP II, § 528). (3) In a change of aspect an object does not show itself from different angles, but is alternately a duck or a rabbit, foreground or background (RPP II, § 475). Although the drawing contains (geometrically) the figure of both a duck and a rabbit, the characteristic feature of an aspect is that the drawing is the figure of a rabbit, not of a duck, or vice versa. The surprising thing, therefore, is not the flexibility of interpretations and perspectives, but their *exclusivity*. The ambiguity as such cannot be seen; at most one can switch back and forth between two alternative and exclusive ways of seeing. For there to be astonishment and so seeing-as, one has to become conscious of the identity of these exclusive ways of seeing. If one merely sees duck and rabbit consecutively, as two different but not yet mutually exclusive interpretations, one has not yet experienced a change of aspect. The importance of seeing-as, says Wittgenstein (LW, § 172), is that the problems of the concept of seeing come to a head in this phenomenon. And in fact, only when seeing a change of aspect does one become conscious of an aspect and so of the complicated relationship between seeing and thinking, seeing and knowledge or interpretation. For here an optical picture seems to remain stable, while something different, a way of seeing, changes. And with this realization a wedge seems to be driven between seeing and thinking.

2. Seeing-as and organization

Attempts by psychologists to explain 'seeing-as' often come down to a resolution of factors. Some, like Köhler, explain the change of aspect by a sensory change – a change in organization and the visual field; others, like James, explain it by an intellectual change – only a change in the imagination takes place, optically everything stays the same. In this section I concentrate on Köhler, since Wittgenstein debates with him extensively. The following section is devoted to the Meaning-theory.

Köhler's introduction of 'organization' in the discussion about perception follows from his conviction that there is something fundamentally wrong with the Meaning-theory. The meaning which in everyday life seems inherent in all kinds of objects was explained away by the introspectionists as the product of associations and experience. The real perception is much plainer, since it remains true to the patterns on the retina, patterns which admit of one interpretation only. It is the psychologist's task to separate carefully these simple and neutral sensations from their associative ballast. But microscopic attention to simple sensations leads to short-sightedeness, most notably in the case of ambivalent images and, more generally, 'Gestaltqualitäten',[12] according to Köhler. For if, as the introspectionists assume, the perception is unambiguously determined by the mosaic on the retina, this creates the problem that the pattern has to correspond with two alternating perceptions. But if length and form are unambiguously determined by the mosaic on the retina, right angles cannot suddenly seem obtuse and lines cannot switch, almost gratuitously, in their relative lengths. Gestalt properties are also overlooked in this way. Similarly, a number of striking features of perception cannot be accounted for on the basis of isolated sensations, aroused by equally isolated local stimuli. If one dissolves a piece of soap in a glass of water, the water appears clouded, says Köhler (Köhler, p. 145). But this aspect disappears if one covers the glass with a carton containing a small hole, so that only a fragment of the water can be seen. The same applies to the property of a surface which feels rough to the hand. In a purely local contact we feel no roughness. More of such properties with a 'supra-local' character are: symmetrical, round, angular, graceful,

---

12 According to Köhler, this term was introduced by von Ehrenfels to emphasize specific qualities of wholes. Examples of such qualities are 'major' and 'minor' (Köhler 1929, p. 147), which are also discussed by Wittgenstein (PI II xi, p. 209).

slender, minor and major. In all these cases the phenomenal reality shows properties which lack a one-to-one relation with the physical reality.

According to Köhler, they are not the product of associations or, as James said about ambivalent figures, the illusory effect of imagination. A much more fundamental principle is operative here: a process of organization. A striking property of visual fields is that certain areas belong together. When I look at my desk, I perceive a number of shaded units standing detached and segregated in a field: a brown book against the background of a desktop, a fountain pen, a cup, and tissues. The existence of such units implies their segregation in the environment. The specific reality of this kind of organization becomes all the more clearer when one tries – in vain – to form other units than those given in the original organization.

Köhler expressly denies the effect of knowledge and meaning on the formation of the original organizations. One might object, after all, that these organizations have a psychological reality, but that they are not actually a part of the sensory perception. We have long been acquainted with the objects on the desk, so that they are loaded, so to speak, with projected meanings. But Köhler believes that the perception as such cannot be explained on the basis of meaning. As a sensory unit the object exists prior to the process of meaning-acquisition. Köhler goes so far as to claim:

> ... that it is precisely the original organization and segregation of circumscribed wholes which makes it possible for the sensory world to appear so utterly imbued with meaning to the adult, because, in its gradual entrance into the sensory field, meaning follows the lines drawn by natural organization. It usually enters into segregated wholes. (Köhler, pp. 115-116)

So meaning is not explained by prior association, but association by prior *organization*. If a change of aspect occurs, the person in question experiences a change in the organization of the visual impression. This change is visual in kind, according to Köhler, but not comparable to a change of parts in the visual field, like form and colour. For in a change of aspect the parts of the visual field do not show any change. A change takes place in another visual feature, organization, which, although more fundamental than form and colour, is 'just as' visible (Köhler, pp. 30, 201).

The importance which Köhler attaches to 'organization' is taken seriously by Wittgenstein. An example of organization aspects is when I suddenly see the solution of a puzzle picture. Before there were only branches and twigs, now there is suddenly a human shape: 'My visual impression has changed and now I recognize that it has not only shape and colour but also a quite particular organization' (PI II ix, p. 196). A change has occurred in the sense that the lines now belong together differently from when the shape was still unnoticed.

Wittgenstein wonders whether this change of shape can be attributed to a change of organization, as Köhler would have it. Is the use of the term right here? 'Why does one here need a word – *essentially* – that already has another meaning?' (RPP I, § 1119). Normally organizing means arranging something, getting to know one's way around in something, describing something via a system or rule. Now all these are activities that one might expect of a secretary, but not of somebody who suddenly perceives an aspect. Strictly speaking, this person does not organize anything, does not do anything with the picture. If one asked somebody to 'organize' a few lines on paper in this sense, what would he do? 'Perhaps he is to count them two by two, or put them in a drawer, or look at them etc.' (RPP I, § 1120). The meaning of the term in 'The organization of my visual impression changes' does not therefore have the same application as in 'The organization of this club has changed'. Something has clearly been done in the latter case and it can also be specified *in what way* the organization has given the club a different appearance. But this specification cannot be given when the row of dots changes shape. The 'change' of organization does not really change here, in the way that a shirt and even somebody's face may lose colour. It is impossible to indicate with regard to what other organization the new organization is different. With colour, however, this is possible: one can compare colours by means of a sample; but one does not show a sample of an organization. One does not for instance tell somebody to look especially at that part of a drawing,

so that he will get the same impression of an organization that
you had.

To call the organization of a visual impression a visual property itself is not only unilluminating but also mystifying. For if
organization is put on a par with form and colour, it must also be
visible. Not only form and colour remain identical in a change of
aspect, but the organization too need not change (LW, § 515). If
one now maintains that the organization of the impression is
perceived, but no longer as an optical property of a physical object,
then it becomes tempting to call organization a property of an
inner object – the visual sensation itself. It is this line of reasoning which informs the following fragment:

> If you put the organization of a visual impression on a level with shapes and
> colours, you are proceeding from the idea of the visual impression as an inner
> object. Of course, this makes the object into a chimera, a queerly shifting
> construction. For the similarity to a picture is now impaired. (PI II xi, p. 196)

Wittgenstein calls 'inner picture' a mystification, not because it is
said to be inner, but because it is an imitation of what is understood by a physical picture. Belonging to the same category, it is
also a thing, it also has properties by means of which it can be
specified, such as organization. In this way one secret is explained
by another and the problem is not solved but merely shifted to
new ground, for instead of a physical picture an inner picture now
has to be investigated.

For all his criticism of Köhler, Wittgenstein too recognizes the
importance of 'organization' for the perception of aspects. Often
aspects can in fact be described via an arrangement and segregation of parts in the visual field. But the objection to Köhler's
emphasis on organization, says Wittgenstein, is that other kinds
of aspects – conceptual aspects – are left out of consideration (RPP
I, § 1113). And since conceptual aspects illustrate so well to what
extent the logic of 'seeing-as' is bound up with 'thinking' and
'interpreting', it is no surprise that Köhler has trimmed off these
branches of the concept and so wrongly reduces 'seeing-as' to
'seeing'. A second objection, I think, is aimed against Köhler's
use of the term organization. Köhler makes it seem as if the
description of an organized visual picture is the description of
something that we *do*: the taking together of initially chaotic

elements. Now the organization of the visual impression is certainly related to the notation of an aspect, but it is not true that the change of aspect can only be described in terms of organization, foreground or background, if these concepts occur in a description of aspect at all (cf. RPP I, § 1023). Ironically, Wittgenstein accuses Köhler here of making an error similar to one discovered by Köhler in an explanation of aspects which he rejected. For Köhler the attempts of some psychologists to explain aspects by eye movements inadmissibly reduce 'seeing-as' to a marginal phenomenon.[13] Wittgenstein's criticism of the theory of eye movements is also instructive as regards his objections to Köhler. He says that there can be no doubt that aspects are often evoked by an eye movement, by a shifting of one's gaze (RPP I, § 974, 997). This causal connection has led some psychologists to believe that such experiences are purely optical and that they can also be described as such. Wittgenstein concludes that in that case one can replace the order 'See this figure as...!' by the order: 'Follow the figure with your eyes in such and such a way'. But one does not and in fact cannot give such an order, since one would have to demonstrate the shifting of one's own gaze and that is not something one normally thinks about. One simply does not notice the trajectory of one's own gaze, especially in the case of smaller pictures. Hence this conclusion:

> But it is not true that an experience which is traceably connected with the movement of the eyes, an experience that can be produced by such a movement, can for that reason be described by means of a sequence of optical images.
> (Any more than someone who imagines a note is imagining a sequence of disturbances of the air.) (RPP I, § 990)

According to Wittgenstein, the experience can only be described analogically, with the help of concepts which do not belong to the

---

[13] Köhler writes of eye movements: 'I was once told that all the observations of gestalt psychology are very old and have long been explained by the kinesthetic experiences which occur during eye-movements' (Köhler 1929, p. 129). His criticism of this view is Wittgensteinian, or rather, Wittgenstein's criticism is Köhlerian: 'But we see that, instead of having solved the problem, we have only shifted it from one place to another, for now we have to solve the problem of the segregation of wholes in the temporal and spatial extension of kinesthetic experiences' (*ibid.*).

description of the figure itself nor to the description of 'organiza-tional' or organic changes.

3. Seeing-as and interpretation

Köhler's theory was a reaction to the Meaning-theory. There were many supporters of this theory, one of whom was William James.[14] In a change of aspect, according to James, the object of perception remains the same, but something changes in one's imagination and one's thinking. What changes is that the same visual experience is subjected to a different interpretation. For introspective psychologists too the problems of perception come to a head in the seeing of aspects, for only there is the psychologist vividly confronted with the effect of association and interpre-tation on perception. This effect must be combatted so as to guarantee the purity of sensations.

Wittgenstein refers to the Meaning-theory when he asks whe-ther it is introspection which tells him that in a change of aspect genuine seeing or interpretation is involved (RPP I, § 2). He himself prefers to speak of a genuinely different visual experience and not just of interpretation. His reason for this is the first step towards a logical specification of 'seeing something according to an interpretation': '... interpreting is an action ... Seeing isn't an action but a state' (RPP I, § 1). The logical specification of 'seeing something according to an interpretation' results at first in the view that there is no question of 'interpretation' in the case of seeing-as. In accordance with a fairly established meaning of

---

[14] According to Köhler, Helmholtz and Wundt are supporters of the Meaning-theory (Köhler 1929). He does not explicitly rank James with them, but in his final chapter he observes that James, despite his attack on psychological atomism, 'clearly fails to recognize natural segregations in the sensory field' (p. 283). Though James is opposed to atomism, his psychology remains introspective, as his explanation of ambiguous figures shows: 'We may then sum up our study of illusions by saying that they in no wise undermine our view that every spatial determination of things is originally given in the shape of a sensation of the eyes. They only show how very potent certain imagined sensations of the eyes may become' (James 1890, II, p. 266). The imagined sensations are the effect of 'habit or probability', according to James (p. 258).

interpretation Wittgenstein states: 'When we interpret, we make a conjecture, we express a hypothesis, which may subsequently turn out false' (RPP I, § 8). And in a protoversion of this fragment he says: 'Interpreting is an articulated process, like translating, deciphering; to see a drawing as this and this is amorphous' (MS 123, 17-5-1941). This might for instance be a hypothesis about a text which at first seems to resist clarification or which seems to conceal more than one meaning. Interpretation in this sense is a purely intellectual process by which the intention of a text is reconstructed. Often this is a laborious process of fitting the pieces together. In this juridical-exegetical sense the question of whether one can see something according to an interpretation seems almost paradoxical: 'The question represents it as a queer fact; as if something were being forced into a form it did not really fit. But no squeezing, no forcing took place here' (PI II xi, p. 200). And in the case of seeing-as there is not only no fitting together of pieces, but there is no hypothesizing either, nor verifying, nor falsifying. For Wittgenstein this is reason enough to say that seeing-as does not involve interpretation as defined above.

Yet he continues to talk about a relation between 'seeing' and 'interpreting' in 'seeing-as': 'Well, the expression of this seeing *is* related to the expression of interpreting' (LW, § 179). The relation is distinctly logical, not psychological. The fact that the formulations are related means that a relation in language-games is involved. And what other relation can Wittgenstein have in mind than *vertical* relations between language-games? The language-game of seeing-as is complex and presupposes vertical relations with other language-games. 'Seeing-as' is vertically constituted by 'seeing', but also by 'thinking', 'interpreting', and 'imagining'. Partly on account of these vertical ramifications, the visual experience cannot be specified separately from 'interpretation'. If one does try to separate the interpretative from the 'purely' visual, one ignores the vertical relations which constitute 'seeing-as' and commits the ground-floor fallacy (see chapter 2, § 2). And that is exactly what introspectionism does.

The following diagnosis of the problem shows that the inclination to specify 'seeing-as' separately from 'interpretation' is in fact due to a disregard of vertical relations. The illustration in a text-book of physics can be seen in various ways: as an open box without a lid, as a cube made of wire, etc.

> Now how remarkable it is, that we are able to use the words of the *interpretation* also to describe what is immediately perceived!
> Here at first we should like to reply: This description of the immediate experience by means of an *interpretation* is only an indirect description. (RPP I, § 9)

It is indirect in the sense that the experience supposedly has an intrinsic character which at most favours a certain interpretation. In that case it would be possible to specify the nature of the experience *without* applying such interpretations. For instance, three interpretations 'A', 'B', 'C' might be given of a picture in a book, corresponding to three ways of seeing or experiencing, A, B, and C, such that A favours interpretation 'A', B 'B', and C 'C'. The idea that 'seeing-as' has an intrinsic character that can be identified separately from interpretation presupposes that the concept functions on the same level as 'seeing'. However, as Wittgenstein rightly remarks, many people have learned the word 'seeing', but have never used it to describe aspects (RPP I, § 12). Now suppose, he goes on to say, that somebody does not know the use of seeing-as. I ask him to see a cube as a wire frame. Can he understand this request? And what can I do if he doesn't understand? It doesn't help to point to the picture, or to instruct him to inspect his mind.

> And if he does understand me, how is that manifested? Isn't it just in this, that he too says he is now *seeing* the figure as a wire frame? (RPP I, § 12)

> Thus the inclination to use that form of verbal expression is a characteristic utterance of the experience. (And an *utterance* is not a *symptom*.) (RPP I, § 13)

The verbal formulation is constitutive for seeing-as and since this formulation is akin to that of interpretation, the experience cannot be identified independently of an interpretation. The formulation 'I see it as a wire frame' constitutes the change of aspect and is not an indirect description of it. If it were, a more direct specification would have to be possible. In a first draft of *Remarks on the Philosophy of Psychology*, § 9 and 12, Wittgenstein explicitly states that a more direct description is impossible:

'Now I see this line as a wire, now as the side of a prism.' – Is that not simply a case of seeing different three-dimensional figures? But how is it with this? Is it an *indirect* description when I say I see this figure now as this, now as that prism? Could I say more directly: 'Now as figure A, now as figure B' – while avoiding to use a word that is connected with other sensations. (MS 123, 18-5-1941)

But a 'more direct' description, for instance indication of the form or organization of the picture or the introspection of visual experiences, is still not a description of an aspect, as is clearly shown by the case of somebody who has yet to learn the meaning of 'seeing-as'. The essential thing about an expression of an aspect-experience, as the following section will make clear, is that the experience is compared via a verbal formulation with the experience of other visual objects. This comparison is not an indirect description in the way that an interpretation is, but a primary expression of the experience:

> The question whether what is involved is a seeing or an act of interpreting arises because an interpretation becomes an expression of experience. And the interpretation is not an indirect description; no, it is the primary expression of the experience. (RPP I, § 20)

This kind of primary expression is obviously not on a par with, say, an expression of pain, but presupposes skill in many other language-games. In this respect seeing-as functions within a complex language-game, a language-game that has vertical relations with other language-games. If a 'direct' description is impossible, then 'I see it as ...', contrary to appearances, cannot be called indirect either.

4. Seeing and thinking

According to Wittgenstein, the problem of 'seeing-as' is not solved by reducing the concept to a different concept, but by describing the similarities and differences between 'seeing-as' and 'seeing' and 'seeing-as' and 'thinking'. 'Seeing-as' is a highly peculiar concept, since it has vertical relations with more than one concept: 'It is seeing, *insofar as*... It is seeing, only insofar *as*... (That seems to me to be the solution.)' (RPP II, § 390). Wittgenstein also emphasizes the relations with both 'seeing' and 'thinking', 'interpreting' or 'imagining', when he writes that the situation in which 'seeing-as' is used is the same as that in which 'seeing' is used, except that the technique is somewhat different (RPP II, § 371). Or when he writes that what would otherwise be the description of a perception is now the expression or formulation of an experience (LW, § 176). First I will talk about the relations of 'seeing-as' with 'interpreting' or 'thinking'.

Wittgenstein expresses the relation between seeing-as and thinking very cryptically when he says that 'what I perceive in the dawning of an aspect is not a property of the object, but an internal relation between it and other objects' (PI II ix, p. 212). The following protoversions of the same idea are instructive:

(a) What I see, I might say, has an occult property besides the one that is easily described; a property that is indicated by saying: 'I see it as...' – which, however, is of course only indicated by that because, to be sure, what one means has nothing to do with a box. (MS 123, 17-5-1941)

(b) Well, we describe the impression; but how do we describe it? This kind of description is the curious phenomenon. Normally one would say that under circumstances different physical bodies can make the same visual impression; but here the impression seems to be defined by its possibly belonging together with a specific body.
Our case is thus at any rate *similar* to a case of association. (MS 123, 18-5-1941)

(c) It is characteristic of the aspect that it is comparable with the seeing of this object and not that, although both are contained in our perception. (MS 137, p. 9)

'Occult property', 'non-causal connection', 'belonging together', and 'comparability' are all terms with which Wittgenstein wants to dismiss an explanation in terms of 'association', and as such they are metaphorical for 'internal relation'. Internal relations are characterized by three features (see chapter 3, § 1): the relation is between two objects; the relation is not mediated by a third term; and the relation exists in a practice and not in the mind or in some abstract medium. The first question therefore is which two 'objects' are involved. For an example we can return to the duck/rabbit drawing. In my view there are three possibilities. (i) One object is the geometrical constellation, the other is either the duck or the rabbit. (ii) One object is the duck, the other is the rabbit. (iii) One object is the change of aspect, the other is either the duck or the rabbit. (i) is out of the question. A characteristic of internal relations is that the two members of the relation cannot be identified independently of each other. But the geometrical constellation of the drawing can be identified independently of either the duck or the rabbit. As an example of a geometrical statement Wittgenstein mentions the statement 'that in the drawing he does see there is a form which he hasn't yet seen' (RPP II, § 438). Thus it is possible for somebody not to see a duck in the drawing until he has reconstructed piece by piece how the duck is geometrically contained in the drawing (cf. RPP I, § 1042). First he independently identifies the geometry of the figure and then he reconstructs a duck. The geometrical constellation is therefore external to the perception of an aspect. Moreover, as we saw earlier, the geometrical constellation is usually not even involved in the description of aspects: a painter can render staring without necessarily being able to describe the required geometrical forms. (ii) is impossible as well, since the duck and the rabbit are alternative and mutually exclusive ways of seeing. If one sees the duck, one does not see the rabbit; if one sees the rabbit, one does not see the duck. Both are identified independently of each other. So the answer must be and is in fact (iii). Wittgenstein wrote that an aspect is characterized by its comparability with this and not that object. The internal relation therefore concerns the relation between an aspect and a specific object that excludes another object which is also geometrically present. We saw earlier that one only becomes conscious of an aspect in a change of aspect. The change of aspect is therefore internally linked to *this* object, not to another one. To put it differently, the change of an aspect, the experience of an aspect, is internally constituted by an *analogical* formulation: 'now it is duck', 'now it is a rabbit'. The use of 'now' or somesuch word is essential, since the formulation of an aspect is essentially temporal, as opposed to the non-temporal meaning of a geometrical statement (RPP II, § 439 ff.). A statement is non-temporal if 'These two faces are similar' cannot be replaced by 'These two faces are now similar'. The latter sentence is typical of the experience of an aspect-change and this change is necessarily related to its comparability with seeing a duck and not a rabbit, regardless of the fact that both are equally real from a geometrical point of view.

The second question is in what way the internal relation between the experience of an aspect-change and an analogical formulation is not mediated by a third term. This third term might be an optically and geometrically observable part of the figure – I leave aside here an inner picture as third term. But Wittgenstein is explicit that no (physical) property of the object is observed in the perception of an aspect. And in fact it was characteristic for an aspect that form, colour, and organization of the figure remain unchanged, while nevertheless something new is seen. In this sense in which an aspect does not involve the perception of a physical property, I take 'seeing-as' to be closely related to 'thinking' or 'interpreting'. For if really something different were perceived, then it would have to be possible to make two different reproductions of the perception before and after the change of aspect, for instance different in colour or form. And of course this is impossible. Nevertheless it is possible, according to Wittgenstein, to see in the way that the drawing is reproduced that something different has been seen after the aspect as compared with before:

> The fact that I produce a different copy (a different result) accords with the concept of the visual state. The fact that I produce the same copy, but in a *different* way – by drawing the lines in a different sequence – points to the concept of *thinking*. (RPP II, § 369)

To sketch the outlines of the duck in a different order from the outlines of the rabbit is evidence of a different 'treatment' or 'conception'. Obviously, identification of this difference is very subtle and only suited to certain media: a photo always shows the same thing.

The third question is in what way 'seeing-as' is based on a practice. Seeing aspects is built on other language-games (RPP II, § 541). But it is a concept that vertically presupposes more language-games than usual and in this respect it is based on a highly complicated practice: '"Now he's seeing it like *this*", "now like *that*" would only be said of someone *capable* of making certain applications of the figure quite freely' (PI II xi, p. 208c). Mastery of a practice is the logical condition for seeing aspects. In order to see a random letter, for instance,

as being organized in a certain way, carelessly or in a typically childish fashion, the child first has to know the more literal meaning of 'taking together' (PI II xi, p. 210). He has to take blocks together literally and pretend they form a house, to pretend literally that a block is a car, that a doll is a baby sister. He has to be able to play with things literally to be able to see the same object differently, to substitute it for something else. And 'according to the fiction' with which he surrounds the object, we will take him to be capable of pointing out different aspects. For the child the same thing stands for something else if he is capable of 'surrounding it with a different fiction', in other words, if he is capable of seeing and treating it in a context of other concepts and actions. One can also instruct a child to take part in this kind of fiction: one can ask him to see a circle as an opening and not as a disc. The ability to carry out this instruction implies that 'seeing-as' depends to a certain extent on the will, just as imagination does. In this respect too seeing-as is related to thinking and not to seeing. The instruction 'see this tomato as red' is pointless. That is why Wittgenstein writes: 'Wherein lies the similarity between the seeing of an aspect and thinking? That this seeing does not have the consequences of perception; that it is similar in this way to imagining' (LW, § 177). The consequence of perception is that some piece of information about reality is communicated to us, something about form, colour, or organization. But anything that can be said about form, colour, or organization still fails to produce a description of an aspect.

Finally, in what way is seeing-as related to seeing? In the first place both duck and rabbit are contained in the object of perception. If I want to tell somebody else that I have seen a duck in the figure, then inevitably I will have to point to the drawing or make a second drawing which is obviously more or less identical to the first: 'The fact that I produce a different copy (a different result) accords with the concept of the visual state' (RPP II, § 369). There is an affinity with perception in the sense in which it is possible to express an aspect in a picture. In the second place there is an affinity in that 'seeing-as', like 'seeing', is a state; a state which can suddenly change into a different one (RPP II, § 43). Grammatically considered, thinking or interpreting is not a state but an action (RPP I, § 1). Like the state of a visual impression, an experience of aspect can be expressed in terms of real duration (see chapter 7, § 1). The difference compared with seeing is, again, that an experience of aspect lasts very briefly, and not accidentally but essentially so: an aspect does not remain fixed, but dawns in a change of aspect and can at most be balanced in this unstable position for a short while. Seeing an aspect is essentially new, whereas seeing objects need not be so. Somewhat puristically Wittgenstein therefore proposes to speak not of seeing but of noticing aspects: 'One doesn't say "I noticed it for five minutes"' (RPP II, § 443).

The conclusion is that both the Meaning-theory and Gestalt psychology have failed to do justice to the vertical complexity of 'seeing-as'. When Köhler equates seeing aspects via the organization of the visual impression with the perception of form and colour, he has trimmed off the logical relations with 'thinking' and has squeezed the concept into a form which does not fit it: when an aspect is registered, the optical image remains to an important extent the same. Nevertheless it is correct to speak of seeing or rather noticing a shift of gaze. The representation of what is seen covers a large number of cases and certainly not just form and colour (PI II ix, p. 200). The unchanged structure of the optical image after a change of aspect has wrongly led the Meaning-theory to reduce 'seeing-as' to thinking and to decide that every description of aspects is indirect and replaceable by a more direct and purer account. But it *is* true that aspects are not 'just as' visible as form and colour, as Köhler asserted.

5. Secondary meaning and aspect

Justice can only be done to the meaning of aspects via the descriptions of vertical relations to 'thinking' and 'perceiving'. In this final section I will show that secondary meanings of words are vertically related to primary meanings in a similar way. Because of these vertical relations, secondary meanings are not reduced to a language-game where they do not belong and are not eliminated as trivial, pointless games either. Both aspects and secondary meanings derive their significance from being connected with important facts of human life. By tracing vertical relations, Wittgenstein shows that they are embedded in a form of life, though he does not say whether the language-games of aspects and secondary meanings themselves can be described via rule-guided horizontal relations. The following four similarities between aspects and secondary meanings specifically indicate how they are vertically related to other language-games.

1. The language-game of seeing-as is built on other language-games, in particular that of perception. There is a similar logical vertical relation between primary and secondary meanings. With reference to 'thin Tuesday' and 'fat Wednesday' Wittgenstein comments:

> In both cases the explanation of the word is that of its primary meaning. It can only have a secondary meaning for someone if he knows its primary meaning. That is, the secondary use consists in applying the word with *this* primary use in new surroundings. (LW, § 797)

I take the 'new surroundings' to consist of other horizontal relations and so of another language-game, the language-game of expression. The 'new meaning' of the word, Wittgenstein wishes to say, consists precisely in the old meaning being used in a new situation. The secondary meaning is not a new and different meaning, just as no new and different property of the object is noticed in the change of aspect. The meaning of 'fat' and 'thin' can only be indicated in the usual way; in any case it cannot be indicated by pointing to Tuesday or Wednesday. The same applies to the description of a certain kind of feeling:

> The feeling of the unreality of one's surroundings. This feeling I have had once, and many have it before the onset of mental illness. Everything seems

somehow not *real*; but not as if one *saw* things unclear or blurred; everything looks quite as usual. (RPP I, § 125)[15]

The choice of 'unreal' is interesting. Wittgenstein does not choose the word for its sound; words with the same sound but with a different meaning would not serve his purpose. Nor does he choose it for its meaning; one has not learned to use 'unreal' in the sense of a feeling: 'The fact is simply that I use a word, the bearer of another technique, as the expression of a feeling' (RPP I, § 126). 'Unreal' is a word which we have learned to use in a certain horizontal context and now use in a *new context*, that of the expression of feelings. The similarity with seeing-as is clear: there too what is normally the description of a perception is used as the expression of an experience. And it is obvious that one is only capable of the secondary use if one is first thoroughly familiar with the primary use: one can only say 'Schubert' as if the word were an adjective if one has already learned to use it as proper noun.

2. The secondary use of words is internally related to what they express and cannot be described as figurative or metaphorical. Figurative language cannot do justice to the internal relation. Secondary meanings do not involve figurative language. The meaning of the word is transferred to a different context. This is not metaphorical:

> But the relationship here is not like the one between 'cutting off a piece of thread' and 'cutting off someone's speech', for here one doesn't *have* to use the figurative expression. And if you say 'The vowel e is yellow', the word yellow is *not* used figuratively. (LW, § 799)

One argument against a metaphorical interpretation is the phenomenological fact that secondary meanings have a persistent hold over us. But a more decisive argument is the logic of internal relations. Via a metaphor two more or less related meanings are compared and connected by the same word. Via a metaphor a word is used in a broader sense. But if one says 'Schubert fits Schubert', one is not using the word in a broader sense. One is not using 'to fit' in a figurative sense, as if Schubert does not fit

---

[15] James (1902, pp. 63-64) discusses this feeling too, in a work with which Wittgenstein was familiar.

Schubert. The secondary meaning is not used 'besides' or 'after' the primary one and compared with it. Any comparison in terms of association disregards the specific nature of the internal relation: 'Would it be more correct to say that yellow "corresponds" to *e* than "*e* is yellow"? Isn't the point of the game precisely that we express ourselves by saying *e is* yellow?' (LW, § 59). Words which are used in a secondary sense do not refer to comparisons or similarities which can be identified independently of the secondary use.

3. The experience of secondary meanings is not that two things are persistently called by the same name. Somebody who repeats the word 'bank' time and again while alternately looking at a money bank and a river bank,[16] in order to impress on his mind the ambiguous meaning of the word, has still not used the word in a secondary sense: 'But if the inflection of voice, for example, seems to me to determine whether I mean one thing or another – then I would be experiencing meaning' (LW, § 60). This brings us to a third similarity between aspects and secondary meanings: there is often an apt formulation for the experiences concerned. In the case of secondary meanings the apt word typically consists in an expression. As it happens, Wittgenstein is conveniently supported in this recognition of the expressive character of secondary meanings by a great introspective writer, Marcel Proust. In the third part of *Du Côté de chez Swann*, 'Nom de Pays: le Nom', Proust minutely describes how in 'cette syllabe lourde du nom de Parme, où circule aucun air', an entire life story is nevertheless absorbed. But the story is only brought to life by pronouncing the word in a certain way: 'Je n'eus besoin pour les faire renaître que de prononcer ces noms: Balbec, Venise, Florence, dans l'intérieur desquels avait fini par s'accumuler le désir que m'avaient inspiré les lieus qu'ils désignaient' (Proust, p. 457). The expression is constitutive for the experience and cannot be dissociated from it, just as the expression with which somebody sings a phrase does not exist independently of it. A more direct representation does not exist, just as 'I see it as ...' is not an indirect description, but a primary description or formulation of the visual experience.

---

[16] In German (and Dutch) the word 'bank' may mean either 'bench' or 'money bank'.

4. Although Wittgenstein does not specifically mention it, there seem to be no criteria for the secondary use of words. For if the meaning of a word does not change in its secondary use (see 1) and if there need not be any similarity between the objects of its primary and secondary applications (what does 'Wednesday' as 'day in the week' have in common with 'Wednesday' as 'fat'?), then it follows that the secondary use cannot be justified on the basis of criteria. Perhaps that is why Wittgenstein speaks of our inclination to use words in a secondary sense; inclinations, after all, are not yet criteria. We are not to infer from this that the secondary use of words is absurd and has to be explained away. This is far from being Wittgenstein's view. In the first place the secondary use of words is not entirely chaotic, since it is vertically related to the rule-guided primary use. In the second place it is not entirely eccentric, since Wittgenstein has shown that this use of words, for instance the atmosphere of proper names (see p. 162 ff. above), plays an important role in our form of life and that rather people who do not understand this use of words are to be called eccentric (aspect-blind).

CHAPTER 7

THE GRAMMAR OF PSYCHOLOGICAL CONCEPTS

Systematic definitions of psychological concepts are rare in psychology. Rather they are systematically neglected in favour of a systematic specification of experimental techniques. The probable reason for this all but deliberate neglect is that psychologists recognize in these definitions the conventions of everyday human knowledge, to which they are professionally disinclined to conform. Psychologists ought not be led by the archaeology of the memory in Proust, the Odyssey of here and now in Joyce, and in general by the lexical contingencies of language.

So, a task for philosophy! But the much-discussed Cartesian tradition in the philosophy of mind has remarkably few definitions. And if there is any attempt at classification, it is not undertaken as a goal in itself, but serves to support a more general epistemological position. Thus Descartes' deficient treatment of the emotions and the will is the consequence of his dualism of thought and extension;[1] and Hume's reduction of all psychological phenomena to sensations is the direct result of his empiricism. Exceptions are formed by Brentano,[2] James, and, to a lesser extent, Spinoza. The classifications of psychological concepts by philosophers and psychologists, writes Wittgenstein (Z, § 462), are like descriptions of clouds according to their forms. And more than once he calls the use of such concepts confusing: as if

---

[1] According to Wilson (1978, p. 181), Descartes was firmly committed to the possibility of providing physiological accounts of *all* mental occurrences except the exercise of pure understanding. Only pure understanding has no connection at all with the brain.

[2] See Brentano (1971, II). There are some interesting parallels between Brentano's description of psychological concepts and Wittgenstein's. See further chapter 4, § 3.

the word 'violin' refers not only to the instrument, but also to the violinist, the sound, and the playing of the violin (RPP II, § 730). Wittgenstein's criticism is not aimed at the lack of mere terminological agreement – he himself is not always consistent either – but addresses the inadequate logical specification of the various concepts. The result is that, for instance, 'representations' are not individuated from 'sensations' or that the crucial distinction between 'states of consciousness' and 'dispositions' is lost. He therefore sets himself the task of untangling the many errors of classification and pointing out the many misleading analogies within traditional categories. His aim is a view of the whole: 'The genealogical tree of psychological phenomena: I strive, *not for exactness*, but for a view of the whole' (RPP I, § 895).

An 'Übersicht' is achieved by describing horizontal and vertical relations of language-games. Wittgenstein does not pursue precision in the sense that the description of language-games does not provide a psychological or physiological explanation of language-games and does not increase the degree of predictability. Causal explanations are irrelevant to the logic of concepts. On the other hand the logical genealogy of psychological concepts *can* be relevant to empirical research. So far as empirical psychology makes use of (everyday) concepts, it too benefits from a logical specification of these concepts. In fact, Wittgenstein is convinced that the problems in psychology are largely conceptual in kind. He does not compare the situation in psychology to the early stages of physics or chemistry, like Köhler:[3]

> The point is not that we still have to be prepared for all sorts of unexpected discoveries (Köhler) – as if the *laws of nature* that psychology teaches (?) were to be treated as provisional. Köhler himself is not in the least clear about the nature of such discoveries. As was said before, the difficulty in psychology is similar to the one concerning the foundations of mathematics. (MS 130, 1-8-1946)

---

[3] See Köhler (1929, p. 30), where he asks why the problem of behaviourism has no parallel in physics: 'The answer is simple enough: Physics is an old science and psychology is in its infancy'. Wittgenstein refers to Köhler's 'young science' theory without mentioning him by name in *Philosophical Investigations* II xiv, p. 232.

Rather he compares it to certain branches of mathematics. The problem in psychology is that the experimental methods are not adequately geared to the problems in hand. The deficiency is not technical but logical: the empirical method ignores the mainly logical nature of the problem. In Wittgenstein's view psychologists turn too readily to experiments, while being insufficiently aware of what is exactly mysterious about, for instance, thinking: 'The experimental method does *something*; its failure to solve the problem is blamed on its still being in its beginnings. It is as if one were to try and determine what matter and spirit are by chemical experiments' (RPP I, § 1093). To resort to physiological explanations is misleading. We already saw instances of this: the problem of 'seeing-as' was not solved by explaining it via the physiology of eye movements, but by a description of horizontal and vertical relations of language-games. Wittgenstein's antidote to this is therefore a kind of physiological *agnosticism*:[4] he pretends to be completely ignorant as to whether humans have a nervous system (RPP I, § 1063).

This agnostic strategy is not surprising in the light of the work of Wittgenstein's main opponent: William James's *Principles of Psychology*[5], which Wittgenstein uses as a rich source of confusions: 'James is a goldmine for the psychology of the philosopher' (MS 124, p. 292). Although this two-part monument subjects the realm of the mind to a more extensive and systematic inquiry than ever before – it is more sophisticated than, for instance, the work of Berkeley, Hume, Reid, and Mill, authors whom James nevertheless saw as his legators – the inquiry itself shows a great confusion of logical and empirical matters. James sells conceptual inquiry as empirical science:

> How necessary the work of philosophy is is shown by James's Psychology. Psychology, he says, is a science. But he discusses almost no scientific questions. His movements are merely attempts to free himself from the cobweb of

---

[4] This agnosticism does not imply *that* there are no physiological causes for psychological phenomena, for it does not imply any *ontological* commitment. Indeed, it is precisely a strategy for dispensing with ontological claims.

[5] The highly speculative character of James's physiological explanations is also commented on by Myers (1986).

metaphysics in which he is caught. He cannot yet walk, or fly at all, he only wriggles: not that that is not interesting. Only it is not a scientific activity. (MS 165, pp. 150-151)

In *Philosophical Investigations* I and II Wittgenstein criticizes James's views on 'willing', 'kinaesthetic sensations', the 'stream of thought', though without systematically mentioning his name. Unfortunately, Wittgenstein's criticism is too concise. James's explanations of these phenomena are rather eccentric to begin with, so that Wittgenstein's highly incomplete and reduced account of James only helps to make his own views more opaque. But in *Remarks on the Philosophy of Psychology* I and II and the *Last Writings* he deals with the problems at greater length and moreover adds a critique of James's theory of emotions and Russell's theory of psychic images to his 'genealogy' of psychological concepts. Nonetheless it will be necessary to describe James's position and, to a lesser extent, that of Russell. I will do this not in general but for each subject individually, that is to say for each psychological concept as it is analysed. But before presenting the analyses in the following six sections, I first wish to give a more general introduction to Wittgenstein's organization of psychological concepts.

Wittgenstein presents his 'genealogy' mainly on the basis of concrete psychological concepts such as 'sensation' and 'emotion', but in one case[6] he draws a more formal distinction: 'states of consciousness' versus 'dispositions'. As examples of 'states of consciousness' Wittgenstein gives: '... the seeing of a certain picture, the hearing of a tone, a sensation of pain or of taste, etc.' (RPP II, § 45). As examples of 'dispositions' he mentions: '... believing, understanding, knowing, intending, and others, ...' (RPP II, § 45). States of consciousness are temporary phenomena

---

[6] In fact there is another fragment, besides *Remarks on the Philosophy of Psychology* II, § 63 and 148, in which he gives a summary account of his classification of psychological concepts, namely *Remarks on the Philosophy of Psychology* I, § 836. I think this summary is less satisfying, less comprehensive, and more ambiguous in its terminology (e.g. Wittgenstein's use of 'Erlebnis-begriffe' versus 'Erfahrungsbegriffe') than § 63 and 148. Nevertheless in the figure below I also borrow from § 863.

occurring at a certain moment; dispositions are more or less persistent phenomena which manifest themselves at (regular) intervals in certain events or states, but without being events or states themselves. A general feature of dispositions, according to Wittgenstein, is that one does not have to ascertain by spot-check whether they are still going on, as with states of consciousness (RPP II, § 57). States of consciousness are characterized by 'genuine duration': 'Where there is genuine duration one can tell someone: "Pay attention and give me a signal when the picture, the rattling etc. alters"' (RPP II, § 50). The duration of pain can be measured with a stopwatch in one's hand, so to speak. One gives continuous attention to the duration, development, beginning and end of the pain. But in order to ascertain whether one still knows the alphabet, there is no need to test the 'duration' of this knowledge.[7] Knowledge of the alphabet is a skill. The predicate 'continuous' does not apply to a skill, since a skill is not an event or a state and so does not occur. A disposition is persistent in the sense that it is not interrupted by an interruption of consciousness or a shift in attention (RPP II, § 45). Even if a disposition does not manifest itself, even if somebody gives no evidence of knowing the alphabet, there still need not be any gap in his knowledge. However, dispositions do persist in different ways; they can remain constant or change and mature or recede. In view of this 'life' of dispositions, Wittgenstein concludes that it is experience which teaches us that we have certain inclinations or skills (RPP II, § 178). A shift in attention or a restriction of consciousness during pain, on the other hand, does entail a gap in the sensation of pain: for this sensation *is* a form of consciousness. In technical terms, the relation between sensation and consciousness is

---

[7] Wittgenstein distinguishes between *two* meanings of the term 'duration'; one being reserved for the duration of dispositions and abilities, the other for the 'genuine duration' of states of consciousness. This distinction becomes very clear in a protoversion of a fragment of part 2 of the *Investigations*, x, p. 191: 'Believing is a state of mind. It has duration; and that independently of the duration of its expression in a sentence, for example. So it is a kind of disposition ...'. In MS 169, pp. 16-17 he uses, instead of 'Dauer', 'existiert eine Zeit', which is a less ambiguous characterization of the 'duration' of dispositions.

internal, whereas the relation between disposition and consciousness is not. Therefore if one says that somebody feels pain, is
afraid, in short, experiences something that has genuine duration,
then this automatically implies that he has consciousness. Hence
the choice of the term 'state of consciousness'. Wittgenstein does
not employ the distinction systematically; in particular he seems
unhappy about the term disposition.[8] In any case he does not
employ the distinction between disposition and state of consciousness like Ryle's dichotomy between dispositions and occurrences.[9]
On the contrary, as Wittgenstein sees it, there are many
psychological concepts which cannot be accommodated within
such a dichotomy. In fact, he only gives one explicit example of a
disposition: the inclination toward jealousy (RPP II, § 178).[10] And
although he mentions 'knowledge' and 'understanding' as
examples of dispositions, he is not happy about it. In fact his
analysis of these concepts suggests that they should rather be
called *abilities*, expressing our 'know-how', than dispositions.
Concepts which in my view are equally not included[11] in such a
dichotomy by Wittgenstein are 'feelings of tendency' (a variant of
'intending') and 'volition'. In order to distinguish them from
states of consciousness and dispositions I call these last concepts
'mental activities'. By this (misleading) term I do not mean that
we are dealing here with 'psychic acts', as in certain forms of
phenomenology, or with actions in a non-mental sense. What
Wittgenstein wants to emphasize, in my view, is that 'being on
the verge of saying something', 'looking for a word that is on the

---

[8] He uses it more or less as a provisional term, for he says that he calls knowledge, etc. 'for the moment ... "dispositions"' (RPP II, § 45).

[9] I mean Ryle's distinction between 'occurrences' and 'dispositions'. See Ryle
(1949, chapter 5). But for a similar use, see also Armstrong (1968, pp. 82-89).

[10] He calls the inclination toward jealousy a disposition 'in the true sense'.

[11] Directly after his summary account Wittgenstein expresses doubt about the
classification of what I shall call 'mental activities' within the categories of
states of consciousness and dispositions (RPP I, § 836). In § 837 he says: 'But
where does *memory* belong, and where *attention*? One can remember a situation
or occurrence *at a moment*. To that extent, then, the concept of memory is like
that of instantaneous understanding or decision.' Some of these concepts I shall
call mental activities (see figure 1).

tip of one's tongue', or 'trying to perform an action' are concepts for something that we initiate (e.g. bodily movements) or bring about (e.g. a memory experience), at any rate in the way that concepts for dispositions or states of consciousness are not (see especially § 5). In the figure below I have represented Wittgenstein's classification of psychological concepts.[12] However, it

---

[12] The terms marked with a dotted line are concrete psychological concepts, i.e. concepts that refer to determinable psychological items. I have given only some examples of these and the list is far from exhaustive. The terms marked by straight lines refer to more abstract of formal psychological concepts. Emotions are rather difficult to classify. In *Remarks on the Philosophy of Psychology* I, § 836 Wittgenstein does not subsume them under the category of 'Erfahrungen', i.e. 'states of consciousness' like impressions and images. And yet many of the features of 'emotions' are those of states of consciousness: genuine duration, development, and characteristic expression. I think Wittgenstein's main reason for not subsuming them under the category of states of consciousness in § 836 is his criticism of the James-Lange theory of emotions (see section 2), in which emotions are equated with (organic) sensations. Hence Wittgenstein emphasizes in § 836 that emotions *are not* 'Erfahrungen' but they *have* characteristic 'Erfahrungen'. Unlike sensations, emotions are constituted by beliefs, and via these beliefs emotions are essentially related to an object. And although he maintains this crucial difference between emotions and sensations in *Remarks on the Philosophy of Psychology* II, § 148, he is much more positive there about the similarities between emotions and states of consciousness. He suggests that emotions can be called *both* states of consciousness *and* dispositions. For instance: 'It is one thing to feel acute fear, and another to have a "chronic" fear of someone' (RPP II, § 148). In the former case 'fear' is a state of consciousness and as such cannot be put to the test; in the latter case it is a disposition like love and hate and as such can be put to the test (cf. RPP II, § 152).

'Forms of conviction' is a term Wittgenstein borrows from James (1890, II). For instance: 'In its inner nature, belief, or the sense of reality, is a sort of feeling more allied to the emotions than anything else. Mr. Bagehot distinctly calls it the "emotion" of conviction ... It would naturally be described by such terms as "willingness" or the "turning of our disposition"' (p. 283). 'Doubt' is 'the true opposite' of belief (p. 284). I will not further discuss these 'forms of conviction' in this chapter.

'Feelings of tendency' is a name Wittgenstein borrows from James (see section 5). The classification of the concept of expecting is rather disputable, since it can also be categorized as a disposition, as an emotional attitude ('anxiously expecting' or 'harren'), and as a form of conviction. For my reasons for classifying 'expecting' as a mental activity, see section 4.

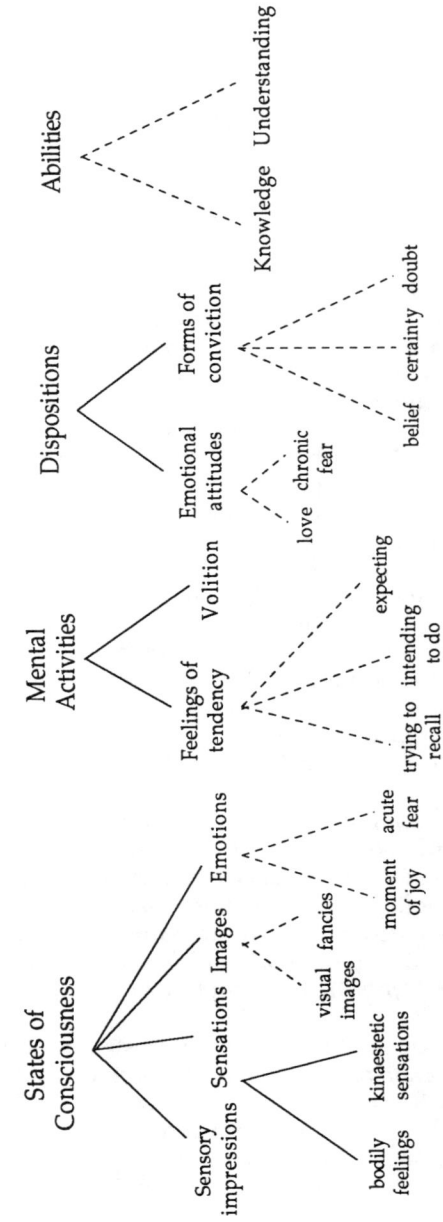

should not be thought of as being conclusive. His description of family resemblances, similarities and differences lays so much emphasis on the many subtle ramifications between psychological concepts that a four-way division remains too artificial an abstraction as well.

1. Sensations and impressions

'Sensation' occupies a crucial position in the tradition of Hume-James-Russell-Ayer. Sensations are the genetic origin of knowledge and the bedrock to which the entire psychological repertoire can be reduced: sensations are the *terminus a quo* and the *terminus ad quem* of experience. A theory which does not start with sensations and does not end with them is, as James puts it, a bridge without piers.[13]

The genetic question is of course disregarded by Wittgenstein. What he does address is the infiltration of such genetic aspects in the specification of the concept 'sensation' in the work of James and his associates. He is struck by the fact that the concept is far from being the solid foundation on which empiricism hopes to base itself. On the contrary, the concept is used loosely in empiricism, like the terms process, state, something, and fact (RPP I, § 648). A clarification of the concept is therefore urgently required.

Wittgenstein distinguishes three meanings of 'sensation': (1) visual and auditory impressions, (2) kinaesthetic sensations, (3) bodily feelings. Of course, the term impression is used by Wittgenstein not to refer to an inner 'sense-datum', but in such a way that no meaningful distinction can be made between perception and a 'sense-datum'. I shall therefore reserve the term 'sensation' for (2) and (3). Wittgenstein's favourite examples for (1) are colours, for (2) sensations of pressure and movement, and for (3) fatigue. As I shall not be going into (3), I note here that the difference between (2) and (3) resides in the fact that bodily

---

[13] See James (1890, II, p. 7).

sensations are diffusely located – in any case not in a specific part of the body – whereas kinaesthetic sensations (K-sensations) are specifically located. The problem of sensations and impressions, finally, can be split up into three parts: (A) the problem of the relation between impressions and the external world, (B) the problem of the description of impressions and sensations, (C) the problem of K-sensations. (A) involves only (1), (B) (1) through (3), (C) mainly (2).

In the view of many philosophers (A) is no problem whatsoever; Wittgenstein agrees, but for different reasons. Schopenhauer,[14] for instance, holds that sensations – in discussing (A) I use the term sensation as it is used by Wittgenstein's opponents, to refer to (1), where Wittgenstein would speak of impression – have no cognitive value at all, so that there can be no question of a relation to the external world, let alone a problematical one. The territory of sensations is inside the body and can never contain anything outside of it. Perception of the external world is an intellectual process, the product of the mind. Schopenhauer can only arrive at this contempt of sensations by choosing (2) and (3), the most internal and subjective meanings, as the paradigm of sensations. For other philosophers (A) is no problem for an even simpler reason: sensations do not exist. Wittgenstein rejects both the idea that sensations are devoid of any cognitive content and the idea that they do not exist. According to him, however, there is only a problem (A) when impression is defined as 'sensation', as 'sense-datum'. He finds this identification in the work of James and his supporters.

According to James, sensations do have a cognitive content. They offer information about the external world, in particular about its spatial proportions. The origin of this dimensionality is not explained in the classical empiricistic way. According to the empiricist A. Bain,[15] for instance, sensations do not originally have dimensions. Only later do they acquire expansion, helped by

---

14 See Schopenhauer (1888, pp. 52-57). Schopenhauer, as so many others, is quoted by James (1890, II, pp. 273-275).
15 See Bain (1855, p. 183).

muscle contractions in the eyes. James is a nativist[16] and regards the explanation of dimensionality by elements originally devoid of dimension as hocus pocus. Sensations are spatial from the word go. Thus a warm bath feels more massive than a pin-prick and a neuralgic pain in the face has less volume than the raw pain produced by piles. Likewise the rumbling of thunder has more volume than the scratching of a pen on paper. Our awareness of this dimensionality is primordial; what we learn is a more artificial knowledge of space.

Wittgenstein's view seems to be in line with that of James when he too says that the constitutive rule for impressions is their informative nature: 'What is common to sense-experiences? – The answer that they acquaint us with the outer world is partly wrong and partly right. It is right inasmuch as it is supposed to point to a *logical* criterion (RPP I, § 702). One notices the difference between James and Wittgenstein when listening to James's definition of 'sensation'. A sensation is 'the mental affection that follows most immediately upon the stimulation of the sense-tract. Its antecedent is directly physical, no psychic links, no acts of memory, inference, or association intervening' (Pr II, p. 216). A sensation is what is immediately given and most concrete, what one needs only to look at in order to know it – thus Wittgenstein describes James's position (cf. RPP I, § 807). This definition leads to a dualistic epistemology in James: the information provided by sensations is indirect: they represent the external world. The old and familiar problem of this representationalism is to show how we can ever reach beyond these inner sensations and get in touch with what they are copies of.

One example of this 'sense-data theory' has attracted particular attention. It was invented by G.E. Moore, but James, Köhler and Wittgenstein mention it too.[17] In his essay Moore notes that when we internally perceive a sensation of blue, we see only the sensation; the other element – our consciousness of the sensation

---

16 James's nativism opposes the empiricism of Spencer, Brown, Bain, and Mill. The original elements of experience postulated by the empiricists are 'extensionless' feelings.

17 See Moore (1903, p. 450).

– is not seen by us; it is diaphanous. Yet it can be noticed, if only we concentrate enough. In Moore's view the experience is internally divided; there is a consciousness and a content, the sense-data.

Wittgenstein puts a different interpretation on this example, more related to the use which Köhler makes of it. 'Look how blue the sky is,' he writes in *Philosophical Investigations*, § 275. If you do this without philosophical intentions, the idea never crosses your mind that the colour impression is located inside you, only belongs to you, and is placed in between you and the world like a membrane (PI, § 276). What Wittgenstein seems to be saying is that the impression itself is not a visual object, is *not itself seen*. The sensation of blue is internally related to the blue sky in the same way that the sensation of pain is internally related to the expression of pain. This internal relation between sensations and the physical reality described is constitutive for the original language-game: we learn the use of the concept of seeing in internal relation to the description of what we see. In other words: 'The words which describe what we see are properties of things. We don't learn their meaning in connection with the concept of "inner seeing"' (RPP II, § 68). We see the blue sky, not the sensation of blue and the sky. In this language-game the sensation cannot be detached from the fact that I see the blue sky. It is precisely on this internal relation between sensations and physical reality that Wittgenstein's logical criterion that impressions give information is based. The informative nature of impressions is conceptually related to the way in which these concepts are learned. Hence mutual agreement is constitutive for this original language-game: the sky *is* blue and does not merely seem blue.

Nevertheless a sensation is not 'nothing' (cf. PI, § 304). There are two reasons for this. In the first place Wittgenstein by no means concludes from the internal relation between sensations and descriptions of physical reality that there are no sensations. Without any hesitation Wittgenstein speaks of 'Erlebnisinhalt'. He merely warns against the conceptual confusion between the *content* of experience and the *object* of experience. An experience is something one has, an object is something one perceives.

Experiences are not 'nothing', but they can only be described or referred to in internal relation to the object of experience. In the second place sensations are not 'nothing' since, besides the original language-games in which the object of experience is central, there are also language-games in which the content of experience is central. In *Philosophical Investigations*, § 278 he asks again whether 'I know how the colour green looks to me' is a meaningless proposition. Not at all. The only question is: 'what use of the proposition are you thinking of?'. In other words, to what kind of language-game does the proposition belong? We know the answer now: language-games in which the content of experience is described are vertically based on language-games in which physical objects are referred to. This vertical relation is also reflected in pedagogy: a child is not taught from the outset 'This looks red to me' (RPP II, § 315), or 'That's probably a chair', but he is taught 'That's a chair' (RPP II, § 319). And 'probably' is not left out because it is still too difficult for the child, so that he is taught something which is not really correct. The point is a purely logical one: the technique for the use of 'It looks red to me' presupposes the technique for the use of 'It's red'. Only against the backdrop of this fundamental agreement can less unanimous descriptions of the content of experience be learned. 'The red visual impression is a new *concept*' (RPP II, § 316).

The content of experience can be described (B). Like James and Köhler, Wittgenstein distinguishes a subjective and an objective aspect in sensations (LW, § 396).[18] In an objective sense

---

[18] Wittgenstein borrows his use of the terms 'subjective' and 'objective' from Köhler (1929, pp. 15 ff.). Köhler introduces these terms in order to find a way out of the dilemma between introspective psychologists and behaviourists. Their use of the term 'direct experience' is misleading. The former use it to refer to what is 'in' us, as do the latter, but they conclude that the object of psychology thus conceived becomes impervious to public scrutiny and dissolves into idealism or solipsism. According to Köhler, this discussion rests on a confusion of the meaning of the terms 'subjective experience' and 'genetically subjective'. Everything, even the objective world of behaviourism, is 'genetically subjective', that is, originates from processes happening within us. But what is genetically subjective is *not* part of what we experience, subjectively or objectively. Hence the behaviouristic rejection of what is genetically subjective as the object of psychology does not

impressions and sensations often describe the outer world, in a subjective sense they often indicate 'what it is like' to see a colour, to feel warm, or to hear music. This subjective aspect of sensations and impressions can be described: 'You do it every day. But how? Well, we have to think about particular cases' (LW, § 397). Thinking about particular cases is necessary, or one might lapse into the false generalization that all sensations are capable of description and all in the same way. Nothing could be less true, as the following synopsis shows:

> Sensations: their inner connexions and analogies.
> All have genuine duration. Possibility of giving the beginning and the end.
> Possibility of their being synchronized, of simultaneous occurrence.
> All have degrees and qualitative mixtures. Degree: scarcely perceptible – unendurable.
> In this sense there is not a sensation of position or movement.
> Place of feeling in the body: differentiates seeing and hearing from sense of pressure, temperature, taste and pain. (RPP II, § 63).

These predicates can be safely used to describe impressions and sensation without a categorial mistake being made. Such a mistake occurs as soon as the terms by which the object of experience is referred to are predicated of the content of experience: as soon as the experience of the blue sky is called blue itself. The memory of a warm holiday is not warm itself either! Predicates which *can* be meaningfully applied to the content of experience are: (i) genuine duration, (ii) quantative gradation or intensity, (iii) qualitative gradation or shades, (iv) location.

---

imply the rejection of subjective experience as a suitable object for scientific research. Wittgenstein refers sympathetically to Köhler's distinctions in this way:

> What is more real, the subjective or the objective? – Nonsense! – Can only the objective be represented in language, not the subjective? – But we do *talk* after all of the subjective! And what we say about that in daily life is all right as it is and is just as little in need of correction by the philosophers as the statements about chairs and tables. But one thing must be emphasized: that the grammar of sentences about the subjective objects is *not the same* as that of the sentences about the objective objects. Or, which comes to the same: the language-games are different. (MS 124, pp. 251-252)

I have already discussed (i) and only add that this predicate is not applicable to all sensations. K-sensations do not have genuine duration. Compare the genuine duration of a sound experience with the 'duration' of the feeling of a bent knee: 'And here again we have a reason why we should like to say of the sensation of posture that it has no content' (RPP I, § 948). Although you may keep your knee bent for a certain period, this does not mean that you experience the genuine duration of the bending; you may have been married for twenty years, but nobody would wish to speak of the genuine duration of a feeling of being married either. Predicate (ii) is not applicable to kinaesthetic sensations either.[19] A toothache can be faint or intense, bearable or unbearable, and a visual impression can be sharp or vague, but the feeling of a bent knee is neither faint nor intense (RPP I, § 771). Wittgenstein is saying here that the sensation of bending or the sensation of movement while I am waving my arm cannot be an observation of bending or movement (see (C)). If there is no observation, there is no description either. By contrast, the sensations which can be caused by bending and movement and which can be observed are sensations of pain, pleasure, etc (RPP I, § 772). Sensations can also be described in terms of qualitative gradations or shades (iii). Gradations of quality do not indicate a change in intensity or faintness. Colours, writes Wittgenstein, are not only green or blue, they are also described as greenish and bluish. In the same way there are shades of smells, sounds, and tastes (RPP I, § 783).

> 'a is between b and c, and is closer to b than to c' – this is a characteristic relation between sensations of the same kind. That is to say, there is, for example, a language-game with the order: 'Produce a sensation between *this* one and *this* one, and closer to the first than to the second.' And also: 'Name two sensations, such that *this* one comes between them.' (RPP I, § 856)

Wittgenstein discusses these shades most extensively in his study of colours.

---

[19] For the distinction between quantitative and qualitative gradations, see *Remarks on the Philosophy of Psychology* I, § 783.

The background of this study is the antithesis between the phenomenological theory of colours set out by Goethe and Brentano and Helmholtz's physicalistic theory.[20] Unfortunately, I cannot say more about it here than the following. An important point of debate was the question of how many primary colours there are. According to Helmholtz, Hering, and Mach, there are six – red, blue, yellow, green, black, white. According to Brentano, there are five. He excludes green from the select few because it is a mixture of yellow and blue. Helmholtz and the others consider mixed colours to be impossible from a physical point of view. Wittgenstein's approach is neither phenomenological – he does not appeal to inner evidence – nor physicalistic – he does not base himself on the physics of the colour circle either. The question whether or not green is a primary colour is resolved by studying language-games (ROC III, § 158). And in particular the language-games of shades give a conclusive answer. The language-games with colours are characterized by what we can and cannot do with colours (Z, § 345). Wittgenstein's conclusion that there are four primary colours – excluding black and white for the moment – is based on the possibilities offered by the language-games. Green is a primary colour because it cannot be used in the language-game of shades, that is to say, it cannot be described as 'bluish yellow' or 'yellowish blue'. This language-game is characterized by the use of the suffix '-ish', the terms 'shade', 'nuance', and 'hue'. One learns to use these terms in language-games of colour arrangements (ROC III, § 110). For example, one learns to describe the various transitions from yellow to red, compared with a brownish yellow. A distinctive feature of primary colours is that one can depict or select pure red spontaneously, without checking it against one's memory or a colour sample (ROC III, § 133). Mixed colours are generally less easily recognized or constructed. Now if green were no primary colour, but a mixture of blue and yellow, one would have to be able to indicate what a bluish yellow or a yellowish blue is. According to Wittgenstein, we are incapable of this (ROC III, § 27). What we can do, mostly roughly, is select a reddish

---

[20] Brentano discusses the subject in his 'Vom Phänomenalen Grün' (1907, pp. 5-44).

yellow from a selection of colour samples, but we are at a loss what to do with 'yellowish blue'. We are unable to accommodate these words in any language-game; they mean as little to us as a 'southwesterly northwind' or 'white water' (ROC I, § 21, 23).

Sensations, finally, can also be located (iv). This locating is a delicate matter and I will deal with it at greater length under (C). But it is clear that we locate a toothache in a tooth and a lump in our throat. In any case visual and auditory impressions cannot be located: we see with our eyes and hear with our ears, but we do not see in our eyes and hear in our ears. What is perceived by a part of the body is never a sensation in the body and what is perceived in a part of the body is never the same as the perception of it by that part of the body.

We are left with the problem of K-sensations (C). James's proposition that sensations have cognitive value also applies to K-sensations, in his view. Perceptions of pressure, movement, and position supply information about the state and position of limbs and other parts of one's body. Wittgenstein rejects this account on logical grounds (PI II, viii). However, his arguments presuppose familiarity with the discussion conducted by James. The fact is that the problem of K-sensations was as hotly debated at the end of the last century as the problem of colours.[21] We will talk further about this problem now.

James's metaphysics of sensations serves to isolate sensations not only from the external world, but also from one another. The sensations of the various senses represent so many individual, independent spatial worlds. A sensation is a little world, a Leibnizian monad, an isolated, windowless world. James aptly expresses this isolation by the image of a hollow tooth;[22] the size of the cavity as it is felt by the tongue is incommensurable with the size perceived in the mirror. The question, of course, is whether and how both 'measurements' can be aligned, so as to result in an intersubjective knowledge of one's body. According

---

[21] See James (1890, II, pp. 181-182), chapter XX.
[22] See James (1890, II, pp. 181 ff.). Given his view that sensations have a cognitive relation with the outer world from the outset, his image of the 'little world' of sensations is rather peculiar.

to James, there are two ways in which equivalences and dis-
crepancies are reduced to a common scale.[23] By feeling parts of the
body with one's palm and fingers, by drawing lines across it, the
dimensions felt from inside the body can be compared with the
dimensions measured by one's fingers. This sense of touch is pre-
eminently used by the blind, but the non-blind use it as well,
according to James. The question is how, having once achieved a
coordination of sensations, we arrive at the construction of this
single public space, how we relate the size of the cavity to the
dimensions reported later by the dentist. In James's theory this is
effected by our feeling of position or place.[24] According to this
principle, it is our habit to locate heterogeneous, simultaneously
experienced sense-data in one place. In this way, via its feeling-in-
one-place, its smell-in-one-place, and its taste-in-one-place, a
morsel of cheese in the mouth is fused together into one and the
same physical object.

The second way has to do with the fact that 'position' is not an
intrinsic feature of sensations, like dimensionality, but a relative
one. 'No single *quale* of a sensation can, by itself, amount to a
consciousness of *position*' (Pr II, p. 154). Sensations do not have a
built-in position, do not speak up and say 'I am here' or 'I am
there'. The question, therefore, is how perception of place is to be
explained.

The explanation subscribed to by James is the local-sign
theory,[25] a theory also accepted by Helmholtz, Lotze, and, in our
day, G. Ryle. The theory is that although sensations do not carry
their position with them in an actual sense, they do carry it poten-
tially. Every sensation derives from its topographical position a
peculiar shade or feeling, a local colour which it does not possess
in a different environment. This local colour is a pure *quale* and
has nothing to do with position as such. But it does offer clues as
to where the sensation is to be located – Helmholtz talks about
'Anhaltspunkte' and Lotze about 'Lokalzeichen'. One notices a

---

[23] See James (1890, II, pp. 183 ff.).

[24] See James (1890, II, p. 154).

[25] See James (1890, II, p. 157). According to Vesey (1965, pp. 49-57), Ryle too
endorses the local-sign theory.

local colour only by touching two corresponding places on, for instance, one's left and right arm: the resulting sensations are similar but never identical. A local colour keeps them distinct. The internal organs too have their specific *qualia*: 'Internal pains, whose seat we cannot see, and have no means of knowing unless the character of the pain itself reveal it, are felt *where* they belong' (Pr II, p. 156). In this genetic explanation of our knowledge of our body James rejects yet another source. According to some psychologists, a separate 'muscular sense' is the source and origin of spatial determinations.[26] If, for instance, I close my eyes and draw a figure in the air with my index finger, I am aware of the geometrical path followed by my finger tip. Yet the skin surface receives no sensations. The muscle contractions do vary, so that a muscular sense must be the source of all knowledge. The evidence for this sense is too inconclusive, according to James. Other experiments show that we locate our finger tip in successive positions through sensations from the joints. The fact that we do not feel these there but in the skin, says James, is due to the negligible part which joints have in our feelings (Pr II, p. 194). The information value of K-sensations cannot be attributed to muscle contractions, therefore.

The following two objections against James's explanations can be reconstructed from Wittgenstein's work. (a) James's thesis that K-sensations teach us the position and state of our body presupposes the possibility of a private ostensive definition of those sensations; (b) the local-sign theory is based on a categorial mistake. Before discussing these points, I want to draw attention to the fact that not all of James's insights are actually denied by Wittgenstein. Thus he not only accepts that we experience K-sensations, but also that we can reproduce them. Especially when we repeat a movement of our fingers (in piano playing) under the same circumstances and after brief intervals, we are able to reproduce K-sensations (RPP I, § 387). Locating K-sensations is not a problem either, only we hardly ever locate them in the joints but mostly in the skin – which is clearly perceived when we blow out

---

[26] James (1890, II, pp. 189 ff.) means the psychologists Brown and Delboeuf.

our cheeks. Wittgenstein agrees with James in this respect too. And finally, Wittgenstein does not deny that there is such a thing as knowledge of the position and state of one's own body: 'One *knows* the position of one's limbs and their movements. One can give them if asked, for example. Just as one also knows the place of a sensation (pain) in the body' (RPP II, § 63). Problems only arise when we consider the specific use of 'knowing' in James's psychology.

James's idea is that we know that our elbow is bent *because* we feel it; we judge the position and movement of limbs by K-sensations (a). But – asks Wittgenstein – what is the criterion for James's assumption that K-sensations play the role of premiss in our knowledge of our bodies? (RPP I, § 698). James's criterion is that of introspective attention and this paves the way for private ostensive definitions of K-sensations (RPP I, § 393). Through the filter of concentrated attention, says James, it ought to be possible to distinguish a sensation in the left thumb from one in the right and to judge whether bending one's knee forty-five degrees always produces the same feeling. Wittgenstein compares this intro-spective and private appeal to K-sensations with the judgement of a man who wants to gauge the depth of a water course by means of a dowsing rod. The man has walked through water courses several times and has felt various tugs at his dowsing rod. 'He associated the tug with the depth and now draws conclusions from the tug to the depth' (RPP I, § 401). Although he may well estimate the depth of the water courses correctly each time, it is equally possible that he fails to judge the strength of the tug correctly. For instance, although the tug is the same each time, he continually indicates a different measure, as if weighing weights in his hand. 'In this (latter) case one will not say he judges the depth by the tug. (At least not "consciously".)' (RPP I, § 403). The point of the example is that although the tug does play a role – if the dowsing rod failed to stir, it would not be possible to gauge the depth in this way either – yet the gauging is not based on the separate consultation of sensations in the hand. For in that case the man would have to be able to indicate that the water course is a meter deep given this strength of the tug, and two meters deep given that strength of the tug. Therefore he must be able to specify the gradation and intensity of the tug. Otherwise his claim to knowledge means no more than the trivial observation that the depth of the water cannot be gauged as long as no tug is perceived.

According to Wittgenstein, James's inevitable appeal to a private ostensive definition results from a misleading analogy with the observation of objects. For if asked where somebody's glasses are, we indicate the spot on the basis of prior observation. In this way observation can also tell us something about our bodies: if I have turned my face away and have therefore been unable to see that I moved my arm, though I am convinced of it, I can subsequently verify it by observation. Observation can tell me whether I have carried out the intended movement and reached the place I wanted to reach. A bodily feeling cannot do this:

> I feel that I am moving all right, and I can also judge roughly *how* by the feeling – but I simply *know* what movement I have made, although you couldn't speak of any *sense-datum* of the movement, of any immediate inner picture of the movement. And when I say "I simply *know*..." "knowing" here means something like "being able to say" and is not in turn, say, some kind of inner picture. (RPP I, § 390)

'Knowing' in this case is not underpinned by a separate familiarity with a sense-datum of position or movement. For that one would have to have a criterion for the identity of sense-data, just as a drawing can be a criterion for a visual impression. There is no such independent criterion for K-sensations; their identity cannot be distinguished from the *movement* which is carried out: 'But as for giving someone, or oneself, the feeling that is characteristic of the arm's being bent at an angle of 30°, I mean without bending the arm – that one can't do' (RPP I, § 391). If the criterion for the identity of K-sensations is the movement which is carried out, then the relation between the two is *internal* and the 'knowledge' of one's own body cannot be separated from one's skill at carrying out all kinds of movements, just as knowing what 'red' is cannot be separated from the description of a red object or knowledge of pain from the expression of pain.

A similar error is made in the local-sign theory (b). The idea that some or other feature of pain indicates its place in the body is like the idea that some or other feature of a memory flash indicates the time in which an event occurred (PI II viii, p. 185). Wittgenstein rejects this theory: 'No local sign about the sensation. Any more than a temporal sign about a memory-image. (Temporal signs in a photograph.)' (RPP II, § 63). It may be that the nature of the pain indicates where somebody has injured or hurt himself, but this is certainly not the normal situation. In the same way it is not normal, though possible, that feelings tell somebody about the position of his arm: somebody who does not know whether his arm is bent because it is anaesthetized may find out through a piercing pain in his elbow (PI II viii, p. 185). These situations are not common and the knowledge gained in this way is based on external relations – just as it external that a yellow colour shows the age of a photo. The local-sign theory rests on a category mistake as well as on a private ostensive definition: terms specifying the circumstances under which feelings are talked about are assigned as predicates to the feelings themselves. Wittgenstein gives a striking illustration of how easily one is led up this garden path. He asks whether it is possible to imagine a pain with all the characteristics of rheumatism, but without locality. 'When you begin to think this over, you see how much you would like to change the knowledge of the place of pain into a characteristic of what is *felt*, into a characteristic of the sense-datum, of the private object that is there before my mind' (RPP I, § 440). The suggestion is not, I think, that there is no feeling – on the contrary – but that predicates by which the feeling is located do not indicate properties of a sense-datum. We feel the pain, we can also say where it hurts, but we do not feel the 'whereabouts' of the pain. Because I feel that I am pricking my finger with the point of a pencil, I know where it hurts, but this is not the same as a feeling of place. 'And if there is no such thing as a feeling of place, why must there be a feeling of position?' (RPP I, § 785). Somewhat oddly, I can say that I feel my arm in a certain position in space and could represent this feeling by making a cast of the position of my arm in plaster (RPP I, § 784). What Wittgenstein rejects is the idea that I feel and *therefore* know the position of my arm. I feel the arm and I know its position; I also know where it hurts. I do not know it by a separate identification of a private bodily feeling. Knowledge of the place of pain cannot normally be divorced from the act of indicating the place. The relation is internal and the action a criterion for the identity of the feeling.

2. Emotions

The ideology of empiricism is the world of the buried distinction, of the fully automatic reduction. James's explanation of emotions is so close to that of bodily feelings that there is ultimately no difference: emotions *are* sensations. Such reductions are prey to Wittgenstein's passion for distinctions. And again he is not concerned with hypothetical explanations of emotions; his aim is a much more modest one: to restore the similarity between the concepts of emotion and sensation to its proper proportions, that is to say, to crucial logical differences. First I will briefly summarize James's theory of emotions.

James's first publication on emotions was the essay 'What is an Emotion'. In the relevant chapter of the *Principles* he mentions that a similar but independent study was published by the Danish author C. Lange in 1885, a year after his own essay. Since then it has been customary to speak of the James-Lange theory.[27] Although both authors differ on points of detail, they agree about the following essential elements: an emotion is 'the effect of the organic changes, muscular and visceral, of which the so-called "expression" of the emotion consists. It is thus not a primary feeling, directly aroused by the exciting object or thought, but a secondary feeling indirectly aroused by the exciting object or thought; the primary effect being the organic changes in question, which are immediate reflexes following upon the presence of the object'.[28] This is the sum and substance of the theory to which James would remain committed.

---

[27] James's article appeared originally as 'What is an emotion' (1884) and as 'The physical basis of emotion' (1894), both published in James (1920).
[28] See James (1920, p. 346).

Not only what the theory asserts is important, but also what it rules out: the existence of 'disembodied' emotions. The theory was born out of resistance to common sense psychology and traditional introspective psychology. A psychologist like Wundt regards emotions as states of consciousness with physical side effects.[29] According to this theory, observation of an event, an object, causes a pure and primary feeling; pure because as a mental entity it exists independent of physiological processes; primary because the feeling is the direct effect of the observation and is in turn the cause of bodily reactions.

James objects not to the ingredients of this causal chain, but to their order. We do not cry because we feel sad, but because we cry we feel sad and because we lash out we are angry.   These formulations in the *Principles* seem the dramatic outgrowth of James's rhetoric rather than of deliberate arguments; later he would put it differently, if not so very differently.[30] Nevertheless the underlying idea of his inversion is 'that *the bodily changes follow directly the perception of the exciting fact, and that our feeling of the same changes as they occur* is *the emotion*' (Pr II, p. 449).   An emotion consists therefore of bodily components and owes its existence to the fact that these bodily components are felt; the emotion cannot occur until those bodily events are caused by the perception of some or other event. James's most characteristic argument for the primacy of the bodily reaction is that if one abstracts from feelings of bodily events, such as quick breathing, trembling, and burning cheeks, nothing remains of the emotion but a cold-blooded and indifferent cognition that a certain event is unfortunate or the opposite. This kind of 'purely disembodied' emotion is a nonentity' (Pr II, p. 452).

James's equation of emotions and sensations is a convenient arrangement. It is only when asking where exactly the similarity lies that we find ourselves in the dark. Wittgenstein asks this question and from his answer four clear distinctions can be

---

[29] See Wundt (1874).

[30] See James (1920, pp. 351-352), where he confesses to be dissatisfied with the example, but maintains his view that the felt emotion is some or other organic change.

reconstructed. (1) Emotions, unlike sensations, are not localized. (2) Emotions, unlike sensations, are directed at an object. (3) Emotions, unlike impressions, give no information about the external world. (4) Emotions, unlike sensations and impressions, form a conglomerate, a syndrome of causes, characteristic (facial) expressions, and actions. On account of these four logical features the language-game of emotions possesses an autonomy which James's theory completely fails to respect.

In the first place (1) Wittgenstein says about emotions: 'Distinction from sensations: they are not localized (nor yet diffuse!)' (RPP II, § 148). He advances three arguments for this constitutive rule: (i) in an emotional state we are often quite unaware of bodily feelings; (ii) awareness of bodily feelings is not the same as being emotional; (iii) the meaning of emotions is not some or other identification, either with bodily feelings or with mind stuff.

It is true that emotions often go with a certain physical state: joy with physical well-being and sadness with physical discomfort (RPP II, § 322). But this empirical regularity does not imply that one is actually aware of locatable feelings (i).[31] In any case the meaning of 'joy' and 'sadness' is not the geography of feelings which can only be mapped after an introspective act. Wittgenstein confirms this when he compares emotions in the study with emotions in the cinema: in the former case one will be aware, while imitating sadness, of the tension in one's face; in the cinema, where one's emotional involvement in a scene is genuine, one is hardly even aware of having a face (cf. RPP I, § 925).

But suppose that one makes oneself aware of such feelings: is it in that case true, as James has it, that mere arousal of them leads to an emotion? Does somebody who turns up the corners of his mouth feel glad for that reason? And, conversely, is somebody who feels glad and who suppresses all the concomitant physical symptoms no longer glad? (ii) Wittgenstein admits that if you

---

[31] In the early stages of his development Wittgenstein shows much more sympathy with the James-Lange theory (and especially with the idea that the experience of locatable feelings is important) than in his later work; see *The Brown Book*, p. 103.

imagine being sad and at the same time try to feel cheerful – by taking deep breaths and imitating a beaming face – it is no longer possible to imagine being sad (RPP II, § 321). But this does not mean that the emotion is the bodily feeling. In the first place emotions do not primarily derive their meaning from the artificial imitation-game prescribed by James: 'If the death of a friend and the recovery of a friend equally caused us to rejoice or – judging by our behaviour – both caused us sorrow, then these forms of behaviour would not be what we call the expressions of joy or sorrow' (RPP II, § 321). Wittgenstein is saying that the original meaning of emotions in our form of life is connected with a pattern of natural reactions, reactions expressing conviction, spontaneity, sympathy or antipathy. These patterns do not admit of sudden interruptions. In view of these patterns it is not so easy to switch from one emotion to the next merely by grimacing differently. If you are sad and at the same time you feel glad merely by pulling a different face, then either you were not really sad or you are not really glad. Someone who is genuinely sad cannot laugh convincingly and someone who is genuinely glad cannot be convincingly down. Exceptions only serve to confirm the rule here. The second reason why James is wrong in granting primacy to bodily feelings is that a genuine emotion need not disappear through mere imitation of another feeling. In fact, ostensibly conflicting emotions can even intensify a certain emotion: 'Couldn't the mere attempt to laugh while one was feeling grief bring about an enormous sharpening of the grief?' (RPP II, § 321).

The meaning of emotions is not an identification; it is not an identification of something in the body, a feeling, nor of something shown by the body, behaviour (iii). The tendency to anchor emotions in the body is due to unfounded concern about a dualistic, i.e. psychic status of emotions: if an emotion is not felt somewhere, it is nowhere and so it is in the mind (RPP I, § 803). Wittgenstein does acknowledge a metaphorical location of emotions. In a fragment reminiscent of Plato's tripartition of the soul he writes that, if asked to locate emotions, he would locate grief in the stomach, love in the breast, and a bright idea in the head (RPP

I, § 438). But we do not literally speak of a bodily place of grief. We do not have an organ in which or by which we experience emotions. And this is not because emotions are diffusely located. Even if the feeling that goes along with joy is located, joy is not (Z, § 486). The emotion of joy is not a feeling around the eyes and the corners of the mouth. Nor is emotion behaviour, even if joy manifests itself in facial expressions. Joy refers neither to something inner nor to something outer (Z, § 487). The reason for this is made clear by Wittgenstein's second argument.

In Z, § 511 Wittgenstein remarks that if we must needs locate emotions, we should locate them not in the mind or the body, but rather in the 'object' of the emotion (2). He sums up the meaning of 'object' as follows: 'Among emotions the directed might be distinguished from the undirected. Fear at something, joy over something. This something is the object, not the cause of the emotion. The language-game "I am afraid" already contains the object' (RPP II, § 148). There are two important points: what is meant by (a) the distinction between cause and object and (b) the distinction between directed and undirected?

The emphasis on the object of emotions is not intended to replace a causal explanation of emotions (a). I take the point of the distinction to be that, on account of their object, emotions cannot be reduced to sensations. The concept of emotion is internally related to an object at which the emotion is directed. If the relation is internal, this entails that the description of an emotion is *at the same time* the description of the object of emotion – not of the cause. In other words, it is normally speaking impossible for somebody to be glad *without* knowing what he is glad about, in the way that it is possible to be thirsty but not for anything in particular, or to feel pain without knowing what exactly hurts. This is not to reject a causal explanation, but merely to put it in its place: an inventory of causes is not constitutive for the language-game of emotions. We could, for instance, describe all the causal happenings when we cry without mentioning what we are crying about (BLB, p. 22). But as long as we have not mentioned what we are crying about, we have not described an emotion. This is not to deny James's insight that when we are sad, we are immediately aware of bodily feelings, nor that this awareness is important. The point is only that this awareness of bodily processes would not be able to tell me that I was sad without telling me what I was sad about.[32] That is, not until we have indicated the object, have we described the emotion. And although there are cases in which object and cause of the emotion refer to a single state of affairs,[33] the link between emotion and object is not causal. This can be seen from the fact that the objects of emotions can be and often are non-existent states of affairs, which obviously cannot cause anything. In such cases one could say that one has certain thoughts and beliefs about something non-existent, and it is this something that is the object of the emotion. That would mean that cognitions are an important part of what we call emotions and I think that Wittgenstein emphasizes just that. For instance, he says that emotions are 'characters of thought' (RPP I, § 836) or that emotions can *colour* thoughts, whereas bodily pain cannot (RPP II, § 153). Indeed, emotions can consist only of thoughts or beliefs, and what those beliefs are about is at the same time the object of the emotion. The conceptual tie-up between beliefs or thoughts and emotions that is emphasized by Wittgenstein in contrast to James, thus explains quite adequately what the object of an emotion is and also the enormous diversity of objects, for one can believe almost anything.

Wittgenstein shows through a number of examples that the cause of an emotion is not the same as its object and that the cause is in a certain sense irrelevant within the language-game. Only by way of a joke might one say: 'I feel much happier today, the muscles around my mouth feel better' (RPP I, § 454). And it

---

[32] James seems to confuse cause and object, for he calls for instance heartbeats the objects of anger. But as Myers (1986, p. 241) rightly remarks, we have to distinguish between the awareness of heartbeats and the feeling of anger. The relation between the emotion and the bodily feeling is contingent and hence the emotion can exist alongside the bodily feeling. In that case the 'objects' postulated by James are not required. Wittgenstein would call these 'objects' causes.

[33] Wittgenstein does admit that there are typical cases in which the object of emotions is identical to their cause (RPP II, § 148).

hardly makes sense to replace 'This fear is unbearable' by 'If only I didn't have this feeling in my stomach!' (RPP I, § 728). In these cases one fails to follow the rules which are constitutive for the language-game of emotions. These rules also imply certain reactions on the part of others. If one wants to reassure somebody who has had a fright, one does not so much treat the body: 'Doesn't one much more soothe him about the event, the occasion?' (RPP I, § 924). Once again, causes are not altogether banished from the explanation of emotions. Gland secretion is rightly called a cause of emotions and it may be that the glands of a depressed person produce a different secretion compared with the glands of somebody who is relieved (RPP II, § 322). People may also start crying over onions and even become sad and start thinking about depressing matters. 'But then the *sensations* of crying would not thereby have turned into a part of the "feeling" of grief' (RPP II, § 323). Nor has the cause become the object: one is sad because one is crying, but crying is not *what* one is sad about.

A possible objection to the relation between emotion and object is that some emotions seem to lack an object, for instance anxiety. Is that what Wittgenstein means by 'undirected' emotions? (b). As the conversations with Waismann show,[34] Wittgenstein was aware of the idiosyncratic meaning of 'anxiety' ('angst') in certain existentialist writings. But 'undirected' already indicates a different view: it does not mean 'without object' but 'indefinite'. Someone who cries 'This anxiety is frightful' will not, if asked why, point to his stomach or chest, but 'perhaps at what gives us our fear' (RPP I, § 729). Although we are not always capable of this, because the object has been repressed or because there are so many that they efface each other, fade into each other, it could still be said that there is an object, but it loses its identity: it is indefinite. Or rather: *indefinable*. And even in cases of objectless 'Angst' one could argue, as Kenny does, that they are parasatic cases of emotion, dependent upon cases where fear has an object (Kenny, 1963, pp. 61ff.).

---

[34] Wittgenstein mentions Heidegger in his conversations with Waismann. See McGuinness (1979, pp. 67-68).

Emotions do not give information about the external world
(RPP II, § 148) (3). Wittgenstein does not enlarge on this point, but
its logic is evident. The statement 'I know that there is a man
behind the window, because I saw a dark shape' makes sense, but
the statement 'I know that there is a man behind the window,
because I was scared stiff' does not. It is possible to say this, but
other people will hardly accept it as information. Of course, the
absence of information value in the language-game of emotions
does not mean that emotions have nothing to do with reality, that
they are merely a physical reaction or a psychic defence
mechanism. On the contrary, emotions are directed at an object,
real or unreal, definite or indefinite. Wittgenstein's position here
is in fact closer to that of Heidegger and Sartre than to that of
James.

Finally (4), emotions form part of a conglomerate of causes,
expressions, and actions. Wittgenstein's distinction between emotions and emotional attitudes is relevant here. In both cases the
description of an emotion is the description of a pattern, a
development. Somebody bursts into rage, cools down, and is calm
again (RPP II, § 148). 'If a man's bodily expression of sorrow and of
joy alternated, say with the ticking of a clock, here we should not
have the characteristic formation of the pattern of sorrow or of the
pattern of joy' (PI II i, p. 174). Wittgenstein is saying that the
pattern of life in which emotions are embedded cannot be defined
exhaustively or described in mathematically delimited segments.
The duration of emotions is 'measured' in a different way from
the duration of sensations.[35] Sounds and pains can be counted in
seconds, but there is no point in setting one's watch by a feeling of
dissatisfaction or impotence. Our concept of emotion does not fit
into a language-game where for hours on end people rapidly
alternate feelings of deep sorrow and intense joy or are continually sad, regardless of the circumstances. In that kind of
language-game emotions do not have the characteristic historical
development which they show in our form of life. That is why
emotions are not identical for us with behaviour. For the

---

[35] The duration of emotions, as 'states of consciousness', is 'genuine'.

development also entails that behaviour is only characterized as emotional under certain circumstances. Description of those circumstances is logically bound up with the use of concepts of emotion: hearing a child cry, we do not yet know why he is crying and only when we know that he is crying because he has bumped his head or because he feels abandoned can we establish that the crying is an expression of pain or of fear (RPP II, § 148).

The conglomerate of causes, expressions, and actions is, if possible, even vaster in what Wittgenstein calls emotional attitudes or 'Gemütsdispositionen', such as love and hate. 'Love is not a feeling. Love is put to the test, pain is not' (RPP I, § 959).[36] The idea is that love forms more of a skill than a bodily feeling or a 'simple' emotion like sorrow. For even emotions like fear and rage are not tested like love. One can consult natural expressions to verify whether somebody is afraid and whether he is genuinely afraid, but a caress need not indicate genuine love. In their love people are tested for their skill, a skill which does not show itself in the instant presence of a feeling or in an expression. Love is therefore a disposition rather than a state of consciousness.

3. Images and fancies

If the critical literature has generally neglected Wittgenstein's psychological concepts, 'Vorstellung' ('image', 'idea') and 'Einbildung' ('fancy') have been least discussed of all. Critics have probably assumed that nothing is said about these concepts in the *Philosophical Investigations*.[37] They are wrong. On a number of occasions (PI, § 364, 366, 385, 386, p. 216, p. 220) Wittgenstein discusses 'calculating in the head' and calculating in the head, as he says elsewhere (RPP I, § 649), is perhaps the only instance where imagining is used regularly in everyday life. Between *Remarks on the Philosophy of Psychology*, § 63-147 he undertakes a remarkably exclusive analysis of 'image', 'to imagine' and 'fancy'.

---

[36] See also *Remarks on the Philosophy of Psychology* II, § 152.

[37] 'Images' are only commented on in the larger context of the private language argument.

Before I venture an interpretation of this analysis, something
needs to be said about the terminology.

The meaning of the German 'vorstellen' is 'to place something
before one's mind', 'to form an idea of something', 'to imagine
something'. In this sense 'to imagine something' is a certain
activity and one which is directed at people or situations in reality.
Thus we sometimes imagine the face of a friend or the flight of a
bird (RPP II, § 72). In English 'to imagine' can also refer to an
activity which is directed at something fictional. This fiction may
be quite ordinary, like somebody who imagines himself making
the winning goal for his home team; it may also be artistic.
Imagination in the artistic sense is usually referred to in German
as 'Vorstellungskraft' or 'Einbildungskraft'. Wittgenstein does not
use these terms; his analysis is more related to the first kind of
imagining directed at reality. Besides this meaning of 'to imagine', he also talks about 'Einbildung' ('fancy'). He uses this term
to denote, not an active imagination, but something passive:
phantasms, delusions, etc. A third important term is the substantive of 'vorstellen', 'Vorstellung'. This term is mainly used in a
philosophical sense, to refer to contents of the mind which can be
inspected 'in' the mind. As such the term is equivalent to the
English term 'image' or 'idea' as used in the British empiricism of
Hume and Russell. When he specifically has this empiricistic
tradition in mind, he also talks – somewhat ironically – about
'Vorstellungsbild', the mental, inner picture in the mind. In
discussing Wittgenstein's analysis of 'Vorstellung', I shall first
address the active aspect and later the passive aspect, 'Einbildung'.

Hume, James, and above all Russell are Wittgenstein's opponents in his analysis of 'image' and 'fancy'. First I briefly summarize their views. Next I discuss Wittgenstein's criticism and
his own more constructive description of these concepts by means
of three propositions: (A) images are distinguished from impressions 'Not by "vivacity"'; (B) 'Images are not pictures'; (C)
'Images tell us nothing about the external world' and 'Images are
subject to the will'. It will become clear later what the connection
is between the two propositions of (C), which will also be
rephrased less ambiguously.

In his chapter on imagination James mentions Galton's experiment, in which a number of scientists are asked to call their breakfast-table to mind: most of them do not even understand the question and dismiss 'mental images' as a poetic fiction.[38] James, who was himself bad at visualizing, moreover observes great individual differences in the ability to imagine something: some people have an auditory rather than visual imagination, others have a 'motile' imagination. Thus James tells of a Viennese professor who could only imagine a marching soldier if he imagined himself marching behind the soldier; if he suppressed the muscle contractions in his legs, the imagined soldier was immediately paralyzed. This kind of inquiry has always been under suspicion; widely different authors like Watson and Köhler question whether it is possible to generalize from such introspective findings.[39] And although, under the influence of Shepard and Kosslyn,[40] psychologists have started using their imagination again – after the drab era of behaviourism – the consensus of opinion is still sceptical.

Psychologists are not clear about the status of mental images. Our suspicion of this only grows when we consider that the philosophical model underlying such psychologies is in effect still the Humean one: a model which hardly excels at making conceptual distinctions. I call this model the 'copy model' and ascribe three theses to it. An image V is an image of an object O iff: (1) there is a similarity between V and O; (2) O has a certain role in the causal history of V; (3) V and O have certain effects in common. (1) is Hume's old and familiar criterion: since in empiricism the perception of O is always the perception of a sense-datum of O, there is hence a similarity between images and sense-data (impressions). The only difference, according to Hume, is a gradual one: the 'force and liveliness' with which images present themselves lacks the intensity of impressions.[41] Even so, images are impressions, if pale-faced and featureless ones. Russell agrees

---

[38] See James (1890, II, pp. 51 ff.).
[39] See Köhler (1929, pp. 5-6).
[40] Kosslyn (1973) endorses the 'picture-theory' rather explicitly.
[41] See Hume (1978, p. 1).

with this characterization, but he adds (2) and (3).[42] By means of
(2) Russell tries to describe the relation between V and O in
external terms. Unlike impressions, which are neither purely
mental nor purely material, images are purely mental and purely
private, which Russell holds to be the same thing. Yet they have
an external, causal relation to the outer world: images are causally
related to physical objects in that they are copies of impressions
from the past; they are not brought about directly by a stimulus
external to the nervous system, but indirectly via association with
impressions. By (3) Russell means that V and O may for instance
elicit the same statements from somebody. Just as one can say 'I
see the furniture of my room' (O), one can also say 'I see the
furniture of my room in my mind' (V), or 'I rely on my
impressions' (O) and 'I rely on my images' (V), etc. And since
impressions can give information about reality, according to
Russell, so can images. Therefore images can be used, like impressions, to verify situations in reality. The empiricistic reduction of
emotions to sensations amounts in Wittgenstein's view to an
unacceptable levelling of language-games. The same ground-floor
fallacy (see chapter 2, § 2) is committed here: 'The *tie-up* between
imaging and seeing is close; but there is no *similarity*' (RPP II, §
70).

By 'tie-up' Wittgenstein refers to the logical, *vertical* relation
between both kinds of language-games; he rejects the idea of a
similarity, since the *horizontal* relations of both differ radically. I
will deal with a number of the logical differences between 'seeing'
and 'imagining' under (B) and (C), confining myself here to
Wittgenstein's idea that the gradual difference introduced by
Hume and Russell is irrelevant to the constitution of both
concepts (A). 'Auditory images, visual images – how are they
distinguished from sensations? Not by "vivacity".' (RPP II, § 63).
Wittgenstein's argument, identical for that matter with James's
correction of the Humean criterion,[43] is that the 'criterion' is
empirical - and therefore a symptom – and that it is inadequate
even in this respect: impressions can be vaguer than images and

---

42 See Russell (1948, pp. 107-109). The same view can be found in Russell (1921,
pp. 145 ff.).
43 See James (1890, II, pp. 70-71).

images more intense than impressions. Naturally, Wittgenstein admits that images are often dim reflections of impressions and that normally we cannot draw somebody's face from memory nearly as accurately as we draw it from life. Yet seeing a person may be much less clear than one's image of him. A similar phenomenon presents itself on Sunday mornings: after the church bells have stopped ringing, one continues to reproduce the rhythm of the sound for a while; often it is impossible to indicate when the last stroke actually took place. Images can also be more vivid than impressions. Wittgenstein is *not* referring here to Hume's examples – cases of hallucination and drunkenness – for he will describe those as fancies (see pp. 232-233 down). He means that the statement 'My images are as vivid today as real visual impressions' need not be nonsense (RPP II, § 99). In art this reversal is quite normal. And so the only empirical difference that empiricists recognize between 'seeing' and 'imagining' is irrelevant.

For the empiricist the world of the image is a world in inverted commas. Images are not pictures, like paintings, but they are 'pictures'; one cannot see these 'pictures', but one can 'see' them. Imaginary colours are like shadows of colours: we 'see' them in our mind's eye; imaginary sounds are like echoes of real sounds: we 'hear' them in our head. This world of shadows and echoes is derided by Bergson, Sartre, and Ryle,[44] and also by Wittgenstein. But Wittgenstein, unlike Ryle, does not claim that images do not exist; he limits himself to the logic of the concept. This logic cannot be described on the basis of inner pictures (B). 'Images are not pictures. I do not tell what object I am imagining by the resemblance between it and the image-picture.[45] Asked "What image have you?" one can answer with a picture.' (RPP II, § 63).

'Image-picture' refers to the empiricistic use of 'inner picture', 'mental copy'; 'picture' is a physical representation. According to Wittgenstein, the copy model results from the application of the logic of physical representations to the world of the image: this

---

44 Ryle's position (1949, chapter 8) seems to be more in line with that of Watson.
45 The English translation writes 'image' here. The same word is translated in § 84 as 'image-picture' and in § 110 as 'imagination-picture'.

world is thus populated by 'inner representations'. Circuitously, via impressions, these 'inner representations' subsequently refer to reality. According to Russell, such 'inner representations' can be identified if the similarity between these representations and their prototype is recognized: recognized in the sense that the causal relation between prototype and representation is detected. It is this causal relation which Wittgenstein wants to reject by asking 'What makes my image of him into an image of *him*?' (PI II iii, p. 177). His answer is that (a) since images are not inner pictures, (b) the relation to the object of imagination is not external but internal.

Wittgenstein sees two absurd consequences inhering in a theory which talks about inner pictures (a): (i) it must be possible to see these images and (ii) it must be possible to compare them with their prototypes. In what sense is it impossible to see them (i)?

> Forming an image of something is comparable to an activity. (Swimming.)
> When we form an image of something we are not observing. The coming and going of the pictures is not something that *happens* to us. We are not surprised by these pictures, saying 'Look!...' (RPP II, § 88)

The reason why seeing is out of the question is that 'seeing' and imagining have different horizontal relations. 'Seeing' is horizontally related to 'observing' and 'looking' (RPP II, § 68, 135). Thus one teaches a child the use of the expression 'trying to see something' by saying 'take a good look' or 'keep your eyes open'. But the expression 'trying to imagine something' is more likely to be taught by saying 'shut your eyes' (RPP II, § 72). 'Seeing' is related to 'observing' and 'looking' precisely because the observation supplies information about reality. In the sense in which seeing is related to looking the observation has the logical feature of being able to *surprise* us. For objects never present themselves *en masse*, but always from a particular perspective. Thus we do not possess one sense which can take in the whole form of a human head at once, so that a sculptor would not have to walk around a model and touch it in order to make a bust (RPP I, § 260). One perspective conceals the other; that is why the observation is often able to surprise us. And in being surprised we are passive. Images do *not* surprise us. They do not surprise us because they have nothing to hide: anything 'contained' in an image is of our own making;[46] images depend on the will (see (C)).

'Observation' and 'seeing' (and so also an object of seeing, an inner picture) do not belong to the language-game of imagining, but the description or representation of the image does (RPP II, § 145). In this sense there *is* a relation between imagining and (physical) images. This relation does not mean an embargo on all kinds of experiences characteristic of imagining. Wittgenstein himself talks about an 'experiential content' of images (RPP II, § 109, 113). Experiential content is not meant here in the sense of 'inner picture'. This is shown by the remark that the meaning of experiential content for image and impression is the same or in any case related (RPP II, § 114). The idea is that if the experiential content for image and impression are the same, this is not because of an introspective similarity but because of the fact that one and the same *outer* picture can represent what I see and what I imagine. This does not mean that image and expression can be interchanged; no more than drawing and seeing can be. But what one sees and what one draws may be the same (RPP II, § 113).

The logical difference between image and observation is therefore pinned down neither by an analysis of inner pictures (for image and impression are not inner pictures) nor by an analysis of outer pictures (for they may be identical for image and observation). The difference is pinned down by tracing the difference in *horizontal* relations between seeing and (outer) picture and imagining and (outer) picture. The observation of pictures then proves independent of the will and the imagining of pictures proves dependent on the will (see (C)). Experiences of images are not observations of inner pictures, therefore. But real pictures, gestures, and sounds are typical media for representing one's images. That is obviously not to deny that in the language-game of imagining one regularly hears somebody saying: 'I can form an exact image of it, but I simply cannot describe it' (RPP II, § 145). A game permits of borderline cases and a rule of exceptions.

---

[46] There is a striking resemblance here between Wittgenstein and Sartre. The latter writes for instance that in the imagination 'je n'y trouverai jamais que ce que j'y ai mis' (1940, p. 23).

If images are not inner pictures, then it makes no sense to say
with Russell that these pictures are identified by their similarity
with a prototype (ii). Wittgenstein's first objection would be that
in that case it must be possible to place and see the inner picture
side by side with the prototype of which it is a representation, as is
usual when two things are compared for their similarity. Clearly,
such a manipulation of 'inner pictures' is absurd. In the second
place Russell's method of identification is based on the wrong
assumption that images 'give information about reality'. For if
the degree of similarity with a real prototype decides whether
somebody is imagining something, then both images and impressions, in the sense of perceptual judgements, can be qualified
as true or false. According to Wittgenstein, these predicates do not
apply in the language-game of imagining, and this is related to the
fact that images 'do not give information about reality' and 'are
dependent on the will' (see (C)).

(b) What makes my image of him into an image of *him* (PI II
iii, p. 177)? In a nutshell the answer is: not an external, causal
relation but an internal relation. A further comment on this
question in the *Investigations* says: 'Is there anything here I could
investigate to see whether it was my mental image of him?' (LW,
§ 314). Wittgenstein is referring here to the identification of the
image on the basis of an inner similarity with a prototype. In
imagining something one is not trying to track something down.
Wittgenstein's treatment of the relation between image and what
it is image of is analogous to his treatment of the relation between
statements in which an intention is reported and the object of
intention, such as 'What makes this sentence a sentence that has
to do with *him*?' (LW, § 308). If you want to know whom he
meant, ask him: 'And his answer would be decisive' (PI II iii, p.
177). And this final sentence is followed in *Last Writings*, § 318 by:
'It would tell us of his intention'. In the answer the relation
between image and what it is image of is expressed internally. In
other words, it is impossible for somebody to have an intention
and not to know whom or what he means. (C) tells us more
about this.

In the final analysis Wittgenstein's criticism of the empiricistic
explanation and characterization of images is that the meaning of

'image' cannot be described via an isolated inquiry of mental images *per se*; it can only be described via a description of language-games in which we imagine something (PI, § 370). The empiricistic inspection of mental images makes for too passive as well as too introspective an account of the imagination: 'The concept of imagining[47] is rather like one of doing than of receiving. Imagining might be called a creative act. (And is of course so called.)' (RPP II, § 111). Wittgenstein also emphasizes the activity and creativity of imagining through the proposition that images are subject to the will (C) (RPP II, § 63). The implication of this dependence is the following: 'It is just because imagining is subject to the will that it does not instruct us about the external world' (RPP II, § 80).[48] First I generally discuss the exact meaning of 'dependence on the will' and the implication that the imagination does not and perception does tell us about reality.

As I noted at the beginning of this section, the labels 'dependence on the will' and 'no information about reality' involve a certain ambiguity. The first might be read as if there is a separate act of the will and a mental image which it can manipulate.[49] But it is clear that Wittgenstein does not intend this kind of dualistic interpretation (see also § 6). The second label might be read as if images have nothing to do with reality and are therefore of no consequence to our view of reality. This is not what Wittgenstein means either. What he does mean, I take it, is the following. Images are dependent on the will in the sense that one can will *both* the imagining *and* what is imagined. In other words, both the *activity* of imagining and the *content* of the image are subject to the power of the will. The image therefore supplies no information about reality in the sense that, given the dependence of the image's content on the will, images cannot serve as a touchstone or means of verification of what takes place in reality – which is not to say that images cannot lead to knowledge about

---

[47] Rather arbitrarily, the English translation writes here 'imaging'. For the sake of consistency I have substituted 'imagining'.

[48] Perhaps Wittgenstein was influenced by this aphorism of Weininger (1904, p. 67): 'Dualism consists in the fact that we do not create our sensations'.

[49] For an explicit rejection of the view that we bend images to our will, see *Remarks on the Philosophy of Psychology* I, § 900.

reality. Impressions can also be dependent on the will, according to Wittgenstein, but only as far as the perceiving is concerned, and not what is perceived. Rephrased: the activity of perceiving can depend on the will, but *not* the percept. Perceiving therefore gives information about reality in the sense that, given the percept's independence of the will, impressions can serve as a touchstone or means of verification of what takes place in reality. The situation for the category of fancies, as we shall see later, is that *neither* the fancying *nor* what is fancied depends on the will.

Wittgenstein's position is best illustrated by looking at two objections which he discusses. The first is that images sometimes force themselves on us and have an obsessive character and seem independent of the will. 'Yet the will can struggle against them' (RPP II, § 86). The awareness that such images – though really these are no longer images but fancies – force themselves on us against our will shows that the relation with the will is still intact. Of course, we need not fight these intruders straightaway; we may be spellbound by them. But we can banish them. Furthermore, for all that they sometimes force themselves on us, we do not assume an observational attitude. And it is this incompatibility of observing and imagining which Wittgenstein expresses in 'dependent on the will'. For since what is imagined depends on the will too, it is also possible not to will certain images. This does not apply to impressions: 'We do not banish visual impressions, as we do images' (RPP II, § 89). We do not create impressions, and so they cannot be banished either.

The second objection links up with this last remark: is it not possible that impressions can be banished after all and that in that respect they too are dependent on the will? If I look at my hand and slowly move it out of my field of vision, have I not then voluntarily banished a visual impression? But there is an important difference between impressions and images here. One could say, writes Wittgenstein (RPP II, § 91), that the will moves images directly, whereas it is *objects* that obey my will when I banish impressions. Impressions therefore have a different relation to the will compared with images. Impressions are only *indirectly* dependent on the will: only by manipulating the bowl of peanuts can I remove the tantalizing impression on my retina

and tastebuds. The manipulation of an object in reality is necessary, since the content of the perception is independent of the will.
I can banish a merely imagined bowl of peanuts without having
to manipulate anything in reality. But that is because images do
depend on the will for their content. If impressions depended
directly on the will, they would no longer give information about
reality. And it is doubtful whether we would still call these
'impressions' impressions, for 'Would things have colours if we
could see them as we wished?' (RPP II, § 79). In the absence of
impressions everything in the world is fiction and nothing is
truth (RPP II, § 92). As we said before, the phrase 'gives no
information about reality' does not mean that the imagination
has no value for our knowledge of reality.[50] This is already indicated by the choice of the term information: observations supply
data and information, which is not necessarily the same as supplying knowledge ('Kenntnis'). That images are not used in the
language-game of supplying information is also expressed by
Wittgenstein in the following way: 'Image and intention. Forming an image can also be compared to *creating* a picture in this way
– namely, I am not imagining whoever is like my image; no, I am
imagining whoever it is I mean to imagine' (RPP II, § 115). The
similarity between prototype and image on which the copy theory
is based is irrelevant to the language-game of imagining. If
somebody draws a portrait of his wife from memory, we do not
judge whether in fact he drew it from memory by the likeness
between portrait and prototype. And analogous to this is the fact
that even if somebody has an utterly wrong image of the face of a
friend, he nevertheless has an image of it (RPP II, § 82). Images are
neither true nor false (RPP II, § 63).

Although the language-games of impressions and images are
radically different, there is a connection between the two (RPP II, §
71). By connection, I take it, Wittgenstein means *vertical* relations: the language-game of imagining presupposes the language-
game of perception. How would I have to describe my images and
how would children be able to learn the language-game if we

---

[50] Wittgenstein's favourite method, the description of fictitious language-
games, testifies clearly to the value he attaches to the imagination as an
enlargement of our views of the possible.

have not first mastered the language-game of perception? Even though I am able to attribute the most illogical forms and colours to things in my imagination, this skill presupposes that I – and not only I but all who share the same form of life – know what colours and forms are. Descriptions of images form an essential part of the language-game of imagining and in those descriptions the vertical relations with the language-game of impressions are made visible. Wittgenstein gives many striking examples. Saying something in your imagination presupposes speech ability (PI II ix, p. 220), since it is essential to inward speaking that, if asked, you can tell somebody what you said to yourself. One typically teaches a child to calculate in his head by ordering him to calculate, on paper or aloud (RPP I, § 655). These vertical relations are also clearly seen in the often highly imaginative games which children play in the street. Wittgenstein gives the example of 'tennis without a ball' (LW, § 116, 854). Children are standing on a make-believe tennis court. They have sticks in their hands, but there is no ball. They react to and anticipate each other's movements as if a ball is being hit and they also call balls 'in' and 'out'. This kind of game can be played and the description of it reveals the vertical relations with real tennis. 'Tennis with a ball' and 'tennis without a ball' are radically different games, but they are connected – in a vertical sense.

Finally, there is the category of fancies. The consequence of the difference in the relation to the will is that images and impressions should not be confused with one another. Yet psychologists have done just that. I mention the experiment carried out by Titchener and Perky.[51] Subjects were asked to imagine the picture of a banana on a screen, while at the same time, unknown to them, the picture of a real banana was projected onto the screen, at first faintly but with increasing intensity. The psychologists hoped that the subjects would call out 'Yes, I see it before me as plain as daylight'. Wittgenstein parodies this experiment on several occasions (RPP II, § 96, 119). His point is that images and impressions should not be logically confused with one another – just as drawing cannot be equated with seeing. 'The dagger which

---

[51] See Perky (1910). Sartre (1940, p. 108) also criticizes this experiment.

Macbeth sees before him is not an imagined dagger. One can't take an image for reality nor things seen for things imagined. But this is not because they are so dissimilar' (RPP II, § 85). The reason is not empirical – degree of similarity – but logical – the difference in the relation to the will. Macbeth is not troubled by a lively imagination but by a fancy. The visions of the drunkard, hallucinations, and after-images do not belong, as Hume thought,[52] to the (extremely lively) imagination, but to the category of fancies. For fancies do not obey the will (RPP II, § 100, 101). After-images, for instance, can be observed, can surprise one, and one can wait till they change shape or colour. Wittgenstein's reason for distinguishing fancies – his use of the term is stipulatory and somewhat confusing in English, since fancies can also belong to the active imagination (see p. 222) – is that there is a certain category of 'images', including dreams, daydreams, and flashes of intuition, which do not depend on the will either for their activity or for their content. If their activity is independent of the will, they cannot be part of the active imagination: fancies are passive. And despite the fact that fancies, like impressions, are independent of the will in terms of their content, they cannot be classified as impressions. To be perfectly clear, therefore, fancies should not be called independent of the will, like impressions, but *disobedient* to the will, or contrary to the will: 'And of course if I *fancy* something to be the case, that does not obey my will' (RPP II, § 101).

4. 'Inner states' and expecting

Emotions, feelings, impressions, and images can be called states of consciousness. Wittgenstein distinguishes states of consciousness from dispositions. States of consciousness have genuine duration. If someone feels pain, he is *eo ipso* conscious of the pain and can express this present sensation in terms of duration. Dispositions and abilities do not have genuine duration. Someone who knows the alphabet does not know it in a continuous state of

---

[52] See Hume (1978, p. 2).

present experiences. He can display his knowledge of the alphabet at irregular intervals, but this need not indicate a gap in his knowledge. An interruption of pain does indicate a gap in the pain: pain is constituted by consciousness. The distinction between states of consciousness, dispositions and/or abilities is by no means a strict dichotomy for Wittgenstein as it is for Ryle (see p. 196). Only inclinations, like jealousy, are called dispositions in the proper sense. In his view concepts for expecting,[53] intending, and willing cannot be accommodated within such a dichotomy. He does not have a name for these three concepts (I do: mental activities), but his individual analyses of them clearly show that they are to be treated as a separate category. By making these distinctions Wittgenstein not only moves away from Ryle but also, emphatically, from the empiricism of Russell and James. For Russell and James do not recognize such distinctions – on the contrary, they lump all psychological concepts into one category: that of sensations and impressions.[54] Sensations are even considered to be their paradigm. Nowhere, according to James, does the bodily sounding-board of organic feelings reverberate so clearly as in the case of pain; and in fact it is quite easy to define the meaning of sensations in private harmony with the sounding-board.[55] For less audible phenomena such as hoping, expecting, intending, and thinking, one merely needs to listen very attentively. And then one also hears a sounding-board of sensations and vibrations, so that they too can be defined ostensively via present sensations.

Wittgenstein's answer to this jumbling together of concepts is his distinction between states of consciousness, dispositions and/or abilities and intending, expecting and willing. In just about the shortest fragment of the *Philosophical Investigations* he indicates that the language-games of the psychological categories in question are widely different: 'An "inner process" stands in need of outward criteria' (PI, § 580). No single statement in the

---

[53] Expecting, however, is not as clear an example of a mental activity as feelings of tendency and volition. See note 64.

[54] Russell's main thesis is that 'all psychic phenomena are built up out of sensations and images alone' (1927, p. 279).

[55] For this sounding-board metaphor, see James (1890, II, p. 471).

Investigations has been more subject to critical bandying about. A very common assumption is that it provides a uniform solution for all psychological concepts.[56] I submit, on the contrary, that *Philosophical Investigations*, § 580 is for Wittgenstein a means of *differentiating* between kinds of psychological concepts. In order to show this I shall indicate (i) why 'inner states' have been put in quotation marks and (ii) why criteria are necessary. Finally, I give an interpretation of Wittgenstein's analysis of the concept of expecting.

Wittgenstein has put 'inner states' in quotation marks because the terms 'state' and 'process' derive from physics and have subsequently been applied to psychological phenomena without sufficient regard to the differences in language-games for psychological concepts and physical concepts. In MS 120 he talks at length about the misleading analogy between physical states and processes and 'inner states':

> An inner process, that would be one of which nothing can be said; neither that it is a process, nor something inner. We have words that, according to their form, seem to describe a process and a process in the normal sense of the word does not correspond to them. (MS 120, p. 239)

> 'You always seem to say that there is only the expression of the memory, not the inner process' – I do *not* say that; for it would mean that someone who says he has now precisely a recollection of...is always lying. I only make clear the distinction between the grammar of 'inner process' and 'outer' physical processes. These distinctions do not appear as distinctions of the *games*, which they are, but as distinctions of the *properties* of 'inner' and 'outer' processes, as the use of the adjectives 'inner' and 'outer' seems to indicate. (MS 120, pp. 251-252)

The quotation marks of 'inner states' do not serve to exclude such inner states; Wittgenstein is not a behaviourist who takes everything between stimulus and response to be superfluous or even non-existent. On the contrary, he considers the introspective appeal to 'inner states' *just as misleading* as the behaviouristic

---

[56] An exception must be made for Hintikka (1986, pp. 289 ff.). But Hintikka also wants to accommodate the whole of psychological concepts within the categories of either episodic private experiences or propositional attitudes. His use of the latter is rather dispositional, as evidenced by his examples: belief, hope, and expectation. At any rate it leaves out 'mental activities' and 'abilities'.

denial of their existence. Wittgenstein's specification of criteria for 'inner states' seems to deny their existence only from the point of view of the introspective dualist or mentalist.

There is a clear parallel here between psychology and Wittgenstein's philosophy of mathematics.[57] In philosophy of mathematics there is a controversy between Platonists and nominalists comparable with the controversy between dualists and behaviourists. The controversy in philosophy of mathematics arises when philosophers ask questions like: 'What kind of entities (numbers) are denoted by numerals?' Platonists hold that numerals stand for numbers in the sense of timeless, abstract realities. For nominalists an abstract reality is an absurdity and their negation of it necessarily leads to the position that numbers are nothing but numerals. In practice the expression 'stand for numbers' is harmless, but it becomes dangerous in metaphysical speculations. There the reference of numerals is apt to be put on a par with the reference of words like 'chair' or table'. Like 'chair' and 'table', 'numerals' refer to objects, but there is a crucial difference: the objects (numbers) to which numerals refer cannot be specified in time and space. Nominalists too retain the name-object model of meaning, but deny the existence of the objects which the Platonists believe in. According to Wittgenstein, this controversy can only be resolved if we stop searching for entities and facts to which numerals are supposed to correspond. Instead, the circumstances should be explored in which propositions containing numerals are put forward. Several fragments in MS 120 deal expressly with the analogous confusions in philosophy of mathematics and psychology:

> But how can I deny that there are inner processes? That would be like denying 'that there are numbers' and not only numerals. Someone who denies 'that there are numbers' obviously expresses himself in a misleading way. For he certainly does not wish to deny that such and such, which can be described, really exists in the world, but he wishes to deny that the word number is being used in such and such a way at all or: that it makes sense to say 'there are numerals and numbers', but of course he may not say: 'There are numerals but no numbers'. (MS 120, p. 247)

---

[57] Despite von Wright's general view that Wittgenstein wrote separately about these two fields. See chapter 1.

And a few pages further on: '"Surely you mean an inner process" – Of course I mean an inner process. Just as by "3" I mean a number' (MS 120, p. 255). Just as the use of number and numeral is different, so the use of 'inner states' and outer or physical states is different. And this difference in use is discovered by specifying the criteria for the use of these terms.

The reason why 'inner processes' need outward criteria (ii) is not that we would otherwise remain unsure of whether others have an inner life, nor that we do have that certainty if we have criteria, and more so than if for instance we merely had symptoms.[58] The reason why criteria are needed is that 'inner process' is not *distinctive* enough as a concept and therefore fails to do justice to the individual features of the various psychological concepts. 'Inner' is a vague term.[59] Impressions, perceptions, feelings, thoughts, emotions, moods, intentions, etc., are all indiscriminately called 'inner states' by philosophers and psychologists. Wittgenstein's idea is that 'intention', for instance, cannot be called an 'inner state' in the same way as 'pain' can. The context of *Philosophical Investigations*, § 580 should already make it clear that Wittgenstein here wants to draw boundaries between psychological concepts, such as states of consciousness, dispositions, and mental activities. We also clearly see this demarcation in progress in two manuscripts (MS 128 and MS 180b) which are at the root[60] of many fragments around *Philosophical Investigations*, § 580. In the course of a long discussion on the logic of intending Wittgenstein writes that intentions seem elusive: 'And why is it elusive? (Tooth)aches do not appear elusive in this sense. Or I could say: an intention does not appear to us a bit more elusive than pain. That is surely only too questionable' (MS 128, p. 24). And a few pages further down: '*When* do you have the intention. Always or intermittently? Look in the drawer where you expect it. The

---

[58] This epistemological view of Wittgenstein is held by many authors, such as Albritton (1964), Malcolm (1950; 1954), and Kenny (1975).

[59] See *Last Writings*, § 959.

[60] See chapter 1, pp. 16-17 for a general description of the content of MS 128. MS 180b is exclusively devoted to feelings of tendency and expectation. The first few pages contain some remarks about the secondary meanings of words (see chapter 6, pp. 161-162 ± 3ff.).

drawer is empty. You looked for it among the sensations' (MS 128, p. 27).

The specification of criteria is a specification of *what we say* when we attribute 'inner states' to others.[61] What we attribute to others when we say that their 'inner state' is an emotion like grief must be distinguished, according to Wittgenstein, from the situation in which we call this 'inner state' understanding or expecting. The difference in use stands out, I think, when we remember the way in which concepts for sensations and understanding are learned. Verbal expressions replace natural expressions and both kinds of expressions are internally related to sensations and feelings. But what is a natural expression of understanding, expecting, or intending? Of course, there are rudimentary symptoms of intending. A cat stalking a bird is an example (PI, § 647). But precisely because the symptoms are no more than rudimentary, we are reluctant to attribute intentions to cats. Similar symptoms can be observed in human beings – looking out of the window impatiently can be a sign that one is expecting somebody – but there are no natural expressions: there is no typical facial expression for understanding or intending. There is a certain intonation, but it requires speech: the expression of dispositional concepts is typically verbal. This linguistic basis does not rule out the possibility that various more or less characteristic feelings may go with the verbal formulations. Wittgenstein does not deny this. His point is that the use of the concepts for dispositions cannot be compared with the use of concepts for states of consciousness and that in turn these two must be marked off from the use of 'intending', 'expecting', and 'willing'. For suppose one has a very special experience each time one understands something, how does one know that it is the experience we call 'understanding'? One might retort by asking how we know which experience we should call 'pain': 'That is different – I know that, because my spontaneous behaviour in certain situations is what is called the expression of pain' (RPP I, § 304). The two cases are incommensurable. Owing to the natural expression of pain it is unnecessary, in the first person, to learn to identify the feeling introspectively and we

---

[61] In this non-epistemological interpretation of criteria I mainly follow Cavell (1979, chapter 1).

possess, in the third person, a fairly unambiguous criterion: the expression of pain *is* the pain. That is why the child need not guess the meaning of the word 'pain' in his own case or in that of others; the parents need not devise impossible procedures to teach the child the connection between feeling and expression.

Dispositional concepts and concepts for abilities, on the other hand, do not refer to momentary 'inner states', but say something about somebody's inclination or skill. The extent to which somebody has mastered a skill, according to Wittgenstein, is shown by his actions in certain situations, and often only by recurrent actions. The situation is yet again different for concepts like 'intending', 'willing', and 'expecting'. I shall illustrate this by first discussing 'expecting'. 'Intending' and 'willing' are dealt with in the next and the last section respectively.

Wittgenstein gives analyses of 'expecting' from very early to very late in his career.[62]   In the beginning his opponent is invariably Russell, who offers a causal analysis in *The Analysis of Mind*.[63]   According to Russell, expectation, like desire, is a feeling of discomfort. And as such expectation and desire are externally related to the physiological state which will release the tension. What is crucial for Russell, therefore, is not the relation of these 'states' to external reality, but their relation to the body. For the point is not what or whom I expect, but *that* I expect – and that I hope the expecting will soon end. How it will end remains hypothetical, in Wittgenstein's view, since there is not just one situation or one event which can put an end to my bodily discomfort. If, for instance, I feel like an apple and somebody punches me in the stomach, so that I lose my appetite and the feeling of discomfort vanishes, this means it was the punch in the stomach which I initially felt like (PR, § 22). The point of this absurd example, according to Wittgenstein, is that the meaning of 'expecting' can never be described in causal terms. No matter how accurately one measures it, the secretion of saliva in the mouth is not what Wittgenstein calls expecting (PR, § 32). What is expected

---

[62] Wittgenstein writes on 'expecting' as early as 1929 in MS 107 and MS 108 and as late as 1944 in MS 180b.
[63] As a matter of fact Russell gives an analysis of desire, which Wittgenstein takes to be an analysis of expecting.

is internal to the expectation: for instance, the verbal expression of the expectation shows directly *what* is expected or, as Wittgenstein puts it, it is in language that an expectation and its fulfilment make contact (PI, § 445). Therefore the criteria for the identification of expecting do not reside in measurements of physiological responses and reactions, but in horizontal relations within the language-game.

Later, around 1945, Wittgenstein starts to pay more attention to the description of these criteria. And in my view these descriptions show that expecting can neither be called a disposition nor a state of consciousness, but is rather what I have called a mental activity, though not as clearly as a 'feelings of tendency' and 'volition'. It is not a disposition in the proper sense since one does not learn through experience that one expects something, as in the case of jealousy. It cannot be called a state of consciousness either, although there is a similarity. The similarity is all the more striking when Wittgenstein talks about 'harren' – to await eagerly – instead of 'erwarten' (PI, § 577). If one eagerly awaits somebody's arrival, one is occupied ('beschäftigt') with the arrival in one's thoughts, feelings, and actions. Wittgenstein talks here about a conglomerate of actions with a certain intention (RPP II, § 175). To the extent that others can infer from this conglomerate that somebody is not only expectant, but also in a restless or excited mood, there is a similarity with states of consciousness.[65] But expecting is a less momentary condition than a state of consciousness (cf. PI, § 583). Wittgenstein expresses this by saying that an expectation is embedded in a situation, which is to be taken in a more specific sense than the fact that all concepts are embedded in a practice: expecting is characterized by being embedded in highly specific situations. The expectation of an explosion arises, for example, from a situation in which an explosion is to be expected (PI, § 581). By 'embedded' Wittgenstein must mean that an expectation is both typically *preceded* and typically *followed* by certain events. The situation in which an explosion is to be expected is

---

[65] But there is also a similarity with dispositions, for we know 'what to expect' of someone who is expecting something. Moreover, we learn about his *views* on the outcome of some or other situation or event, which is also characteristic of dispositions.

normally preceded by certain events. Somebody who cries out for no reason at all that he expects an explosion and, when asked why, does not answer but merely repeats his assertion, will not be recognized by us as somebody who expects something. He has not mastered the technique necessary for the rule-governed application of the concept. The situation in which an explosion is to be expected also has a typical follow-up. Hence Wittgenstein points out: 'The words "I expect an explosion" will often just mean "Be prepared for an explosion" or "I believe there will now occur an explosion"' (MS 180b, p. 40). This *alertness* to what is *about to happen*, this beginning of an action, makes expecting more a mental activity than a state of consciousness or a disposition.[66] In any case one does not attribute expectations to others because they have a certain skill or are in a certain state of mind. Expecting does involve states of consciousness, but the decisive criterion here is what precedes and what follows these possible states. In many cases one can therefore replace a state-ment of expectation by stating what follows. Of course, an ex-plosion need not always follow – the language-game is proof against its failure to occur; but it is not proof against perpetual non-occurrence of the expected consequences. Expectations which always run counter to expectations are no longer expectations.

5. Feelings of tendency

Expectations are not the only phenomena which cannot be subsumed under states of consciousness or dispositions. Sudden flashes of insight, intentions which temporarily fail of expression, words at the tip of one's tongue, and names which defy recall can-not be accommodated within Ryle's (and Hintikka's) dichotomy either. The name which Wittgenstein attaches to these intriguing phenomena, discussed in *Philosophical Investigations* § 633-656 and II ix, pp. 217-219, is 'Keimerlebnisse' (germinal feelings) or 'Tendenzerlebnisse' (feelings of tendency). 'Tendenzerlebnisse' (PI,

---

[66] Therefore Wittgenstein calls the verbal expression of expecting an action: 'When I say "I expect him anxiously", one can often call these words an action of expectation' (MS 180b, p. 39).

§ 591) derives from James, who in his chapter 'The Stream of Consciousness' indicates the importance of 'feelings of tendency' for the process of thinking.[67] More about him now.

In the face of the prevailing tradition of atomism and associationism, James stresses the continuity and integrity of consciousness. What was true of Heraclitus' river is true of the stream of consciousness: we never have the same feeling twice.[68] In the stream of consciousness feelings and sensations change without cease. This continuity and mutability becomes clear when we shift introspection from the substantive to the transitive parts of consciousness. The substantive parts consist of the classical atomistic furniture: words, images, and impressions. The transitive parts consist of feelings of relations between the substantive parts. James compares both to the life of a bird: flying and perching alternate; the periods of rest are occupied by words and images, the periods of flight by feelings of relation between these more stable elements of the mind.[69] It is easy to grasp the substantive parts introspectively, but the transitive parts are elusive: trying to fix them is like turning on the light to see what the dark looks like.[70] Yet the transitive sensations are the most important. They give direction and reference to thought. They lead from image to image, from image to word, from word to word, and from word to action. A striking example of this sense of direction is a name on the tip of one's tongue. One tries to recall the name and feels a gap. But it is no mere gap: the empty space carries the mould of the name and rejects every name not belonging in it and so gives direction to the memory (Pr I, p. 251). The feeling itself has no name, for to be able to name it we need the name which the feeling is putting us on to. The feeling of an absence is not the same, therefore, as the absence of a feeling. Another example is the intention of saying something before one has said it. This anticipatory intention is very definite and distinct as well. And yet we can hardly say anything about it without using words that belong to the later result. 'The intention *to-say-so-and-so* is the

---

[67] See James (1890, I, pp. 249 ff.).

[68] See James (1890, I, p. 233).

[69] See James (1890, I, p. 243).

[70] See James (1890, I, p. 244).

only name it can receive' (Pr I, p. 253). Finally, feelings of tendency also – indeed pre-eminently – go with conjunctions and prepositions. According to James, we ought to speak of a feeling of 'and', of 'if', of 'but', of 'by', and not just of 'blue' (Pr I, p. 245). These feelings give direction to our thought and guarantee the main feature of transitive sensations: the feeling of harmony or disharmony, of right or wrong directions in our thought.

As the examples make abundantly clear, transitive sensations are above all intentions and the meaning of language and thought is sought in these elusive flights of consciousness. Not surprisingly, therefore, Wittgenstein is eager to take up these examples. I shall first demonstrate that Wittgenstein recognizes germinal feelings or feelings of tendency as a special category (1); next, what temptations James was unable to resist, according to Wittgenstein, when he gave this special category an introspective description (2); finally, on what grounds James's description in terms of introspective judgements is wrong and what description is logically more adequate (3).

Wittgenstein calls feelings of tendency a special category of psychological phenomena (1) (RPP I, § 777). Examples are: words on the tip of one's tongue (PI II xi, p. 219), being interrupted by somebody and then finishing what one wanted to say (PI, § 633), and the related philosophical assumption that the thought is already complete prior to the spoken or written sentence (Z, § 1). 'Here, as in many related cases, there is something we might call a *germinal experience*: an image, a sensation, which *grows* little by little into a full-fledged explanation' (LW, § 843). Retrospectively the gain in these situations is not an addition to one's knowledge, but a specification of what was often there from the beginning. Wittgenstein does not deny this. For he would then have to say that the name or whatever one wanted to say after being interrupted was not germinally present and that one did not find out or remember one's intention until later. And that is not what he wants to say (LW, § 844). Wittgenstein does not wish to trivialize the special nature of these phenomena, but James's characterization of them. Although James may do justice to the special nature of such phenomena from an introspective point of view, he fails to regard the logical demarcation of them from other concepts:

intentions are lumped together with experiences. The language-games in which concepts for feelings of tendency are used are too subtle and idiosyncratic to be subsumed under experiences in this way. Growing words and germinating intentions are not experiences (cf. LW, § 841). Wittgenstein's view, as I see it, is that intentions, and particularly the kind that refers to a certain point in time – 'Now I know', 'What I really wanted to say then' – can neither be called experiences, nor states of consciousness, nor dispositions. They are not experiences or states of consciousness since they have no experiential content. For the content, an image say, which often goes hand in hand with the intention is not the intention itself (PI II xi, p. 217). Moreover, 'I intended' is not the expression of an experience as 'I feel pain' is, which clearly appears from the fact that there is no natural expression of intention. What one *can* call an experience, according to Wittgenstein, is the decision with which an intention frequently begins (cf. RPP II, § 179). Similarly, intentions – and in particular feelings of tendency – are not dispositions: 'And yet neither is it a disposition, like knowing. For the intention was present when I said "Bank"; now it is no longer present; but I have not forgotten it' (RPP II, § 243). A disposition and an ability, as we saw before, typically manifest themselves in certain situations, for instance when somebody shows in a conversation that he knows Freud's theories. Obviously, he may forget this knowledge, so that later he will have to make an effort to recall it. Now, according to Wittgenstein, if we were also to call feelings of tendency dispositions, they would *not* be *distinct* from memories – at least so far as Wittgenstein would call memories dispositions.[71] But we do *not* *forget* feelings of tendency, as the explicit time reference shows: 'My actual intention then was ...'. The conclusion must be that the explicit time reference aligns feelings of tendency to states of consciousness: such a feeling is attributed to somebody partly on the basis of the state of mind he was in. Dispositions, on the other hand, can be attributed to somebody without his being in a certain state of mind. But the attribution of a feeling of tendency not only depends on somebody's state of mind at a given time, but also and

---

[71] That this is not evident at all can be seen from *Remarks on the Philosophy of Psychology*, § 837 (quoted in note 11).

above all on the specific situation.   In this respect feelings of
tendency are less like states of consciousness and closer to
dispositions.   So that it seems useful to put them in a separate
category (mental activities) (see 3).

Two comparisons have put James on the wrong track (2).   In
the first place there is the syntactic form of statements like 'Now I
know'.   Statements containing an explicit time reference are often
related to events which are taking place somewhere at that
moment.   'Now he is receiving the ball', 'They are starting now',
etc.   The statement 'Now I know' also makes reference to a point
of time, but no event referred to or spoken of by the statement is
happening in physical reality (RPP I, § 244).   Given the doctrine
that the meaning of words is their reference, such statements can
only mean something if they refer to events in the mind – thus
Wittgenstein diagnoses James's idea.   But as we have already seen,
the meaning of feelings of tendency can be formulated neither in
terms of introspective experiences nor in terms of dispositions.   In
the second place James has got carried away by fertility metaphors.
Thus he writes that the horizon of the mind with all its various
parts is immensely broad.   'The present image shoots its perspective far before it, irradiating in advance the regions in which lie
the thoughts as yet unborn' (Pr I, p. 256).   Intentions, therefore, are
the germs of thoughts, as seeds are the germs of plants.   Wittgenstein does not object to this metaphor as such; his criticism is
aimed at James's introspective interpretation of the 'birth' of
thoughts.   James supposes that conceptualization and introspection of the germ can reveal the future, just as an ultra-sound scan
can show whether the baby is a boy or a girl.   'When I say "I meant
it thus" – Do I judge the seed and say, that is the seed of such a
plant; or do I let it grow and *show* which plant comes out of it?'
(MS 128, p. 6).   It may well be that experts inspect the seeds,
Wittgenstein is saying, but most laymen will let them grow.   And
if they can say what plant will come out, they usually know the
'previous history' of the seed: they know what packet it comes
from.   As we shall see later, the knowledge of feelings of tendency
too is largely based on their *previous history*; in any case it is not
based on introspective inspection.

Why is it that reconstructions of initial intentions and continuations of interrupted stories are not introspective judgements
of inner experiences (3)? Wittgenstein's first answer is easily
given: if judgements are involved at all, they cannot, for reasons
which are by now familiar, be introspective judgements. But his
second and decisive answer is that no *judgements* are involved at
all. For if formulations of feelings of tendency were judgements
of something that happened a while ago, they could no longer be
distinguished from memories. And one reason why this distinction is necessary is that, as was mentioned above, we have not
forgotten feelings of tendency when we express them by saying 'I
wanted to deceive you then'; the explicit reference to a point of
time shows that we have not forgotten. And if we have not
forgotten these experiences, then we do not, properly speaking,
remember them either. According to Wittgenstein, there are
certain criteria for memories which determine whether my recall
is correct and these criteria do not apply to feelings of tendency:

> I think the main problem is in the question: What is a criterion for the
> memory of my intention being correct or incorrect – If there is *no* such criterion,
> then one can speak of an interpretation instead of memory. (MS 128, p. 23)

This is important. The point of the fragment is that feelings of
tendency involve interpretations, not memories. The term 'interpretation' is ambivalent, however. In my view Wittgenstein does
not mean that when we say we were then about to deceive somebody, we interpret certain inner and outer facts and subsequently
draw our conclusions. Viewed in this way, interpretation all but
equals a memory: a memory in the sense that we have an
assumption and draw up a hypothesis about the course of an
event from the past. Interpretation in the sense of memory is not
involved here, according to Wittgenstein. His example of a
feeling of tendency in *Philosophical Investigations*, § 638 is that
somebody says 'For a moment I was going to deceive you'. A
Jamesian explanation of this statement would say that one infers
the initial malicious intention from certain introspective facts.
Wittgenstein's first reaction to this is to ask whether the facts may
not be too scanty (PI, § 638). His criticism, of course, is that we do
not base ourselves on facts here at all, nor on introspective or
observable fragments of behaviour. For if we did draw such

conclusions, it might always be the case – as indeed it is – that the facts are far too thin. But the reaction which ought to follow this is absurd: I would have to admit that I have erred in the interpretation of my intention, or that I do not have enough facts to determine whether or not I intended to deceive somebody. The fact that one rarely hears such confessions has nothing to do with chronic mendacity or an arrant lack of self-knowledge; it has everything to do with the way we have learned the meaning of concepts for feelings of tendency. And this is not that we interpret inner or outer facts hypothetically, make an assumption, and then draw conclusions. We learn *that* in the language-game of remembering.

The question is: what *are* the criteria for what James calls feelings of tendency? I contend that when Wittgenstein calls the formulation of a feeling of tendency an 'interpretation', the criteria for such an interpretation do not lie in a correct or incorrect judgement of inner and outer facts, but in the correct or incorrect *continuation* or *elaboration* of the thoughts and feelings in the initial situation. The following example is the beginning of his answer.

> A band at the end of a ceremony has the intention of playing the national anthem. The music sheets are unfolded; the first bar has already been sounded; then this is interrupted by a natural disaster. Were it not possible that the conductor had not the intention of playing the national anthem, but of interrupting it after the first bars? And if this were not the case, he had the intention of playing the national anthem. But what did this intention consist of? We might say: it was already completely implied in the situation. (MS 180b, p. 21)

This description is by no means behaviouristic. An intention is not partly embedded in a situation, but *wholly*. A behaviouristic explanation, on the other hand, reduces intentions to parts, units of response, just as a mentalistic explanation reduces them to specific experiences. Wittgenstein's approach is more in line with Gestalt psychology. The horizontal relations of the language-game in question form a logical Gestalt of rule-guided behaviour; not a spatial but a temporal Gestalt. The meaning of 'I was about to come and see you' cannot be described by mere present experiences or units of response. An intention develops, says Wittgenstein (PI, § 639). He means that an intention is not given in the present, but in a characteristic history – and in a characteristic continuation of this line. Although statements of intention seem bound to the present by such words as 'now' or 'at this moment', the present needs to be supplemented by the past if their meaning is to be traced. Wittgenstein is not led astray by the germ metaphor: an intention does not evolve in the sense that the things to come are already germinally present and can also be judged as such; an intention develops in the sense that its meaning is only given by a characteristic prior history. The events making up the history of the intention do not constitute facts on the basis of which somebody says 'For a moment I was going to deceive you' (PI, § 638). The criterion for such statements does not lie in a correct or incorrect judgement but in a correct or incorrect continuation of them. And to recognize this continuation as a continuation one must in turn know what has gone before. Yes, it was the bandmaster's intention to play the national anthem; the criterion is that he can – and will – continue his conducting in the right way. The schoolmaster's reprimand 'I mean you' is also a continuation of a previous situation and not an introspective report. 'Somebody is trying to waste our time. I mean you'. Raising a hand in class is also an expression of an intention for which the criterion lies in the overall situation: in the teacher's preceding questions and in the correct continuation of this situation by the pupil. The raised hand is an expression of an intention if the gesture in this situation moreover has predictive value: normally the pupil has an answer or a question ready (RPP I, § 245). And the same obtains to 'The word is on the tip of my tongue'. Such statements are mental activities in the sense that their meaning is internally related to what they *bring about*, the finding of a word, the execution of a movement. They are mental activities since they are followed by an action (broadly speaking) and in this sense have *predictive* value: the words 'The word is on the tip of my tongue' are often followed by the finding of the right word (PI II xi, p. 219). Not that it always follows, of course, but if the word is never found, it will never be on the tip of one's tongue either.

Wittgenstein's emphasis on the highly specific context of intentions should be understood along the same lines as the holism of the Gestalt concept. Somebody who remembers something he was once going to say remembers various details, but all of them together do not show the intention (PI, § 635). However, these details are not irrelevant, like other details which one also remembers (PI, § 636). The point is that a certain detail can only be called an expression of intention in the specific situation. Wittgenstein gives this example:

> Consider the experience of wishing to say something in a conversation, but then deciding to say nothing. It is a characteristic experience to breathe in and to hold your breath. But if you then decide to say nothing after all, you breathe out again. Someone who observes you can clearly see that you wanted to say something. So did the intention consist of holding one's breath? No. But in this entire situation this intention for instance was this action. (MS 180b, p. 32)

Holding one's breath is not yet what Wittgenstein would call a feeling of tendency, since it is not in every situation a tendency to say something. It is only that in a situation with appropriate motives and consequences. In one fragment Wittgenstein makes an explicit link with the Gestalt tradition. He describes a situation identical to the many experiments in which Gestalt psychologists have shown that Gestalt qualities are holistic.

> Let a human being look furiously and arrogantly and ironically; and now cover up his face with a cloth, but leave the eyes, in which the entire expression appeared to converge, uncovered. You will see how surprisingly ambiguous the expression of the eyes now is. (MS 128, p. 12)

The relevant situation in this kind of concept is therefore not a totality of separate elements, but a logically coherent whole.

The primacy of the Gestalt of rule-governed applications means that the description of intentions is internally related to the description of situations. In *Philosophical Investigations*, § 636 and § 642 Wittgenstein notes that we can reproduce such situations and he even talks about scenes, thus stressing the analogy with the stage. Playing such a scene is a different kind of description from explicitly naming the intention via the statement 'For a moment I was going to deceive you'. But Wittgenstein is saying that the verbal expression is not always necessary. Often the verbal formulation does no more than the non-verbal actions do (cf. PI II xi, p. 219). His idea is that the verbal formulation is not superior in status to the action. The verbal formulation is not a more detached introspective or behaviouristic description which provides more certainty and conclusiveness than actions. On the contrary, often intentions are more plainly illustrated by non-verbal than by verbal expressions:[72]

> I climb the stairs with a patient. He stumbles. I make the beginning of a movement to support him, but he automatically recovers his balance and I withdraw my arm again – How do I know that the movement was the beginning of an attempt to help. Well, it was the same sort of thing that a third person would also have recognized it to be. (MS 180b, p. 24)

It is even conceivable that somebody else may be more sure of my intentions than I myself, that he has seen certain intentions in my actions without my having said anything. If he imitates my actions in order to convince me, he reproduces my intention without, of course, having the intention himself at that moment. If he experiences any intention at all, it is in acting out the entire situation. The description which he gives in this way, through the imitation of actions and characteristic thoughts, is the description of the intention. But if an intention can be depicted without mentioning a single word, the reverse is also true: no 'intention' need be mentioned when words *are* used. Novelists and playwrights are masters of this art. Without once putting the expression 'I mean ...' in the mouth of their main character, they describe the history of his actions merely by describing situations. As Wittgenstein remarks, a good example of a psychological intention is often a quotation from a play (cf. LW, § 38).

6. Willing

The only psychological concept already analysed in the *Tractatus* period is 'willing'. *Tractatus Logico-Philosophicus* 5.136 ff. and 6.37 ff. contain the definitive version of notes from the *Notebooks* pp. 73 ff. In one day (4.11.1916) in the same *Notebooks* (pp. 86 ff.) Wittgenstein subjects his earlier views on the will to an extensive critique which already bears the imprint of his most mature ideas

---

[72] Because of this emphasis on the non-verbal, Hintikka's terminology of 'propositional attitudes' (see note 56) seems misleading, i.e. too linguistic.

(PI, § 611-632). Other sources also show that these later ideas evolved at an early stage, earlier than his ideas about all other psychological concepts. Many fragments from *Philosophical Investigations*, § 611-632 assume their definitive form as early as 1933 (MS 115) and 1934 (MS 157b).[73] The early definitive form of these fragments is all the more striking when compared with the endless corrections made to most other concept analyses. This long history of 'willing' makes it necessary to say something about the *Tractatus*. After that I discuss James's analysis of the will, since he was again an important source of inspiration for Wittgenstein's views. Finally, the later work is dealt with.

In relation to causality the free will is in a somewhat paradoxical situation. As the governing principle of our actions the will ought to be exempt from causality, if it itself is not to be an effect. At the same time the will can only bring about modifications via causality, so that it seems to be a kind of cause after all. Kant solved this problem by the dualism of a phenomenal and noumenal reality, as did Weininger, with whose work Wittgenstein was thoroughly familiar. Weininger palpably influenced Wittgenstein's first ideas about the will, particularly his distinction between the will as the vehicle of the ethical and the will as phenomenon. The first will cannot be spoken of, the second is only of interest to psychology (T, 6.423). In *Tractatus* 5.5421 Wittgenstein talks about 'superficial psychology', a pejorative qualification which puts one in mind of Weininger's condescending remarks about psychology.[74] By psychology Weininger means above all the psychologism of British empiricism and he considers it pernicious because it breaks down logic and ethics. The I and the Will can only be conceived from a logical and ethical point of view; any attempt to construct these principles on an empiricistic-atomistic foundation is therefore doomed to fail. Wittgenstein endorses this view when he asserts that the subject as conceived in 'superficial psychology' is an absurdity. For a composite soul would no longer be a soul (T, 5.5421). Wittgenstein is not

---

[73] See chapter 1, note 26 for the correspondence between the *Philosophical Investigations* and these two manuscripts.
[74] See Weininger (1903, p. 100) for his remarks about psychology. He writes on the will in (1904, pp. 153-156).

following Hume here, as is often thought.[75] Hume proceeds from
the parts and concludes that no whole can be inferred;
Wittgenstein says that *if* one proceeds from the parts, it will in fact
be impossible to find the whole. Hume's argument is purely
destructive and aimed at liquidation of the subject; Wittgenstein's
argument is constructive and aimed at refuting the atomic
interpretation of the subject as a thing and *ipso facto* at saving the
non-composite subject. If the subject is interpreted as a thing, it
becomes an 'Unding', an absurdity. But the genuine subject is not
a thing and therefore not an 'Unding' either: 'The I is not the
object' (N, p. 80).

The philosophical I is not the man, the human body, or the
soul discussed by psychology, but the metaphysical subject. And
this subject is not a part of the world but its limit (T, 5.641). This
subject is the will as vehicle of the ethical, which cannot be
spoken of. The will as vehicle of the ethical is a transcendental
will.[76] Nothing can be said about it because this will does not put
us in contact with any aspect of states of affairs in the world, but
only with the world conceived as a whole. The transcendental
will makes my world into an entirely different one according to
whether I am happy or unhappy, but this change takes place at the
limit of the world, not in some or other constellation of facts. In
Wittgenstein's terms: 'In brief, the world must thereby become
quite another. It must so to speak wax or wane as a whole' (T,
6.43). As a transcendental perspective on the world as a whole,
the ethical will is in a certain sense entirely free with regard to the
states of affairs in the world. And since it is only possible to talk
about states of affairs, according to the *Tractatus*, the ethical will
cannot be talked about. The will which *can* be talked about is
phenomenal. But this will has no power over the events in the
world. Events in the world are said by Wittgenstein to be independent of my phenomenal will in the same way that they are
independent of each other. Wittgenstein does not deny empirical
causality here in the sense of regularity; he denies only that this
causality is equal to logical necessity. For an analysis of the

---

[75] See for instance Mounce (1981, p. 88) and Hacker (1972, pp. 59-60).

[76] A satisfying interpretation of the ethical will is given by Bouveresse (1973,
chapter 3).

relation between voluntary acts and events in terms of cause and effect shows that such a relation can never lead to more than psychological convictions and habits, and certainly not to 'knowledge' of what will happen in the future (T, 5.1361 and 6.3631). Only logical deduction can lead to 'knowledge' of what must necessarily happen in the future.

It is specially relevant to what follows that Wittgenstein arrives at such a causal description of the will by his equation of willing and wishing.[77] According to *Notebooks* p. 77, the wish bears no logical relation to its fulfilment. He radically breaks with this identification of willing and wishing on 4.11.1916. But it is not the only break. Wittgenstein will also dismiss James's reduction of willing to various kinds of bodily sensations and in particular his 'ideo-motor theory'. That is our next subject.

Bodily movements are for James the most directly observable manifestations of the will, so that he concentrates on their explanation.[78] In saying that sensations can effectively guide action, James departs from the introspective tradition according to which actions must be preceded by explicit thoughts. These sensations can be divided into direct effects of the movement, in particular kinaesthetic sensations in muscles and joints, and more indirect ones, such as kinaesthetic ideas or memories of the sensation. As we become more and more trained in certain movements, the direct effects increasingly escape our observation and the movement comes mainly to be guided and led by the indirect effects, as is illustrated by the fact that professional dancers are purely guided in their performances by their (kinaesthetic) memory of bodily feelings and not by the direct sensations of their present movements. James is convinced of the absolute necessity of guiding sensations for the successful execution of voluntary movements (Pr II, p. 490). An example of this necessity is the case of an anaesthetic boy, who only had sensations in his right eye and left ear and no kinaesthetic sensations in his limbs; if his eye was closed, he would maintain that he was opening and shutting his hand, although his hand was being held in one position. Thus

---

[77] This equation is also commented on by Winch (1968).
[78] See James (1890, II, pp. 487-488).

the open eye was a condition for correct observations but also for voluntary movements.

According to James, such indirect effects suffice for the execution of movements. In this he opposes Wundt, Helmholtz and Mach, who moreover postulate a 'feeling of innervation' as a condition, a feeling of a current of energy from the brain to the muscles.[79] There is hardly any introspective evidence for this, according to James. The only element we need appeal to is an anticipatory idea of the effects of a movement, a kind of shadow of the movement to be executed. These shadows also explain our surprise when a box that does not look heavy, at first resists our efforts to lift it up. The surprise is the result of a sensation which runs counter to the expected sensation (shadow). The gist of the 'ideo-motor theory'[80] which James goes on to argue is that such shadows are enough for the carrying out of movements. No separate act of the will, no special fiat, no ready-set-go such as dualists believe in, is needed. The theory is that as soon as an idea is stably fixed in the mind, it will automatically seek release in an action (cf. Pr II, p. 522). That is, if the idea prevails over others and is not blocked by contradictory notions. Willing therefore remains confined to the purely mental sphere. The will has finished its job, according to James, when after much effort and attention a certain idea has been stably fixed in the mind and possible rivals have been eliminated. An aphasic patient who wants to say something and summons up the idea of the word, opens his mouth, but nevertheless produces unintelligible and wrong sounds, is, despite this lack of success, exercising his will. Hence the very mentalistic conclusion that the essential task of the will has been fulfilled once attention has put a stable idea before the mind (Pr II, p. 561). A final example is: wanting to get out of bed on a cold winter morning.[81] For this we focus our

---

[79] Wittgenstein's argument against the feeling of innervation differs from James's in not appealing to introspection: 'Can't rest be just as voluntary as motion? Can't abstention from movement be voluntary? What better argument against a feeling of innervation?' (RPP I, § 845).

[80] Lotze is also mentioned by James as a supporter of the ideo-motor theory (1890, II, p. 523).

[81] See James (1890, II, pp. 524-525).

attention on a cup of tea, normally an easy thing, but difficult now because of the idea of the cold floor which goes with it. But once the tea is stably fixed in our mind, we find ourselves standing in the kitchen before we realize it. Volition has ended as soon as the image of tea refuses to leave us. James's theory of the will as an attempt at conscious fixation of mental ideas, regardless of the physical continuation, is therefore mentalistic, if not dualistic.

Wittgenstein has objections both to the classical theory of mental acts of volition and to its correction in the ideo-motor theory. In both cases a relation which should be internal is described as external, in his view. I first discuss his criticism and then his constructive description of internal relations.

Wittgenstein formulates the traditional problem of voluntary, goal-oriented, or intentional actions as follows: 'what is left over if I subtract the fact that my arm goes up from the fact that I raise my arm?' (PI, § 621; MS 115, p. 108; MS 157, p. 37). The opposition created here is between the voluntary raising and the involuntary going up of the arm. What is left over of a voluntary action if the fact *that* the arm goes up is subtracted; and, conversely, what must be *added* to the fact that the arm goes up for a voluntary action to be involved? The question is deliberately formulated in this way so as to show how philosophical problems arise here. For the immediate implication of the question seems to me to be that the opposition between doing and happening, active and passive, or voluntary and involuntary can only be fought out in the realm of inner experiences. In fact, the answer of most thinkers is that 'raising' is distinguished from 'going up' by the addition of a mental cause.

The opposition thus formulated is spurious, according to Wittgenstein. People have been thrown off track by expressions like 'I do this' or 'I raise my arm' and 'My arm goes up' or 'I see my arm going up'. '"I do ..." seems to have a definite sense, separate from all experience' (PI, § 620; MS 115, p. 107). In more graphic terms, doing itself seems to have 'no volume of experience'. The meaning of this metaphor is that doing is an inner, mental activity which has a sense *per se*, regardless of its relation to the experience of carrying out actions. The willing subject is imagined here as a motor which has no inertia in itself to overcome, writes

Wittgenstein. It need not overcome the inertia of the body either, for with Augustine one can say 'I will, but my body does not obey me', but never 'My will does not obey me' (PI, § 618). Again Wittgenstein is referring to the traditional idea that willing is pure activity and completely independent, in contrast to, for instance, seeing and hearing. One cannot always see or hear something at will. Thus someone can be told to wait patiently for the right moment when he will be able to hear or see something. Waiting patiently for the moment when one is able to will something seems absurd. According to the classical theory, willing is possible at any moment. For I am the one who wills, and 'I' does not mean my body. This mental activity supposedly lays the groundwork which distinguishes voluntary actions from involuntary ones. The presupposition here is that one cannot tell by the physical action as such whether it is voluntary or involuntary. The addition which makes an action voluntary is of course invisible too; it must be experienced 'from within'. The reasons for speaking of such mental actions and ideas are plain. Although it is not clear 'from the outside' whether an action is voluntary, it *is* clear for the agent. There can be no question for him whether he knows what he wants; he knows. And he knows this on the basis of the relation between willing and the mental idea of the willed action, according to Wittgenstein's diagnosis: 'The will seems always to have to relate to an idea. We cannot imagine e.g. having carried out an act of will without having detected that we carried it out' (N, p. 86). The action has been carried out mentally *before* it is carried out in reality. If these mental acts of volition are considered superfluous, as by James, then alternatively the action has been prepared or anticipated in a mental idea. The common principle of the theory of voluntary acts and the ideo-motor theory is therefore that willing is a mental affair which can be identified *independently* of actions and intended actions. The differences between the two theories are minimal and merely gradual. Even so Wittgenstein aims his criticism at each individually.

For Wittgenstein (but also for James), the theory of voluntary acts is a classic example of a philosophy which fails to fuel itself with enough examples (cf. BRB, pp. 150-151).[82] The prototype of a voluntary action is taken to be one which requires a distinct effort: lifting a weight or robbing a bank. In these cases the action is in fact preceded by effort, concentration, one attempt or more, deliberation, in short: activities of the will. Wittgenstein has two objections to this. Many, if not most, actions which we call voluntary are not preceded by mental activities: 'When I'm writing, walking, eating, talking, gazing here and there (normally), I no more *try* to perform these actions than the face of an old friend *"strikes* me as familiar"' (LW, § 848). Voluntary actions not only often lack preparatory activities, sometimes they even lack a very sense of voluntariness. Writing, a voluntary activity, is not or scarcely preceded by acts of the will; rather it feels automatic (RPP II, § 267). Similar experiences of 'causal' acts of volition are also lacking in voluntary actions like lighting a cigarette with one's hand or bringing a spoon to one's mouth. 'And how different it is again when I want to reflect, to remember, etc.' (MS 115, p. 102). 'Voluntary' therefore applies to actions which can only be described via family resemblances, not via a prototype, like weight lifting.

The ideo-motor theory is subject to the same criticism insofar as it appeals to preparatory mental ideas and impressions. But Wittgenstein has an extra point of criticism. In the *Brown Books* he mentions James's getting-out-of-bed example and takes particular exception to the phrase 'he finds himself getting up' (BB, pp. 51 ff.). James suggests by it that we assume an observational attitude to our own actions and that we can therefore be surprised about them. But Wittgenstein holds that we are more likely to be surprised about reflex movements, like slipping, and that it is this kind of action which involves observation.

However, his fundamental objection to dualistic and mentalistic theories is that they see volition as an inner action – as James does when he describes willing in terms of a fixing of one's attention. In this way the activity of willing is wrongly modelled on the activity of the physically observable result of volition, so that besides the publicly observable action there is also an inner

---

[82] See also the more elaborate German version of this part of *The Brown Book* in MS 115, pp. 287-292.

and primary action, willing or the fixing of one's attention. This view is due to the fact '... that the word willing is being conceived of falsely here, like the word "time" when one thinks that time must move at a certain speed' (MS 157, p. 44). Willing is not an 'action' which, as an inner motor, causes the publicly observable action: 'Doubtless I was trying to say: I can't will willing; that is, it makes no sense to speak of willing willing. "Willing" is not the name of an action; and so not the name of any voluntary action either' (PI, § 613). The point being that if the will is an action, the predicates voluntary-involuntary also have to be applicable to this action. Just as it makes sense to say that one raises one's arm voluntarily, it would have to be possible to say that one wills voluntarily or involuntarily. The latter statement is of course absurd. It makes no sense to say that one wills voluntarily or that one wills at will. It does make sense to say that an action takes place at my will and that I choose to let it take place, but not that I choose the choice.

There is a second respect in which the traditional view leads to absurd consequences. Authors like Augustine, James, and the Wittgenstein of the *Tractatus* are also aware that the relation between willing and what is willed is necessary: to will is to know what is willed. But these authors locate the necessity in the sphere of the mental preparations or executions of the real actions. Necessity is guaranteed because I know mentally what I want, either through an explicit act of volition or through intense concentration on the inner representation of the outer action. In Wittgenstein's view this does not yet make the relation between willing and doing an internal one. On the contrary, it remains *external*. No matter how far voluntary acts and mental representations cast their shadows before, yet they are still shadows. For if willing is represented as an action, there must also be an instrument used in performing the action, a wish, a mental picture, etc. Like every action, willing ought to be able to manipulate, produce, banish such pictures. But Wittgenstein counters: 'The fact that I will an action consists in my performing the action, not in my doing something else which causes the action' (N, p. 88). The relation between willing and doing is not mediated by a third term, a mental cause, since the cause need not lead to the effect. Although acts of volition are meant to form a stable link with actions, they can only bring about an external relation.

> Let us consider too that the activity of deliberating is independent of the experiences which we have while actually carrying out the movement. I.e., this deliberating, consulting, choosing, might occur, even a decision could be made, and yet the voluntary action might not take place. Conversely, the voluntary action could be carried out without *any* preceding consideration. (MS 115, p. 108)

Willing is incapable of failure, not because the resulting actions are necessarily successful, but because failure and success are only applicable to *actions*. Always to be able to will something – *the* distinctive feature of the will in many accounts – can only mean that one can *never try* to will something, in the way that actions must be learned and tried (cf. PI, § 619). But willing is neither an inner action nor a publicly observable one.

In thus rejecting the idea that willing is an inner action, Wittgenstein also revokes his earlier views in the *Tractatus* and the *Notebooks*. Both works initially showed a confusion of willing and wishing. As from 4.11.1916 Wittgenstein starts to distinguish between wishing and willing and he maintains this distinction in the *Philosophical Investigations*. For instance, he writes that the wish is not the middle term between willing and the execution of the will (PI, § 614). His reason for making this distinction I take to be that wishing and acting are *not* internally related, whereas willing and acting are. For one can wish without acting and act without wishing. And the incompatibility of wishing and willing also appears from the fact that an involuntary movement may be wished – for instance, I may wish my heart to stop beating. But it is impossible to will without doing (N, p. 87). However, Wittgenstein now takes doing or acting in a broader sense. For he does not mean that it is impossible for us to will something and only carry it out much later – though admittedly he does not say a great deal about this form of willing (see ii). As he already remarks in the *Notebooks*, the will must have an object and this object is the 'intended action' (N, p. 87). This relation between willing and the intended action is internal. The action internally related to the willing is no longer the extensionless point, the point of the needle (PI, § 620), but action in the ordinary sense:

> If it is the action, then it is so in the ordinary sense of the word; so it is speaking, writing, walking, lifting a thing, imagining something. But it is also trying, attempting, making an effort, – to speak, to write, to lift a thing, to imagine something etc. (PI, § 615).

Wittgenstein is not saying in this fragment that willing is nothing more and nothing less than the action. His point is that willing is not only acting in the sense of actually performing something, but *also* acting in the sense of choosing, deliberating, and trying. So the meaning of willing also refers to these preparatory 'mental activities' of the action, but the willing has not finished after this: it is internally related to the (intended) action; nor does the meaning of willing refer only to the part following the preparatory phase, the actual action *tout court*: it is action only in a certain context, a context of deliberation, choice, trial, etc. The opposition between voluntary and involuntary actions is no longer being played out in the sphere of mental acts of volition and ideas. On the contrary, the concept of action is primary and the meaning of the predicates voluntary-involuntary is described on this basis: 'The antithesis happening-acting obviously belongs to the realm of actions' (MS 157, p. 42). This reaccommodation raises two questions: (i) what are the criteria for voluntary as opposed to involuntary actions; (ii) how do voluntary actions relate to causal explanations? The criteria for voluntary as opposed to involuntary actions are not only widely divergent, but above all very numerous (i). This is not surprising given the enormous range of voluntary actions: imagining something, bringing something to mind, thinking, deciding, and all kinds of physical actions are normally voluntary. The meaning of 'voluntary' must therefore be *aspecific*. In the language-game the concept is nevertheless used in the conceptual vicinity of a number of other concepts: ordering, intending, deciding, learning, trying, acting. Reading, for instance, is voluntary, because it is an activity which must be learned and which one can decide to do (cf. RPP I, § 759). The operation of the memory is involuntary, but calling something to mind is deliberate and voluntary (RPP I, § 848). But one cannot order somebody to have an attack of angina and one cannot decide to have an attack oneself (RPP I, § 805). One does not bring about voluntary movements in oneself: I do not employ a means to make my legs move. If I do employ a means – inhaling pepper and sneezing, slicing onions and crying – the movement is involuntary (cf. RPP I, § 806). Involuntary movements are typically reflexes that cannot be prevented or movements and reactions one is unaware of (RPP I, § 761). Especially this last fact is interesting in connection with James's characterization of ideo-motor actions. A reaction one is unaware of may be a look which one has given someone and which has made an impression on others that was no part of one's intentions. Told about this, one is surprised or even perplexed. 'I really meant nothing by it' is a typical reaction, or 'Tell me, how did I look at her?'. Curiosity, surprise, and an observational attitude are typical of involuntary movements, but not of voluntary ones, like James's account of getting out of bed. Hence this conclusion: 'One makes quite different inferences from involuntary movements and from voluntary ones: this *characterizes* voluntary movement' (RPP I, § 850).

If acting is no longer explained by willing – a mental act of volition, a mental idea – but willing is described in terms of a certain type of action, then what is Wittgenstein's position with regard to the classical debate between determinists and indeterminists (ii)? For it would seem that Wittgenstein rejects indeterminism insofar as this view appeals to free, mental acts of volition, but does not conform to determinism either insofar as it considers free actions impossible – since Wittgenstein talks expressly about voluntary actions. In my opinion Wittgenstein opts neither for determinism nor for indeterminism, but shows how these philosophical positions are largely based on a misleading use of concepts. The problem for my approach, perhaps, is that none of Wittgenstein's later work seems explicitly preoccupied with determinism versus indeterminism. But the Nachlass contains a number of fragments in which he deals more explicitly with this problem and which appear to allow more than fragmentary conclusions.[83]

In the following fragment Wittgenstein offers a fairly complete diagnosis of the opposition between determinists and indeterminists:

---

[83] The manuscripts concerned are MS 115 (1) and MS 157a. There are also lecture notes on the freedom of the will by Smythies (1945-1946).

Is it impossible for a voluntary action to be caused? – And is it thereby
compelled? If I am arrested and taken away by the police, I go along under
compulsion. Is it the same situation when I go for a walk in the garden? Is
then the cause a compulsion. Is it right to say: 'I merely do not *feel* myself
compelled in this case, because I am ignorant of the cause of my moving the
way I do'? Would the knowledge of a natural law be a feeling of compulsion?
Is the feeling, the experience of compulsion the immediate perception of the
cause that is otherwise just inferred from the coincidence? (MS 115, pp. 108-
109)

Determinists and indeterminists are led astray by two comparisons: the cause of an action is compared to compulsion and the
knowledge of a cause, a law of nature, to a sense of compulsion.
Prompted by these comparisons, the determinist asserts that if
there is a cause for every action, no action can be free; causes
compel actions and compulsion is incompatible with freedom.
The indeterminist, on the other hand, asserts that there is not a
cause for every action, for otherwise no action can be free; causes
compel actions and compulsion is incompatible with freedom.
The above quotation shows that Wittgenstein rejects both comparisons: a cause *does not* compel and the knowledge of a cause is
not a sense of compulsion. For Wittgenstein, laws of nature and
other hypothetical propositions – at any rate as far as they are
discussed in the *Philosophical Grammar* and the *Philosophical
Remarks* – are rules or schemes for the construction or deduction
of propositions (PG, p. 219).[84] A law of nature gives a correct
description of some or other observed regularity. But the fact that
the movements of a certain object can be described and also
predicted in accordance with laws of nature does not mean that
laws of nature compel the movements of objects or people.[85] If
the comparison between cause and compulsion is rejected, as
Wittgenstein does, there is also less of a contradiction in the idea
that voluntary actions can have causes.[86] Although he is not

---

[84] For this interpretation, see von Wright (1982, p. 151).

[85] In the lecture notes of Smythies Wittgenstein says: 'to say that the natural
law in some way compels the things to go as they do is in some way an absurdity'
(p. 1). 'What on earth would it mean that the natural law compels a thing to go
as it goes. The natural law is correct and that's all.' (p. 2)

[86] Wittgenstein's view is thus similar to forms of compatibilism or soft
determinism.

explicit about it, Wittgenstein's position seems to come down to a contrast between actions – or rather movements – which can only be explained and described via causes and actions which must moreover be described via reasons and motives, a contrast between involuntary movements and voluntary actions. The traditional contrast between actions with causes (determinism) and actions without causes (indeterminism) is thus cancelled.

Wittgenstein's analysis of voluntary actions cannot be viewed in terms of classical indeterminism either. He not only dismisses the indeterministic idea that causes are incompatible with the voluntary nature of actions, but also the idea that it is meaningful to speak of a free will in the extreme sense of voluntarily willing or choosing a choice:

> My choice is free means nothing other than: I can choose. And that I often choose is surely unquestionable. What one calls 'free' is *just* the choice in itself. To say: 'we only believe that we choose' is nonsense. The process that we call 'choosing' does take place, whether the result of the choice can be predicted according to natural laws or not. (MS 115, pp. 110-111)

Wittgenstein does not – or at least this seems to me the implication of his philosophy – discuss the concept 'voluntary action' and related concepts like 'responsibility, 'guilt', and 'punishment' in terms of the *presence* or *absence* of causes, but relates them to certain ways of thinking and acting, i.e. language-games and forms of life. For Wittgenstein, the question of whether or not an action is free is not answered by looking for some or other causal or quasi-causal, isolable element prior to the public criteria for the action. Public criteria also apply to the ethical aspect of willing. In his later work Wittgenstein no longer draws a boundary, as in the *Tractatus*,[87] between a phenomenal will inside the world and an ethical will outside of it. The ethical will too only has meaning *within* language-games. In his published work after the *Tractatus* Wittgenstein no longer talks about the ethical aspect of the will; in his unpublished work I have found one fragment – all too few, I admit – where this aspect is dealt with:

> 'The will is free' in fact means: 'There is a will'. Instead of saying to a person 'Your will is free' one could also say to him 'You have a will'; and perhaps

---

[87] See T, 5.1362.

there are people that express it this way. Maybe also like this: 'You don't
have to'. And yet what I said is not correct; for what does 'There is a will'
mean? To whom does one explain this? One says to somebody that his will is
free in whom one wishes to strengthen the feeling of responsibility, one wishes
to change his life. It is not quite unlike teaching someone: 'Against illness
nothing can be done; you can take medicine or not, the illness comes and goes
when it pleases' – and another: 'You can fight illness and if there is not yet a
remedy against it, it is only a matter of time and one will be found'. If both
teachings are effective, they will Iproduce I very different attitudes towards
illnesses. And in the same way when someone says: '*You* are the one who acts'
and another 'You only act the way you have to'. (MS 134, 2-4-1947)

The language-games in which this ethical aspect occurs are obviously different from the language-games of involuntary movements. But I think they are also different from the language-
games of voluntary movements which Wittgenstein describes in
the *Investigations*. The language-games which centre on the
ethical are not so much concerned with concrete actions like
eating, writing, or walking, but with a way of life in general, or
rather, a (different) *attitude* to a way of life. And if the later
philosophy is silent on this ethical aspect, it is not because the
ethical lies outside the world, as in the *Tractatus*, but precisely
because it only shows itself *in* a way of life.

A summary of this long chapter is called for. In the first place I
have argued that Wittgenstein sees public criteria as applying to
the use of all psychological concepts, and secondly that Wittgenstein's originality consists in a further specification of the kinds of
criteria for the various psychological concepts. On this last point
he departs from both a classical and a more modern tradition:
from the first so far as it defines the mental sphere in general as
'the inner'; from the second so far as it splits up the mental sphere
into states of consciousness and dispositions (the dichotomy of
Ryle and Hintikka). 'Inner state' is a vague term for Wittgenstein,
since it fails to differentiate between the different uses of the
various psychological concepts. Although Ryle's dichotomy is an
improvement on the tradition, yet it still tries to accommodate
too many different concepts within one and the same category.
'Expecting', 'feelings of tendency', and 'willing' cannot be classified
with dispositions, according to Wittgenstein. Only inclinations

and forms of conviction are called dispositions in the proper sense. The category 'states of consciousness' is not as uniform as the name suggests either. In fact, Wittgenstein's main concern is to highlight the differences between what, for the sake of convenience, he refers to as states of consciousness: sensations and impressions, images, emotions. Thus he sharply opposes the empiricism of Hume and Russell, who recognize only a gradual difference between impressions and images, and the empiricism of James, who ranks emotions with sensations. Wittgenstein's analysis of language-games shows that there are different criteria for each of these three concepts, so that they cannot in this sense be derived from each other. 'Expecting' and 'feelings of tendency' (together with 'willing' I called these concepts 'mental activities') are related to both states of consciousness and dispositions. The meaning of willing, finally, is especially complicated since it involves an ethical as well as a psychological component. Wittgenstein mainly focuses on the psychological component. As with most of the preceding concepts, he first dispenses with James's introspective account of the concept and arrives at a description of willing in terms of a highly specific type of action; an action in a conceptual environment of 'trying', 'choosing', and 'deliberating'. The ethical aspect of the will, the notion of freedom and responsibility, is no longer described as a metaphysical principle, as in the *Tractatus*, but in the context of a very specific practice, for instance a practice in which one wishes to change one's own life or that of others.

CHAPTER 8

CONCLUSION: WITTGENSTEIN AND THE TURING TEST

After dealing at length with the interpretation of Wittgenstein's work, I will now show in what way his analysis of psychological concepts is important for present-day developments in psychology and philosophy. The relevance of conceptual analyses of ordinary psychological concepts to empirical psychology has already been illustrated in previous chapters by reconstructions of the criticism which Wittgenstein levels at the psychology of notably James and Köhler. My view is that all empirical research makes use of concepts and can therefore benefit from logical specification of them. The importance of specification is all the greater when the concepts are largely rooted in the context of everyday life, as so often in psychology. In everyday life the use of concepts like 'thinking', 'observing', 'hoping', or 'imagining' is highly complex and related in the most subtle manner to ways of life and specific situations that are difficult to pinpoint. If there is an inadequate grasp of the complicated way in which these concepts are embedded in language-games and forms of life – and in fact there is, according to Wittgenstein – the transfer of these concepts to empirical psychology will often be problematic too. And even if a purely technical use of concepts is achieved – though often it is a quasi-technical use, as Wittgenstein shows in his criticism of the way Köhler uses 'organization' (see chapter 6) – a conceptual analysis of everyday concepts is still important for translating technical vocabulary back into everyday language.[1]

---

[1] Psychology in particular is dominated by a 'horror sensus communis' and psychologists are supported in this by philosophers, for instance Stich (1983) and Churchland (1979, 1981), who try to eliminate concepts that stem from what they call 'Folk psychology'. However, as Fodor remarks in a quite Wittgensteinian mood – though he would take exception to this adjective, but that is because he misunderstands Wittgenstein completely –: 'the predictive adequacy of common-

In this final chapter I want to demonstrate the relevance of Wittgenstein's philosophy to the latest developments in psychology: cognitive psychology. I am not concerned with cognitive psychology in general, however, but with one particular facet of it: the procedure of the Turing test.[2] This test relates to a specific situation, but one to which many cognitive psychologists and philosophers attach fundamental convictions and far-reaching consequences. I therefore consider the Turing test an exemplary case of a more general tendency in cognitive psychology and the philosophy of mind associated with it.

So instead of entering into a general discussion of the foundations of cognitive psychology, I confine myself to testing the relevance of Wittgenstein's analysis of psychological concepts to the exemplary debate over the Turing test. This first of all calls for a thumbnail sketch of cognitive psychology. Next I dwell more specifically on the Turing test and the metaphor which it partly inspired: that of the human mind as a computer. The philosophy of mind underlying much of cognitive psychology and the Turing test in particular is generally referred to as 'functionalism'. I will also briefly discuss functionalism before considering and criticizing these recent developments from a Wittgensteinian point of view.

It would be easy to amplify the following account of cognitive psychology. But instead of an exhaustive account we need one which links up with Wittgenstein's philosophy. Cognitive psychology is a branch of cognitive science, the beginning of which is usually dated around 1960. In very general terms, cognitive science deals with the study of information-processing systems. More specific definitions are a matter of controversy,[3] so

---

sense psychology is beyond rational dispute ... If you want to know where my physical body will be next Thursday, mechanics ... is *no use to you at all*. Far the best way to find out (usually, in practice, the *only* way to find out) is: *ask me'* (1987, p. 6). At any rate I think it important that there is a language in which the psychologist can make himself understood to his client.

[2] Prof. Dr O. Duintjer has pointed out to me the relevance of Wittgenstein's philosophy to the problems concerning the Turing test.

[3] See Gardner (1987, pp. 5-6).

I will merely draw a picture in terms of a family resemblance. In any case the family portrait shows the following three features.

1. Internal representations. Intelligent behaviour can (only) be explained by appealing to internal cognitive processes – symbols, rules, images, in short: representations. This appeal to intermediate processes between input and output was above all a reaction to behaviourism. Behaviourism described output (response or behaviour) mainly as a function of input (stimulus or environment). But the fifties gave way to an awareness that this scheme of stimulus and response was too restrictive: many facets of human conduct could not thus be accounted for. Human conduct, it was thought, is in the first place a function of intentions, deliberations, wishes, and emotions. Cognitive psychology focuses on the study of these psychic processes and states, if no longer in the classical mentalistic idiom – which proved too vague for scientific purposes – but in terms of exact programming languages which can be cast in the form of a computer program.

2. The computer metaphor. If behaviourism was strongly inspired in its experimental research by an analogy between man and animal (notably mouse and pigeon), cognitive psychology draws on an analogy between man and computer. The term artificial intelligence (AI) is used to refer to computer programs capable of carrying out intelligent tasks, and designing these programs is part of the discipline of cognitive science. This part is especially important for cognitive psychology, since adequately programmed computers can carry out tasks which require a high degree of intelligence in human beings. Thus the behaviour of computers bears a certain resemblance to that of humans, and from this and also from the Turing test it is inferred that the behaviour of humans is guided by a program – internal representations or rules – similar to that which guides the intelligent behaviour of a computer. In using this computer metaphor, many cognitive scientists commit themselves, sometimes quite explicitly, to the epistemological position that knowledge of reality is acquired indirectly.[4] The computer and the mind are first confronted with isolated, meaningless facts or, rather, components of

---

[4] See for instance Neisser (1967, pp. 3 ff.) and Neisser (1976, chapters 2 and 4).

facts, usually called input. Next, meaning is given to these components of facts by the rules of the program and, analogously, by
internal representations in the mind. Like a computer program,
the mind is conceived of as an information-processing system that
applies rules or representations to input. Some cognitive scientists believe that knowledge of input should also be explained by
underlying neurophysiological structures as well as by internal
representations.[5] But most scientists and philosophers have
avoided this cooperation with neurophysiology. There is a respec-
table tradition that maintains that since computer programs can
be studied apart from their realization in some or other material
(the hardware), the mind too can be investigated apart from its
realization in the central nervous system. This idea, called
functionalism, need not therefore go together with physicalism –
physicalism being roughly the idea that psychic states are type-
identical to brain processes.[6] On the contrary, authors like
Putnam, Fodor, and Block go so far as to argue that if functionalism is right, physicalism is wrong.[7] Functionalism specifically means that psychic processes and states are defined as the
processes and states which play a certain functional role in relation to certain stimuli and responses and to other internal cognitive states. Now 'functionalism without physicalism' has been
inspired by the computer metaphor. The program of a computer
is a functional property of the computer. This functional property
is non-physical in the sense that the program can be effectuated in
systems made of widely varying materials. In other words, the
physical realization does not really matter. If pain, for instance, is
called a functional property, it cannot be a cerebral state, since pain
would then also have to be realizable in systems without a brain –
computers, for instance. Although the many versions of functionalism currently on offer make for confusion, there is general

---

[5] See for instance Johnson-Laird (1988).
[6] According to Fodor (1975), there is no evidence for any '... but the grossest
correspondence between types of psychological states and types of neurological
states ...' (p. 17). Moreover, he endorses a token-token identity, that is, the
physicalistic thesis that every psychological event is a neurological event.
[7] See Putnam (1975, pp. 386-408), Putnam (1981, pp. 78 ff.) and Fodor and Block
(1980).

agreement about 'functionalism without physicalism'. But there is disagreement as to how literally we should take the computer metaphor of the mind. The philosopher Searle has introduced a distinction which reflects this lack of concord; he talks about 'weak artificial intelligence' (WAI) and 'strong artificial intelligence' (SAI).[8] WAI is scarcely controversial and entails the view that designing intelligent programs is a heuristic tool for the construction of psychological theories (see for instance Boden, 1978, 1987). SAI implies that the mind is a computer program. Searle, who opposes this view, describes it as follows: 'the appropriately programmed computer really is a mind in the sense that computers given the right programs can be literally said to understand and have other cognitive states' (Searle, p. 282). A program is now not merely a tool for the explanation of human behaviour, but is the explanation itself. This view is explicitly argued by Pylshyn (1980) and McCarthy, but is implicitly heard in many other authors.[9] In the rest of this chapter I confine myself to the controversial view of SAI.

3. Interdisciplinary research. Cognitive science is a highly interdisciplinary science. Here I only want to discuss a connection put forward by many authors, that between philosophy and AI. Dennett points out the common interest of philosophy and AI in epistemological problems and claims rather too optimistically that AI has the wherewithal to solve the traditional problems once and for all.[10] Authors like Boden (1987) and Bolter (1984) lay emphasis on moral and cultural-philosophical implications of AI. I would like to mention a third point of contact between philosophy and AI. AI can benefit greatly from philosophical conceptual analyses of psychological concepts. For the simulation of human thinking, intending, recognizing, etc. requires first of all a thorough knowledge of the various logical distinctions between these concepts. But in the case of SAI, as we shall see, the possible heuristic value of philosophical analyzing for AI is subject to a

---

[8] See Searle (1981) and Searle (1984, chapter 2).
[9] See for instance Dreyfus's discussion of Schank's program for a visit to a restaurant (1975, pp. 42 ff.).
[10] See Dennett (1978, chapter 7).

large number of critical reservations, to the extent that SAI must be considered untenable.

The method for justifying the computer model of the mind is largely derived from the Turing test. The inventor of this test, the British logician and mathematician Alan Turing, proposed to replace the question 'Can computers think?' by a question 'which is closely related to it and is expressed in relatively unambiguous words' (Turing, 1981, p. 53). According to Turing, the new form of the problem can be described in terms of an imitation-game. In this game a human subject is seated at the console of a punch card reader, where he is able to communicate with two other card readers operated from separate rooms. One of these is operated by a human being, the other by a computer. The subject is unable to see or hear either the other person or the computer and does not know which one is in which room. Via his console he can ask any question he likes to find out whether he is dealing with a human being or a computer. The computer does its very best to convince the interrogator that it is a human being. It imitates as best it can the behaviour of a human being and is even permitted to lie: if asked 'Are you a computer', it may answer, 'No, I am an assistant in the laboratory here'. Now suppose that the interrogator is unable to distinguish between the output of the computer and the human output. This indistinguishability allows us to conclude, according to SAI, that man and computer are identical. In turn this identity allows us to conclude that the output of computer and man can be explained by the same mechanism. In short, if the computer passes the Turing test, SAI claims that there are sufficient grounds for attributing real consciousness to computers.

Turing predicted that in the year 2000 computers would be so proficient at the game that an average interrogator would have no more than a 70% chance of giving the right identification after five minutes of questioning. Yet there is still no program capable of passing the test.[11] In fact, optimism about the test is not based on empirical grounds, but mainly on *a priori*, conceptual

---

[11] See Boden (1987, pp. 97-106) on the only serious but failed attempt by K. Colby's paranoiac program 'PARRY'.

assumptions. In view of these *a priori* assumptions[12] there is every reason to confront SAI with Wittgenstein's conceptual analysis of psychological concepts. What I want to see is whether the conceptual assumptions on which the Turing test often implicitly rests can stand the test of Wittgenstein's criticism – the Wittgenstein test, so to speak. If they cannot stand the Wittgenstein test, then it would seem to me that the Turing test is not a legitimate method for justifying the computer model of the mind. In that case SAI is untenable. I do not want to attach far-reaching consequences to the Wittgenstein test, like questions about the possibility of cognitive psychology; such questions go beyond the scope of this book. But it may well be asked on what grounds I take the Wittgenstein test as criterion for the (in)correctness of the Turing test. The answer is: not at all so as to defend a 'conceptual conservatism',[13] but because of the fact that supporters of SAI have become *entangled* in the rules for using certain words. The Turing test and the SAI view derived from it make frequent use of commonsense psychological concepts, but never specify their meaning. The computer is said to have intentions, to be able to think, hope, expect, or have emotions, but we are never told what it means to transfer these concepts from the human form of life to the laboratory situation of the Turing test. As a result, logical properties of psychological concepts which possibly resist application to computers are smoothed over. In this way the application of psychological concepts to computers is made to seem less problematic than it actually is. The failure to specify the meaning of concepts also makes for ambivalence. Often it is quite unclear whether concepts like 'processing information' and 'simulation' are used in a special technical sense or in a normal sense.[14] From a philosophical and scientific point of view, this vagueness and this ambiguity are unacceptable. So a philosophical analysis is necessary and recourse to the Wittgenstein test seems the obvious step, since Wittgenstein has most thoroughly investigated the meaning and use of psychological concepts in the human form of life. The result of the Wittgenstein test will be that SAI is

---

[12] See Dreyfus (1975) on *a priori* assumptions.

[13] See also chapter 2, § 1.

[14] See Dreyfus (1975, pp. 166 ff.).

untenable if the meaning of the psychological concepts in question has been investigated and they turn out to be used in the normal rather than technical sense. If they are used in a technical sense – which in that case ought to be indicated – only WAI seems to me tenable. But I will not discuss WAI any further.

The Turing test will be subjected to the Wittgenstein test on the basis of several crucial concepts. But first I want to take a closer look at the third person perspective in the Turing test. In effect the Turing test is an experimental reproduction of a situation familiar to us in everyday life: our cognitive relation to other minds. The Turing test presents this knowledge of other minds as if it is based on *indirect* grounds. The interrogator infers indirectly via behavioural signs what is going on in someone else's mind (the program of the computer). As Hofstadter puts it, the Turing test 'treats the mind as a "target" that is not directly visible but whose structure can be deduced more abstractly. By "scattering" questions off a target mind, you learn about its internal workings just as in physics' (Hofstadter & Dennett, p. 79). The abstract structure proper to thinking and many other mental processes is hypothetically demonstrated or suggested by the observation of behavioural signs. For supporters of SAI, this indirect approach to other minds is entirely consonant with the situation in *everyday life*, as is shown by Dennett's endorsement of Turing and Hofstadter that 'we treat *each other* as black boxes, relying on our observation of apparently intelligent behavior to ground our belief in other minds' (*ibidem*, p. 94). And not only this indirect access to other minds but also the questions which must be put to the computer agree with everyday life: 'If our question is about whether some entity is intelligent, we will find no more direct, telling probes than the everyday questions we often ask each other' (*ibidem*, p. 94).

In its view of the third person perspective the Turing test therefore *relies* heavily on its view of the situation in actual reality. But the popular position that knowledge of other minds is indirect has been dismissed by Wittgenstein as a wrong 'picture' proceeding from a deficient specification of the use of the shadowy concepts 'inner' and 'outer' (see especially chapter 5). I will not subject this indirect position to the Wittgenstein test in general terms but will look instead at the use of specific concepts. The Wittgenstein test consists of the following three questions, of which the first is the most important. (a) What does it mean to say that people think or feel in a 'real' or 'simulated' way? (b) What does it mean to say that people 'simulate', 'pretend', or 'lie'? (c) What it does it mean to say that people are 'machines'?

a. Confronted with two outputs in the Turing test, an interrogator is instructed to distinguish between the output which shows real thinking or feeling and the output which shows simulated thinking or feeling. In Parry's experiment, for instance, a psychiatrist has to discriminate between the answers of a paranoid patient and those of a machine simulating paranoia. Thus the procedure of the test largely depends on the use of the recurrent terms 'real-simulated'. Both are *everyday* concepts, like the 'human signs' and 'robot signs' which the subject is asked to detect. We are never given a logical specification of these concepts. Indeed, it is suggested that such a specification is impossible. Around 1950 – the year in which Turing published his famous article – Wittgenstein devoted himself to a full specification. In chapter 5 we saw that his analysis produced two results in particular: (i) the application of 'real-simulated' to other minds is based on clear but not generally specifiable evidence; (ii) knowledge of human nature, which is necessary for distinguishing between real and simulated, cannot be formalized. I subject the use of 'real-simulated' in the Turing test to these two logical characteristics.

My principal argument against SAI as based on the Turing test is derived from Wittgenstein's analysis of the logical conditions for a meaningful use of the concepts 'real-simulated' (i). Those conditions entail that the use of 'real-simulated' in connection with psychological concepts is mainly based on imponderable evidence. Wittgenstein calls this clear but imponderable and not generally specifiable evidence 'subtle shades of behaviour' (see chapter 5, § 4), extremely subtle evidence like facial expressions, vivacity and variability of face and gesture, characteristic glances, intonation of the voice, striking choice of words, rhythm of a spoken sentence, interpunction of written sentences, etc. These subtle shades of behaviour are eliminated by the punch card readers of the Turing test; in the card reader, behaviour is nothing more than written output. In Turing's words: 'In order that tones of voice may not help the interrogator the answers should be written, or better still, typewritten' (Turing, p. 54). The Turing test therefore fails to fulfil the conditions for the meaningful use of the terms 'real-simulated' and the subject cannot be meaningfully asked to distinguish between 'real' and 'simulated'. This means in turn that SAI cannot rely on the Turing test for its claim that computers can 'really' think or feel and that man and computer are identical. And since SAI is mainly, perhaps exclusively, underpinned by the Turing test, SAI is in this respect untenable. I am not saying that there are no analogies at all between man and computer, but only that the conclusions drawn from these analogies can never go beyond WAI, i.e. the scarcely controversial view that computers have heuristic value for the construction of psychological theories about man.

Now one might concede that in most cases no distinction is possible between 'real' and 'simulated' in the Turing test and yet object that in a small number of cases the distinction can be made. But if the distinction can be made, this means that there are, after all, signs differentiating human output from computer output. And in that case the test result again serves to refute SAI. An example can illustrate this. The small number of cases that might be appealed to are formed by simulations of situations which are so closely geared to the intellectual solution of specific problems that a written reaction is entirely adequate. And in written output the computer may be a match for humans. An example of such a program is Winograd's SHRDLU, the robot which can arrange geometrical blocks according to instructions and can also converse in English on a level comparable to that of a child or an assiduous Frenchman. Despite the clearly limited syntax, Margaret Boden has admitted to being impressed by the robot's conversation. 'That conversation so restricted may eventually strike one as somehow "flat", "prosaic" or "dull", is a largely aesthetic rather than a purely linguistic criticism' (Boden, p. 123). The aesthetic aspect of language may be less important from the perspective of the heuristic value of computers for psychology, but from the point of view of SAI it is *crucial*, since even in fairly technical conversations aesthetic aspects will discriminate between human output and machine output. The 'prosaic' nature of the machine language will not escape the attention of the subject in the Turing test, unless he is 'aspect-blind'. Rather the subject may be expected to note the 'aspect-blindness' of the computer, the fact that its choice of words is not apt but stereotype and its interpunction not musical or rhythmical but mechanical. Thus subtle shades of behaviour also play a role in written language.[15]

The knowledge of human nature needed to discriminate between real and simulated cannot be formalized (ii). But the Turing test does put knowledge of human nature, so far as it comes into question, on a par with formalizable knowledge. The concepts of knowledge, proof, hypothesis, rule, and verification are used in the same way as they are in natural science. This equation of 'Menschenkenntnis' with formalizable knowledge is impermissible and further weakens the case for SAI. For while SAI (tacitly) appeals to knowledge of human nature when asking a subject to discriminate between real and simulated, it is unable to incorporate in its experiments the straightforward but nevertheless largely imponderable evidence for this knowledge. In fact, human beings are not computers for the very reason that 'knowledge of human nature' is conceived as formalizable knowledge in the Turing test.

That the Turing test takes knowledge of other minds and specifically knowledge of human nature to be formalizable knowledge is shown by the fundamental principle of SAI that the mind 'processes information' in the same way as the computer: through the application of exact rules to input. In this connection it is interesting to consider a computer simulation of human perception, for instance the perception of a facial expression – so important for our knowledge of other people. The computer program here abstracts the expression (the pattern) from a classification of special characteristics. The program deduces the expression from the classification of the exact geometry of anatomical proportions. But Wittgenstein has shown at length that we recognize and can imitate expressions *without* being able to describe the expression

---

[15] The subtle shades of behaviour are also relevant to our identification of more cognitive psychological states. For we do speak of a convincing opinion, of someone who is really thinking in contrast to someone who merely acts as if.

with geometrical precision. And even if we could, the fact remains that the specific expression depends so much on the context of the whole face and the situation in which somebody is laughing or thinking that no list of context-independent, crucial geometrical features can be drawn up. The observation of facial expressions is not indirectly deduced from a sum of geometrical relations; facial expressions and other examples of visual and auditory aspects are seen directly. This holds good not only in everyday life, but also for professional observers like (portrait-)painters: a painter is quite capable of representing staring without being able to analyze the expression geometrically (RPP I, § 1077). This is not to say that a portrait cannot be described in geometrical terms, for instance via a computer program. But that kind of geometrical description is a subsequent abstraction and not by any means a 'simulation' of actual reality.

Yet cognitive scientists claim that their simulations of human perception support SAI. Johnson-Laird (1988, p. 114), for instance, says that perception simulations by Roberts and Oatley operate on the same principles as the painter Cézanne. Cézanne, according to Johnson-Laird, was guided by the Platonic doctrine that all forms can be decomposed into a primitive vocabulary of stereometrical figures. This reduction of Cézanne's work to an abstraction imposed by him on nature is absurd and merely attests to the unreasoned dogma of cognitive scientists that their programs have reality content, *are* reality. A few quotations from Cézanne make this painfully clear. One of the principles he followed in order to paint the 'Mont Sainte-Victoire' was that 'Pour bien peindre un paysage, je dois d'abord en découvrir les caractéristiques géologiques' (Cézanne, p. 63). *Geological*, not geometrical characteristics. For this purpose Cézanne took many walks around the Mont Sainte-Victoire, so that he was able to take in the landscape as a whole from varying perspectives. On these walks Cézanne was not at all concerned with an identification of individual geometrical lines or surfaces; *that* marks a computer's method. Instead, it is such elusive factors as the smell and colour of a landscape which determine its composition on the canvas. Cézanne's aim is to paint a landscape 'Où le parfum tellement prenant des pins dans le soleil doit se mêler à l'odeur des prés, à celles des pierres et au charme des rochers de la montagne Sainte-Victoire dans le lointain ... C'est cela qu'il faut rendre ... Et seulement par le couleur, sans litérature' (Cézanne, p. 36). His principle that form and colour are inseparable and that form is determined by colour applies *a fortiori* to nature's most complex figuration: the human face. The computer cannot even come close to an imitation of Cézanne's method here. Not that I want to detract from the computer's method; I am only saying that the strong analogy between computer simulations of perception and human perception fails to obtain even to the perception of 'professionals' like Cézanne. In this respect too SAI is untenable.

b. Up till now I have assumed that the frequent use of the term 'simulation' in AI is unequivocal. But it is not. As with many terms in AI, 'simulation' vacillates between a technical and an everyday meaning. I am concerned with the everyday meaning here. The frequent but implicit everyday use of 'simulation' is supplemented by terms like 'pretending', 'wool-pulling', 'fooling', and 'lying'. But in accordance with Wittgenstein's analysis of this concept, computers cannot be said to pretend in the same sense as human beings. I am not sure what computers can be said to do, but at any rate they are not just like people in the case of 'pretending' either and SAI is again untenable here. This is made clear by a further comparison of man and computer. Wittgenstein has shown that the meaning of 'pretending' and 'lying' presupposes an intention or special motive. But one cannot ascribe intentions to computers in any meaningful sense: the intentions one attributes to them merely *derive from*[16] the use which human beings and in particular programmers make of computers. If real intentions cannot be ascribed to them, then neither can behaviour, lies, or histrionic talent. Nevertheless there are cognitive scientists, like McCarthy, who hold that computers

---

[16] Many authors now believe that computers have only 'derived intentionality', as opposed to 'intrinsic or original' intentionality. Dennett, however, does not believe in the distinction (1987, pp. 289-297). But the arguments of Searle and Dretske and Fodor in support of intrinsic intentionality differ from Wittgenstein's view that we say only of human beings that they have consciousness, etc. The former base their argument on neurophysiological hypotheses, whereas Wittgenstein bases his claim on the description of our practice.

genuinely have intentions. McCarthy is corrected on this count by the cognitive scientist Johnson-Laird: 'It seems more accurate to say that they act as though they had intentions' (1988, p. 365). But is it more accurate? I think not. If by 'acting as though' Johnson-Laird means 'giving someone a wrong idea', he presupposes that computers have intentions and begs the question. If by 'acting as though' he means something like 'merely imitating', this fails to prove that an intention is involved. As Wittgenstein notes, a clever dog can be taught to give a whine of pain without ever achieving a conscious imitation (RPP II, § 631). Mere imitation need not be characterized by an intention.

c. Finally, what does it mean to regard human beings as computers and computers as human beings? I want to discuss this question with reference to Wittgenstein's distinction between 'opinion' and 'attitude' and show that both the Turing test and less extreme comparisons of man and machine fail to respect this logical distinction, so that conceptual confusion results. The contrast between 'opinion' and 'attitude', as we saw in chapter 5, is specifically geared to the problem of other minds, but generally goes back to the logical, vertical relations between 'knowing' and 'certainty'. An 'Einstellung zur Seele' logically *precedes* an opinion, assumption, or hypothesis about someone else's mind. Now in the Turing test the subject is put in a position where he must draw up hypotheses in order to verify or falsify who the human being is and who the computer. In other words, the Turing test reduces the third person perspective to a situation where it is only possible to talk about others in terms of 'guessing', 'erring', 'supposing', 'knowing', 'proving', or 'verifying'. But Wittgenstein has shown that the use of these epistemic concepts presupposes an 'Einstellung zur Seele' and that this kind of attitude cannot be said to involve doubt or error; one immediately treats the other person as a human being, which is shown by all kinds of more or less primitive reactions of sympathy and antipathy to 'subtle shades of behaviour'. These subtle shades of behaviour cannot be incorporated into the test, so that the test cannot be said to involve an 'Einstellung zur Seele' either – which makes the SAI view that man and computer are identical even less convincing. This is not to say that we never find ourselves in situations analogous to the Turing test and that we never base our psychological judgements of others on explicit hypotheses. Far from it. But the fact that there are situations in which we adduce and argue explicit grounds for our opinions means that there are also situations in which we are sure without being able to adduce reasons. In other words, there are situations in which we say that the behaviour of other 'looks' or 'seems' genuine, but we can only say this if there are also conclusive criteria for genuineness: 'it seems genuine' only makes sense if we can also say 'it is genuine'. The latter statement is not normally based on an opinion or hypothesis, but is grounded in an 'Einstellung zur Seele'. One is sure of oneself, one approaches the other with complete certainty, but one is unable to adduce grounds for this certainty since one's attitude is not based on assumptions either. Views akin to SAI are guilty of confusing 'assumption' and 'attitude' too, as in the physicalism of D. Dennett. Moreover, Dennett culpably confuses what Wittgenstein has called constitutive rules and modifying (culinary) rules (see chapter 3). Dennett claims that we can adopt the 'intentional stance' both toward (chess) computers and toward other human beings: 'One predicts behavior in such a case by ascribing to the system *the possession of certain information* and supposing it to be *directed by certain goals*, and then by working out the most reasonable or appropriate action on the basis of these ascriptions and suppositions' (Dennett, 1978, p. 6). The confusion between 'assumption' and 'attitude' is partly due to the fact that Dennett introduces his version of 'intentionality' with primary reference to chess computers and then goes on to claim that computers are treated as intentional systems just like other human beings. Dennett does not first explain how we ascribe intentions and emotions to other people and can therefore maintain that computers and human beings are equally regarded as intentional systems. For as his definition plainly shows, his comparison between computers and humans is only relevant to a highly specific level: the level which Wittgenstein calls the language-games of 'supposing', 'knowing', or 'doubting', in short, the level which is based on 'assumptions'. Although I do not deny that it may be very efficient to approach computers on the basis of an intentional 'assumption', it does not follow that computers are intentional systems in the same way that human beings are. Other people are often, perhaps even usually, approached with an 'Einstellung zur Seele' and this level cannot be merely explained in terms of hypotheses, predictions, verifications, or falsifications. Indeed, this level is the presupposition of every intentional 'assumption' and so of what Dennett refers to as the 'intentional stance'.

Dennett's pragmatism moreover rests on a confusion between constitutive rules and modifying rules. According to Dennett, an intentional stance is only 'chosen' for the pragmatic reason that ascribing intentions to some or other system is a highly efficient way of explaining and predicting its behaviour. So the 'choice' of an intentional stance is justified by its purpose or usefulness. But, says Dennett, if there turns out to be another perspective which is more efficient, we will abandon the 'intentional stance' in favour of it. And for the physicalist Dennett there can be no doubt which perspective will ultimately be most efficient: the so-called 'physical stance', the explanation and prediction of behaviour in purely physical terms.[17] A Wittgensteinian diagnosis of Dennett's confusion between constitutive and modifying rules takes the following form. Dennett's description of intentionality plainly indicates that this perspective is part of the human form of life: 'what I will call intentions here, meaning to include hopes, fears, intentions, perceptions, expectations etc.' (1978, p. 271). The language-games to which these everyday concepts belong are governed by constitutive rules. But Dennett treats these concepts as if they are merely governed by modifying rules. For their use in the intentional stance is justified by something in reality, their purpose or usefulness. Thus Dennett treats rules for psychological concepts as analogous to, say, culinary rules. Culinary rules are justified by a purpose or usefulness independent of the rules, so that if the rules are changed, we can still say that cooking is involved; the same purpose is achieved by different means. But Wittgenstein's analysis of the rules for psychological concepts shows that if these rules are changed, we can no longer say that the same activities or purposes are involved: in that case an

---

[17] See Dennett (1978, pp. 253-255).

entirely different game is being played. Inasmuch as they admit of no alternatives, constitutive rules are autonomous and cannot be defined as a means to an end in the way that Dennett does. For that is to equate psychological rules with, for instance, traffic rules, which *can* be regarded as a means of preventing accidents and traffic chaos. But in the absence of the constitutive rules for psychological concepts no 'accidents' are capable of arising: for without these rules we do not just have deficient or inefficient psychological traffic, but we have no psychological traffic at all. And by the same token Dennett cannot claim that other rules, i.e. physical regularities, will make for better and more efficient psychological 'traffic' and that we will still speak of rationality and responsibility. Dennett's discussion as to whether the existing (constitutive) rules establish the meaning of psychological concepts correctly or efficiently is in fact pointless; as is his idea that we have 'chosen' these rules and can also 'choose' others. Wittgenstein calls constitutive rules arbitrary in a quite different sense: they are arbitrary because they give concepts meaning in the first place. Without these rules the concepts do *not* yet have a meaning, and if different rules are 'chosen', the concepts have an entirely *different* meaning or none at all. Thus there is no question of choice here. The implication of this autonomous and arbitrary nature of our form of life is not that changes are precluded. The implication is only that such changes would have to be contemplated on the basis of our existing form of life; but in turn this means that they cannot be contemplated in any meaningful way, since a form of life admits of no alternatives. Only if there were really another form of life would there be other concepts; but in that case – and this is the paradox – no change would be involved. And also the question of how and when our form of life might change is regarded as pointless by Wittgenstein: 'Thus the question is: Would we change our form of life if that and that were put our disposal? – How could I answer this question?' (MS 176, p. 52).

Finally, I want to talk about Searle's objection to the Turing test. Searle is not a functionalist or physicalist and his criticism concerns the SAI notion that the brain has no bearing on the explanation of cognition. The mind's intentionality, the feature by which mental processes are directed at reality, is caused by operations of the brain and is also effected in the structure of the brain, according to Searle.[18] Therefore cognition cannot be studied without considering the role of the brain. SAI leaves the brain out of the picture and so, in Searle's view, is altogether on the wrong track. Searle refutes the idea that computers have real consciousness by arguing that computers do not have a brain as we have. In the Turing test we might be tempted to assign consciousness to a robot, says Searle, but if we knew that the robot has no brain and is merely loaded with a formal program, we would immediately revoke the predicate 'conscious'. By way of comparison Searle indicates why we are ready to assign consciousness to animals. The main reason we are ready to do so is 'the assumption of the same causal stuff underlying it, we assume both that the animal must have mental states underlying its behavior, and the mental states must be produced by mechanisms made out of the stuff that is like our stuff' (Searle, p. 297). And again we would at once retract our mentalistic interpretation of the animal's behaviour if we knew that it was supported by a formal program rather than a brain. Wittgenstein already warned that thinking in terms of physiological hypotheses easily projects wrong problems and solutions. Physiological hypotheses only serve to distract our thinking about problems in psychology. The best remedy, according to Wittgenstein, is to pretend that other people do not have a brain. Clearly this strategy is a far cry from Searle's approach. But it is important to note that Wittgenstein does not *deny* that thinking, willing, or intending may correspond to physiological structures. His point is that we should not claim dogmatically that 'understanding', for instance, is a physiological structure. The deceptive inference from this compulsive physiological hypothesis is that since we are (still) baffled by the physiological structure and since 'understanding' is identical with this structure, we are also baffled by the psychological phenomenon. But this does not follow. On the contrary, Wittgenstein's conceptual analysis shows time and again that our puzzlement over psychological concepts is chiefly caused by their extremely

---

[18] See Searle (1983, p. 265).

complicated embedment in language-games and forms of life and
that a description of this embedment can go far to solve the problems. 'Understanding' is an ability and this technique can be described via criteria and specific rule-governed actions in specific
situations. Ignorance of the nature of 'understanding' can therefore be remedied by a description of criteria without needing to
appeal to physiological processes. The same applies to the 'problem' of other minds. Wittgenstein has shown that particularly
the comparison of the mind to an invisible quasi-physical structure leads to crippling sceptical problems. The existing problems
are soluble or at least visible and have to do with the often inconclusive signs of behaviour, with the long experience required for
knowledge of human nature, and with the participation in a form
of life as a condition for knowledge of others. The grounds for
psychological qualifications of other people's behaviour do not
reside in physiological assumptions, but in the contexts of skills,
actions, facial expressions, etc. described by Wittgenstein. Searle's
view that such qualifications rest on a physiological hypothesis
about other people is therefore unfounded.

And one wonders whether Searle realizes the implications of
his physiological hypothesis. He seems to suggest that we are
more confident about our psychological qualifications of animal
or human behaviour if we know that it is supported by a brain
instead of a formal program. Suppose that we know this explicitly, that we go behind the 'casing' to establish whether we are
dealing with a man or a robot, would we still apply our psychological concepts to these beings? Wittgenstein has demonstrated
the extreme doubtfulness of this via a great number of hypothetical language-games. Our psychological concepts are so embedded in a form of life where insight into the brain plays no role
that a society in which knowledge of other minds *is* based on
physiological grounds takes on an entirely different appearance.
So much so that we would not be able to take part in this
'physiological' form of life. Insight into brain processes is therefore unlikely to confirm us in our psychological judgements;
instead, it is more likely to reduce the number of leads for such
judgements. A comparison with animals is instructive, but the
conclusions it leads to are opposite to the ones that Searle draws.

A dog, says Wittgenstein, is closer to human beings than a being in human form that behaves mechanically. We are ready to ascribe feelings and intentions to dogs and other higher animal species, not on the basis of a physiological assumption, but because we can live with them. We do not share a form of life with them, but we can, after some experience, learn what to expect from their reactions and expressions and we can learn to live with them in this sense.

Agreement in forms of life is the guiding principle of Wittgenstein's later philosophy. In this book I have above all been concerned to show how, according to Wittgenstein, problems in philosophy and psychology about the relation between language and reality, rules and their application, mind and body, inner and outer, need not arise if the agreement in language-games and forms of life is appreciated in the right way. The last chapter has shown, I hope, that Wittgenstein's philosophy is also relevant to present-day developments in science and culture, where the problem of inner and outer re-emerges in the form of the computer model of the human mind.

BIBLIOGRAPHY

Albritton, R.: 1968, 'On Wittgenstein's Use of the Term Criterion', *The Journal of Philosophy*, 22, 845-857.

Armstrong, D.M.: 1968, *A Materialist Theory of the Mind*, Routledge and Kegan Paul, London.

Austin, J.L.: 1967, 'Pretending', in D.F. Gustafson (ed.), *Essays in Philosophical Psychology*, MacMillan, London, pp. 99-117.

Ayer, A.J.: 1971, 'Can there be a Private Language', in O.R. Jones (ed.), *The Private Language Argument*, MacMillan, London, pp. 50-61.

Ayer, A.J.: 1985, *Wittgenstein*, Weidenfeld and Nicolson, London.

Baker, G.P. and Hacker, P.M.S.: 1985, *An Analytical Commentary on the Philosophical Investigations*, vol. 2, *Wittgenstein, Rules, Grammar and Necessity*, Basil Blackwell, Oxford.

Baker, G.P. and Hacker, P.M.S.: 1984, *Skepticism, Rules and Language*, Basil Blackwell, Oxford.

Baker, G.P. and Hacker, P.M.S.: 1983, *Wittgenstein: Understanding and Meaning, an Analytical Commentary on the Philosophical Investigations*, Basil Blackwell, Oxford.

Bartley, III, W.W.: 1985, *Wittgenstein*, The Cresset Library, London.

Block, N. (ed.): 1980, *Readings in the Philosophy of Psychology*, vol. I., Harvard University Press, Cambridge.

Boden, M.A.: 1987, *Artificial Intelligence and Natural Man*, The MIT Press, London.

Boring, E.G.: 1929, *A History of Experimental Psychology*, The Century Co, New York.

Bouveresse, J.: 1973, *Wittgenstein: la Rime et la Raison*, Les Éditions de Minuit, Paris.

Brentano, F.: 1973, *Psychologie vom empirischen Standpunkt, erster Band*, Felix Meiner Verlag, Hamburg.

Brentano, F.: 1971, *Psychologie vom empirischen Standpunkt, zweiter Band*, Felix Meiner Verlag, Hamburg.

Brentano, F.: 1974, *Psychologie vom empirischen Standpunkt, dritter Band*, Felix Meiner Verlag, Hamburg.

Brentano, F.: 1979, *Untersuchungen zur Sinnespsychologie*, Felix Meiner Verlag, Hamburg.

Budd, M.: 1987, 'Wittgenstein on Seeing Aspects', *Mind*, 381, 1-17.

Bühler, K.: 1934, *Sprachtheorie*, Gustav Fischer, Jena.

Carnap, R.: 1959, 'Psychology in Physical Language', in A.J. Ayer (ed.), *Logical Positivism*, The Free Press, New York, pp. 165-199.

Carnap, R.: 1966, *Scheinprobleme in der Philosophie. Das Fremdpsychische und der Realismusstreit*, Suhrkampf, Frankfurt am Main.

Cavell, S.: 1979, *The Claim of Reason: Wittgenstein, Skepticism, Morality and Tragedy*, Oxford University Press, Oxford.

Cézanne, P.: 1978, *Correspondance*, Paris.

Churchland, P.: 'Eliminative Materialism and the Propositional Attitudes', *Journal of Philosophy*, 2, 67-90.

Churchland, P.: *Scientific Realism and the Plasticity of Mind*, Cambridge University Press, Cambridge.

Dennett, D.C.: 1978, *Brainstorms: Philosophical Essays on Mind and Psychology*, The Harvester Press Limited, Hassocks, Sussex.

Dennett, D.C.: 1987, *The Intentional Stance*, MIT Press, Cambridge.

Dilman, I.: 1974, 'Wittgenstein on the Soul', in G.N.A. Vesey (ed.), *Understanding Wittgenstein*, Cornell University Press, Ithaca, pp. 162-193.

Donagan, A.: 1966, 'Wittgenstein on Sensation', in G. Pitcher (ed.), *Wittgenstein: A Collection of Critical Essays*, Doubleday and Company, Inc., New York, pp. 324-351.

Dreyfus, H.L.: 1979, *What Computers Can't Do: the Limits of Artificial Intelligence*, Harper & Row Publishers, New York.

Duintjer, O.D.: 1988, *Rondom Metafysica*, Boom, Amsterdam.

Duintjer, O.D.: 1977, *Rondom Regels*, Boom, Meppel.

Finch, H. le Roy: 1977, *Wittgenstein. The Later Philosophy: an Exposition of the Philosophical Investigations*, Humanities Press, New York.

Fodor, J.A.: 1975, *The Language of Thought*, Harvester University, Cambridge.

Fodor, J.A.: 1987, *Psychosemantics, the Problem of Meaning in the Philosophy of Mind*, MIT Press, Cambridge.

Fodor, J.A.: 1981, 'Methodological Solipsism Considered as a Research Strategy in Cognitive Psychology', in J. Haugeland (ed.), *Mind Design: Philosophy, Psychology, Artificial Intelligence*, Bradford, Cambridge, pp. 307-339.

Fodor, J.A. and Chihara, C.S.: 1967, 'Operationalism and Ordinary Language: a Critique of Wittgenstein', in H. Morick (ed.), *Wittgenstein and the Problem of Other Minds*, Harvester Press, Sussex, pp. 170-202.

Fogelin, R.: 1976, *Wittgenstein*, Routledge and Kegan Paul, London.

Frege, G.: 1978, *Die Grundlagen der Arithmetik*, Basil Blackwell, Oxford.

Gardner, H.: 1987, *The Mind's New Science; a History of the Cognitive Revolution*, Basic Books, Inc., New York.

Garver, N.: 1984, 'Die Lebensform in Wittgensteins Philosophische Untersuchungen', *Grazer Philosophischen Studien*, 21, 33-54.

Gibson, J.J.: 1950, *The Perception of the Visual World*, Houghton Mifflin, Boston.

Gustafson, D.F.: 1986, '"Pain", Grammar and Physicalism', in D.F. Gustafson and B.L. Tapscott (eds.), *Body, Mind and Method*, Reidel, Dordrecht, pp. 149-166.

Hacker, P.M.S.: 1972 (1987), *Insight and Illusion: Wittgenstein on Philosophy and the Metaphysics of Experience*, Oxford University Press, Oxford.

Hallett, G.: 1977, *A Companion to Wittgenstein's Philosophical Investigations*, Cornell University Press, Ithaca.

Hanson, N.R.: 1965, *Patterns of Discovery*, Cambridge University Press, Cambridge.

Hark ter, M.R.M.: 1990, 'The Development of Wittgenstein's Views about the Other Minds Problem', *Synthese* (forthcoming).

Hilmy, S.S.: 1987, *The Later Wittgenstein*, Basil Blackwell, Oxford.

Hintikka, J. and Hintikka, M.B.: 1986, *Investigating Wittgenstein*, Basil Blackwell, Oxford.

Hofstadter, D.R. and Dennett, D.C.: 1981, *The Mind's I: Fantasies and Reflections on Self and Soul*, Penguin, Harmondsworth.

Hume, D.: 1978, *A Treatise of Human Nature*, Clarendon Press, Oxford.

James, W.: 1920, *Collected Essays and Reviews*, Longmans, Green & Co, New York.

James, W.: 1904, 'Does "Consciousness" Exist?', *Journal of Philosophy, Psychology and Scientific Methods*, 1, 477-491.

James, W.: 1894, 'The Physical Basis of Emotion', *Psychological Review*, 1, 516-529.

James, W.: 1950, *The Principles of Psychology*, 2 Vols., Dover Publications, Inc., Dover.

James, W.: 1982, *The Varieties of Religious Experience*, Penguin, Harmondsworth.

James, W.: 1884, 'What is an Emotion', *Mind*, 10, 188-205.

Janik, A.: 1985, *Essays on Wittgenstein and Weininger*, Rodopi, Amsterdam.

Johnson-Laird, P.N.: 1988, *The Computer and the Mind; an Introduction to Cognitive Science*, Fontana Press, London.

Kenny, A.: 1963, *Action, Emotion and Will*, Routledge and Kegan Paul, London.

Kenny, A.: 1975, *Wittgenstein*, Penguin, Harmondsworth.

Knight Dunlap (ed.): 1922, *The Emotions*, Williams and Wilkins, Baltimore.

Köhler, W.: 1929, *Gestaltpsychology*, Bells and Sons, London.

Kosslyn, S.M.: 1975, 'Information Representation in Visual Images', *Cognitive Psychology*, 7, 341-370.

Kripke, S.: 1981, 'Wittgenstein on Rules and Private Language', in I. Block (ed.), *Perspectives on the Philosophy of Wittgenstein*, Basil Blackwell, Oxford, pp. 238-313.

Lewis, P.B.: 1976, 'Wittgenstein on Seeing and Interpreting', in G.N.A. Vesey, *Impressions of Empiricism*, London, pp. 93-108.

Locke, D.: 1968, *Myself and Others*, Clarendon Press, Oxford.

Malcolm, N.: 1986, *Nothing is Hidden*, Basil Blackwell, Oxford.

McGinn, C.: 1984, *Wittgenstein on Meaning*, Basil Blackwell, Oxford.

McGuinness, B. (ed.): 1979, *Ludwig Wittgenstein and the Vienna Circle: Conversations Recorded by Friedrich Waismann*, Basil Blackwell, Oxford.

Moore, G.E.: 1959, 'A Defense of Common Sense', in G.E. Moore, *Philosophical Papers*, Routledge and Kegan Paul, London, pp. 32-60.

Moore, G.E.: 1959, 'Proof of an External World', in Moore (1959), pp. 127-151.

Mounce, H.O.: 1981, *Wittgenstein's Tractatus: an Introduction*, Basil Blackwell, Oxford.

Myers, G.E.: 1986, *William James: his Life and Thought*, Yale University Press, New York.

Neisser, U.: 1967, *Cognitive Psychology*, Appleton-Century-Crofts, New York.

Neisser, U.: 1976, *Cognition and Reality. Principles and Implications of Cognitive Psychology*, Freeman and Company, San Francisco.

Nyiri, J.C.: 1982, 'Wittgenstein's Later Work in Relation to Conservatism' in B. McGuinness (ed.), *Wittgenstein and his Times*, Basil Blackwell, Oxford, pp. 44-69.

Odgen, C.K. and Richards, I.A.: 1923, *The Meaning of Meaning*, Routledge and Kegan Paul, London.

Pears, D.: 1970, *Ludwig Wittgenstein*, Fontana, New York.

Perky, C.W.: 1910, 'An Experimental Study of Imagination', *American Journal of Psychology*, 21, 422-452.

Pitcher, G.: 1972, 'About the Same' in A. Ambrose and M. Lazerowitz (eds.), *Ludwig Wittgenstein: Philosophy and Language*, George Allen and Unwin, London.

Proust, M.: 1954, A la Recherche du Temps Perdu, Paris.

Putnam, H.: 1975, *Mind, Language and Reality*, Cambridge University Press, Cambridge.

Putnam, H.: 1960, 'Minds and Machines', in S. Hook (ed.), *Dimensions of Mind*, MacMillan, New York, pp. 138-165.

Putnam, H.: 1981, *Reason, Truth and History*, Cambridge University Press, Cambridge.

Rhees, R. (ed.): 1984, *Recollections of Wittgenstein*, Oxford University Press, Oxford.

Rimbaud, A.: 1973, *Poésies*, Paris.

Russell, B.: 1921, *The Analysis of Mind*, George Allen and Unwin, London.

Russell, B.: 1948, *Human Knowledge: its Scope and Limits*, Clarion Book, Simon and Schuster, London.

Ryle, G.: 1949, *The Concept of Mind*, Hutchinson, London.

Sacks, S. (ed.): 1978, *On Metaphor*, The University of Chicago Press, Chicago.

Sartre, J.P.: 1940, *L'imaginaire*, Gallimard, Paris.

Searle, J.: 1983, *Intentionality: an Essay in the Philosophy of Mind*, Cambridge University Press, Cambridge.

Searle, J.: 1980, 'Minds, Brains and Programs', in Haugeland (1981), pp. 282-307.

Searle, J.: 1984, *Minds, Brains and Programs*, Harvester University Press, Cambridge.

Spengler, O.: 1931, *Der Mensch und der Technik*, Deutscher Taschenbuch Verlag, Munich.

Spengler, O.: 1923, *Der Untergang des Abendlandes*, Deutscher Taschenbuch Verlag, Munich.

Staten, H.: 1985, *Wittgenstein and Derrida*, Basil Blackwell, Oxford.

Stich, S.: 1983, *From Folk Psychology to Cognitive Science*, MIT Press, Cambridge.

Strawson, P.F.: 1959, *Individuals*, Methuen, London.

Strawson, P.F.: 1983, *Skepticism and Naturalism: some Varieties*, Methuen, London.

Stroud, B.: 1981, 'Wittgenstein's Philosophy of Mind', in G. Floistad (ed.), *Contemporary Philosophy*, vol. 4: *Philosophy of Mind*, Nijhoff, Den Haag, pp. 319-343.

Tilghman, B.R.: 1984, *But is it Art?*, Basil Blackwell, Oxford.

Vesey, G.N.A.: 1965, *The Embodied Mind*, George Allen and Unwin, London.

Vesey, G.N.A.: 1976, *Meaning and Understanding: Locke and Wittgenstein*, Milton Keynes.

Von Wright, G.H.: 1982, 'The Origin and Composition of the Philosophical Investigations', in G.H. von Wright, *Wittgenstein*, Basil Blackwell, Oxford, pp. 111-137.

Von Wright, G.H.: 1982, 'The Wittgenstein Papers', in von Wright (1982), pp. 35-63.

Von Wright, G.H.: 1982, 'Wittgenstein on Probability', in von Wright (1982), pp. 137-163.

Weininger, O.: 1980, *Geschlecht und Charakter*, Matthes & Seitz, München.

Weininger, O.: 1980, Über die Letzten Dinge, Matthes&Seitz, München.

Winch, P.: 1958, The Idea of a Social Science and its Relation to Philosophy, Routledge and Kegan Paul, London.

Winch, P.: 1984, 'Wittgenstein: his Treatment of the Will', in T. Honderich (ed.), *Philosophy through its Past*, Penguin, Harmondsworth, pp. 485-504.

Wittgenstein, L.: 1979, *Bemerkungen über Frazers Golden Bough*, The Brynmill Press, England. (BFGB)

Wittgenstein, L.: 1965, *The Blue and Brown Books*, Basil Blackwell, Oxford. (BLB)

Wittgenstein, L.: 1980, *Briefe*, Suhrkampf, Frankfurt am Main. (B)

Wittgenstein, L.: 1980, *Culture and Value*, Basil Blackwell, Oxford. (CV)

Wittgenstein, L.: 1982, *Last Writings*, Basil Blackwell, Oxford. (LW)

Wittgenstein, L.: 1962, *Notebooks 1914-16*, Basil Blackwell, Oxford. (N)

Wittgenstein, L.: 1979, *On Certainty*, Basil Blackwell, Oxford. (OC)

Wittgenstein, L.: 1982, *Philosophical Remarks*, Basil Blackwell, Oxford. (PR).

Wittgenstein, L.: 1978, *Philosophical Grammar*, Basil Blackwell, Oxford. (PG).

Wittgenstein, L.: 1971, *Philosophical Investigations*, Basil Blackwell, Oxford. (PI).

Wittgenstein, L.: 1977, *Remarks on Colour*, Basil Blackwell, Oxford. (ROC)

Wittgenstein, L.: 1967, *Remarks on the Foundations of Mathematics*, Basil Blackwell, Oxford. (RFM)

Wittgenstein, L.: 1980, *Remarks on the Philosophy of Psychology*, 2 vols., Basil Blackwell, Oxford. (RPP)

Wittgenstein, L.: 1961, *Tractatus Logico-Philosophicus*, Routledge and Kegan Paul, London. (T)

Wittgenstein, L.: 1976, 'Ursache und Wirking: Intuitives Erfassen', *Philosophia*, vol. 6, 391-408.

Wittgenstein, L.: 1967, 'The Wittgenstein papers', Cornell University Microfilms, Ithaca (N.Y.).

Wittgenstein, L.: 1981, *Zettel*, Basil Blackwell, Oxford. (Z)

Wollheim, R.: 1974, *On Art and the Mind*, Harvard University Press, Cambridge.

INDEX

APPENDIX

ORIGINAL TEXT OF QUOTED PASSAGES

p. 2   Dieses Buch stellt meine Anschauungen über die Philosophie dar, wie sie sich in den letzten acht Jahren entwickelt haben. Ich habe es so gut gemacht als ich konnte; aber es ist dennoch //doch// in vielen Beziehungen unbefriedigend ausgefallen. Es mangelt treffende Kürze //Treffsicherheit des Ausdrucks//, der Ausdruck ist weitschweifig. Was mit einem Strich hätte gezeichnet werden sollen, musste ich mit zehn Strichen also undeutlich. (MS 152, p. 13)

p. 2   Wenn ich für mich denke ohne ein Buch schreiben zu wollen, so springe ich um das Thema herum; das ist die einzige mir natürliche Denkweise. In einer Reihe gezwungen fortzudenken ist mir ein Qual. Soll ich es nun überhaupt probieren?? Ich *verschwende* unsägliche Mühe auf ein Anordnen der Gedanken das vielleicht gar keinen Wert hat. (MS 118, 15-9-1937)

p. 3 (n. 2)   Fühle mich beim Kompilieren meiner Bemerkungen nicht ganz wohl. (MS 118, p. 84)

p. 8   ...die unscharfen Grenzen gehören zu meinem Begriff der Pflanze, so wie er jetzt ist, d.h. so, wie ich dieses Wort jetzt gebrauche, und es charakterisiert diesen Begriff, dass ich z.B. sage: ich habe darüber keine Bestimmung getroffen, ob dieses Ding eine Pflanze heissen soll oder nicht. (TS 213, p. 251)

p. 8   Die Bedeutung eines Wortes verstehen, heisst seinen Gebrauch kennen, verstehen. (MS 153a, p. 117)

p. 12   Wenn wir vom Gesichtsraum reden, so werden wir leicht zu der Vorstellung verführt als wäre er eine Art von Guckkasten den Jeder mit //vor// sich herumtrüge. D.h. wir verwenden dann das Wort 'Raum' ähnlich, wie wenn wir ein Zimmer einen Raum nennen. (MS 113, p. 248)

p. 12   Mein Gesichtsfeld weist keine Unvollständigkeit auf die mich
         dazu bringen könnte mich umzuwenden und zu sehen was
         hinter mir liegt.   Im Gesichtsraum gibt es kein 'hinter mir'...
         (MS 113, p. 249)

p. 12   Der Übergang von den Zahnschmerzen zur Aussage 'Ich habe
         Zahnschmerzen' ist eben ein ganz anderer als der vom
         Geräusch zur Aussage 'in diesem Zimmer ist jemand'.   Das
         heisst die Übergänge gehören ganz andern Sprachspielen an
         (gehören zu ganz verschiedenen Sprachspielen). (MS 113, p.
         104)

p. 13   Ich habe ja die Worte 'Ich habe' nicht gelernt dass man mir etwa
         gesagt hätte: beobachte wer Schmerzen hat und wenn Du's bist
         zeig auf Dich etc.   Sondern diese meine Worte sind die direkte
         Übersetzung einer aussgestossenen Klage. (MS 120, p. 33)

p. 13   'Sagst Du, also, dass das Wort "Schmerz" ursprünglich das
         Schreien des Schmerzes bedeutet?' – Im Gegenteil. Es ersetzt
         das Schreien, aber sagt nicht dass Einer schreit.   Die Worte 'ich
         habe Schmerzen' werden zu einem Teil des Schmerz-Beneh-
         mens; und sagen daher nicht, dass jemand sich so benimmt.
         Und so sind alle sprachlichen Äusserungen der Empfindungen
         mit den ursprünglichen Empfindungsäusserungen verknüpft
         worden. (MS 124, pp. 223-224)

p. 26   Es gibt eine Art der Philosophie – man könnte sie psycho-
         logistische Philosophie nennen, aber den eigentlich guten
         Namen für sie habe ich noch nicht gefunden – die immer von
         Assoziationen und dem gleichzeitigen oder ungefähr gleich-
         zeitigen Auftreten von Ereignissen A, B und C spricht, von den
         ähnlichen Bestandteilen zweier Ereignisse die zur Folge haben,
         dass uns das Ganze einfällt wenn ein Teil vor unseren Augen
         tritt.   Eine typische philosophische Sackgasse. Die Mischung
         von angestrebter Exactheit und tatsächlicher Irrelevanz. (MS
         107, p. 235)

p. 26   Der Gedanke ist durch seinen Ausdruck vollständig be-
         schrieben. Eine Beschreibung die ausserhalb des Ausdrucks des
         Gedankens liegt, geht uns nichts an, da sie zur Psychologie oder
         Physiologie gehört. (MS 109, p. 210)

p. 26   ...diese interessieren den Psychologen, uns nicht. Insofern haben Odgen & Richards mit ihrer kausaler //Theorie// Ansicht recht, nur, dass sie den anderen Aspekt nicht sehen. (MS 109, p. 210)

p. 29   Haben wir hier nicht das Wesen des Motivs im Gegensatz zur Ursache. Offenbar ja. Der Befehl wird, wenn ich ihn befolge, zum Motiv meiner Handlungsweise.
Und das Motiv ist nicht hypothetisch. In dem Motiv kann ich mich nicht irren, es ist in meiner Handlung enthalten, aber nicht so ihre Ursache.
(Odgen & Richards und Russells Theorie der Bedeutung beruht also auf einer Verwechslung, oder Gleichsetzung von Motiv und Ursache.) (MS 110, p. 94)

p. 29   Solange man sich unter der Seele ein *Ding*, einen *Körper* vorstellt der in unserem Kopfe ist solang ist diese Hypothese *nicht* gefährlich. Nicht in der Unvollkommenheit und Rohheit unsrer Modelle liegt die Gefahr sondern in ihrer Unklarheit (Undeutlichkeit).
Die Gefahr beginnt wenn wir merken dass das alte Modell nicht genügt es nun aber nicht ändern sondern nur gleichsam sublimieren. Solange ich sage, der Gedanke ist in meinem Kopf, ist alles in Ordnung; gefährlich wäre es, wenn wir sagen: der Gedanke ist nicht in meinem Kopfe aber in meinem Geist. (MS 107, pp. 238-239; PR, § 229)

pp. 29-30 Wenn man sagt, der Gedanke sei eine seelische Tätigkeit, oder eine Tätigkeit des Geistes, so denkt man an den Geist als an ein trübes, gasförmiges Wesen, in dem manches geschehen kann, das ausserhalb dieser Sphäre nicht geschehen kann. Und von dem man manches erwarten kann //muss//, das sonst nicht möglich ist...
Es ist //wäre// gleichsam der Gedanke der organische Teil des Symbols, das Zeichen der anorganische. Und jener organische Teil kann Dinge leisten, die der anorganische nicht könnte. (TS 213, p. 286)

pp. 30-31 Die Bedeutung ist eine Festsetzung, nicht Erfahrung. Und damit nicht Kausalität. Was das Zeichen suggeriert, findet man durch Erfahrung. Es ist die Erfahrung, die uns lehrt, welche Zeichen am seltensten missverstanden werden. Das Zeichen, soweit es suggeriert, also soweit es wirkt, interessiert uns nicht. Es interessiert uns nur als Zug in einem Spiel: <u>Glied</u> in einem System, das <u>selbständig</u> ist //Glied in einem System: das seine Bedeutung in sich selbst hat// Glied in einem System das <u>selbstbedeutend</u> ist: das seine Bedeutung in sich selbst hat.

Ich könnte mir denken, dass ein Philosoph glaubte //Ein Philosoph könnte glauben// einen Satz mit //in// roter Farbe drucken lassen zu müssen, da er erst so ganz das ausdrücke, was der Autor sagen will. (Hier hätten wir die magische Auffassung der Zeichen statt der logischen.) (Das magische Zeichen würde wirken wie eine Droge, und für sie wäre die kausale Theorie richtig. [deleted])

Die Untersuchung, ob die Bedeutung eines Zeichens seine Wirkung ist, ist eine grammatische Untersuchung.

Ich glaube, auf die kausale Theorie der Bedeutung kann man einfach antworten, dass wir, wenn Einer einen Stoss erhält und umfällt, das Umfallen nicht die Bedeutung des Stosses nennen. Der Sinn der Sprache ist nicht durch ihre Wirkung bestimmt. Oder: Was man den Sinn, die Bedeutung in der Sprache nennt, ist nicht ihre Wirkung. (TS 213, pp. 40-41)

p. 31   Das Exakte ist die interne Beziehung. (MS 153a, p. 136)

p. 31   Frege über die psychologische Logik. Seine Bemerkungen beziehen sich alle auf die Inexactheit der psychologischen Betrachtungen im Gegensatz zu der Logik. (MS 153a, p. 228)

p. 32   Es gibt Grade der Erwartung //Hoffnung//, aber es ist unsinnig von einer Messung der Hoffnung zu reden, wenn wir dem Wort 'Hoffnung' seinen [deleted: normalen] Gebrauch lassen. (MS 115, p. 73)

p. 33   Ob ein Phänomen ein Symptom des Regens ist, lehrt die Erfahrung; was als Kriterium des Regens gilt ist <u>Sache der Abmachung</u> //unsere Bestimmung (Definition). (MS 115, p. 72)

p. 33   Was in der Logik, nicht nötig ist, hilft auch nicht //ist auch nicht von Nutzen//. Was nicht nötig ist, ist überflüssig. (TS 213, p. 90)

p. 33   'Dadurch, dass ich den Satz *meine*, erhält er Leben'. Aber ich muss ihm ja ein ganz *bestimmtes* Leben geben, nicht nur Leben. *Einen* Sinn und nicht einen anderen. Wenn ich ihn meine, muss ich ihn so meinen. Die Worte müssen auf ihre Bedeutungen blicken. – Aber der lebendige Blick des Wortes auf seine Bedeutung beruht auf den stetigen Bewegungen im Felde der Anwendung. (MS 129, p. 94)

p. 37 Freilich ist der Satz von irgendwo hergenommen, und wenn man will, so spielt er nun auch ein Spiel mit sehr primitiven Regeln; denn es bleibt ja wahr, dass ich auf die Frage 'wer ist N' eine Antwort bekam, oder eine Reihe von Antworten, die nicht gänzlich regellos waren. – Wir können sagen: Untersuchen wir die Sprache auf ihre Regeln hin. Hat sie dort und da keine Regeln, so ist das das Resultat unsrer Untersuchung. (TS 213, p. 254)

p. 37 Ist es richtig zu sagen: Einer folgt einer Regel nur dann, wenn er bestimmte Dinge tun *kann*. (Und diese Klausel bezieht sich natürlich auf eine Zeitdauer.) (MS 165, pp. 68-69)

p. 37 Wir lernen als Kinder zugleich die Begriffe und was man mit ihnen macht. (MS 169, p. 71)

p. 38 'Warum nimmst Du an dass er besserer Stimmung sein wird, weil ich Dir sage dass er gegessen hat? ist denn das ein Grund?' – 'Das ist ein guter Grund, denn das Essen hat erfahrungsgemäss einen Einfluss auf seine Stimmung.' Und das könnte man auch so sagen: 'Das Essen macht es wirklich wahrscheinlicher, dass er guter Stimmung sein wird'.
Wenn man aber fragen wollte: 'Und ist alles das, was Du von der früheren Erfahrung vorbringst ein guter Grund, anzunehmen dass er sich auch diesmal so verhalten wird', so kann ich nun nicht sagen: ja, denn das macht das Eintreffen der Annahme wahrscheinlich. Ich habe aber meinen Grund mit Hilfe des Standards für den guten Grund gerechtfertigt; jetzt kann ich aber nicht den Standard rechtfertigen. (MS 113, p. 113)

p. 40 Wer eine Seele hat, muss des Schmerzes, der Freude, des Kummers etc. fähig sein. Und soll er dazu auch fähig sein zu erinnern, Entschlüsse zu fassen, sich etwas vorzunehmen, so braucht er den sprachlichen Ausdruck. (MS 173, pp. 41-42)

p. 42 Gewisse Begriffe //die Grundbegriffe// sind so eng mit dem Fundamentalsten in unsrer Lebensweise verflochten, dass sie darum unangreifbar sind. (MS 169, p. 71)

p. 43   Wenn ich nun eine Extension bilde, was heisst es ich bilde sie
         nach jenem allgemeinen Ausdruck?
         Das ist wie wenn man fragt: wie gehorcht man einem – oder
         diesem – Befehl? Wie ist, was ich tue, mit diesen Worten
         verbunden //verknüpft//? (Ich meine aber nicht kausal ver-
         bunden.) Nun doch nur durch eine allgemeine Praxis. (MS 165,
         p. 79)

p. 46   Ich erkenne also es ist *so*. Und nun muss ich zu Worten, oder
         Handlungen //Handlungen: Worten z.B.// übergehen.
         Ich war (früher) in der Schwierigkeit, dass eine Regel keine
         Handlungsweise bestimmen könnte, da eine jede mit der Regel
         in Übereinstimmung zu bringen sei. Die Antwort war: ist jede
         mit der Regel in Übereinstimmung zu bringen, dann auch zum
         Widerspruch. Daher verlören hier 'Widerspruch' und 'Über-
         einstimmung' ihren Sinn völlig.// Daher gäbe es hier über-
         haupt weder Übereinstimmung noch Widerspruch//. (MS 180a,
         pp. 72-73)

p. 47   Es scheint hier so klar: dass, 'das Wort *verstehen*' Eins ist, und
         'es *anwenden* können', ein Anderes. Und dies kommt wieder
         daher, dass wir gewohnt sind die hinweisende Erklärung als
         endgültige Antwort der Frage: 'Verstehst du das Wort ...?'
         anzunehmen. Denn es scheint als könnten wir uns auf die
         Frage: 'Verstehst du was "Erinnerungsbild" (oder: Schmerz, etc.)
         bedeutet', sogleich selbst die hinweisende Erklärung geben,
         indem wir uns (so) ein Bild vor die Seele rufen. (MS 116, pp.
         144-145)

p. 49   Es ist mit dem Begriff des Befehls wohl vereinbar, dass Befehle
         nicht befolgt werden, aber nicht, dass nie oder fast nie ein Befehl
         befolgt wurde. (MS 165, p. 81)

p. 49 (n. 5) Wie weiss ich, dass ich im Verfolg der Reihe +2 200004,
         200006 schreiben muss und nicht 200004, 200008?
         Die Frage ist ähnlich der: wie weiss ich dass diese Farbe rot ist.
         (MS 118, p. 1)

p. 50   ...kommt plötzlich zu einem Ende. Und nun sagt mein Freund:
         'Alles was du zu tun hast, ist jetzt noch von hier aus den Weg
         nach Hause zu finden.' (MS 180a, p. 70)

p. 50   Die Regeln lassen uns im Stich, weil es keinen Übergang gibt von Sehen, dass es *so* ist zum Sehen, dass es *rot* ist. (MS 180a, p. 74)

p. 50   Der Übergang von jenem Gesehenen zu den Worten ist ein *privater*. Darum hängen hier die Regeln in der Luft.
Die Regeln lassen mich im Stich; denn kann der Übergang von Schauen zum Wort 'rot' nicht unvermittelt gemacht werden, dann auch nicht über Regeln. (MS 180a, p. 75)

p. 50   Darum beziehen sich die Worte 'einer Regel folgen' auf eine Praxis der nicht durch den Schein einer Praxis ersetzt werden kann. (MS 180a, p. 76)

p. 51   Soll ich nun sagen dass die Bedeutung des Wortes 'rot' auf der Übereinstimmung der Menschen beruht? Das nämlich die Praxis auf der Übereinstimmung beruht? (MS 165, p. 82)

p. 52 (n. 8) Die Worte 'sicher sein dass' kann man nur von einer Hypothese gebrauchen. Es heisst nichts zu sagen 'ich bin sicher dass ich Zahnschmerzen habe' ausser in einem Sinne in dem es doch möglich ist zu zweifeln ob ich Zahnschmerzen habe...
Was heisst es, sicher zu sein, dass man Zahnschmerzen haben wird. *Kann* man nicht sicher sein, dann erlaubt es die Grammatik nicht das Wort in dieser Verbindung zu gebrauchen. (MS 110, pp. 31-32)

p. 53   Das Spiel beginnt nicht mit dem Zweifel, ob einer Zahnschmerz hat, denn das entspräche – sozusagen – nicht der biologischen Funktion des Spiels in unserm Leben. Seine einfache //primitive// Form ist eine Reaktion auf die Klagelaute und Gebärden des Andern, eine Reaktion des Mitleids oder dergl. Wir trösten, wollen helfen. Man kann denken: weil der Zweifel eine Verfeinerung, in gewissem Sinne, Verbesserung des Spiels ist, so wäre es wohl das allerwichtigste mit dem Zweifel gleich anzufangen. (Ähnlich wie man denkt, weil es oft gut ist, wenn ein Urteil begründet ist, so müsste zur vollkommenen Rechtfertigung eines Urteils die Kette der Gründe in's unendliche weitergehen.) (MS 119, pp. 111-112)

p. 53 (n. 9) Ich könnte auch so fragen: Warum verlangst Du Erklärungen? Wenn diese gegeben sein würden, wirst Du ja doch

wiederum vor einem Ende stehen. Sie können dich nicht
weiter führen als Du jetzt bist. (MS 110, p. 96)

p. 53 (n. 9) Die Kette der Grunde kommt zu einem Ende und zwar in
diesem Spiel (und zwar dem Ende des Spiels) (und zwar (an)
der Grenze des Spiels). (MS 112, p. 221)

p. 54 Die Vernunft – möchte ich sagen – gibt sich uns als Gradmesser
par excellence, an welchem alles was wir machen und alle
Sprachspiele sich selber messen und beurteilen. – Wir können
sagen: wir sind mit der Betrachtung eines Masstabes so präoccu-
piert, dass wir unsre Blicke nicht an gewissen (Erscheinungen
oder) Bildern *ruhen* lassen können. Wir sind, sozusagen, ge-
wöhnt dies damit 'abzutun', sie seien unvernünftig, entsprechen einem niedern //niedrigen// Stande der Intelligenz
etc. Unser Blick wird von dem Masstabe gefangen gehalten und
durch ihn immer wieder von diesen Erscheinungen, gleichsam
nach oben hin abgezogen. (MS 119, pp. 127-128)

p. 54 Man möchte Gründe und Gründe und Gründe angeben! In
dem Gefühl: wo ein //solange ein// Grund ist //da ist//, ist
alles in Ordnung. Ist kein Grund vorhanden, so ist die Sache
irrational, und daher für uns nicht interessant. (Der Gebrauch
von 'irrational' ähnlich dem des Wortes 'fallen' im Satz: 'Wenn
die Erde nicht irgendwie gehalten würde, müsste sie fallen'.)
Wir möchten nicht einfach beschreiben was geschieht, sondern
wir möchten immer (nur) erklären. (MS 116, p. 128)

p. 55 Nun aber denken wir uns die Mutter, die von vornherein
skeptisch ist: Wenn das Kind schreit, zuckt sie die Achseln und
schüttelt den Kopf; eventuell //manchmal// sieht sie es
forschend //prüfend// an, untersucht es; in Ausnahmefällen
//ausnahmsweise// macht sie auch vage Versuche des Tröstens
oder Pflegens. – Sähen wir ein solches Verhalten, so würden
wir es durchaus nicht das der Skepsis nennen, es würde uns
(nur) seltsam und närrisch anmuten. 'Das Spiel kann nicht mit
dem Zweifel anfangen' heisst: wir würden es nicht 'Zweifel'
nennen, wenn das Spiel damit anfänge. (MS 119, pp. 114-115)

p. 56 Aber dann brauchen wir ja nicht von den *Anfängen* des Spiels
zu reden, sondern wir können sagen: Das Spiel 'die Ursache
aufsuchen' *besteht* vor allem und hauptsächlich darin, dass wir

eine gewisse Praxis ausüben //in einer gewissen Praxis, in einer gewissen Methode//. Es erscheint darin auch etwas, was wir Zweifel und Unsicherheit nennen können, aber dies ist ein Zug zweiter Ordnung //Grösse//. Wie es zwar charakteristisch für das Funktionieren der Nähmaschine ist, dass sich ihre Teile abnützen und verbiegen, und die Achsen in den Lagern schlottern können, aber doch ein Charakteristicum zweiter Ordnung verglichen mit dem normalen Gang der Maschine. (MS 119, p. 145)

p. 56   Die primitive Form des Sprachspiels ist die Sicherheit, nicht die Unsicherheit. Denn die Unsicherheit könnte nie //nicht// zur Tat führen. (MS 119, pp. 147-148)

p. 57   Ich will sagen: es ist charakteristisch für unsere Sprache, dass sie auf dem Grund fester Lebensformen, regelmässiger Handlungsformen //regelmässigen Tun's// //Formen des Handelns//, emporwächst. Ihre Funktion ist *vor allem* durch die Handlung, deren Begleiterin sie ist, bestimmt. Wir haben eben einen Begriff davon, was für Lebensformen primitive sind, und welche erst aus solchen entsprossen sind //entspringen konnten//. Wir glauben, dass der einfachste Pflug vor dem komplizierten da war. (MS 119, pp. 148-149)

p. 59   Ich weiss = Ich bin sicher dass es so ist und es ist so. (MS 171, p. 9)

p. 61   Was aber ist der Unterschied zwischen einer Einstellung und einer Meinung?
Ich möchte sagen: Die Einstellung kommt *vor* der Meinung. Eine Meinung kann sich irren. Aber wie sähe hier ein Irrtum aus? (MS 169, p. 60-61)

p. 64   Wenn man jemandem fragt 'wie weisst du, dass diese Beschreibung wiedergibt, was du siehst', so könnte er etwa antworten 'ich *meine* das mit diesen Worten'. Aber was ist dieses 'das', wenn es nicht selbst wieder artikuliert, also schon Sprache ist. Also ist 'ich *meine* das' gar keine Antwort. Die Antwort ist eine Erklärung der Bedeutung der Worte. (TS 213, p. 190)

p. 64   Kann man denn etwas Anderes als einen Satz *verstehen*? Oder aber: Ist es nicht erst ein Satz, wenn man es versteht. Also: Kann man Etwas anderes, als Satz verstehen? (TS 213, p. 2)

p. 64   Gesprochenes kann man nur durch die Sprache erklären, darum kann man die Sprache (in diesem Sinne) nicht erklären. (TS 213, p. 2)

p. 64   Ich will doch sagen: Die ganze Sprache kann man nicht interpretieren. Eine Interpretation ist immer nur eine im Gegensatz zu einer andern. Sie hängt sich an das Zeichen und reiht es in ein weiteres System ein. (TS 213, p. 2)

p. 65   Es ist klar, dass nichts anderes erwartet werden konnte und dass die Antwort den Gebrauch der Sprache //des bestimmten Sprachspiels// voraussetze. Wie alles, was zu sagen ist // was wir sagen können. (TS 213, p. 3)

p. 66   Es ist etwa eine Regel, dass man Eier 3 Minuten lang kocht, um weiche Eier zu erhalten; wird aber durch irgendwelche Umstände das gleiche Ergebnis durch 5 Minuten langes Kochen erreicht, so sagt man nun nicht 'das heisst dann nicht "weiche Eier kochen"'. (TS 213 p.236)

p. 66   Der Zweck der Grammatik ist nur der Zweck der Sprache. (TS 213, p. 194)

p. 67   Man kann die Regeln der Grammatik 'willkürlich' nennen, wenn damit gesagt sein soll, der *Zweck* der Grammatik sei nur der der Sprache. Und es sei //ist // Unsinn etwa zu sagen: die Sprache müsse Substantive, Eigenschaftswörter, Verben und Zahlwörter enthalten, weil es Dinge, Eigenschaften und Tätigkeiten und Zahlen gebe, u. dergl. Als sei der Fall vergleichbar dem: Die Astronomie muss von 4 Jupitermonden sprechen, weil es 4 Jupitermonde gibt. (MS 116, pp. 134-135)

p. 67 (n. 13)   Du vergisst was Einstein, wie ich vermute, die Welt gelehrt hat: dass die Methode //Art und Weise// der Zeitmessung zur Grammatik der Zeit-Ausdrücke gehört. (MS 119, pp. 226-227)

p. 69   'Contrat sociale'. Auch hier ist in Wirklichkeit *kein* Vertrag geschlossen worden; aber die Situation ist mehr oder weniger ähnlich, analog, der in welcher wir wären, wenn ... Und sie ist mit grossen Nutzen unter dem Gesichtspunkt eines solches Vertrages zu betrachten. (TS 213, p. 196)

p. 71   Wenn Menschen wirklich, wie ich annahm, das Nervensystem des Andern funktionieren sehen könnten und danach ihr Verhalten zum Andern einrichteten, so hätten sie, glaube ich, gar nicht unsren Schmerzbegriff (z.b.), obgleich vielleicht einen verwandten. Ihr Leben *sähe eben ganz anders aus* als das unsre. D.h. ich betrachte dieses Sprachspiel als autonom. Ich will es nur beschreiben, oder betrachten, nicht rechtfertigen. (MS 169, p. 65)

p. 75   Es gibt Fälle in welchen wir sagen, Einer ermahne sich selbst; befehle, gehorche, bestrafe, tadle, frage und antworte sich selbst. Dann kann es also Menschen geben, die nur die Sprachspiele kennen, die jeder mit sich selbst spielt. Ja es wäre denkbar, dass solche Menschen ein reiches Vokabular hätten. Wir können uns denken, dass ein Forscher in ihr Land käme und beobachtete, wie jeder von ihnen seine Tätigkeiten mit artikulierten Lauten begleitet, sich aber dabei nicht an Andere wendet. Der Forscher kommt irgendwie auf den Gedanken, dass diese Leute Selbstgespräche führen, belauscht sie bei ihren Tätigkeiten und es gelingt ihm eine wahrscheinliche Übersetzung ihrer Reden in unsere Sprache. Er ist durch das Lernen ihrer Sprache auch in den Stand gesetzt Handlungen voraus zu sagen, welche die Leute später ausführen, denn manches was sie sagen ist der Ausdruck von Vorsätzen und Entschlüssen. (Wie die Leute ihre Sprache haben lernen können ist hier gleichgültig). (MS 124, pp. 213-214)

p. 76   Die Private Sprache, die ich oben beschrieben habe ist eine solche, wie sie etwa Robinson auf seinen Insel hätte mit sich selbst sprechen können. Hätte ihn jemand belauscht und beobachtet, er hätte diese Sprache Robinsons lernen können. Denn die Bedeutungen der Worte zeigten sich im Verhalten Robinsons. (MS 124, p. 222)

p. 77 (n. 4) Mozart in einem berühmten Briefe schreibt, er sähe ein ganzes musikalisches Werk mit einem Schlage vor seinem Geiste. – Wie ist das möglich, hörte er es in rasendem Tempo gespielt vor //in// seinem Geiste; oder gar so dass alle Töne gleichzeitig erklängen? Und mit welchem Rechte sagte er dann er habe ein Musikstück im Geiste wahrgenommen? Wie wusste er, dass ein Musikstück dem entsprach was er wahrnahm. (MS 124, pp. 216-217)

p. 78   Stell dir das Denken nicht vor wie den Text, der die Melodie des Lieds begleitet, sondern eher wie den 'Ausdruck' mit welchem das Lied gesungen wird. (MS 124, p. 215)

p.79   Das Gebiet in dem wir uns hier befinden, gilt mit Recht als eines der schwersten der Philosophie; darum nämlich, weil die Oberflächengrammatik hier ungemein irreleitend ist und der Boden //die Erde// von den unzähligen, einander kreuzenden Wagenspuren der philosophierenden Menschen so aufgewühlt ist, dass es beinahe unmöglich ist hier irgendwelche *Wege* zu erkennen.
Wollte man von einer persönlichen Erfahrung reden in einem Sinne, in welchem ihre Grammatik vom Ausdruck der Erfahrung ganz unabhängig wäre, dann wäre es ganz gleichgültig, *was für eine* solche Erfahrung wir hinter dem Ausdruck stehend annehmen und gleichgültig, ob wir annehmen, ich erkenne sie richtig oder falsch wieder. Ich mag mich in *diesem* Sinne immer wieder irren, wenn ich sage ich habe Zahnschmerzen, weil ich jedesmal eine grundverschiedene Erfahrung habe; aber es mache gar nichts. – Was ist das aber für ein Sinn des Wortes persönliche Erfahrung, der *so* funktioniert? Woher nehmen wir ihn; wie entsteht er? (MS 119, pp. 226-227)

p. 81   Oder eigentlich hundert irreführende Vergleichungen scheinen sich hier zu treffen: Man hält etwas für hinweisende Erklärung, was keine ist, und etwas für Beschreibung was keine ist, und etwas für eine Personsbezeichnung, was keine ist, und etwas für ein Wissen, was keines ist. ('innen und aussen'). (MS 120, p. 67)

p. 82   Oh, wie schwer ist es hier, aus der Metaphysik in die Grammatik zu treten. (MS 120, pp. 122-123)

p. 82   Die Philosophie arbeitet gegen die Mythen bildenden Tendenzen in unserem Verstand. (MS 158, p. 49)

p. 83   Phänomenologische Sprache: Die Beschreibung der unmittelbaren Sinneswahrnehmung, ohne hypothetische Zutat. (MS 113, p. 246)

p. 83 (n. 9) Es ist nun ein Satz zu sagen: Rot ist hier. Dabei ist 'hier' die Bezeichnung eines Wortes im Gesichtsfeld und diese Bezeichnung, bezeichnet auch die Gestalt des roten Flecks denn aus der

Lage der Farbe Rot geht diese Gestalt hervor. Wie aber ist diese Lage wirklich zu beschreiben? (MS 105, pp. 49-51)

p. 84 (Von welcher Wichtigkeit ist denn diese Beschreibung des *gegenwärtigen* Phänomens die für uns gleichsam zur fixen Idee werden kann. Dass wir darunter leiden, dass die Beschreibung nicht das beschreiben kann, was beim Lesen der Beschreibung vor sich geht. Es scheint als wäre die Beschäftigung mit dieser Frage geradezu kindisch und wir in eine Sackgasse hineingeraten. Und doch ist es eine bedeutungsvolle Sackgasse, denn in sie lockt es alle zu gehen, als wäre dort die letzte Lösung der philosophischen Probleme zu suchen – Es ist als käme man mit dieser Vorstellung des gegenwärtigen Phänomens in einen verzauberten Sumpf, wo alles Erfassbare verschwindet.) Anderseits brauchen wir eine Ausdrucksweise die Phänomene //Vorgänge// des Gesichtsraums getrennt von den Erfahrungen andrer Art darstellt. (MS 113, pp. 247-248)

pp. 84-85 Wenn wir vom Gesichtsraum reden, so werden wir leicht zu der Vorstellung verführt als wäre er eine Art von Guckkasten den jeder mit sich herumtrüge. D.h. wir verwenden dann das Wort 'Raum' ähnlich wie, wenn wir einen Zimmer ein Raum nennen. In Wirklichkeit aber bezieht sich doch das Wort 'Gesichtsraum' nur auf eine Geometrie, ich meine, auf einen Abschnitt der Grammatik unserer Sprache. In diesem Sinne gibt es keine 'Gesichtsräume' die etwa jeder seinen Besitzer hätten. (Und etwa auch solche vagierende, die gerade niemandem gehören). (MS 113, p. 248)

p. 85 'Nichts im Gesichtsraum deutet darauf hin etc.' (L.Ph.Abh.) Das heisst sozusagen: Du wirst vergebens im Gesichtsraum nach dem *Seher* suchen. Er ist nirgends im Gesichtsraum zu finden. Aber die Wahrheit ist: Du *tust* nur als suchtest du nach etwas. (MS 120, pp. 113-114)

p. 85 Der Solipsismus könnte durch die Tatsache widerlegt werden, dass das Wort 'Ich' in der Grammatik keine zentrale Stellung hat, sondern ein Wort ist wie jedes andere Wort. (TS 213, p. 508)

p. 85 Wie im Gesichtsraum, so gibt es in der Sprache kein metaphysisches Subjekt. (TS 213, p. 508)

p. 86   Ich will sagen: 'Hinter dem was die Beschreibung meiner Erfah-
           rung heisst, steht etwas, was keinen Nachbar, was einzig ist,
           womit ich die Beschreibung vergleiche'. (MS 156b, p. 114)

p. 86   Die Tendenz ist zu sagen 'nur was *ich* sehe ist wirklich'. Ich
           schaue auf meine Umgebung und sage '*das* ist gesehen'. Wenn
           jemand andrer sagt, er sieht das und das, sage ich '*gesehen* ist
           nur das. Das Gesehene hat keinen *Nachbar*'. (MS 156b, p. 88)

p. 86 (n. 12)   Denn es ist ja eben darum dass wir denken, wir *entdeckten*
           es, weil wir uns seiner nicht immer bewusst sind. (MS 120, p.
           87)

p. 87   Kann ich, was ich sehe, einem Andern zeigen?   Nicht in dem
           Sinne, in dem nur ich es sehen kann.
           Kann ich es aber *mir* zeigen, wenn niemand andrem? ('Das ist
           hier'). (MS 156b, p. 104)

p. 87   Wir wehren uns gegen die Auffassung, dass mein Gesichtsfeld
           seinem benachbart ist.   D.h. wir wollen 'Gesichtsfeld' in einem
           Sinne gebrauchen in dem es nicht ein Teil des physischen
           Raums bedeutet.   Wir müssen uns wieder fragen: wie ge-
           brauchen wir das Wort 'Gesichtsfeld'? (MS 156b, p. 111)

p. 88   Aber inwiefern ist der Gesichtsraum nur mit *Dir* besonders
           verbunden? Denn von welchem 'ich', von deiner Person in
           welchem Sinne redest du hier? Von Deinem Bild im Ge-
           sichtsraum? Nein.   Von dem Körper L.W.? (MS 156b, pp. 94-95)

p. 88   Mit welchem Recht aber sage ich 'Nur ich sehe...' Wer ist ich?
           Wohl könnte ich sagen, W sieht und meinen, dass sein Leib
           jetzt um das geometrische Auge sichtbar ist. 'Ich sehe' sagt mir
           überhaupt nichts, wenn ich nicht weiss wer ich bin. (MS 156b, p.
           89)

p. 88   Ich habe hier (in meinem Zahn) Schmerzen.   Dass ich sie in
           meinem Körper habe, gehört zur Erfahrung.   Aber auch, dass
           ich sie habe? (MS 156b, p. 76)

p. 88   Die Person tritt als Gegenstand der Erfahrung auf, scheint aber
           auch anders aufzutreten: wesentlich als Subjekt, nicht Objekt.
           (MS 156b, p. 73)

p. 89 Was soll es heissen: er hat diese Schmerzen? ausser, er hat solche Schmerzen: d.h. von solcher Stärke, Art, etc. Aber nur in dem Sinne kann auch ich diese Schmerzen haben.

Das heisst, die Subjekt-Objekt Form ist darauf nicht anwendbar. Die Subjekt-Objekt Form bezieht sich auf den Leib und die Dinge um ihn, die auf ihn wirken.

In der nicht-hypothetischen Beschreibung des Gesehenen, Gehörten – diese Wörter bezeichnen hier grammatische Formen – tritt das Ich nicht auf, es ist hier von Subjekt und Objekt nicht die Rede. (TS 213, p. 508)

p. 90 Kommt nicht alles drauf hinaus, dass die Worte 'Ich habe...' einem Stöhnen oder Schrei entsprechen? Dass, wenn ich aus Mitleid stöhne, man daraus nicht entnehmen kann, wer der Leidende ist, sondern dafür ein Zeigen oder dergl. nötig ist //wäre//, während der Schrei des Leidenden (uns) zu ihm führt. (MS 120, p. 30)

p. 90 Man kann eben sagen: Ich kann sagen, dass ich Schmerzen habe, ohne zu wissen *wer* sie hat //Man könnte über Schmerzen klagen ohne zu wissen *wer* sie hat//. (MS 120, p. 31)

p. 90 Ich könnte mit einer hinweisenden Geste //Gebärde// definieren //erklären//: '"meine" Nase ist *diese* Nase'. Könnte ich nun auch ähnlich //analog// erklären: '"meine" Schmerzen sind *diese* Schmerzen'? Ich könnte (doch jedenfalls) erklären: '"Meine" Klage ist die, die *dieser* Mund ausstösst'. Das Wesentliche an dieser Erklärung wäre //ist//, dass die zeigende Geste *reflexiv* ist.

Anders, wenn ich sage: '"Meine Bücher" nenne ich *diese* Bücher'.

'"Meine Bücher" nenne ich *die* Bücher, weil *ich* sie immer benütze'.

'Mein' reflexiv oder possessiv.

'Mein' ist das, was ich *habe*; und *das* (mit einer reflexiven Geste) bin ich. Willst Du also wissen, ob etwas mein ist, so sieh nach, wer es besitzt; *habe ich es*, so ist es *mein*. Diese Erklärung könnte man (etwa) auf jene Bücher anwenden: Wenn Du findest, dass *ich* sie lese, so weisst Du, dass sie mir gehören //die meinen sind//. Aber kann man die Erklärung auch auf den Ausdruck 'mein Gesicht' anwenden? Und auf 'meine Schmerzen'? (MS 120, pp. 159-161)

p. 91   'Aber Du gebrauchst doch "ich" im Gegensatz zu "er". Also, unterscheidest Du doch (damit) zwischen Personen' (MS 158, p. 158)

p. 91   'Habe ich denn behauptet, *ich* habe etwas'? Ich habe nur geklagt und man hat mich die Klage gelehrt 'Ich habe Schmerzen'. (MS 120, p. 203)

p. 91   'Aber Du lässt doch nicht offen, ob Du oder ein Andrer die Schmerzen hat'? – Ich lasse alles offen, ich *klage* bloss. (MS 120, p. 204)

p. 91   Die Klage //Schmerzäusserung// 'Ich habe Schmerzen' ist eine Aussage über mich in *übertragenem Sinne* //ist ein Satz, der von mir *in übertragenem Sinne* etwas aussagt.// Die Klage //Schmerzäusserung// 'Ich habe Schmerzen' redet von mir und davon dass ich etwas habe, in übertragenem Sinne. Sie wird aber nicht als Aussage über mich, d.h. über meinen Körper, angewendet. (MS 116, p. 175)

p. 92   Wie ist es: teile ich jemand mit wer klagt indem ich sage: 'ich klage'? Teile ich jemand mit wer das Wort 'ja' //'Au'// sagt, indem ich sage 'ja' //'Au'//? (MS 120, p. 217)

p. 93   'Das visuelle Zimmer hat keinen Besitzer' heisst soviel als: es hat keinen Nachbar.
Wie aber wird der Ausdruck 'das visuelle Zimmer' *gebraucht*?
Wie, wenn Du jemandem sagst: 'Ich habe *diese* Vorstellung...' und nun eine Vorstellung beschreibst, während Du dich in sie versenkst – also hast Du diese Vorstellung – aber die Vorstellung ist nicht Objekt eines Subjekts. Man kann auch sagen: Der Körper vor deinen Augen ist Objekt und Dein Sinn Subjekt. Aber im Gegensatz dazu ist die Vorstellung nicht Objekt: man kann von ihr nicht sagen, sie werde *gesehen*, noch steht sie sonst *vor* einem Subjekt, denn sie *grenzt an nichts*, ist nicht Teil eines Raumes. Ich stehe vor diesem Ofen, aber nicht vor der Vorstellung von diesem Ofen.
Es steht etwa mein visuellen Körper vor dem visuellen Ofen – aber mein visuellen Körper kann nicht sehen. Darum möchten //haben// wir ja sagen //den Eindruck//: es gibt hier kein Subjekt – und also auch kein Objekt. (MS 120, pp. 79-81)

p. 93   Ich sehe etwas vor mir; das ist doch *gesehen*; aber ist es nicht nur *da*, ist es tatsachlich *gesehen*? Siehst man, dass es gesehen ist? 'Sehen' hängt mit einem Bild der Wirkung des Objekts auf das Subjekt zusammen. Ich sage 'ich sehe den Vorhang'; soll ich aber auch sagen 'ich sehe eine Vision'?
Ich möchte sagen: im visuellen Raum wird nichts gesehen, gehen keine Lichtstrahlen von einem Objekt zum Sehenden.
Was habe ich dann für gewöhnlich vor mir: den visuellen Raum, oder den physikalischen Raum? Nein, so ist es nicht. Der visuelle Raum ist nicht quasi ein andrer Guckkasten als der physikalische. Wenn ich sage: 'durch den visuellen Raum gehen keine Lichtstrahlen', so heisst das nur, dass ich nur von einer Gesichtserscheinung sage, sie sei im visuellen Raum.
Und da nur das Gesehene ein Gegenstand im visuellen Raum ist, so kann man nicht sagen, es werde etwas im visuellen Raum *gesehen*. (MS 120, pp. 114-115)

p. 95   Ich möchte mich auf das momentane Erlebnis berufen, aber dieses erscheint wieder unfassbar, etwas, was man nicht festlegen kann, was als ein Stein im Spiel nicht funktionieren kann.
Oder auch: es ist das Resultat einer falschen Sprachdeutung. Man will nämlich sagen: es gibt etwas, was nur Gegenwart hat und keine Vergangenheit (noch Zukunft). (MS 179, pp. 42-43)

p. 96 (n. 17)   Frage nicht so sehr: 'Wie kann man Empfindungen benennen?' als: 'wie kann man die Namen der Empfindungen anwenden'? (MS 179, p. 25)

pp. 96-97   Wie benennt man denn (nun) eine Vorstellung? Etwa so: Man hat sie gerade, konzentriert die Aufmerksamkeit auf sie und spricht dabei die Worte: 'das soll "Z" heissen'. Ist sie nun benannt? Und wozu hilft uns dieser magische Vorgang? Wir vergessen ja ganz wozu das was wir Benennen eines Gegenstandes nennen eigentlich dient. Es ist als ernennten wir Puppen oder auch andere Gegenstände zu Leutnants, Hauptleuten und Generälen, indem wir ihnen die Distinktionen dieser Chargen anhefteten. (MS 119, pp. 257-258)

p. 99   Aber beurteilen wir nicht, dass etwas das gleiche innere Erlebnis ist einfach durch die Erinnerung? Die Erinnerung ist wohl ein weiteres inneres Erlebnis? Und was heisst es denn nach der

Erinnerung 'beurteilen'? Ist beurteilen doch wieder ein inneres Erlebnis so weiss ich nicht wie ich endlich zur Benützung von *Worten* kommen kann //werde//. Heisst aber beurteilen bereits: etwas *sagen* so weiss ich nicht was es heissen soll mich mit dem was ich sage noch nach dem innern Erlebnis *richten*, wenn die *Regel* fehlt nach der ich mich richte und die ja dann das innere Erlebnis dem Wort – im Form einer Tabelle *etwa* – zuordnen müsste. (MS 119, pp. 209-210)

p. 99   Denk Dir wieder ein Tagebuch und die Aufzeichnung privater Gefühle. Das Wiedererkennen zeigt ihm ja nicht dass dies dasselbe Gefühl ist welches er hatte, sondern es ist nun bloss ein neues inneres Erlebnis. Aber wir dürfen dafür nicht das Wort 'Wiedererkennung' gebrauchen, denn dies war für gewissen öffentlichen Gebrauch bestimmt. Also müssten wir ihm einen neuen Namen geben, mit dem aber nichts anzufangen ist. Er kann ein Zeichen in das Tagebuch eintragen und die Zeichen wieder anschauen, und mehr wissen wir nicht von dem was vorgeht zu sagen. Aber ist das ein Tagebuch? (MS 119, pp. 237-238)

p. 100   'Er hat die gleiche Empfindung wie ich.' – Kriterien der Identität. Was ist aber das Kriterium der Identität, wenn ich sage: 'Ich habe jetzt den gleichen Schmerz wie früher?' Soll ich sagen: 'ich *erkenne unmittelbar*, dass es der gleiche ist'? Also erkenne ich unmittelbar, dass das Wort 'gleich' auf ihn passt? Oder, dass das Bild ++ auf ihn passt? Und *wie* passt? – Aber willst du sagen, ich *sage* bloss das Wort 'gleich' ohne dass es irgendwie gerechtfertigt ist? Das Wort 'bloss' ist hier falsch //schlecht// angewendet. Das Wort, dass der Ausdruck 'gleich' hier nicht gerechtfertigt ist gibt dir das gleiche Unbehagen wie manchen Menschen der Ausdruck dass die Erde ohne gestützt zu werden frei im Raum schwebt. (Und darin ist nichts Lächerliches). (MS 121, pp. 42-43)

p. 102   Der Satz: 'Hinter der Äusserung der Empfindung steht nichts' ist ein *grammatischer* – er sagt also nicht, dass wir nichts empfinden. (MS 124, p. 6)

p. 102   Ja, ihr Gebrauch ist *verschiedener*, als die Philosophen, welche gegen den Behaviourismus <u>sprechen</u>, es darstellen. //verschie *dener*, als die Philosophie es darstellt, die gegen den Behaviourismus spricht//. (MS 124, p. 20)

p. 102 Es ist, als wäre hier etwas unfassbares – Man fragt: 'Ist hier etwas, oder nichts?' und keines passt. Das Wort 'Schmerz' bezeichnet weder ein Ding noch eine Leere. (MS 121, p. 41)

p.103 Wenn man nur sagte 'Ich habe Schmerzen' und nicht auch Schmerzen *hätte*, wäre gar nichts Schreckliches an den Schmerzen' – Freilich, wenn man keine Schmerzen hat so ist daran nichts Schreckliches. 'Wenn man nur das Schmerzbenehmen hätte und sonst nichts, so wäre daran nichts Unangenehmes.' – Freilich: sich die Wange halten ist nicht unangenehm – der Zahnschmerz ist das Unangenehme. (MS 121, pp. 7-8)

p. 105 Wenn nun jemand erwiderte: 'Nun, er hat eben die Erlebnisse //das bestimmte Erlebnis// die //dass// wir "Erinnerungserlebnisse" nennen' – so wären wir hier plötzlich geneigt, das als eine irrelevante Bemerkung beiseite zu schieben; wir wüssten mit der Idee des //dieses// innern Erlebnisses nun nichts anzufangen, und sind geneigt, sie fallen zu lassen. Es wird hier plötzlich unnötig von 'einem bestimmten inneren Erlebnis' zu sprechen (James' Zitat aus Ballard). (MS 116, p. 203)

p. 106 Denken wir uns ein Tagebuch mit Hilfe von einer Zahl, von einander unabhängiger Satzzeichen //Signalen// geführt. Jede Seite trägt ein Datum und ist, gleichsam wie ein Stundenplan, in 24 Abschnitte //Kästchen// eingeteilt; und nun heisst 'A' in unsrer Sprache: ich gehe schlafen, 'B': ich stehe auf, 'C': ich esse; etc. Wie weiss er, dass es immer dasselbe ist, was er mit //durch// 'A' notiert? Er befragt sein Gedächtnis. Aber das führt uns nicht weiter. Die Aussage des Gedächtnisses gesellt sich dann eben zu dem Zeichen (Denke, statt des Gedächtnisses diente ihm ein Würfel, und er würfle (nun), was er zu schreiben hat. (MS 116, p. 135)

p. 107 Bei 'Erinnerungserlebnis' denkt man (natürlich) vor allem an so etwas wie – Erinnerungsbild. Nun gibt es freilich //natürlich// Erinnerungsbilder, – ich kann mir leicht welche vor die Seele rufen. Aber wie rufe ich es mir vor die Seele, in welcher Umgebung von Gedanken? Und wenn ich es nun isoliert betrachte, festhalte, ist es selbst die Erinnerung? Ich sage etwa: 'Ich sehe mich mit einem Freunde da und da spazieren gehen'. Aber – wie weiss ich, dass *ich's* bin und mein Freund? Sind die Portraits so gut getroffen? Natürlich nicht. Aber ich *sage*, dass ich's bin mit meinem Freund, ich mache diesen Übergang vom Bild (von der Vorstellung) zu Worten, oder von diesem Bild zu gewissen andern Bildern, etc... (MS 116, p. 137)

pp. 107-108   'Die Erinnerung ist doch ein innerer Vorgang' ist eine grammatische Bemerkung; sie sagt eigentlich, dass der *Ausdruck* der Erinnerung das Sprachspiel beginnt.
Der Satz scheint es aber zu rechtfertigen, dass wir irgend eine Annahme über die innern Vorgänge einer Person machen. – Man kann aber sagen: *Weil* die Erinnerung ein innerer Vorgang ist, drum hat eine Annahme über Erinnerungsvorgänge keinen Sinn, wenn sie keine Annahme über den Ausdruck dieser Vorgänge ist. (MS 120, p. 121)

p. 108   Man könnte diese Art von Aussagen 'Äusserung' nennen. 'Schmerzäusserung', 'Erinnerungsäusserung', u.a. (MS 120, p. 206-207)

p. 108   Wie ist es aber mit: 'Ich *hatte* Schmerzen'. Dies ist doch keine Klage. Es wird im allgemeinen eine Aussage der Erinnerung sein. Wer aber sagt: 'ich erinnere mich...' der spricht eine Erinnerung aus und sagt //behauptet// nicht der und der erinnere sich... (MS 120, p. 206)

p. 108   Der Gebrauch der *Äusserung* wird Dich nicht gelehrt, indem Dir ein Phänomen gezeigt wird, dass man durch diese Worte beschreibt //darstellt//. (MS 120, p. 227)

p. 110   Ich habe ja die Worte 'Ich habe' nicht so gelernt dass man mir etwa gesagt hätte: beobachte wer Schmerzen hat und wenn Du's bist zeig auf Dich etc. Sondern diese meine Worte sind die direkte Übersetzung einer ausgestossene Klage. (MS 120, p. 33)

p. 110   'Sagst Du also, dass das Wort "Schmerz" ursprünglich das Schreien des Schmerzes bedeutet?' – Im Gegenteil. Es ersetzt das Schreien, aber sagt nicht, dass Einer schreit. Die Worte 'ich habe Schmerzen' werden zu einem Teil des Schmerz-Benehmens; und sagen daher nicht, dass jemand sich so benimmt. Und so sind alle sprachlichen Äusserungen der

Empfindungen mit den ursprünglichen Empfindungs-
äusserungen verknüpft worden. (MS 124, pp. 223-224)

p. 111 Es handelt sich nicht um das, was ich ihm sage; sondern um das
was er damit tut. (MS 158, p. 15)

p. 112 ...ich brauche kein äusseres, aber auch kein inneres Kriterium.
Wenn ich ein solches 'inneres Erlebnis ausdrücke' so ist es eben
dieser Ausdruck der im Spiel fungiert und ich muss nun für
den Andern annehmen, dass er auch einen Ausdruck gebraucht
den man Ausdruck des Erinnerungserlebnis nennt. (MS 119, p.
223)

p. 113 Ist der Schrei wahr, oder falsch? Wie, wenn ich sagte, er sei
echt, oder nicht echt.
Nicht, natürlich, als sei das Wort 'echt' richtiger als 'wahr'! Es
erinnere uns nur an einen grammatischen Unterschied, der
übersehen, oder nicht verstanden wird. (MS 124, p. 280)

p. 116 *Wie* kann //gehört// die innere Gebärde zum Satz gehören?
wie zum Sprachspiel? Sie 'begleitet ihn' nicht in dem Sinne, in
welchem eine Gebärde ihn begleitet, sie ist eben keine Gebärde.
Eine rezeptive Einstellung (das Horchen z.B.) kann zwar eine
Gebärde sein und als ein Zeigen funktionieren //fungieren//,
aber der erhaltene Sinneseindruck (das Hören z.B.) //die
Gehörsempfindung// entspricht //ist// dann nicht dem
//der// Gegenstand auf welchen gezeigt wurde //wird//.
Durch die Geste des Lauschens zeige ich nicht auf das was man
'meine Gehörsempfindung' nennt. (MS 120, pp. 188-189)

p. 117 Ja, es geht ein 'inneres Zeigen' vor sich, oder oft vor sich, (und)
dies ist charakteristisch für die Situation, in der diese Worte
ausgesprochen werden. Aber wenn ich fortfahre 'ich habe
meinen Schmerz gemeint' so nicht auf Grund einer Beobach-
tung eines inneren Phänomens des Meinens. Vielmehr setze
ich //substituiere eben nun// nachträglich für das Wort 'er' das
Wort Schmerz. Ich fahre in der Rechnung fort und wie ich im
Kalkül fortfahre das ist //ergibt// die Meinung. (MS 120, pp.
176-177)

p. 120 Man muss die Begriffe 'Schmerz haben' und 'Schmerz
heucheln' in der *dritten und ersten* Person betrachten. Oder

auch: der Infinitiv hat alle Personen und Zeiten hinter sich. Nur das Ganze ist das Instrument der Begriffe. (MS 169, p. 59)

p. 121 Die Hauptschwierigkeit entsteht dadurch, dass man sich das Erlebnis (den Schmerz, z.B.) als ein Ding vorstellt, für welches wir natürlich einen Namen haben und der Begriff also ganz leicht fasslich ist. Wir wollen also immer sagen: Was 'Schmerz' bedeutet wissen wir (nämlich *dies*), und so liegt also die Schwierigkeit nur darin, dass man eben dies im Andern nicht mit Sicherheit feststellen kann. (MS 169, pp. 69-70)

p. 123 Wenn ich mich mit der Sprache dem Andern verständlich mache, so muss es sich hier um ein Verstehen im Sinne des Behaviourismus handeln. Dass er mich verstanden hat ist eine Hypothese, wie, dass ich ihn verstanden habe. (MS 110, p. 8)

p. 124 Behaviourismus. 'Mir scheint, ich bin traurig, ich lasse den Kopf so hängen.'
Warum hat man kein Mitleid, wenn eine Tür ungeölt ist und beim Auf- und Zumachen schreit? Haben wir mit dem Andern, der sich benimmt wie wir, wenn wir Schmerzen haben, Mitleid – auf philosophische Erwägungen hin, die zu dem Ergebnis geführt haben, dass er leidet, wie wir? Ebensogut könnten uns die Physiker damit Furcht einflössen, dass sie uns versichern, der Fussboden sei gar nicht kompakt, wie er scheine, sondern bestehe aus losen Partikeln, die regellos herumschwirren. 'Aber wir hätten doch mit dem Andern nicht Mitleid, wenn wir wüssten, dass er nur eine Puppe ist, oder seine Schmerzen bloss heuchelt.' Freilich, – aber wir haben auch ganz bestimmte Kriterien dafür, dass etwas eine Puppe ist, oder dass Einer seine Schmerzen heuchelt und diese Kriterien stehen eben im Gegensatz zu denen, die wir Kriterien dafür nennen, dass etwas keine Puppe (sondern etwa ein Mensch) ist und seine Schmerzen nicht heuchelt (sondern wirklich Schmerzen hat). (TS 213, p. 509)

p. 126 Das Kennzeichnende des Seelischen scheint zu sein, dass man es im Andern nach Äusserem erraten //raten// muss und nur von sich her *kennt*.
Aber wenn durch genaueres Überlegen diese Ansicht in Rauch aufgeht, so ist zwar nicht das Innere zum Äusseren geworden,

aber es gibt für uns nicht mehr direkte innere und indirekte äussere Evidenz des Seelischen. (MS 173, p. 33)

pp. 127-128   'Ist die Unmöglichkeit zu wissen, was im Andern vorgeht eine physische oder eine logische. Und wenn beides – wie hängen sie //die beiden// zusammen?'
Vorerst: es liessen sich Möglichkeiten der Erforschung des Andern denken, die in Wirklichkeit nicht bestehen. Also gibt es eine physische Unmöglichkeit.
Die logische Unmöglichkeit liegt in dem Fehlen exakter //klarer// //scharfer// Regeln der Evidenz. (Daher drücken wir uns manchmal so aus: 'Wir können uns immer irren; wir können nie sicher sein, was wir betrachten, kann immer noch Verstellung sein'. Obgleich Verstellung nur eine von vielen, möglichen Ursachen eines falschen Urteils ist.) (MS 176, pp. 50-51)

p. 128   Man kann sagen 'Er versteckt seine Gefühle'. Das heisst aber, dass sie nicht apriori immer versteckt sind. Oder auch: Es gibt zwei Aussagen die einander widersprechen: Die eine ist, dass die Gefühle wesentlich versteckt sind; die andre, dass jemand seine Gefühle vor mir versteckt. (MS 169, pp. 55-56)

p. 129   Das Innere ist uns verborgen, heisst, es ist uns verborgen in einem Sinne in dem, es ihm nicht verborgen ist. Und dem Besitzer ist es nicht verborgen in dem Sinne, dass er *es äussert* und wir der Äusserung unter gewissen Bedingungen Glauben schenken und es da den Irrtum nicht gibt. Und diese Asymmetrie des Spiels bringt man mit dem Satz, das Innere sei uns //dem Andern// verborgen, zum Ausdruck. (MS 169, pp. 56-57)

p. 129   Es ist nicht so, als hätte ich in mir direkte, er für mein Seelisches aber nur indirekte. Sondern er hat dafür Evidenz, ich (aber) nicht. (MS 173, p. 42)

p. 130   Bedenke, dass wir den Andern nicht nur dann nicht verstehen, wenn er seine Gefühle versteckt, sondern oft auch dann nicht, wenn er sie nicht versteckt, ja wenn er sein Äusserstes tut, sich verständlich zu machen. (MS, 169, p. 43)

p. 130   Man könnte sogar sagen: Die Unsicherheit über das Innere ist eine Unsicherheit über etwas Äusseres. (MS, 174, p. 13) pp. 130-131   Vor allem hat die Verstellung ihre eigenen äusseren Zeichen. Wie könnten wir sonst überhaupt über Verstellung reden? (MS 169, p. 68)

p. 131   Ich sage 'dieser Mensch verbirgt sein Inneres'. Woher weiss man, dass er es verbirgt? Es gibt dafür also Anzeichen und auch Anzeichen fürs Gegenteil. (MS 169, p. 50)

p. 131   Auch was in ihm vorgeht ist ein Spiel, und die Verstellung ist in ihm nicht wie ein Gefühl *gegenwärtig*, sondern wie ein Spiel. (MS 169, p. 49)

p. 132   Die Äusserungen meiner Gefühle können unecht sein. Insbesondere können sie verstellt sein. Das ist ein anderes Sprachspiel als das primitive der echten Äusserungen. (MS 169, p. 63)

p. 132   Wäre die Verstellung nicht ein kompliziertes Muster, so wäre es denkbar dass sich das neugeborene Kind verstellt. (MS 171, p. 1)

p. 133 (n. 10)   Inwiefern kann man sagen, dass das Lügenspiel auf den Spiel ohne Lügen basiert ist? Doch nur darum weil wir das Wort Lüge nicht für etwas gebrauchen würden, was nicht in bestimmter Weise eine Ausnahme wäre. (MS 121, p. 29)

p. 134   Kann ich *nie* wissen was er fühlt, dann kann er sich auch nicht verstellen. (MS 169, p. 56)

p. 134   Ich will also sagen, dass es einen ursprünglichen, echten Schmerzausdruck gibt; dass also der Schmerzausdruck nicht gleichermassen mit dem Schmerz und dem Verstellung verbunden ist. (MS 171, p. 1)

p. 137   Aber wie sähe hier ein Irrtum aus? (MS 169, p. 61)

p. 137   Es gibt doch Fälle, wo nur ein Wahnsinniger den Ausdruck des Schmerzes (z.B.) für unecht halten könnte. (MS 169, p. 51)

p. 138   Mir scheint: wenn man nicht eigentlich *wissen* kann, ob sich jemand ärgert (z.B.), dann kann man es auch nicht eigentlich glauben oder vermuten. (MS 174, p. 7)

p. 142   Man kann wirklich sagen: der *beseelte* Körper hat Schmerzen. Und ob ein Körper beseelt ist, das nimmt man durch die Sinne wahr //das *sieht* man//. (MS 124, pp. 244-245)

p. 143   'Seelisch' ist für mich kein metaphysisches, sondern ein logisches Epitethon. (MS 173, p. 35)

p. 143   Inneres ist mit Äusserem nicht nur erfahrungsmässig verbunden, sondern auch logisch. (MS 173, p. 37)

pp. 143-144   Wenn Miene, Gebärde und Umstände eindeutig sind, dann scheint das Innere das Äussere zu sein; erst wenn wir das Äussere nicht lesen können, scheint ein Inneres hinter ihm versteckt. (MS 173, p. 36)

p. 144   Wenn ich ihn anlüge und er errät es an meinem Gesicht und sagt es mir, – habe ich noch immer das Gefühl, dass mein Inneres vor ihm in keiner Weise zugänglich, verborgen ist? Fühle ich nicht vielmehr, dass er mich ganz durchschaut. (MS 169, p. 52)

p. 145   Es muss etwa so sein dass ich im allgemeinen von meinen Handlungen einen kohärenteren Bericht geben kann als der Andre. In diesem Bericht spielt das Innere die Rolle der Theorie oder Konstruktion, die das übrige zu einem verständlichen Ganzen ergänzt. (MS 169, p. 54)

p. 147   Der Begriff des Lebewesens hat die gleiche Unbestimmtheit, wie der der Sprache. (Verstehe ich nicht ganz). (TS 213, p. 192)

p. 147   Man könnte sich denken, dass zur Feststellung, ob einer 'Schmerzen' habe, eine Art Fieberthermometer verwendet wird. Schreit ein Mensch oder stöhnt er, so legen sie ihm das Thermometer ein, und erst wenn dies den und den Anschlag zeigt, fangen sie an den Leidenden zu bedauern und ihn zu behandeln wie wir den, der 'offenbar Schmerzen hat'. (MS 176, p. 50)

p. 148   Wenn //wo// uns das Messen nicht wichtig ist, dann //dort// messen wir nicht, auch wenn wir es *können*. (MS 176, p. 50)

p. 149   Man könnte sagen: In einem Spiel in dem die Regeln unbe-
         stimmt sind, *kann* man nicht wissen wer gewonnen und wer
         verloren hat. (MS 174, p. 9)

p. 150   'Schau Dir nur das Gesicht und die Bewegungen des //eines//
         Hundes an und Du siehst, dass er eine Seele hat.' Aber was ist
         es am Gesicht? Ist es nur die Ähnlichkeit mit dem Mienenspiel
         des menschlichen? Ist es, wenigstens unter anderen, der
         Mangel an Steifheit? (MS 173, p. 39)

p. 150   Das, was ich mir da vorstellen kann, ist, dass dieser Menschen-
         leib automatenhaft handelt und nicht wie die gewöhnlichen
         Menschenleiber. (MS 173, p. 40)

p. 154   Es gibt Unsicherheit und es gibt Sicherheit; aber daraus folgt
         nicht, dass es sichere Kriterien gibt. (MS 174, p. 11)

p. 154   Wenn ich den Andern lange gekannt habe, wird der
         Gerichtshof wohl auch meine Aussage gelten lassen, ihr
         Gewicht beilegen. Aber meine absolute Sicherheit wird ihm
         nicht ein *Wissen* bedeuten. Denn aus einem Wissen müsste er
         ganz bestimmte Schlüsse ziehen können. (MS 174, p. 12)

p. 155 (n. 27)   Und man kann nicht entgegnen: '*Ich* ziehe bestimmte
         Schlüsse aus meinem Wissen, auch wenn's niemand andrer
         kann' – denn *Schlüsse* müssen für Alle gelten. (MS 174, p. 12)

pp. 155-156   Wichtig ist z.B. dass man einen Menschen '*kennen*' muss,
         um beurteilen zu können, welche Bedeutung einer Gefühlsäus-
         serung von ihm beizumessen //zukommt// ist, und dass man
         doch nicht beschreiben kann, was man in ihm kennt. Ebenso
         wichtig ist, dass man nicht sagen kann, worin die wesentlichen
         beobachtbaren Folgen eines innern Zustandes bestehen. Wenn
         er sich z.B. wirklich gefreut hat, was ist dann von ihm zu
         erwarten, und was nicht? Es gibt natürlich solche charakteris-
         tische Folgen, aber sie sind nicht so zu beschreiben wie die
         Reaktionen, welche einen Zustand eines physikalischen Gegen-
         standes kennzeichnen. (MS 174, p. 14)

p. 156   Wichtig ist dies: Ich mag aus gewissen Anzeichen und der
         Kenntnis einer Person wissen, dass er //dieser Mensch// sich
         freut etc. Aber einem Dritten kann ich nicht meine

Beobachtungen beschreiben; wenn er diesen traut, ihn dadurch von der Echtheit jeder Freude etc. überzeugen. (MS 174, p. 10)

p. 157   Denk dir es handelte sich wirklich um Muster auf einem langen Band.
Das Band zieht an mir vorbei und ich sage einmal 'dies ist das Muster S', einmal 'das ist das Muster V'. Manchmal weiss ich für einige Zeit nicht, welches es ist; manchmal sage ich am Ende 'Es war keines von beiden'.
Wie könnte man mich lehren dieses Muster zu erkennen? Man zeigt mir einfache Beispiele, dann auch komplizierte von beiden Arten. Es ist beinahe, wie ich den Stil zweier Komponisten unterscheiden lerne. Warum zieht man aber bei den Mustern diese *schwer fassliche* Grenze?
Weil sie in unserm Leben von Wichtigkeit ist. (MS 169, p. 69)

p. 158   Aussage: 'Ich weiss, dass die Flasche dort gestanden ist'. – Wie weisst du das? 'Ich habe sie dort gesehen.' – Wenn nun die Aussage ist: 'Ich weiss, dass er sich gefreut hat' und gefragt wird 'Wie weisst du das?'. – Was ist die Antwort? Sie ist nicht einfach die Beschreibung eines physikalischen Tatbestandes. Es gehört z.B. dazu, dass ich den betreffenden kenne. Wenn im Gerichtssaal ein Film vorgeführt werden könnte, in dem die ganze Szene wiedergegeben wäre, sein Mienenspiel, seine Gebärden, seine Stimme, könnte das manchmal ganz überzeugend wirken. Zum mindesten wenn er kein Schauspieler ist. Aber es wirkt z.B. nur wenn die, welche die Szene beurteilen, der gleichen Kultur angehören. Ich wüsste z.B. nicht wie bei Chinezen die echte Freude aussieht. (MS 174, p. 14)

p. 161   Was wollen wir unter 'Bedeutung' eines Wortes vestehen? Ein charakteristisches Gefühl, das das Aussprechen (Hören) des Wortes begleitet? (Das und-Gefühl, wenn-Gefühl. James), oder wollen wir das Wort 'Bedeutung' ganz anders gebrauchen; z.B. sagen, zwei Worte haben die gleiche Bedeutung, wenn diesselben grammatischen Regeln von beiden gelten? Wir können es halten wie wir wollen, müssen aber wissen, dass dies zwei gänzlich verschiedene Gebrauchsweisen (Bedeutungen) des Wortes 'Bedeutung' sind. (Man kann vielleicht auch von einem spezifischen Gefühl reden welches der Schachspieler bei Zügen mit dem König empfindet.) (TS 213, p. 33)

p. 161   Und will man hier von Bedeutung reden, so liegt sie nicht im Gebrauch der Worte. (MS 180b, p. 6)

p. 161   Die Bedeutung eines Wortes, sagte ich, sei sein Gebrauch. Aber dem muss ein wichtiger Zusatz gemacht werden //dazu gehört ein wichtiger Zusatz//. (MS 180b, p. 8)

p. 164   Warum soll ich überhaupt sagen, was die Bedeutung ist? Warum soll ich nicht sagen: Sprache, Musik und vieles was der Sprache ähnlich ist nennen wir bedeutend? (MS 180b, p. 6)

p. 179   Interpretieren ist ein artikulierter Vorgang, wie Übersetzen, Entziffern; die //eine// Zeichnung als das und das sehen ist amorph. (MS 123, 17-5-1941)

p. 181   'Jetzt sehe ich diesen Strich als Draht, jetzt als Kante eines Prismas' – Ist das nicht einfach ein Fall des sehens verschiedenen 3-dimensionalen Gestalten? Aber wie ist es mit diesem? Ist es eine *indirekte* Beschreibung, wenn ich sage, ich sehe diese Figur jetzt als dieses, jetzt als Prisma? Könnte ich direkter sagen: 'jetzt als Gestalt A, jetzt als Gestalt B' – wobei ich vermeide ein Wort zu gebrauchen welches mit anderen Sinneseindrücken verbunden //verknüpft// ist. (MS 123, 18-5-1941)

p. 182   Das, was ich sehe, möchte ich sagen, hat eine okulte Eigenschaft, ausser den leicht zu beschreibenden; eine Eigenschaft die man dadurch andeutet, dass man sagt 'ich sehe es als...' – die aber freilich dadurch nur angedeutet ist//sein kann//, da ja, was man meint //sieht//, mit einer wirklichen Kiste etc. nichts zu tun //schaffen// hat //mit einer Kiste nur einen kausalen Zusammenhang hat//. (MS 123, 17-5-1941)

p. 182   Wohl, wir beschreiben den Eindruck; aber wie beschreiben wir ihn? Das merkwürdige Phänomen ist diese Art der Beschreibung. Normalerweise würde man sagen, dass unter Umständen verschiedene physikalische Körper uns den gleichen Gesichtseindruck machen können; aber hier scheint der Eindruck durch seine *mögliche* Zugehörigkeit zu einem bestimmten //besonderen// Körper definiert zu sein.
Unser Fall ist also jedenfalls *ähnlich* einem Fall von Assoziation. (MS 123, 18-5-1941)

p. 182   Das Charakteristische des Aspekts ist seine Vergleichbarkeit mit dem Sehen *dieses* Objekts und nicht *jenes*, obschon beide in unserer Wahrnehmung enthalten sind. (MS 137, p. 9)

p. 192   Es handelt sich nicht darum, dass wir noch aller möglicher ungeahnter Entdeckungen gewärtig sein müssen (Köhler) – als wären die *Naturgesetze*, die die Psychologie lehrt (?), noch als provisorisch zu behandeln.   Köhler ist dabei selbst ganz im Unklaren, welcher Natur solche Entdeckungen etwa sein könnten.   Wie gesagt, die Schwierigkeit in der Psychologie ist am ähnlichsten den der 'Grundlagen' der Mathematik. (MS 130, 1-8-1946)

p. 193   James ist eine Fundgrube der Psychologie des *Philosophen*. (MS 165, p. 182)

p. 193   Wie nötig die Arbeit der Philosophie ist zeigt James' Psychologie.   Die Psychologie, sagt er, sei eine Wissenschaft.   Er bespricht aber beinahe keine wissenschaftlichen Fragen.   Seine Bewegungen sind lauter Versuche sich vom Spinnennetz der Metaphysik, in dem er gefangen ist, zu befreien.   He cannot yet walk, or fly at all he only wriggles: Nicht, dass das nicht interessant ist.   Es ist nur nicht eine wissenschaftliche Tätigkeit. (MS 165, pp. 150-151)

pp. 203-204 (n. 18) Ist das Subjective, oder Objective wirklicher? – Unsinn! – Lässt sich nur das Objektive durch die Sprache darstellen, nicht das Subjektive? – Aber wir *reden* ja vom Subjektiven!   Und was wir darüber im alltäglichen Leben sagen ist in Ordnung, wie es ist und braucht sowenig eine Richtigstellung durch den Philosophen, wie die Aussagen über Stühle und Tische.   Eines nun muss //ist zu// betont werden //betonen//: dass die Grammatik der Sätze von den subjektiven Gegenständen *nicht die gleiche ist*, wie die der Sätze von den objektiven Gegenständen.   Oder, was dasselbe heisst: die Sprachspiele sind verschieden. (MS 124, pp. 251-252)

p. 235   Ein innerer Vorgang, das wäre einer, von dem sich nichts sagen lässt; auch nicht, dass es //er// ein Vorgang ist oder etwas inneres ist.   Wir haben Worte, die ihrer Form nach einem Vorgang zu beschreiben scheinen und ein Vorgang im gewöhnlichen Sinne des Wortes entspricht ihnen nicht. (MS 120, p. 239)

p. 235 'Du scheinst immer zu sagen, es gebe nur den *Ausdruck* der Erinnerung, nicht den //einen// innern Vorgang' – Das sage ich *nicht*; es hiesse ja, dass Einer, der sagt, er habe sich jetzt gerade an...erinnert //jetzt das und das in der Erinnerung vor sich gesehen// immer lüge. Ich mache nur den //die// Unterschied klar zwischen der Grammatik der 'inneren Vorgänge' und der der 'äusseren' physischen Vorgänge. Diese Unterschiede erscheinen nicht als Unterschiede der *Spiele*, was sie sind //denn das sind sie//, sondern als Unterschiede der //zwischen// *Eigenschaften* der 'äusseren' und (der) 'inneren' Vorgänge, wie die Verwendung der Adjektive 'äusserer' und 'innerer' anzudeuten scheint. (MS 120, pp. 251-252)

p. 236 Wie kann ich denn leugnen, dass es innere Vorgänge gibt. Das wäre so, wie zu leugnen, 'dass es Zahlen gibt' und nicht nur //bloss// Zahlzeichen. Wer leugnet 'dass es Zahlen gibt', drückt sich offenbar missverständlich aus. Denn er will ja nicht leugnen, dass es das und das, was man beschreiben kann, wirklich in der Welt gibt, sondern er will leugnen dass das Wort Zahl überhaupt in der und der Weise gebraucht werde oder: dass es Sinn habe zu sagen 'es gibt Zahlzeichen und Zahlen' aber er darf natürlich auch nicht sagen: 'es gibt Zahlzeichen aber keine Zahlen'. (MS 120, p. 247)

p. 237 'Du meinst doch einen inneren Vorgang' – Freilich meine ich einen innern Vorgang. Wie ich auch mit '3' eine Zahl meine. (MS 120, p. 255)

p. 237 Und warum ist sie //scheint sie uns// ungreifbar? (Zahn)-schmerzen erscheinen uns nicht in diesem Sinne ungreifbar. Oder ich könnte sagen: eine Absicht erscheint uns noch um einen Grad ungreifbarer als Schmerzen. Das ist doch gar zu verdächtig. (MS 128, p. 24)

pp. 237-238 *Wann* hast du die Absicht? Immer oder intermittierend? Schau in die Lade, in der du sie erwartest. Die Lade ist leer. Du hattest sie unter den Empfindungen gesucht. (MS 128, p. 27)

p. 241 Die Worte 'Ich erwarte eine Explosion' werden oft einfach heissen 'Sei auf eine Explosion gefasst' oder 'Ich glaube es wird jetzt eine Explosion stattfinden'. (MS 180b, p. 40)

p. 241 (n.65)   Wenn ich sage: 'Ich erwarte ihn sehnsüchtig' so wird man diese Worte manchmal eine Handlung der Erwartung selbst nennen können. (MS 180b, p. 39)

p. 245   Wenn ich sage 'Ich habe es so gemeint' – beurteile ich den Samen und sage, dass ist der Same einer solchen Pflanze; oder lasse ich ihn wachsen und *zeige*, welche Pflanze aus ihm wird? //*Beurteile* ich den Samen, oder lasse ich ihn weiter wachsen?//. (MS 128, p. 6)

p. 246   Ich glaube das Hauptproblem liegt in der Frage: Was für ein Kriterium gibt es dafür, dass die Erinnerung meiner Absicht richtig oder falsch ist. – Gibt es *kein* solches Kriterium, dann kann man von einer Deutung statt von einer Erinnerung reden. (MS 128, p. 23)

p. 247   Eine Musikkapelle, am Ende einer Feierlichkeit, ist im Begriffe die Nationalhymne zu spielen.   Die Noten liegen auf den Falten; der erste Takt ist schon erklungen; da unterbricht sie ein Elementarereignis.   Wäre es nicht möglich, dass der Dirigent //die Spieler// die Absicht hatte //hatten//, die Hymne nicht zu spielen sondern sie nach den ersten Takten zu unterbrechen?   Und wenn dies nicht //wenn dies aber nicht// der Fall war, so hatte er also die Absicht die Hymne zu spielen. Aber worin bestand diese Absicht?   Wir möchten sagen: sie lag schon ganz in der Situation.' (MS 180b, p. 21)

p. 249   Denke an das Erlebnis in einem Gespräch etwas sagen zu wollen, Dich aber dann zu entscheiden nichts zu sagen.   Ein charakteristisches Erlebnis ist es den Atem einzuziehen und anzuhalten.   Entscheidest du dich dann doch nichts zu sagen, so lässt du den Atem wieder aus.   Jemand der Dich beobachtet kann deutlich sehen, dass du etwas sagen wolltest.   War also die Absicht den Atem anhalten?   Nein.   Aber in dieser ganzen Situation machte diese Handlung etwa diese Absicht aus.' (MS 180b, p. 32)

p. 249   Lass einen Menschen zornig und hochmütig und ironisch blicken; und nun behänge sein Gesicht mit einem Tuch, aber lass die Augen, in denen der ganze Ausdruck vereint //konzentriert// schien, unbedeckt.   Du wirst sehen, wie überraschend vieldeutig nun der Ausdruck dieser Augen ist. (MS 128, p. 12)

p. 250 Ich gehe neben einem Kranken die Treppe hinauf. Er strau-
chelt. Ich mache den Anfang einer Bewegung ihn zu stützen,
aber (er) gewinnt von selbst das Gleichgewicht und ich ziehe
meinen Arm wieder zurück. – Wie weiss ich, dass die
//meine// Bewegung der Anfang einer Hilfeleistung war?
Nun sie war das als was auch der Dritte sie unter diesen
Umständen erkannt hatte. (MS 180b, p. 24)

p. 257 Und wie verschieden ist es wieder wenn ich nachdenken will,
mich erinnern will etc. (MS 115, p. 102)

p. 258 ... dass hier das Wort Wollen falsch aufgefasst wird, wie das
Wort 'Zeit' wenn man denkt, die Zeit müsse sich mit einer //in
einer// bestimmten Geschwindigkeit bewegen. (MS 157, p. 44).

p. 259 Bedenken wir auch, dass die Tätigkeit des Deliberierens von
den Erfahrungen beim wirklichen Ausführen der Bewegung
unabhängig sind. D.h., dieses Deliberieren, Überlegen, Wählen,
könnte geschehen, auch ein Entschluss gefasst werden, und die
willkürliche Handlung doch nicht stattfinden. Und umgekehrt
konnte die willkürliche Handlung ohne *jede* vorausgehende
Überlegung ausgeführt werden. (MS 115, p. 108)

p. 260 Die Antithese Geschehen-Tun ist offenbar im Gebiet der
Handlungen zu Hause. (MS 157, p. 42)

p. 262 Kann nun eine willkürliche Handlung nicht verursacht
werden? – Und ist sie dadurch gezwungen? Wenn ich arretiert
und von der Polizei abgeführt werde, so gehe ich gezwungen.
Ist nun das Gleiche der Fall, wenn ich im Garten spazieren
gehe? Ist denn die Ursache ein Zwang? Ist es richtig zu sagen:
'Ich *fühle* mich im diesem Falle nur nicht gezwungen, weil mir
die Ursache, weswegen ich mich bewege, wie ich es tue, nicht
bekannt ist'? Wäre die Kenntnis eines Naturgesetzes ein Gefühl des Zwanges? Ist das Gefühl, die Erfahrung, des Zwanges
die direkte Wahrnehmung der Ursache, die man sonst nur aus
der Koinzidenz erschliesst? (MS 115, pp. 108-109)

p. 263 Meine Wahl ist frei, heisst nichts anderes als: ich kann wählen
//wähle manchmal//. Und dass ich manchmal wähle, steht
doch nicht im Zweifel. Was man 'frei' nennt, ist *nur* die Wahl
an sich. Zu sagen: 'wir glauben nur, dass wir wählen', ist
Unsinn. Der Vorgang, den wir 'wählen' nennen, findet statt, ob

man das Resultat der Wahl nach Naturgesetzen voraussagen kann, oder nicht. (MS 115, pp. 110-111)

pp. 263-264 'Der Wille ist frei' heisst eigentlich: 'Es gibt einen Willen'. Statt dem Menschen zu sagen 'Dein Wille ist frei' könnte man ihm auch sagen 'Du hast einen Willen'; und vielleicht gibt es Völker, die es so ausdrücken. Vielleicht auch so: 'Du *musst* nicht'. Und doch ist was ich sagte nicht richtig; denn was heisst 'Es gibt einen Willen'? Wem erklärt man das? – Wem man sagt, sein Wille sei frei, in dem will man das Gefühl der Verantwortlichkeit stärken, man will sein Leben ändern //beeinflussen//. Es ist nicht ganz unähnlich, wie wenn Einer lehrte: 'Gegen Krankheiten ist nichts zu machen; du kannst Medizinen einnehmen oder nicht, die Krankheit kommt und geht wenn sie will' – und ein Andrer: 'Gegen Krankheiten kann man ankämpfen und hat man gegen eine noch kein Mittel, so ist es nur eine Frage der Zeit und man wird eins finden'. Haben die beiden Lehren Effekt, so werden sie sehr verschiedene Haltungen Krankheiten gegenüber <u>erzeugen</u>. Und so auch wenn Einer sagt '*Du* bist der Täter' und ein Anderer 'Du handelst nur, wie du musst'. (MS 134, 2-4-1947)

p. 282 Die Frage ist also: Würden wir unsre Lebensform ändern, wenn uns das und das zur Verfügung gestellt würde? – Wie könnte ich diese Frage beantworten. (MS 176, p. 52)

81. S. G. Harding (ed.), *Can Theories Be Refuted?* Essays on the Duhem-Quine Thesis.
1976   ISBN 90-277-0629-8; Pb 90-277-0630-1
82. S. Nowak, *Methodology of Sociological Research*. General Problems. 1977
                                                            ISBN 90-277-0486-4
83. J. Piaget, J.-B. Grize, A. Szemińska, and V. Bang, *Epistemology and Psychology of Functions*. 1977   ISBN 90-277-0804-5
84. M. Grene and E. Mendelsohn (eds.), *Topics in the Philosophy of Biology*. [Boston Studies in the Philosophy of Science, Vol. XXVII] 1976
                                             ISBN 90-277-0595-X; Pb 90-277-0596-8
85. E. Fischbein, *The Intuitive Sources of Probabilistic Thinking in Children*. 1975
                                                            ISBN 90-277-0626-3
86. E. W. Adams, *The Logic of Conditionals*. An Application of Probability to Deductive Logic. 1975   ISBN 90-277-0631-X
87. M. Przełęcki and R. Wójcicki (eds.), *Twenty-Five Years of Logical Methodology in Poland*. 1976   ISBN 90-277-0601-8
88. J. Topolski, *The Methodology of History*. 1976   ISBN 90-277-0550-X
89. A. Kasher (ed.), *Language in Focus: Foundations, Methods and Systems*. Essays dedicated to Yehoshua Bar-Hillel. [Boston Studies in the Philosophy of Science, Vol. XLIII] 1976   ISBN 90-277-0644-1; Pb 90-277-0645-X
90. J. Hintikka, *The Intentions of Intentionality and Other New Models for Modalities*.
1975   ISBN 90-277-0633-6; Pb 90-277-0634-4
91. W. Stegmüller, *Collected Papers on Epistemology, Philosophy of Science and History of Philosophy*. 2 Volumes. 1977   Set ISBN 90-277-0767-7
92. D. M. Gabbay, *Investigations in Modal and Tense Logics with Applications to Problems in Philosophy and Linguistics*. 1976   ISBN 90-277-0656-5
93. R. J. Bogdan, *Local Induction*. 1976   ISBN 90-277-0649-2
94. S. Nowak, *Understanding and Prediction*. Essays in the Methodology of Social and Behavioral Theories. 1976   ISBN 90-277-0558-5
95. P. Mittelstaedt, *Philosophical Problems of Modern Physics*. [Boston Studies in the Philosophy of Science, Vol. XVIII] 1976   ISBN 90-277-0285-3; Pb 90-277-0506-2
96. G. Holton and W. A. Blanpied (eds.), *Science and Its Public: The Changing Relationship*. [Boston Studies in the Philosophy of Science, Vol. XXXIII] 1976
                                             ISBN 90-277-0657-3; Pb 90-277-0658-1
97. M. Brand and D. Walton (eds.), *Action Theory*. 1976   ISBN 90-277-0671-9
98. P. Gochet, *Outline of a Nominalist Theory of Proposition*. An Essay in the Theory of Meaning. 1980   ISBN 90-277-1031-7
99. R. S. Cohen, P. K. Feyerabend, and M. W. Wartofsky (eds.), *Essays in Memory of Imre Lakatos*. [Boston Studies in the Philosophy of Science, Vol. XXXIX] 1976
                                             ISBN 90-277-0654-9; Pb 90-277-0655-7
100. R. S. Cohen and J. J. Stachel (eds.), *Selected Papers of Léon Rosenfield*. [Boston Studies in the Philosophy of Science, Vol. XXI] 1979
                                             ISBN 90-277-0651-4; Pb 90-277-0652-2
101. R. S. Cohen, C. A. Hooker, A. C. Michalos and J. W. van Evra (eds.), *PSA 1974*. *Proceedings of the 1974 Biennial Meeting of the Philosophy of Science Association*. [Boston Studies in the Philosophy of Science, Vol. XXXII] 1976
                                             ISBN 90-277-0647-6; Pb 90-277-0648-4
102. Y. Fried and J. Agassi, *Paranoia*. A Study in Diagnosis. [Boston Studies in the Philosophy of Science, Vol. L] 1976   ISBN 90-277-0704-9; Pb 90-277-0705-7

103. M. Przełęcki, K. Szaniawski and R. Wójcicki (eds.), *Formal Methods in the Methodology of Empirical Sciences.* 1976   ISBN 90-277-0698-0
104. J. M. Vickers, *Belief and Probability.* 1976   ISBN 90-277-0744-8
105. K. H. Wolff, *Surrender and Catch.* Experience and Inquiry Today. [Boston Studies in the Philosophy of Science, Vol. LI] 1976
          ISBN 90-277-0758-8; Pb 90-277-0765-0
106. K. Kosík, *Dialectics of the Concrete.* [Boston Studies in the Philosophy of Science, Vol. LII] 1976   ISBN 90-277-0761-8; Pb 90-277-0764-2
107. N. Goodman, *The Structure of Appearance.* 3rd ed., 1977 [Boston Studies in the Philosophy of Science, Vol. LIII] 1977   ISBN 90-277-0773-1; Pb 90-277-0774-X
108. Kazimierz Ajdukiewicz, *The Scientific World-Perspective and Other Essays, 1931-1963.* Edited and with an Introduction by J. Giedymin. 1978   ISBN 90-277-0527-5
109. R. L. Causey, *Unity of Science.* 1977   ISBN 90-277-0779-0
110. R. E. Grandy, *Advanced Logic for Applications.* 1977   ISBN 90-277-0781-2
111. R. P. McArthur, *Tense Logic.* 1976   ISBN 90-277-0697-2
112. L. Lindahl, *Position and Change.* A Study in Law and Logic. 1977
          ISBN 90-277-0787-1
113. R. Tuomela, *Dispositions.* 1978   ISBN 90-277-0810-X
114. H. A. Simon, *Models of Discovery and Other Topics in the Methods of Science.* [Boston Studies in the Philosophy of Science, Vol. LIV] 1977
          ISBN 90-277-0812-6; Pb 90-277-0858-4
115. R. D. Rosenkrantz, *Inference, Method and Decision.* Towards a Bayesian Philosophy of Science. 1977   ISBN 90-277-0817-7; Pb 90-277-0818-5
116. R. Tuomela, *Human Action and Its Explanation.* A Study on the Philosophical Foundations of Psychology. 1977   ISBN 90-277-0824-X
117. M. Lazerowitz, *The Language of Philosophy.* Freud and Wittgenstein. [Boston Studies in the Philosophy of Science, Vol. LV]. 1977
          ISBN 90-277-0826-6; Pb 90-277-0862-2
118. Not published
119. J. Pelc, *Semiotics in Poland, 1894–1969.* 1979   ISBN 90-277-0811-8
120. I. Pörn, *Action Theory and Social Science.* Some Formal Models. 1977
          ISBN 90-277-0846-0
121. J. Margolis, *Persons and Mind.* The Prospects of Nonreductive Materialism. [Boston Studies in the Philosophy of Science, Vol. LVII]. 1977
          ISBN 90-277-0854-1; Pb 90-277-0863-0
122. J. Hintikka, I. Niiniluoto, and E. Saarinen (eds.), *Essays on Mathematical and Philosophical Logic.* 1979   ISBN 90-277-0879-7
123. T. A. F. Kuipers, *Studies in Inductive Probability and Rational Expectation.* 1978
          ISBN 90-277-0882-7
124. E. Saarinen, R. Hilpinen, I. Niiniluoto and M. P. Hintikka (eds.), *Essays in Honour of Jaakko Hintikka on the Occasion of His 50th Birthday.* 1979
          ISBN 90-277-0916-5
125. G. Radnitzky and G. Andersson (eds.), *Progress and Rationality in Science.* [Boston Studies in the Philosophy of Science, Vol. LVIII] 1978
          ISBN 90-277-0921-1; Pb 90-277-0922-X
126. P. Mittelstaedt, *Quantum Logic.* 1978   ISBN 90-277-0925-4
127. K. A. Bowen, *Model Theory for Modal Logic.* Kripke Models for Modal Predicate Calculi. 1979   ISBN 90-277-0929-7

128. H. A. Bursen, *Dismantling the Memory Machine*. A Philosophical Investigation of Machine Theories of Memory. 1978   ISBN 90-277-0933-5
129. M. W. Wartofsky, *Models*, Representation and the Scientific Understanding. [Boston Studies in the Philosophy of Science, Vol. XLVIII.] 1979
ISBN 90-277-0736-7; Pb 90-277-0947-5
130. D. Ihde, *Technics and Praxis*. A Philosophy of Technology. [Boston Studies in the Philosophy of Science, Vol. XXIV] 1979   ISBN 90-277-0953-X; Pb 90-277-0954-8
131. J. J. Wiatr (ed.), *Polish Essays in the Methodology of the Social Sciences*. [Boston Studies in the Philosophy of Science, Vol. XXIX] 1979
ISBN 90-277-0723-5; Pb 90-277-0956-4
132. W. C. Salmon (ed.), *Hans Reichenbach: Logical Empiricist*. 1979
ISBN 90-277-0958-0
133. P. Bieri, R.-P. Horstmann and L. Krüger (eds.), *Transcendental Arguments in Science*. Essays in Epistemology. 1979   ISBN 90-277-0963-7; Pb 90-277-0964-5
134. M. Marković and G. Petrović (eds.), *Praxis*. Yugoslav Essays in the Philosophy and Methodology of the Social Sciences. [Boston Studies in the Philosophy of Science, Vol. XXXVI]. 1979   ISBN 90-277-0727-8; Pb 90-277-0968-8
135. R. Wójcicki, *Topics in the Formal Methodology of Empirical Sciences*. 1979
ISBN 90-277-1004-X
136. G. Radnitzky and G. Andersson (eds.), *The Structure and Development of Science*. [Boston Studies in the Philosophy of Science, Vol. LIX] 1979
ISBN 90-277-0994-7; Pb 90-277-0995-5
137. J. C. Webb, *Mechanism, Mentalism and Metamathematics*. An Essay on Finitism. 1980   ISBN 90-277-1046-5
138. D. F. Gustafson and B. L. Tapscott (eds.), *Body, Mind and Method*. Essays in Honor of Virgil C. Aldrich. 1979   ISBN 90-277-1013-9
139. L. Nowak, *The Structure of Idealization*. Towards a Systematic Interpretation of the Marxian Idea of Science. 1980   ISBN 90-277-1014-7
140. C. Perelman, *The New Rhetoric and the Humanities*. Essays on Rhetoric and Its Applications. 1979   ISBN 90-277-1018-X; Pb 90-277-1019-8
141. W. Rabinowicz, *Universalizability*. A Study in Morals and Metaphysics. 1979
ISBN 90-277-1020-2
142. C. Perelman, *Justice, Law and Argument*. Essays on Moral and Legal Reasoning. 1980   ISBN 90-277-1089-9; Pb 90-277-1090-2
143. S. Kanger and S. Öhman (eds.), *Philosophy and Grammar*. Papers on the Occasion of the Quincentennial of Uppsala University. 1981   ISBN 90-277-1091-0
144. T. Pawlowski, *Concept Formation in the Humanities and the Social Sciences*. 1980
ISBN 90-277-1096-1
145. J. Hintikka, D. Gruender and E. Agazzi (eds.), *Theory Change, Ancient Axiomatics and Galileo's Methodology*.
Proceedings of the 1978 Pisa Conference on the History and Philosophy of Science, Volume I. 1981   ISBN 90-277-1126-7
146. J. Hintikka, D. Gruender and E. Agazzi (eds.), *Probabilistic Thinking, Thermodynamics, and the Interaction of the History and Philosophy of Science*. Proceedings of the 1978 Pisa Conference on the History and Philosophy of Science, Volume II. 1981   ISBN 90-277-1127-5
147. U. Mönnich (ed.), *Aspects of Philosophical Logic*. Some Logical Forays into Central Notions of Linguistics and Philosophy. 1981   ISBN 90-277-1201-8

148. D. M. Gabbay, *Semantical Investigations in Heyting's Intuitionistic Logic.* 1981
ISBN 90-277-1202-6
149. E. Agazzi (ed.), *Modern Logic – A Survey.* Historical, Philosophical, and Mathematical Aspects of Modern Logic and Its Applications. 1981 ISBN 90-277-1137-2
150. A. F. Parker-Rhodes, *The Theory of Indistinguishables.* A Search for Explanatory Principles below the Level of Physics. 1981 ISBN 90-277-1214-X
151. J. C. Pitt, *Pictures, Images, and Conceptual Change.* An Analysis of Wilfrid Sellars' Philosophy of Science. 1981 ISBN 90-277-1276-X; Pb 90-277-1277-8
152. R. Hilpinen (ed.), *New Studies in Deontic Logic.* Norms, Actions, and the Foundations of Ethics. 1981 ISBN 90-277-1278-6; Pb 90-277-1346-4
153. C. Dilworth, *Scientific Progress.* A Study Concerning the Nature of the Relation between Successive Scientific Theories. 2nd, rev. and augmented ed., 1986
ISBN 90-277-2215-3; Pb 90-277-2216-1
154. D. W. Smith and R. McIntyre, *Husserl and Intentionality.* A Study of Mind, Meaning, and Language. 1982 ISBN 90-277-1392-8; Pb 90-277-1730-3
155. R. J. Nelson, *The Logic of Mind.* 2nd. ed., 1989
ISBN 90-277-2819-4; Pb 90-277-2822-4
156. J. F. A. K. van Benthem, *The Logic of Time.* A Model-Theoretic Investigation into the Varieties of Temporal Ontology, and Temporal Discourse. 1983
ISBN 90-277-1421-5
157. R. Swinburne (ed.), *Space, Time and Causality.* 1983 ISBN 90-277-1437-1
158. E. T. Jaynes, *Papers on Probability, Statistics and Statistical Physics.* Ed. by R. D. Rozenkrantz. 1983 ISBN 90-277-1448-7; Pb (1989) 0-7923-0213-3
159. T. Chapman, *Time: A Philosophical Analysis.* 1982 ISBN 90-277-1465-7
160. E. N. Zalta, *Abstract Objects.* An Introduction to Axiomatic Metaphysics. 1983
ISBN 90-277-1474-6
161. S. Harding and M. B. Hintikka (eds.), *Discovering Reality.* Feminist Perspectives on Epistemology, Metaphysics, Methodology, and Philosophy of Science. 1983
ISBN 90-277-1496-7; Pb 90-277-1538-6
162. M. A. Stewart (ed.), *Law, Morality and Rights.* 1983 ISBN 90-277-1519-X
163. D. Mayr and G. Süssmann (eds.), *Space, Time, and Mechanics.* Basic Structures of a Physical Theory. 1983 ISBN 90-277-1525-4
164. D. Gabbay and F. Guenthner (eds.), *Handbook of Philosophical Logic.* Vol. I: Elements of Classical Logic. 1983 ISBN 90-277-1542-4
165. D. Gabbay and F. Guenthner (eds.), *Handbook of Philosophical Logic.* Vol. II: Extensions of Classical Logic. 1984 ISBN 90-277-1604-8
166. D. Gabbay and F. Guenthner (eds.), *Handbook of Philosophical Logic.* Vol. III: Alternative to Classical Logic. 1986 ISBN 90-277-1605-6
167. D. Gabbay and F. Guenthner (eds.), *Handbook of Philosophical Logic.* Vol. IV: Topics in the Philosophy of Language. 1989 ISBN 90-277-1606-4
168. A. J. I. Jones, *Communication and Meaning.* An Essay in Applied Modal Logic. 1983 ISBN 90-277-1543-2
169. M. Fitting, *Proof Methods for Modal and Intuitionistic Logics.* 1983
ISBN 90-277-1573-4
170. J. Margolis, *Culture and Cultural Entities.* Toward a New Unity of Science. 1984
ISBN 90-277-1574-2
171. R. Tuomela, *A Theory of Social Action.* 1984 ISBN 90-277-1703-6

172. J. J. E. Gracia, E. Rabossi, E. Villanueva and M. Dascal (eds.), *Philosophical Analysis in Latin America*. 1984   ISBN 90-277-1749-4
173. P. Ziff, *Epistemic Analysis*. A Coherence Theory of Knowledge. 1984
                                                                 ISBN 90-277-1751-7
174. P. Ziff, *Antiaesthetics*. An Appreciation of the Cow with the Subtile Nose. 1984
                                                                 ISBN 90-277-1773-7
175. W. Balzer, D. A. Pearce, and H.-J. Schmidt (eds.), *Reduction in Science*. Structure, Examples, Philosophical Problems. 1984   ISBN 90-277-1811-3
176. A. Peczenik, L. Lindahl and B. van Roermund (eds.), *Theory of Legal Science*. Proceedings of the Conference on Legal Theory and Philosophy of Science, Lund, Sweden, 11–14 December 1983. 1984   ISBN 90-277-1834-2
177. I. Niiniluoto, *Is Science Progressive?* 1984   ISBN 90-277-1835-0
178. B. K. Matilal and J. L. Shaw (eds.), *Analytical Philosophy in Comparative Perspective*. Exploratory Essays in Current Theories and Classical Indian Theories of Meaning and Reference. 1985   ISBN 90-277-1870-9
179. P. Kroes, *Time: Its Structure and Role in Physical Theories*. 1985
                                                                 ISBN 90-277-1894-6
180. J. H. Fetzer, *Sociobiology and Epistemology*. 1985
                                             ISBN 90-277-2005-3; Pb 90-277-2006-1
181. L. Haaparanta and J. Hintikka, *Frege Synthesized*. Essays on the Philosophical and Foundational Work of Gottlob Frege. 1986   ISBN 90-277-2126-2
182. M. Detlefsen, *Hilbert's Program*. An Essay on Mathematical Instrumentalism. 1986
                                                                 ISBN 90-277-2151-3
183. J. L. Golden and J. J. Pilotta (eds.), *Practical Reasoning in Human Affairs*. Studies in Honor of Chaim Perelman. 1986   ISBN 90-277-2255-2
184. H. Zandvoort, *Models of Scientific Development and the Case of Nuclear Magnetic Resonance*. 1986   ISBN 90-277-2351-6
185. I. Niiniluoto, *Truthlikeness*. 1987   ISBN 90-277-2354-0
186. W. Balzer, C. U. Moulines and J. D. Sneed, *An Architectonic for Science*. The Structuralist Program. 1987   ISBN 90-277-2403-2
187. D. Pearce, *Roads to Commensurability*. 1987   ISBN 90-277-2414-8
188. L. M. Vaina, *Matters of Intelligence*. Conceptual Structures in Cognitive Neuroscience. 1987   ISBN 90-277-2460-1
189. H. Siegel, *Relativism Refuted*. A Critique of Contemporary Epistemological Relativism. 1987   ISBN 90-277-2469-5
190. W. Callebaut and R. Pinxten, *Evolutionary Epistemology*. A Multiparadigm Program, with a Complete Evolutionary Epistemology Bibliograph. 1987
                                                                 ISBN 90-277-2582-9
191. J. Kmita, *Problems in Historical Epistemology*. 1988   ISBN 90-277-2199-8
192. J. H. Fetzer (ed.), *Probability and Causality*. Essays in Honor of Wesley C. Salmon. 1988   ISBN 90-277-2607-8; Pb 1-5560-8052-2
193. A. Donovan, L. Laudan and R. Laudan (eds.), *Scrutinizing Science*. Empirical Studies of Scientific Change. 1988   ISBN 90-277-2608-6
194. H.R. Otto and J.A. Tuedio (eds.), *Perspectives on Mind*. 1988
                                                                 ISBN 90-277-2640-X
195. D. Batens and J.P. van Bendegem (eds.), *Theory and Experiment*. Recent Insights and New Perspectives on Their Relation. 1988   ISBN 90-277-2645-0

Previous volumes are still available.

KLUWER ACADEMIC PUBLISHERS – DORDRECHT / BOSTON / LONDON